Environmental Policy

An Introduction

Barry C. Field

University of Massachusetts—Amherst

D0145034

WAVELAND

PRESS, INC.

Long Grove, Illinois

For information about this book, contact:
Waveland Press, Inc.
4180 IL Route 83, Suite 101
Long Grove, IL 60047-9580
(847) 634-0081
info@waveland.com
www.waveland.com

10-digit ISBN 1-57766-428-0
13-digit ISBN 978-1-57766-428-4

Printed in the United States of America

7 6 5 4 3

To my students

Contents

SECTION III: THE POLICIES   151

Contents

SECTION IV: THE PROBLEMS   275

SECTION V: INTERNATIONAL ISSUES   347

Preface

Human impacts on the natural world have occurred since there were humans. But in recent years the scale of these impacts, actual and potential, has become magnified. The addition of many more people and the growth of modern, high-consumption economies have expanded and intensified the environmental ramifications of contemporary life. Thus, people around the world, from local village groups to national governments, are struggling to come to grips with these issues and manage the human/environment interrelationship. The study of how governments make decisions about environmental matters comes under the heading of environmental policy—the complex process by which authoritative public action is undertaken toward the objective of protecting the environment.

This book is an introduction to environmental policy in the United States, particularly at the federal level. It covers the basics of the process, the participants and their roles, the primary content of the policies themselves, and some of the important policy problems that currently exist. It is based on a one-semester course in environmental policy that I have taught for many years. My intent has been to provide a broad introduction to the different facets of environmental policy, especially to help students identify the alternative paths they might take if they wished to study the subject more deeply.

This is a book about policy, not advocacy. This is not to diminish the need in the modern world for more and better environmental advocacy. Such a need will grow as economies around the world continue to expand, magnifying the actual and potential impacts on the natural world. Advocacy is especially important on worldwide issues such as the phenomenon of global warming, a new and profound threat to which we have only begun to respond. Paradoxically, the more successful we are in reducing the environmental footprints of our contemporary economies, the more people may come to think of the environment as a back-burner policy issue. This only heightens the need for both advocacy and for designing and implementing effective environmental policies in a world where other issues appear to be more pressing.

My greatest debt is to my students from over the many years I have taught this and other courses related to environmental problems. Their basic common sense and good spirit has served to keep me focused through the years. Thanks also to colleagues John Stranlund, Tom Stevens, and John Hird for many fruitful conversations on environmental policy matters. Thanks also to the good folks at Waveland Press for pushing the book along, and especially Laurie Prossnitz for her superb editing. As always, thanks to Darleen for her work on this manuscript, a continuation of all the great work she has done for me throughout the years. And finally, my family: Martha, Tory, Sidney, and Leslie, whose love has been so sustaining and inspiring.

SECTION I
INTRODUCTION

This first section consists of two chapters, the first of which is an introduction to some basic terms and ideas that are common in the study of environmental policy. This will start to build a foundation for later chapters, where we will discuss issues and ideas in greater detail. The second is a chapter on recent trends in environmental quality in the United States. Since environmental policy is being undertaken with the objective of improving the quality of the environment, we want to start off with a brief understanding of how things have been going over the last three decades or so. This will provide a context for later discussions of policies, the policy process, and policy problems.

1

Environmental Policy

Concepts and Issues

As we move further into the twenty-first century, human communities throughout the globe are struggling to come to terms with the world of nature. The problems vary from the strictly local, such as the pollution of a backyard creek or the air inside of one's own home, to the global, such as the possible impacts of humans on the earth's atmosphere. And the perspective from which people see the natural world varies a lot among countries and peoples of the world. In the developed world many people have achieved relatively high levels of economic security and want a cleaner environment as part of an enhanced standard of living. For people in the developing world, where economic insecurity is still high, a cleaner environment is also a priority, but this goal has to be balanced with the desire for improved economic circumstances.

But in all cases the basic problem is the same: how to manage the impacts of human activity on the natural environment and reduce the damaging effects, present and future, that environmental degradation has on humans and nonhuman elements of the earth's ecosystem.

Nature and Human Society

Human societies rely on nature in two fundamental ways, as depicted in figure 1.1. Nature is a supplier of energy and materials, without which human life cannot be sustained. There are important questions to be asked about how much, and how fast, these natural resource inputs should be used, how much should be preserved for future generations, how much effort we should devote to finding substitutes, and so on. These problems generally come under the heading of natural resource management.

The other role nature has traditionally played is as a sink for wastes, or leftovers, from human (and nonhuman) activities. In modern societies there is a vast array of energy and materials leftovers put back into the water, air, and land resources of the planet. The critical questions here are how to reduce these flows and to what extent, whether to substitute one flow for another, how much to recycle, and so on. These problems generally come under the heading of environmental quality management, or the management of environmental pollution.

In this book we are going to focus on issues of environmental policy. This is not to say that the two sets of issues are independent; obviously they are not. Think of your automobile. It uses inputs from nature to power it: gasoline made primarily from petroleum, and air. It also produces leftovers, or residuals, that come out of the tailpipe: carbon dioxide, nitrogen oxides, unburned hydrocarbons, and so on. Naturally these two phenomena are closely related. If you burn less gasoline, you will produce less air pollution. There are several questions to address on the input side: How fast should we extract petroleum from an underground deposit? To what extent should the

The Natural World

Natural Resource Inputs
Energy, food,
minerals, air, water

**Human Society
and Economy**

Waste emissions into air, water, land

Figure 1.1   Human Societies Depend on Nature in Two Ways

United States try to become "energy independent"? To what extent should we restructure the energy industry to create more competition? The main environmental problem is to manage the residuals coming from the massive, and growing, fleet of automobiles on the streets of this and other countries. What standards should be applied to tailpipe emissions? How should an inspection and maintenance program be structured? How do we encourage manufacturers and consumers to switch to low-polluting vehicles?

Another example is water. On the natural resource side there are important questions about the adequacy of water supplies, especially in arid regions of the world, many of which have rapidly growing populations. Droughts can occur at times, and storage and conveyance systems have to be created and managed with these in mind. On the water quality side we have substantial problems with waterborne emissions from municipalities, industries, and farms. Degraded water quality has a range of impacts, from human health concerns to ecological effects to aesthetic considerations. Clearly the water resource and water quality problems are related, as in the case, for example, of contaminated drinking water supplies. Nevertheless, in this book we will stress the issues of water quality rather than those of water quantity.

Public Policy

Policy is a word that refers to a plan or guideline for action, much like the word *strategy* in military applications. Any individual or group can pursue a policy, a plan of action directed at moving toward and achieving some objective. By public policy we mean actions undertaken in the public arena, by groups of people, to manage activities affecting their welfare. A broad conception of public policy would include situations where groups of people get together under private auspices to pursue some shared goal. A group of homeowners along a private road meet to consider action on how it should be maintained; a group of people get together to buy a piece of land to protect it from development. Private, collective behavior of this type can be facilitated by public action that sets procedures and rules by which groups can organize and function effectively.

More commonly, **public policy** refers to collective actions that are pursued through formal governmental institutions: a law passed by a legislature, a pronouncement by a president or governor, a ruling made by a court. Policy actions are, or at least give the appearance of being, purposeful in the sense that they have objectives and the means with which to accomplish them. But the policy process also incorporates the political posturing, pushing and shoving, and ideological theater to which people and groups resort as they try to increase and extend their influence over events.

Environmental Policy

Environmental policy (or perhaps, more properly, public policy toward the environment) is collective action undertaken to manage human impacts on the quality of the environment. It focuses on issues of pollution control and the ways in which we regulate our production and consumption leftovers in order to lessen their impacts on the environmental resources: water, air, and land. It includes actions of formal **governmental institutions**, such as legislatures and courts. It also encompasses public opinion about the environment, the actions of environmental interest groups, the activities and results obtained by environmental scientists, the reporting of the environmental press, and so on.

The traditional focus of environmental policy is the laws and regulations that have direct impacts on polluters and, thus, on the quality of the environment. Examples include the major environmental laws: the Clean Air Act, the Clean Water Act, the Superfund law, to name a few. In later chapters we will take a look at the major provisions contained in these laws. Within each of these laws are hundreds of regulations promulgated by the EPA and other agencies to implement the general procedures set out in the statutes. It is in this implementation process where some of the fiercest battles take place, often out of view of the general public.

In addition, laws that are not explicitly aimed at the environment can nevertheless impact the environment in major ways. Agricultural subsidies to support farm incomes have important environmental implications. Laws on transportation matters obviously can impact air quality in major ways.

The essential foundation for governmental actions on environmental quality is our legal system: the U.S. Constitution (and the many state constitutions), the courts in which legal battles take place, and the numerous customs and precedents that make up our legal traditions. As we all know, America tends to be a **litigious society**, meaning that we often resort to the courts to resolve our differences. This is certainly true of our environmental laws and regulations; these impinge on people and constrain their behavior in various ways. Proponents want to see them vigorously applied; opponents want to see them applied less stringently. They meet in the courts, and the rulings of these courts effectively set the parameters for environmental protection.

Environmental policy also broadly includes institutional changes that impact the environment. An **institution** is an organization, law, or custom that affects the ability of people to come together and make collective decisions. For example, one of the major institutional changes affecting the environment over the last three or four decades is the rise of large and competent state environmental agencies. In the other direction there are global institutions that impact national environments, for example the World Trade Organization and the many international environmental treaties to which the United States is signatory.

Nor must we forget the role of the government as polluter. We normally think of public agencies as protectors of the environment. As we shall discover throughout the book, however, governmental agencies are frequently the sources of pollution. Examples include the environmental impacts of military bases and the radiation pollution stemming from the nuclear weapons program.

The Layered Nature of Public Action

In most political systems public bodies exist in a layered system starting with neighborhood groups and ending with global organizations. Thus, collective actions to protect the environment can take place at many levels. Some of these are shown in table 1.1. The way that political layers are structured and related to one another varies throughout the country. In some

Table 1.1   Layers of Public Action to Protect the Environment

Group	Institution	Action Examples
Neighborhood homeowners	An informal meeting every Saturday morning to develop plans for protecting the quality of the neighborhood	Voluntary cleanup efforts once a month to pick up trash, followed by a potluck dinner
Citizens of a town or city	The annual town meeting, or weekly meetings of town manager and council members	A local ordinance making it illegal to keep junk cars in backyards
Citizens of a county or group of communities	County board of supervisors	A county regulation restricting residential development in areas where wetlands may be harmed
Citizens of a state	State Department of Environmental Quality	Regulations that require firms to have operating permits if they plan to emit toxic pollutants into the air or water
Collection of states	An interstate compact or regional agreement	A program to control NO_x emissions within a multistate region
Citizens of the country	U.S. EPA and the U.S. Congress	The Clean Air Act of 1990
Groups of countries	An international agreement among all countries in a particular region	The U.N. Regional Seas program, where nations bordering particular seas (e.g., the Mediterranean) act to protect water quality
All the countries of the world	The United Nations Environment Program	The Kyoto agreement to reduce emissions of greenhouse gases

states, local communities are powerful compared to county-level governments; in others, county institutions have greater power. Nor are these differences static; we are currently in the midst of a shift in environmental policy activity and initiative from federal to state levels in the United States.[1]

In a book about environmental policy we would like to study actions at all these levels. But inevitably we will have to specialize somewhat. So although we will occasionally talk about local action, and often talk about actions by the individual states, we will primarily discuss action at the federal level. We will also devote several chapters to international events.

The Evolution of Environmental Policy

Environmental policy is changing. Some observers have described this change as a revolution, or watershed, but it is more accurate to think of environmental policy as continuing to evolve, urged forward by ongoing concern about achieving a healthier environment, by certain political and economic facts of life, and by the accomplishments and problems of past environmental policies.

One fundamental change is the underlying perspective with which governmental action is pursued. The spirit of most federal and state environmental policy for the last quarter century has been to think of pollution reduction as a **technological problem**. According to this view, diligent and resourceful public policy makers and regulators identify the best technological means for reducing the flow of pollutants into the environment. They do this because polluters themselves cannot be relied upon to search for and develop these means. Regulatory authorities then force polluters to adopt and use these pollution-control technologies, using various fines and penalties to bring about compliance. This has come to be called the **command-and-control** approach to policy.

The limits of this approach have become increasingly obvious. There is no doubt that it can get results, especially when both the problems and their solutions seem obvious. But more recently we have come to understand pollution as a **behavioral problem**, in which the main point is to change the incentives faced by polluters. This will not only lead to more cost-effective pollution control, but also enlist the skills and knowledge of the polluters themselves to reduce environmental pollution. It also puts the burden of important pollution-control choices where it belongs—on the polluters themselves rather than on government agencies. Command and control may have been a reasonable way of doing things when environmental problems were readily apparent and easy to comprehend. But we have made progress in ameliorating many of the obvious problems. What is now needed is a system of pollution control in which environmental factors are deeply and thoroughly ingrained into the billions of decisions made every day by producers and consumers.

Environmental policy also is evolving in terms of its locus of action. Before the 1970s the initiative for environmental pollution control lay with the states. The federal role was to backstop the states, providing them with financial aid, research on important pollution-related issues, and technical advice. But the environment emerged as a national concern in the 1960s, prompted by a growing sense that state-level action was not sufficient to deal effectively with the growing problems:

1. Few states had developed any expertise among policy makers and administrators for dealing with environmental issues. It has taken many years for capable and influential state environmental agencies to establish themselves.

2. Environmental interest groups were not particularly strong at the local and state levels. It was, therefore, hard to develop vigorous environmental action among public interest groups at that level.

3. Most states were, and still are, heavily focused on the desirability of economic development, so there was a strong disinclination for individual states to require their businesses to engage in serious antipollution measures that would make them less competitive vis-à-vis firms in other states.

4. But there was growing recognition that pollution problems weren't confined by state boundaries; that actions in one state could produce problems in another.

Thus in the early 1970s the federal role in environmental regulation was greatly expanded. The EPA was created and federal actions and responsibilities became the primary force in environmental policy. This happened in the United States as well as in many other countries around the world. More recently, there has arisen a greater sensitivity to the need for some degree of **devolution**, a shifting of policy initiative and responsibility to state and local levels. This by no means implies that the federal role is going to become insignificant, only that some substantial shifts have taken place as individual states have become much more sophisticated and capable in their environmental actions.

Another trend is in effect the obverse of this. It is the trend toward **international action**, involving coordinated steps taken by groups of nations, sometimes just a few, other times by almost all of them (global policy). Globalization has brought greater connectivity among people and countries, and joint action on international environmental issues has become important. This has led to the growth of international institutions, like the U.N. Environment Program, the proliferation of international environmental nongovernmental organizations (NGOs), and new environmental treaties and agreements among countries. We will focus on international environmental policy in the last section of the book.

Approaches to the Study of Environmental Policy

Environmental policy, or any type of public policy for that matter, can be studied from a number of different perspectives. When discussing policy issues these perspectives can often get tangled up, making it hard to sort out what's being said, where there is agreement, and where there is difference.

Positive vs. Normative Policy Analysis

A critical distinction that needs to be made is between positive and normative policy analysis. **Positive analysis** looks at what is: how policy is enacted, why policies and regulations are what they are and not something else. **Normative analysis**, on the other hand, involves the question of what policy ought to be.

Positive Analysis.   It might seem simple to study the "what is" (or what was) dimension of environmental policy. But it turns out that there are a number of ways one can approach this. One way is from the standpoint of environmental politics. The political process is where interests and institutions clash and cooperate, where environmental policies and regulations emerge from a complex process of coalition building and the exercise of political power. It is important to understand who the main players are, how they typically operate, what the primary rules of the game are, and how the political process functions to yield the outcomes that it does.

Another approach is to emphasize the actual content of the environmental policies that have been enacted over the years at the federal, state, and community levels. We would study what the environmental laws say, how environmental agencies like the EPA have followed up the laws with specific regulations, and how these have been enforced. Particular attention might be focused on how environmental policies and laws have evolved through the years and decades.

Related to this is a third approach that emphasizes current problems in environmental policy and how changes might be made to ameliorate these problems. This approach focuses on the failures and successes of current policies in terms of achieving greater environmental protection, and seeks new policy initiatives that will rectify these failures or duplicate the successes. The emphasis is on effective policy analysis: why policies and regulations have or have not worked well in the past, and how they can be designed to be more effective in the future.

Normative Analysis.   We normally don't study environmental policy just to satisfy idle curiosity. We do it because we want to get somewhere, namely to a cleaner and healthier natural environment. We bring value judgments to our work: what is good and what is bad, what is right and what is wrong. Not only do we have values as observers, but clearly the participants in the policy struggle bring strong values and interests to the fray. So policy discussions need to be clarified in terms of "ought": what ought to be the case. In fact, the notion of ought can be used in two senses: (1) assuming some predetermined objective or set of objectives, what policies ought to be to achieve them, and (2) what policies ought to be in an ethical or moral sense.

Ideally we would pursue each of these policy perspectives in some depth. Inevitably, however, the constraints of space in the book and time in a normal semester make this impossible. Thus, section II looks at the policy process, summarizing the main actors and how they operate. In section III we examine the policies themselves, reviewing their major objectives and content. In section IV there are several chapters discussing the major problems being encountered in contemporary policy arenas. While sections II and III focus on positive aspects of environmental policy, section IV will inevitably incorporate normative questions to a much greater extent. In the last section of the book we will look at some of the international aspects of environmental policy.

Environmental Policy and Politics

One of the most fundamental things one can say about environmental policy is that it is the outcome of a political process. In an open political system such as that of the United States, the political process is an ongoing struggle in which different individuals and groups, with a range of values and beliefs, contend for influence and control over policies and regulations. The parties involved include legislatures, regulatory agencies, public and private research organizations, interest groups, political parties, regional groups, international groups, and so on. Sometimes political differences are muted, and people are able to unite around particular causes of action; often contention and conflict are high, and policy outcomes, if they occur at all, are complex results of shifting alliances and arcane strategies.

In environmental policy, the fact that politics are involved is frustrating to many people. Environmental issues normally involve many technical questions; for example, questions about the impact of humans on complex ecosystems, the corresponding impact of environmental degradation on humans, and so on. There is a natural tendency, especially among environmental scientists, to see clearly the policies that seem to offer technical solutions to many of these problems. Political conflicts over such issues as how restrictive environmental regulations ought to be, how quickly they should be put into effect, how their costs should be distributed among different groups, and so on, often seem to get in the way of sound policy. But in any society that calls itself democratic, policy is the result of some type of group activity, where attitudes, objectives, and competencies will differ among individuals in the group. Policy has to be the result, therefore, of an effort to hammer out a collective course of action from among these individual situations, and that means political action.

Environmental policy is often thought of as an activity that expresses the underlying values of the people involved.[2] It is this, but it is also much more. It is a reflection of the changing circumstances in which people find themselves. One reason that issues of environmental quality became, and have remained, important to people in the developed world is that we have achieved unprecedented levels of material security in the last half century. It is only natural, then, to turn our attention to the environmental impacts of our economic activity. This refocusing is not so much a reflection of a fundamental change in values as it is an acknowledgment of improved economic circumstances: we now have ample resources for cleaning up the environment. It is the reason why people in countries of the developing world may put more emphasis on economic growth and less on environmental quality, not because their fundamental values are so different, but because they are substantially poorer than many people in the developed world.

The other dimension of what we mean by "circumstances" is **strategic possibilities**. The policy process, as we shall see, is a political phenomenon in which different people and groups contend for influence and try to move outcomes in one direction or another. What is possible at any time depends on the tactical and strategic possibilities existing at that time, in terms of such elements as the potential to form alliances, to take advantage of unforeseen events, to develop public opinion, and so on. The 1990 Clean Air Act, for example, may be regarded as having sprung from environmental values, but more directly it was a product of the alignment of political forces at the time and the way in which the policy stalemate of the 1980s on air pollution regulation was resolved.

This is not to say by any means that environmental policy is all just political tactics and short-run advantage. In an open democracy the authority and initiative for public policy, certainly in theory and to a large extent in practice, comes from the public. The ultimate impetus for environmental policy actions, therefore, comes from public attitudes about the environment and the steps that should be taken to protect it. **Public opinion** can reflect both the objective state of the environment and the activities and accomplishments of the policy process itself. Nor is it correct to say that there is a single and unanimous public opinion on the environment among all of the citizenry; rather, there are multiple and changing opinions among different groups and at different times.

The importance of public opinion in environmental policy was beautifully illustrated in the mid-1990s. The Republican victories in the 1994 elections encouraged many in that party to pursue a vigorous antiregulation program in the 104th Congress (1995–96). One of their loudly proclaimed goals was to weaken environmental laws and regulations. They soon discovered, however, that the broad consensus of public opinion did not support this; rather, the general public, or at least a very large majority of it, was happy with the general state of environmental regulations and was not in favor of weakening these laws. The antienvironment rhetoric and actions of this group soon faded away.

Environmental Policy as a Morality Play

In the rhetoric and posturing of the political process, environmental policy often gets reduced to a simplistic morality play. On one side are the good guys: government regulators and environmental groups with clear insight and pure motives. On the other side are the bad guys: private corporations and business interest groups who think only of profits and care nothing about the health and beauty of the natural world. In a variety of ways reality is much more complex.

1. The world of industry and business is not made up entirely of thoughtless profit mongers who care nothing about the environment. Some companies are more progressive than others in being willing to undertake initiatives toward environmental improvement. Moreover, the envirotech industry, the performance of which is critical in developing and applying new pollution-control techniques, is a private-sector operation.

2. Government policy makers are by no means all-seeing and all-competent, nor do the motives of agency workers always move them unambiguously in the direction of the "public good." The pejorative word for federal policy makers is "bureaucrats." Sometimes bureaucracies can indeed stand in the way of progress, even in environmental policy.

3. The fact is that a substantial amount, in some cases even most, of the pollution in the United States comes not from businesses, but from private individuals and public agencies. For example: air pollutants from automobiles, radiation pollution from nuclear weapons sites developed by the Department of Defense, and water pollution from public wastewater-treatment plants.

So it is too simplistic to think about environmental policy as simply a battle between corporate polluters and the rest of the world. As we will see, the real world is more complex, and interesting, than this simple dichotomy.

Summary

The purpose of this preliminary chapter is to introduce the general subject of environmental policy and indicate how it relates to other parts of the policy/political world. We also briefly presented some of the main problems and issues that exist in environmental policy—the role of science; the division of responsibility among federal, state, and local authorities; the problem of managing conflict and encouraging consensus; the issue of enforcement; the difficulty in shifting from command and control to more incentive-based policies; the role of policy analysis; and international issues. We also tried to counter two ideas that sometimes bedevil discussions of environmental policy: that policy consists essentially of passing new environmental statutes (there are many different policy instruments available for use in different circumstances), and that environmental policy can be reduced to a simple struggle between polluters dressed in black and everybody else dressed in white.

Key Terms

behavioral problem
command and control
devolution
environmental policy
governmental institutions
institution
international action
litigious society

normative analysis
policy
positive analysis
public opinion
public policy
strategic possibilities
technological problem

Questions for Further Discussion

1. Suppose you are discussing federal air pollution control policies with a friend. How would you distinguish positive types of issues from normative types of questions?

2. Suppose the homeowners around a lake meet periodically and draw up agreements among themselves to upgrade their individual septic tanks in order to protect water quality in the lake. Is this an example of local public policy in action, or should we regard it as something else?

3. How should we determine at which level (local, state, federal, global) a particular environmental problem ought (primarily) to be addressed?

4. People with higher incomes often are willing to devote more resources to improving the quality of the natural environment. Is this a case of changing values?

5. Explain the following statement: "Effective normative policy discussions often hinge on effective positive analyses."

Web Sites

There are, of course, thousands of Web sites dealing with environmental policy, for example, environmental agencies like the EPA:

www.epa.gov

Congressional committees that deal with the environment, such as the Senate Committee on Environment and Public Works:

www.senate.gov/~epw/

Private interest group sites, such as:
Environmental Defense
www.environmentaldefense.org

Sierra Club
www.sierraclub.org

Environmental think tanks, such as Resources for the Future:
www.rff.org

Scientific organizations involved in environmental issues, such as the Intergovernmental Panel on Climate Change (IPCC):
www.ipcc.ch/

The Environmental Research Foundation has a very comprehensive list of private firms and public organizations involved in environmental issues:
http://www.eco-web.com

Additional Readings

Baumol, William J., and Wallace E. Oates, *Economics, Environmental Policy, and the Quality of Life* (Englewood Cliffs, NJ: Prentice-Hall, 1979): 217–224.

Caldwell, Lynton, and Robert V. Bartlett, *Environmental Policy, Transnational Issues and National Trends* (Westport, CT: Quorum Books, 1997).

Carter, Neil, *The Politics of the Environment: Ideas, Activism, Policy* (New York: Cambridge University Press, 2001).

Chertow, M. R., and D. C. Esty, eds. *Thinking Ecologically: The Next Generation of Environmental Policy* (New Haven, CT: Yale University Press, 1997).

Davis, C., and J. Mazurek, *Pollution Control in the United States: Evaluating the System* (Washington, DC: Resources for the Future, 1998).

Ervin, David E., James R. Kahn, and Marie Leigh Livingston, eds., *Does Environmental Policy Work? The Theory and Practice of Outcomes Assessment*, New Horizons in Environmental Economics Series (Northampton, MA: Edward Elgar, February 2004).

Grant, Jane A., *Community, Democracy, and the Environment: Learning to Share the Future* (Lanham, MD: Rowman and Littlefield, 2003).

Helm, Dieter, ed., *Environmental Policy: Objectives, Instruments and Implementation* (Oxford: Oxford University Press, 2000).

Kettl, Donald F., *Environmental Governance: A Report on the Next Generation of Environmental Policy* (Washington, DC: Brookings Institution Press, 2002).

Lacey, Michael J., ed., *Government and Environmental Politics: Essays on Historical Developments Since World War Two* (Baltimore: Johns Hopkins Press, 1991).

Landy, Marc K., Marc J. Roberts, and Stephen R. Thomas, *The Environmental Protection Agency: Asking the Wrong Questions from Nixon to Clinton,* expanded edition (New York: Oxford University Press, 1994).

Michel, David, ed., *Climate Policy for the 21st Century: Meeting the Long-Term Challenge of Global Warming* (Baltimore: Johns Hopkins University, School of Advanced International Studies, 2005).

Roberts, Jane, *Environmental Policy* (New York: Routledge, 2003).

Rosenbaum, Walter A., *Environmental Politics and Policy,* 4th ed. (Washington, DC: Congressional Quarterly Press, 1998).

Sexton, Ken, Alfred A. Marcus, K. William Easter, and Timothy D. Burkhardt, eds., *Better Environmental Decisions: Strategies for Governments, Businesses, and Communities* (Washington, DC: Island Press, 1999).

Smith, Zachary A., *The Environmental Policy Paradox,* 4th ed. (Englewood Cliffs, NJ: Prentice-Hall, 2004).

Stavins, R. N., and B. Whitehead, *Thinking Ecologically: The Next Generation of Environmental Policy* (New Haven, CT: Yale University Press, 1997).

Vig, Norman J., and Michael Kraft, eds., *Environmental Policy: New Directions for the Twenty-First Century*, 5th ed. (Washington, DC: Congressional Quarterly Press, 2003).

Notes

[1] We will look at this phenomenon in chapter 17.

[2] For example, a recent book on environmental policy is subtitled *Translating Values into Policy.* See Judith A. Layzer, *The Environmental Case* (Washington, DC: Congressional Quarterly Press, 2002).

2

Recent Trends in Environmental Pollution

It has been more than thirty years since the first major federal pollution-control laws were put on the books, and longer since some of the individual states took the first steps to control pollution. An obvious question is: How much have we accomplished? In other words, how effectively have these public policies addressed the various aspects of the environmental pollution problem? If we want to do more and better in the future, we must try to answer this question.

Assessing Policy Effectiveness

You might think it would be easy to figure out what progress has been made; just look at the data on pollution levels and see if they have changed. But it turns out to be harder than you might expect, for a variety of reasons. Perhaps the most important is that to determine how pollution is trending, an adequate monitoring system must be in place and must be in operation over a long enough period that consistent and comparable data can be generated from which to draw conclusions. In the early days of the federal push for pollution control, little emphasis was put on monitoring emissions or on determining the state of the environment; the focus was on getting polluters to adopt less-polluting technologies. It is only more recently that the importance of monitoring has become apparent and more effective monitoring systems put in place. It will take many years before long-run pollution trends can be adequately monitored.[1]

Another problem is that the environment is actually multidimensioned. This raises the distinct possibility that some types of pollution will be getting worse even as other dimensions are showing improvement. Whether you think things are getting better or worse may well depend on which part of the environment you are most interested in. This can also lead to endless arguments among political adversaries, as those who favor more aggressive pollution control point to indices that show conditions getting worse, while those on the other side point to data that show things are getting better.

Before/After vs. With/Without

Another critical component of pollution assessment is choosing a base from which to draw judgments about change. For example, air pollution in a number of U.S. cities is worse now for some pollutants than it was in 1970. Do we conclude, therefore, that we are worse off now than back then?

Certainly comparing air pollution today with what it was in 1970 (a **before/after comparison**) is a relevant comparison. If the average person is breathing more pollutants, we would presumably judge them to be worse off. But perhaps an even more useful comparison is between current pollution levels and what they would have been today if no federal pollution-control program had been put into effect (a **with/without comparison**). For example, the average car produced in 1970 emitted much more pollution than does the average car produced today, thanks to pollution-control regulations of the Clean Air Act. So, despite the great increase in the number of people and the number of cars on the road, air pollution is not nearly as bad as it would have been if cars had remained unchanged. From this standpoint, then, these particular laws may be regarded as successful.

The Attribution Question

Usually we want to know not only whether pollution has increased or decreased but why; to what can we attribute the change in emissions or the change in ambient environmental conditions. We would like especially to know whether the pollution-control programs put into effect have accomplished what we expected them to. Here again, it is not a simple relationship: pollution-control program enacted → two years later an improvement → hence the program has worked. A major difficulty with this line of reasoning hinges on what in economics is called the **sectoral change** phenomenon.[2] In 2004 the total airborne emissions of SO_2 in the United States amounted to 15,200 million tons. That year the U.S. Gross Domestic Product (GDP)[3] was $11,735 billion. This means that the SO_2 output was 2.6 pounds per $1,000 of

GDP. In 1970 this index stood at 17.4 pounds per $1,000 of GDP, so in the intervening period of time there was a very considerable drop-off in SO_2 per dollar of GDP. A first reaction might be to think that this reduction shows how effective environmental policies and regulations have been over time. This could be misleading for the following reason. When we speak of the sectoral composition of an economy, we refer to how the total amount of economic activity is distributed among the various parts of the total; this could be a detailed breakdown into industry categories, or a very broad breakdown into major economic categories. The broad sectoral composition of the U.S. economy in 1970 and 2003 was as follows:

	Percent of Total GDP	
	1970	2003
Primary sectors (agriculture, mining, forestry, construction)	9.6	7.0
Manufacturing and transportation	29.9	23.2
All other (services, trade, government)	60.5	69.8

These data show that the economy changed substantially over this period, with the service sector expanding its percentage of the GDP and primary and manufacturing sectors declining their shares. But the average service-sector firm (an insurance firm, for example) produces far less pollution per dollar of its output than does a manufacturing firm (e.g., a steel mill or chemical plant). Thus, just the sectoral shift alone, without any change in pollution output per firm, would have led to a considerable drop in the pollution output per dollar of GDP, because GDP includes the whole economy.

So in this case the real question is: To what extent is the improved performance in the overall pollution emissions of the U.S. economy a result of environmental policies and regulations, and to what extent would emissions have dropped anyway due to sectoral changes in the economy? We will encounter this question again in the chapters to come.

The Policy Effectiveness Question

Suppose we were to demonstrate with confidence that the Clean Air Act has been effective in giving us better air quality, especially in our urban areas. And suppose we estimate that on average this effort is costing the U.S. economy about $100 billion per year. Many of us would undoubtedly regard this as money well spent; in fact, most of us would probably vote for even larger expenditures.

But there is another relevant question to pose in evaluating past progress: Did we get the maximum impact in terms of pollution control for the money we spent? This is the question of **cost effectiveness**: Do environmental policies and regulations give us the "biggest bang for the buck"? Answering this question conclusively would take us well beyond the scope of this book, which is primarily aimed at describing how the policy system works and what the results have been.[4] We will see, however, that the search for cost effectiveness drives many contemporary changes in environmental policy. It is the key consideration, for example, in the movement to limit carbon dioxide emissions to reduce global climate change.

The Political Implications of Data

There is still another reason why looking at data to assess progress is often problematic. Conclusions about how much progress we actually have made are very political. They have important ramifications for building and projecting support for different points of view within the struggle for new policy initiatives or fights over existing policies. Environmental policy is, like most other types of public policy, a matter of heated political conflict and contestation. All the participants are trying to sway opinion in a way that will favor their positions. Advocates of tougher pollution-control laws will rightly stress that pollution is still a major problem that needs continued strong action. Proponents of weaker laws will try to show that much improvement has been made and that tough new regulations will interfere with the need for economic competitiveness and growth. All of the parties will try to use the facts to paint pictures congenial to their views. So facts, or data, can be very controversial.[5]

Data vs. Public Attitudes

In this chapter we will discuss environmental quality as expressed in terms of physical parameters and how they have evolved. But physical data and public attitudes are quite different phenomena and they do not necessarily change in synchronization. Improving data (e.g., reductions in a particular air pollution parameter) do not necessarily lead to changes in public attitudes about the importance of pollution problems. And public attitudes can shift even in situations where the data do not show any particular trend one way or the other. As society changes, for example as incomes increase, or as information available to the citizenry changes, environmental attitudes among the public also can shift. What might have been acceptable years ago in terms of environmental performance may now be unacceptable, prompting public policy changes despite what the data may say. This is because policy attitudes stem from perceptions, while policy initiatives are often based on strategic and tactical possibilities that present themselves from time to time. All of which is not to say that physical data are not important, just that we must recognize that there are many other elements in the entire policy process.

Having considered all of these complications and caveats about looking at the data to assess past progress, let us now take that look. We must keep several things in mind as we do it. The environment is hugely multidimensional, and in one brief chapter we can consider only a tiny collection of data on these different dimensions. Understand that, behind each bit of data we will present, there is much more that could be presented if we had the time and space. The other thing to keep in mind is that in looking at these data, we will begin to encounter the nomenclature and programmatic details of the different environmental policies and programs. In later chapters we will be discussing many of these details at greater length, so don't be concerned if, in this chapter, you don't reach a full understanding of them.

Air Quality Trends

There are three ways of reporting trends in pollution and pollution control: (1) by looking at trends in emissions, (2) by looking at trends in ambient levels, and (3) by looking at trends in the number of people and other organisms exposed to pollution. **Emissions** are the quantities of pollutant actually discharged into the environment; **ambient conditions** are the levels of pollutants in the environment in which people live; and **exposure** takes into account the number of people living in the environment. One would naturally expect that there would be a close relationship between them, but while it is close it is not exact. Between the emission of some substance and the level of that substance in the environment lies nature, and all the meteorological, hydrological, chemical, and biological processes of which it is comprised. A gradual shift in the direction of the prevailing wind, for example, can change ambient air quality levels over a city even though emissions, in terms of quantity, quality, and location, are unchanged.

The Criteria Pollutants

Six of the most common and widespread pollutants have been designated by the federal government as **criteria pollutants**. These are pollutants for which the U.S. Environmental Protection Agency has been given the responsibility of establishing **National Ambient Air Quality Standards (NAAQS).** They are:

- Sulfur dioxide (SO_2)
- Nitrogen oxides (NO_x)
- Carbon monoxide (CO)
- Lead (Pb)
- Ozone (O_3), formed when volatile organic compounds (VOCs) combine with NO_x
- Particulate matter (PM)

Emissions. Data showing trends from 1970 to 2004 in total emissions of the criteria pollutants are shown in table 2.1. As can be seen, all have gone down. Most notable is the reduction in emissions of lead, which can be attributed to the change to unleaded gasoline. Total sulfur dioxide (SO_2) emissions have been cut in half, as have emissions of volatile organic compounds (VOCs). SO_2 gases are formed when fuels (especially oil and coal) are burned and during metal smelting and other industrial processes. VOCs are major precursors (along with NO_x) of smog, and are emitted from cars and trucks,

Table 2.1   National Air Pollutant Emissions Estimates (Fires and Dust Excluded) for Major Pollutants

	Millions of Tons Per Year				
	1970	1980	1990[a]	2000[a]	2004[b]
Carbon Monoxide (CO)	197.3	177.8	143.6	102.4	87.2
Nitrogen Oxides (NO$_x$)[c]	26.9	27.1	25.2	22.3	18.8
Particulate Matter (PM)[d]	12.2[a]				
PM$_{10}$		6.2	3.2	2.3	2.5
PM$_{2.5}$[e]	NA	NA	2.3	1.8	1.9
Sulfur Dioxide (SO$_2$)	31.2	25.9	23.1	16.3	15.2
Volatile Organic Compounds (VOCs)	33.7	30.1	23.1	16.9	15.0
Lead[f]	0.221	0.074	0.005	0.003	0.003
Totals[g]	301.5	267.2	218.2	160.2	138.7

[a] In 1985 and 1996 EPA refined its methods for estimating emissions. Between 1970 and 1975, EPA revised its methods for estimating particulate matter emissions.

[b] The estimates for 2004 are preliminary.

[c] NO$_x$ estimates prior to 1990 include emissions from fires. Fires would represent a small percentage of the NO$_x$ emissions.

[d] PM estimates do not include condensable PM, or the majority of PM$_{2.5}$ that is formed in the atmosphere from "precursor" gases such as SO$_2$ and NO$_x$.

[e] EPA has not estimated PM$_{2.5}$ emissions prior to 1990.

[f] The 1999 estimate for lead is used to represent 2000 and 2003 because lead estimates do not exist for these years.

[g] PM$_{2.5}$ emissions are not added when calculating the total because they are included in the PM$_{10}$ estimate.

Source: U.S. EPA, *Air Trends* (www.epa.gov/airtrends/2005/econ-emissions.html).

industrial processes, and a host of consumer and commercial products. Particulate matter consists of solid particles or liquid droplets found in the air, some of which is visible as dust or soot, and some of which is so small that it can only be seen with a powerful microscope. These are emitted directly from industrial transportation and energy conversion operations, and indirectly when emissions of SO$_2$, NO$_x$, and VOCs interact with other compounds in the air. PM$_{10}$ consists of particulate matter with particles less than 10 microns in diameter, while PM$_{2.5}$ consists of particles less than 2.5 microns in diameter. Total emissions of both forms of particulate matter have decreased over the last several decades, but appear to have increased somewhat in the last four years. Total carbon monoxide emissions have declined by over 50 percent from 1970 to 2004, while those of nitrogen oxides have gone down by about one-third in this time.

Ambient Conditions.   When determining emission levels it seems reasonable to get a total by adding up all the separate flows. With ambient conditions, however, it is more difficult to find useful ways of characterizing them. Some sort of **averaging** is necessary, but there are many types of averages that could be calculated. Across the country, monitoring stations are operated by federal, state, local, and tribal agencies. At each of these monitoring stations periodic readings are made of ambient concentration; for example, a monitoring station might sample the air every 15 minutes and calculate, each time, the SO_2 concentration in terms of parts per million (ppm). To get a weekly, monthly, or yearly reading for that station, some type of average has to be calculated; it could be a simple average of all the readings, or it could be an average of only the highest daily readings, etc. To find a **national ambient concentration**, then, an average would be calculated of all the individual station averages. Again, this average could be calculated in a number of different ways. So we must understand that the ambient trends we will be discussing are actually the result of a complex process of data gathering and analysis.

Table 2.2 shows changes over the last two decades in the simple U.S. averages of ambient concentrations of the criteria pollutants. The data are either parts per million (ppm) or micrograms per cubic meter ($\mu g/m^3$). Note that the figures for particulate matter (PM) are for the period 1993–2002. The numbers show clearly that there have been substantial improvements in ambient air quality over these periods. The largest decline has been in lead, which went down 94 percent in this time period. While table 2.1 showed emissions of volatile organic compounds (VOCs), table 2.2 shows ppm of ozone, of which VOCs are an important precursor. The ozone data show trends in both the 1-hour average and the 8-hour average. There has been a larger decline in the short-run (1-hour) concentration than there has in the longer-run (8-hour) concentration.

While these numbers clearly show improvements, they need to be interpreted with care. The air quality data in table 2.2 represent averages from hundreds of monitoring stations around the country. So air quality at some monitoring stations could have worsened, even though the average shows improvement. We also should keep in mind that percentage changes like those shown in the table can vary greatly, depending on which years are chosen for comparison; by taking a different base year the numbers can sometimes be made to appear quite different. Also, comparing two end points can often hide important trend information; a 50 percent reduction over 20 years, for example, could actually consist of a very large reduction in the first 10 years and little change over the second decade.

Table 2.2	Changes in Ambient Air Quality, 1983–2002	
Pollutant	**Percent Change**
CO (ppm)	−65
Pb ($\mu g/m^3$)	−94
NO_x (ppm)	−15
O_3 (ppm)	
1-hr. standard	−26
8-hr. standard	−21
PM ($\mu g/m^3$; 1993–2002)	
PM_{10}	−13
$PM_{2.5}$	−8
SO_2 (ppm)	−54

Source: U.S. EPA, *Air Trends* (www.epa.gov/airtrends).

Exposure Conditions. Ambient conditions don't translate directly into exposure levels, because these depend both on air quality and on where people live. Demographic changes occur over time; some places lose population, others grow. Table 2.3 shows recent exposure levels in terms of the number of people who are still exposed to levels of air pollutants that exceed the National Ambient Air Quality Standards (NAAQS) established by the EPA pursuant to the federal Clean Air Act. Note that while exposure to elevated levels of nitrogen dioxide (NO_2) and sulfur dioxide are zero, there are many millions of people still exposed to elevated levels of the other criteria pollutants.

Table 2.3 Number of People Living in Countries with Air Quality Concentrations that Exceeded the NAAQS in 2002

Pollutant	Number of People
NO_2	0
O_3	
1-hr. standard	65 million
8-hr. standard	130 million
SO_2	0
PM_{10}	15 million
$PM_{2.5}$	50 million
CO	700 thousand
Lead	200 thousand
Any NAAQS	140 million

Source: U.S. EPA, "Six Principal Pollutants," *Air Trends*, 2004 (www.epa.gov/airtrends/sixpoll.html).

Toxic Pollutants

Another major dimension of air pollution is **toxic materials**, which include a vast array of chemicals produced and used in varying quantities throughout the economy. Although they may be less widespread than the criteria air pollutants, they are much more hazardous. As part of the Emergency Planning and Community Right to Know Act (EPCRA) of 1986, Congress established the **Toxic Release Inventory (TRI)**, a program requiring companies[6] to report the quantities of a large number of specified chemicals released into the environment.[7] At present there are approximately 650 chemicals on the TRI list. "Released" means toxics disposed of on-site in air, water, or land, plus off-site transfers that are slated for disposal. Table 2.4 shows some recent TRI data. As can be seen, the bulk of the releases were on-site. The total increased during the 1990s but has decreased since then. In particular, airborne emissions declined about 50 percent during this period.

As noted above, release data are not the same as ambient data. It is reasonably easy to characterize total release by adding up the total number of pounds of material introduced into the environment. One cannot do this so readily with ambient conditions, which are normally reported in units such as parts per million (ppm) or micrograms per cubic meter ($\mu g/m^3$). Thus it may not make sense to add together the ambient quantities of different substances. Furthermore, once toxic materials are dispersed in the environment, testing for concentration levels can be costly. There is relatively little in the way of reliable data on long-term trends in the ambient levels of toxic chemicals. One way of estimating exposure levels is to have data on releases disaggregated by small area, for example by U.S. county.

Table 2.4	Toxic Release Inventory Data, 1988, 1998, and 2003		
	1988	1998	2003
	(1,000 pounds)		
On-Site Releases			
Airborne	2,831,070	2,091,165	1,380,546
Other	2,849,124	4,574,879	2,540,224
Off-Site Releases	1,269,425	430,298	522,397
Total	6,949,619	7,096,342	4,443,167

Source: U.S. EPA, *TRI Trends Report*, 2006 (www.epa.gov/triexplorer/trends.htm).

An organization called Environmental Defense has done this in its "Scorecard" program, which can be accessed on its Web site.[8]

It should be emphasized that the TRI covers only manufacturing firms for the most part. It does not cover agricultural firms, which are the source of major amounts of pesticide runoff. The U.S. Geological Survey recently reported that almost all of the streams in the country have been contaminated with agricultural chemicals, frequently at levels that can affect aquatic life and fish-eating animals.[9]

Ozone-Depleting Chemicals

The earth is in balance with the sun as regards incoming and outgoing radiation. One of the prime structures that maintains this balance is the earth's atmosphere. About 20 years ago scientists discovered that the very thin layer of ozone in the earth's atmosphere was being destroyed by a class of chemicals that was being heavily used, especially for refrigeration and air conditioning.[10] In response to this, the countries of the world got together and negotiated the Montreal Protocol to phase out the production and use of these ozone-depleting chemicals.[11] This agreement has been remarkably effective. U.S. production and use of these chemicals have been reduced almost to zero in the last decade, as has happened in many countries around the world. It is an instance of effective global reaction to a major global environmental problem.

Greenhouse Gases

The same cannot be said about "global warming." The buildup of certain gases in the earth's atmosphere, as a result of human production and consumption practices, threatens to alter the chemical content of the atmosphere and change this radiation balance enough to produce a significant warming at the earth's surface. The major expected impact of this effect is a rise in global mean surface temperatures (hence its nickname, the greenhouse effect), sufficient in extent to lead to substantial impacts on the earth's biophysical

**Table 2.5   Total U.S. Emissions
of Greenhouse
Gases, 1990–2003**

Year	Teragrams, CO_2 Equivalent
1990	6,088.1
1997	6,677.5
1998	6,719.7
1999	6,752.2
2000	6,953.2
2001	6,806.9
2002	6,858.1
2003	6,900.2

Source: U.S. EPA, *Inventory of U.S. Greenhouse Gas Emissions and Sinks, 1990–2003*, April 2005 (http://www.epa.gov/globalwarming/publications/emissions).

processes and, thus, on the welfare of human beings. Contrary to the trends in ozone-depleting chemicals and the criteria air pollutants, emissions of greenhouse gases continue to grow at a substantial rate.

The major greenhouse gas is carbon dioxide (CO_2), and the primary source of this is the burning of fossil fuels. Table 2.5 shows the total U.S. emissions of greenhouse gases from 1990 to 2003. These have trended upward with perhaps some flattening out since 2000. These CO_2 emissions are very closely related to energy use in the modern economy which, in the case of the United States and most other countries, is highly dependent on the use of fossil fuels (coal, petroleum, natural gas, wood). We will discuss this, and especially the international efforts to reduce global CO_2 emissions, in chapter 18.

Water Pollution Trends

While an extensive body of reasonably consistent data are being developed for air pollution, the same cannot be said about water pollution. High quality, comprehensive data on waterborne emissions and water-quality parameters are much harder to find. There are many sources of emissions: point and nonpoint sources; municipal and industrial sources; large and small sources; freshwater and saltwater emissions; and so on. Water quality changes are not easy to characterize because of the sheer scope and variety of the nation's water resources. The Clean Water Act applies to about 3 million miles of rivers, from huge main stem rivers to small local streams. It covers 40 million very diverse acres of lakes, 34,000 square miles of estuaries, and 58,000 miles of ocean shoreline. Most of the water quality monitoring is done by the states, which use varying means of sampling and testing, with varying levels of budgetary and political commitment, in their programs. Thus it is not easy to create a database that is readily comprehensible and reasonably comprehensive to give a picture of changing water quality in the United States.

Emissions

Waterborne emissions are normally classified as conventional, nonconventional, and toxic pollutants. **Conventional pollutants** consist primarily of biochemical oxygen demand (BOD, discussed below), total suspended solids, bacteria, and oil and grease. **Nonconventional pollutants** are largely nutri-ents such as phosphorus and nitrogen. **Toxic pollutants** are the natural and synthetic chemicals and metals discharged from industrial sources.

Given the great complexity of pollutants and the water systems into which they are emitted, it is difficult to get a comprehensive picture of water-borne emissions. We can look at some of the important components of the total, however.

Municipal Wastewater Discharges. The best data are for municipal wastewater treatment facilities, owing to the need for monitoring the federal construction grant program. The U.S. population stood at 180.7 million in 1960 and 282.3 million in 2000. This represents a 56 percent increase over these four decades, with obvious implications for the amount of sanitary waste produced and requiring removal and treatment. The Clean Water Act funded a major federal effort to provide municipalities and towns with con-struction grants to fund publicly owned treatment works (POTWs). In the 1980s this was changed to a system of state revolving-fund programs, seeded by the federal government, to be used for the same purpose. Has the program been effective? The data in table 2.6 reveal the story.

The data refer to tons of BOD, which stands for **biochemical oxygen demand**. This is a measure of the quantity of oxygen-consuming organic mat-ter in wastewater. The greater the amount of BOD discharged to a water resource, the greater the oxygen depletion in that resource and the lower its water quality. The oxygen depletion can be temporary or can last a long time, depending on the amount of dissolved oxygen in the water and its rate of replenishment. We will discuss this at greater length in chapter 10. New treat-ment plant capacity involves not only new plants but also upgraded technol-ogy in existing plants. It's customary in wastewater treatment to classify

Table 2.6   Results and Projections of POTW Construction for Selected Years, 1968–2025

	1968	1972	1978	1996	...	2016	2025
Population served by POTWs (millions)	140.1	141.7	155.2	189.7		275.0	295.0
Percent of total population	71	69	70	72		88	88
Influent BOD (tons per day)	34,885	35,306	39,889	46,642		67,607	72,724
Design removal efficiency (%)	39	41	52	65		71	71
Effluent BOD (tons per day)	21,280	20,831	19,147	16,325		19,606	21,090

Source: U.S. EPA, *Progress in Water Quality: An Evaluation of the National Investment in Municipal Waste-water Treatment*, EPA-832-R-00-008, June 2000 (www.epa.gov/owm/wquality/benefits.htm).

technologies as primary, secondary, and tertiary. **Primary treatment**, relying primarily on physical means such as settling ponds, typically can remove up to 30 percent of the BOD load of the incoming wastewater stream. **Secondary treatment** technologies can extract up to 80 to 90 percent of the waste stream, while **tertiary treatment**, involving sophisticated chemical means of handling the wastewater, can remove up to 99 percent of the BOD.

As table 2.6 indicates, the percentage of the total U.S. population served by POTWs has stayed relatively constant at 70 percent over the last four decades, meaning that the total inflow of wastewater handled by these plants has increased along with population increases. The fourth row of the table shows that there has been a substantial increase in the overall treatment removal efficiency, from 39 percent in 1968 to 65 percent in 1996. This appears to be a clear response to the Clean Water Act of 1972, which called for all POTWs to incorporate at least secondary treatment by 1977 (subsequently extended to 1983). As we shall see in chapter 10, there has been some controversy over the actual effectiveness of this program.

Industrial Point Sources. Another major source of waterborne discharges is industrial point sources. Major sources in this category are subject to a discharge permit program; in order to discharge lawfully they must have a discharge permit that specifies emission limits. One development that has occurred since the 1970s is a substantial shift from direct to indirect discharge. **Direct discharge** means point sources discharge directly into rivers, lakes, or other water bodies. **Indirect discharge** means industrial emissions are sent to POTWs for treatment and then discharged. Over the past 25 years or so, there has been a gradual shift away from direct discharge as older plants have been retired and new facilities have opted for connecting to a POTW. Thus at the present time, indirect industrial dischargers greatly outnumber direct dischargers. For this reason, total emissions from direct dischargers probably fell substantially over the last few decades, although the exact numbers are not immediately available. We do have data on direct discharges of TRI chemicals into surface water bodies; these declined from about 337 million pounds in 1988 to 233 million pounds in 2003.

Nonpoint Sources. Even harder to get are data on the changes over time on waterborne pollutants from nonpoint sources. Nonpoint sources include agricultural runoff, urban storm-water runoff, runoff from construction sites, septic tank emissions, discharges from recreational boaters, and so on. By definition these are dispersed and diffused, so measuring quantities and qualities of effluent are problematic. The Environmental Protection Agency now regards nonpoint source water pollution as more damaging than point source emissions.

Surface Water Quality

As mentioned earlier, because of the extreme diversity of water resources (streams, rivers, ponds, lakes, oceans, etc.) it is difficult to derive a comprehensive picture of water quality in the United States and any changes that have occurred as a result of various policy initiatives. There are two primary sources of information on water quality: (1) data collected by the states under terms set out in the Clean Water Act (CWA) and reported to the EPA, and (2) data collection programs of the U.S. Geological Survey.

Information Under the CWA. Section 305(b) of the Clean Water Act requires states to report the quality of their water resources in comparison to quality standards that have been set for these waters. The standards are set in terms of designated uses, such as water that is drinkable, fishable, or swimmable. Section 303(d) of the Clean Water Act requires that states provide lists of all their waters that are "impaired." The act also requires the EPA to issue a biennial report to Congress using these data to assess the state of the country's water quality. The most recent report was the 2002 National Water Quality Inventory Report.[12] In it, EPA reports that 39 percent of assessed (i.e., those that were actually evaluated) rivers and streams, and 45 percent of assessed lakes, did not meet applicable water quality standards and were judged as impaired for one or more desired uses (i.e., fishing, swimming, etc.). While it is reasonably clear that this is an improvement from several decades ago, it is not possible to make a concrete comparison because of the lack of earlier data.

Information from the U.S. Geological Survey (USGS). In 1991 the USGS launched the National Water Quality Assessment (NAWQA), which is intended to be a long-term effort to collect data on water quality in a large number of water resource basins around the United States. According to a researcher who has studied this effort in some detail:

> These results suggest that the Clean Water Act, and in particular its point-source programs, has made at least modest improvements in water quality, especially considering the increase in economic activity during the 1980s. Incomplete implementation of the Clean Water Act during the 1980s was one reason improvements were not larger, but probably a far more important factor was the failure of the Act to do much about nonpoint sources.[13]

Drinking Water

It was only in the latter part of the nineteenth century that the health implications of contaminated drinking water were fully understood. In 1914 the first federal standards were put in place, covering maximum permissible levels of total bacteria and of coliform bacteria. But the standards then were applied only to interstate water carriers. By the early 1970s about 800 public water supply systems in the United States were regulated under federal standards, while many more were regulated by the individual states. In the Safe Drinking Water Act of 1975, federal **water quality standards** became binding for all U.S. public water supplies. These standards now cover almost a hundred different individual contaminants, including organic and inorganic chemicals, microbiological organisms, and radionuclides.

There are no trend data on the quality of drinking water in the country. That quality problems still exist to some extent is evidenced by the occasional outbreak of illness traceable to contaminated water, such as the Milwaukee episode of 1993. In that case the contaminant was an intestinal parasite: protozoa *cryptosporidia*.

One of the few available data trends tracks the number of violations reported by the operators of U.S. public water systems. Violations can be of two types: violations of monitoring and reporting requirements to which these systems are subject under the Safe Drinking Water Act, and violations of the standards for maximum contaminant levels that have been set under the act. Figure 2.1 illustrates the history of violations reported from 1986 to 1998.

It clearly appears that in recent years the number of violations has increased. What is not clear, however, is whether we can take this as evidence of a trend toward lower quality water in the public water supply systems of the country. The Safe Drinking Water Act has been amended regularly by Congress, provisions have been changed, and the reporting system has been improved. What these data may reflect in part is an increasingly effective monitoring and reporting system.

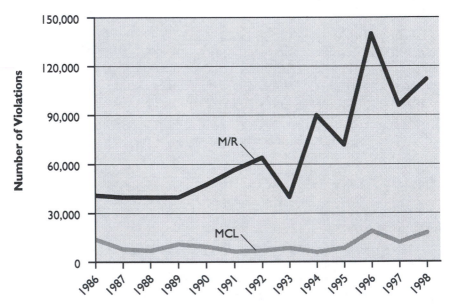

Note: M/R denotes monitoring and reporting violations; MCL indicates violations of maximum contaminant levels.

Source: U.S. EPA, National Public Water System Supervision Program, Annual Compliance Reports.

Figure 2.1   Number of Public Water Supply System Violations Reported to EPA, 1986–1998

Municipal Solid Waste

Municipal solid waste (MSW) consists of the garbage and trash disposed of by families and small firms. It includes domestic waste, lawn and garden material, and used building materials from households. It also includes wastepaper scrap from office buildings and various types of non-hazardous waste from small industrial firms. The handling of the MSW stream has largely been a local responsibility, managed through the initiatives and budgets of communities and states. Major efforts have been undertaken to institute recycling programs to reduce the quantities of MSW requiring disposal. Final disposal has historically been mostly in landfills.

Table 2.7 contains trend data on MSW generated, recovered, and put in landfills for the last two decades. In the 1980s MSW generated per capita increased from 3.7 to 4.5 pounds per day. This, coupled with the population increase, led to a substantial increase in the total quantity of MSW generated. In 1980 about 10 percent of this was recovered, leaving most of the rest to be landfilled. By 1990 the proportion recovered had increased to about 17 percent.

In the 1990s two trends seem to have occurred: the MSW generated per capita leveled off, while recovery rates increased. Since the population continued to increase during this decade, there was about a 12 percent increase in the aggregate MSW generated. The year 1999 also saw an increase in the MSW recovery rate to almost 30 percent. The result was that there was a relatively modest increase in the quantity of MSW sent to landfills during the 1990s.

Table 2.7   Municipal Solid Waste Generated, Recovered, and Landfilled, Selected Years, 1980–2003

	1980	1990	1995	1999	2003
Waste generated					
Total (mil. tons)	151.5	205.2	211.4	229.9	256.2
Per capita (lb./day)	3.7	4.5	4.4	4.6	4.4
Materials recovered					
Total (mil. tons)	14.5	33.6	54.9	63.9	72.3
Per capita (lb./day)	.4	.7	1.1	1.3	1.4
Waste landfilled					
Total (mil. tons)	123.3	139.7	120.9	131.9	150.5
Per capita (lb./day)	3.0	3.1	2.5	2.7	2.5

Source: Franklin Associates, "Characterization of Municipal Solid Waste in the United States, 1999," as reported in the U.S. Statistical Abstract (Washington, DC: U.S. Census Bureau, 2006, table 363): 229.

Hazardous Waste

Hazardous waste (HW) is the name given to a huge variety of mostly chemical wastes generated in the production and consumption activities of a modern economy. These chemicals are of varying composition, concentration, and toxicity, and the routes they take from first manufacture to transportation, use, and finally disposal are also extremely diverse.

There are two major components of hazardous waste policy in the United States, one applying to the handling and disposal of HW that is being generated presently, and the other applying mostly to cleaning up legacy sites that were used in past years to dispose of HW.

Contemporaneous Hazardous Waste

The disposal of contemporaneous hazardous waste in the United States comes under the Resource Conservation and Recovery Act, passed in 1976. This statute does not give the EPA authority to limit the amount of hazardous waste generated, but does govern the means by which it can be handled and disposed. Regulations on these activities can, in turn, affect the incentives generators have to limit the quantities of HW requiring disposal.

Figure 2.2 illustrates recent data on the amount of hazardous waste generated. These figures are subject to a great deal of uncertainty, a situation that affects many data sets dealing with environmental pollution. The data are gathered by the states, which differ in terms of the means devoted to the task and the thoroughness of the effort. The chemicals classified by EPA as hazardous also have changed somewhat over time.

The dark rectangles in the figure show quantities of originally designated HW generated for selected years from 1981 to 1995. These demonstrate a substantial decline starting in the late 1980s and continuing through the 1990s. The lighter rectangles include quantities of HW newly designated and regulated in the 1990s, the volume of which is quite stable up to 1995. Thus it appears reasonable to conclude that the overall quantities of HW have, in fact, declined substantially in the last decade of the twentieth century.

Old Hazardous Waste Dump Sites

In 1980 the U.S. Congress passed CERCLA, the Comprehensive Environmental Response, Compensation and Liability Act, popularly known as Superfund. A major goal of CERCLA was to identify and clean up old hazardous waste sites, many of which had been abandoned and forgotten. We will look closely at the Superfund program in chapter 11; it has been a contentious program costing many billions of dollars thus far. It's not easy to assess the progress that has been made in actual cleanup operations. The program works through a process by which the EPA examines potential Superfund sites around the country and places those that it thinks are serious enough on the National Priorities List (NPL). Cleanup actions are then directed at these NPL sites.

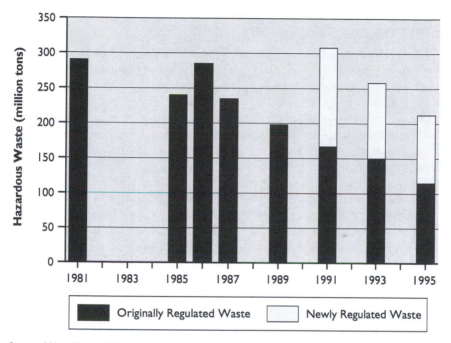

Source: Hilary Sigman, "Hazardous Waste and Toxic Substances Policies," in Paul R. Portney and Robert N. Stavins, eds., *Public Policies for Environmental Protection*, 2nd ed. (Washington, DC: Resources for the Future, 2000):228.

Figure 2.2   Generation of Hazardous Waste, 1981–1995

Since the inception of the program about 1,500 sites around the country have been put on the NPL. Since that time also, cleanup operations have been completed at about 800 sites. This appears to be real progress, and it is. To some extent, however, this is because the EPA has explicitly chosen to reduce the number of new sites put on the NPL, so that the backlog of sites already on the list could be remediated.

Several years ago the EPA estimated that about 3,000 potential sites might qualify for addition to the NPL.[14] This suggests that there is a lot more remaining to be done under Superfund. Complicating this assessment are the actions taken by all of the states to develop their own Superfund-type programs to clean up sites that are contaminated but are not on the NPL. So future progress in cleaning up old hazardous waste sites is going to hinge importantly on how the states and the EPA sort out questions of who will take responsibility for cleaning up specific sites.

Summary

The environment is many faceted. Over the last three decades some environmental parameters have gotten better, some have gotten worse. Progress has been made in reducing many air pollutants, especially the criteria pollutants (with the exception of NO_x) and airborne releases of toxic chemicals. Airborne releases of (atmospheric) ozone-destroying chemicals, particularly chlorofluorocarbons, have been substantially reduced. The one major air pollutant that has not been controlled to any extent is carbon dioxide (CO_2), the primary substance responsible for global warming.

Industrial and municipal sources of water pollution have been controlled to a substantial degree, and the results of this appear to be improvements in water quality in many, though by no means all, water bodies of the United States. Much more needs to be done to control nonpoint sources of water pollution.

One environmental parameter that continues to grow is solid waste, especially municipal solid waste. Major changes have occurred in how it is handled, however, which has probably reduced the risk of environmental damage from this source. Major progress also has been achieved in instituting better programs for handling hazardous waste, though much more remains to be done.

We need to remember that knowing how various environmental parameters have changed does not immediately answer the question of why the changes have happened. In particular, we need to determine the effectiveness of federal efforts to control pollution in comparison with other factors that may account for some of the changes. Federal-level environmental policy is still something of a political football, and policy effectiveness is not necessarily the prime consideration that drives events.

Key Terms

ambient conditions
averaging
before/after comparison
biochemical oxygen demand
conventional pollutants
cost effectiveness
criteria pollutants
direct discharge
emissions
exposure
hazardous waste (HW)
indirect discharge
municipal solid waste (MSW)

National Ambient Air Quality
   Standards (NAAQS)
national ambient concentration
nonconventional pollutants
primary treatment
secondary treatment
sectoral change
tertiary treatment
toxic materials
toxic pollutants
Toxic Release Inventory (TRI)
water quality standards
with/without comparison

Questions for Further Discussion

1. Why do you think it is difficult to get an accurate picture of changes in environmental quality in the United States over the last three or four decades?

2. Under what circumstances might total emissions of some pollutant decline, while at the same time the ambient concentrations of the pollutant increase?

3. If you were the head of EPA and had $100 million to spend, how much of this would you spend on reducing pollution and how much on monitoring emissions and ambient conditions?

4. Suppose you were responsible for reporting on the changes in water quality over the last 20 years of some large river. What are some of the practical problems encountered when doing this?

5. Suppose you find, in question 4, that average dissolved oxygen levels of the river have increased by about 20 percent over the last 20 years. How would you determine whether this was (or how much of it was) a result of federal water pollution-control policy?

Web Sites

The EPA has a number of sites where data on the status of the environment are available, for example:

www.epa.gov/enviro/
www.epa.gov/airnow/
www.epa.gov/ord/htm/monitoring.htm

Other government agencies with relevant information:
National Oceanic and Atmospheric Administration
www.ncdc.noaa.gov/oa/ncdc.html

U.S. Geological Survey
www.usgs.gov

U.S. Fish and Wildlife Service
http://info.fws.gov/databases2.html

For international data one of the best sites is the United Nations Environment Program:
www.unep.org/themes/assessment/

See also the Organization for Economic Cooperation and Development:
www.oecd.org/home

Additional Readings

Blatt, Harvey, *America's Environmental Report Card: Are We Making the Grade?* (Cambridge, MA: MIT Press, December 2004).

Dahl, T. E., *Status and Trends of Wetlands of the Conterminous United States 1986 to 1997* (Washington, DC: U.S. Department of the Interior, U.S. Fish and Wildlife Service, 2000).

U.S. Environmental Protection Agency, *Draft Report on the Environment* (Washington, DC: EPA, 2003). Available on the EPA Web site, www.epa.gov/indicators, especially the data underlying the report.

U.S. Environmental Protection Agency, *The Benefits and Costs of the Clean Air Act 1990 to 2010: EPA Report to Congress* (www.epa.gov/EE/epa/eerm.nsf/vwRepNumLookup/ EE-0295A?Open Document).

U.S. Environmental Protection Agency, "An Examination of BOD Loadings Before and After the CWA," chapter 2 in *Progress in Water Quality: An Evaluation of the National Investment in Municipal Wastewater Treatment*, EPA-832-R-00-008, June 2000 (www.epa.gov/owm/wquality/chap02.pdf).

U.S. Environmental Protection Agency, *Latest Findings on National Air Quality: 2001 Status and Trends*, EPA-454-K-02-001, Office of Air Quality Planning and Standards (Washington, DC: EPA, September 2002).

U.S. Environmental Protection Agency, *Municipal Solid Waste in the United States: 2001 Facts and Figures*, EPA 530-R-03-011 (Washington, DC: EPA, October 2003). (www.epa.gov/epaoswer/non-hw/muncpl/msw99.htm).

U.S. Environmental Protection Agency, *National Water Quality Inventory: 1998 Report to Congress*, EPA-841-R-00-001, Office of Water (Washington, DC: EPA, June 2000).

U.S. Environmental Protection Agency, *Toxics Release Inventory (TRI) Program, 2001 Public Data Release Report* (www.epa.gov/tri/tridata/tri01/pdr/index.htm).

Notes

[1] Over the last few years the EPA has been developing a program called "Environmental Indicators" that would generate and publish scientifically valid data showing how various dimensions of environmental quality are changing. See www.epa.gov/indicate.

[2] For example, some observers strongly believe that significant air pollution reductions actually started well before the federalization of environmental policy in the 1970s, as a result of the local and voluntary efforts of an increasingly affluent and service-based society to reduce emissions. See Indur Goklany, *Clearing the Air: The Real Story of the War on Air Pollution* (Washington, DC: CATO Institute, 1999).

[3] GDP is a measure of the total value of final goods and services produced within an economy.

[4] Cost-effectiveness is a major concept in environmental economics.

[5] This was highlighted recently in a book by Bjørn Lomborg titled *The Skeptical Environmentalist* (Cambridge: Cambridge University Press, 2001). My own reading of this book is that he simply is saying that some progress has been made in combating some environmental problems. But others have interpreted him as saying that many environmental problems are not as serious as they have been made out to be. Whatever the case, the book has been highly controversial, mainly because it challenges the current status of many environmental parameters.

[6] Companies employing 10 or more employees, producing more than 25,000 pounds or otherwise using more than 10,000 pounds of listed chemical.

[7] In the Pollution Prevention Act of 1990, companies also were required to report waste management and source reduction activities. We will look more closely at these programs in chapter 11.

[8] www.scorecard.org

[9] U.S. Department of the Interior, Geological Survey, *Pesticides in the Nation's Streams and Groundwater*, March 2006. (www.usgs.gov/newsroom/article.asp?ID=1450)

[10] In chapter 18 we will look at this problem in more detail.

[11] Among which are chlorofluorocarbons, hydrochlorofluorocarbons, carbon tetrachloride, methyl chloroform, and methyl bromide.

[12] www.epa.gov/305b.

[13] Winston Harrington, *Regulating Industrial Water Pollution in the United States*, Discussion Paper 03-03 (Washington, DC: Resources for the Future, April 2003):22.

[14] The U.S. General Accounting Office has published a number of reports assessing progress under Superfund and identifying places where the program needs to be improved. See its Web site: www.gao.gov and search on "superfund."

SECTION II
THE POLICY
PROCESS AND
ITS PARTICIPANTS

In the next five chapters we will discuss the nature of the public decision process that produces environmental policy. In this section we will highlight the process at the federal level; in a later chapter (17) we will discuss environmental policy at the state level. The first chapter in this section examines the nature of the policy process at the conceptual level. The next four chapters summarize the roles of the important private and public participants in that process. It bears repeating that within the scope of any one book, the discussions are by necessity brief. There are dozens of books and thousands of scholarly articles published each year on various aspects of environmental policy in the United States. What we can accomplish in a few chapters is to provide an overview of the process and the primary roles of the participants.

In this chapter we develop some general concepts about how to think of the governmental processes that are responsible for producing environmental policies and regulations. Our aim is to develop some general ideas about the phenomenon that will move us toward an understanding of its basic outlines and primary features. Policy making is a complicated process, and scholars have made numerous attempts to distill this complicated process into simplified models and theories of various types. While none is completely successful in either description or prediction, a brief overview of some of these models will give readers a good sense of different ways people think about policy making. The greater the variety of perspectives you can bring to environmental policy, the better able you will be to understand how policy making works and how you might become more effectively involved.

The Rational View

A typical view of policy making—long championed by older textbooks on the subject—is like that depicted in figure 3.1. According to this **rational model**, an environmental problem is discovered, information is gathered and analyzed, alternatives are assessed, and policy makers render a decision that reflects a rational response to the problem at hand. Under this view, scientific knowledge may be incomplete; our understanding of how policies work in practice may be limited; participants may disagree on criteria, alternatives, and best solutions; but in any event, a decision will reflect the best possible response to the problem given the constraints involved.

In the first stage, the environmental problem is identified. This may result from a significant environmental event, a policy study, or the gradual accretion of interest group attention and policy-making opportunity that brings a problem to our attention. Regardless of how it comes to be understood, the problem is identified as something that can be addressed by decision makers, and is presented to them as something to be "solved." Some problems, such as natural disasters like hurricanes and floods, cannot be solved, although steps can be taken to ameliorate the consequences.

Once the problem, say climate change, has been identified, the next step in the rational view is to identify the relevant criteria that would be used to assess whether or not any proposed policy solution will be successful. For instance, we may consider factors such as economic efficiency (do economic benefits exceed costs?), effectiveness (is the problem likely to be solved?), equity (are the costs and benefits borne by the appropriate individuals or groups?), organizational capacity (are the organizations entrusted to carry out the policy capable of doing so?), and political feasibility (is the proposed solution politically possible?). Other criteria may be used in different circumstances.

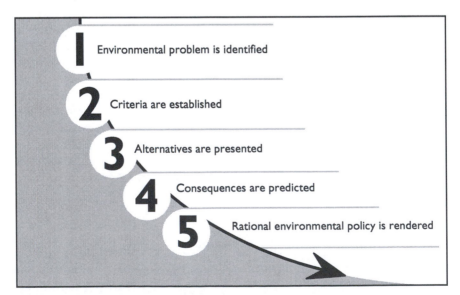

1 Environmental problem is identified

2 Criteria are established

3 Alternatives are presented

4 Consequences are predicted

5 Rational environmental policy is rendered

Figure 3.1   Stages in the Rational View of Policy Making

Once criteria have been established, the policy makers are presented with a series of **alternative policy responses** that can best address the environmental problem. These normally include significant responses (in the case of climate change, a tax on carbon-emitters), some intermediate responses (more moderate actions or studying the problem further), or doing nothing. Like medical practice, the first rule of policy analysis is to do no harm; sometimes doing nothing is the best policy response if it looks like all other responses would make things worse.

At this stage, policy makers have been presented with alternative policy responses and now must begin to understand, as best as possible, what will happen under each of the different scenarios. For example, if a carbon tax is implemented, what effect will this have on energy industries, consumers, specific sectors of the economy (e.g., particularly energy-dependent ones), specific geographical regions, the U.S. economy overall, and so on? Under the rational view, the better the predictions, the better the policy making that will result. Information should be as complete as possible. Even where the option is "do nothing," policy makers need to understand the ecological, economic, and political implications of no action. In the rational view, the role of environmental policy research is critical at this stage.

In the final stage, decision makers render a decision that in their view best reflects the interests of the public. Inevitably, trade-offs must occur (e.g., the benefits of cleaner air may accrue to different regions or groups than those bearing the burden of the tax) and not all parties will be completely satisfied with the outcome. Nonetheless, the policy decision will be one that policy makers decide will best serve the interests of the public.

The virtue of the rational view of policy making is its simplicity, its attention to the role of ideas and information, and its emphasis on the relationship between intentions and outcomes. On the other hand, the rational model often has been depicted as naïve because political actors and interests are ignored and it presumes a rationality in decision making that simply does not comport with reality. Further, arguments about criteria, such as efficiency versus equity, are so fundamental that compromise solutions cannot always be expected to create effective policy responses. To take one brief example, U.S. air pollution policy can be described as having a political rationality, but the Clean Air Act itself (as we will see in future chapters) is not normally viewed as a rational environmental response to the problem of air pollution. If there is any rationality at all, it involves a more complex view of the policy-making process that is ignored by the rational view of policy making, one that recognizes other important dimensions: the process, institutions, and ideas.

Policy Making as a Process

Looking at things from a rational standpoint tells us something about how policy making could take place, but doesn't tell us enough about how actions fit together or their relationship to each other. Further, the rational view is linear, with a beginning and an end, and we know that policies continue for decades and frequently are revised over time. What is the sequence of actions that best describes how policies are enacted and revised? In reality, thousands of policy events (meetings, congressional testimony, lobbying, publishing reports, etc.) are going on at any one time, so it's useful to organize them around a series of primary activities or functions. One approach within this **functional model** is that of a **policy cycle**, a typical example of which is shown in figure 3.2.

The policy cycle consists of a series of events, or activities, arranged in sequence. The steps in the sequence are laid out in a loop, which conveys an important lesson: policy issues are never really over and entirely dispensed with. The policy process is an ongoing struggle where the campaigns and battles wax and wane but never really stop. We will discuss briefly the steps in the cycle.

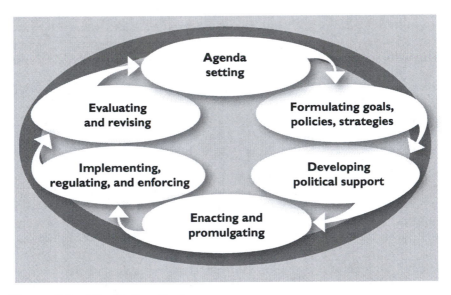

Figure 3.2   The Policy Cycle

Setting the Agenda

For a problem to be addressed it first has to get on the **political agenda** for action. There are many environmental problems, but just being a problem is not sufficient to compel action. As important as environmental problems are, there are literally thousands of "problems" that policy makers may choose to tackle: education, transportation, criminal justice, national security, and so forth. Therefore, getting the attention of policy makers for any one problem is difficult. There are many cases of problems being neglected by policy makers even though by some intrinsic measure they should be regarded as important. Indoor air pollution is a good case in point. Another might be global warming, at least among policy makers in the United States.

One way that specific environmental problems get on the policy agenda is for some galvanizing event or series of events to give it visibility and elevate its importance in the mind of the public. When the Cuyahoga River in Cleveland caught fire in 1969—albeit not for the first time!—and was publicized by *Time Magazine* a week later, the public recognized how awful the water quality in some American rivers had become and called for greater attention to surface water quality. The role of the media in publicizing these events is a powerful one. Visibility requires the combination of an important environmental event that people care about, and media outlets willing to publicize the problem. Love Canal did this for the problem of abandoned hazardous waste landfills, where the media provided images of basement walls in toxic colors and irate residents screaming at government officials to do something. The *Exxon Valdez* tanker grounding clearly did it for the issue of marine oil pollution, as is discussed in exhibit 3.1. These events led to major new U.S. environmental laws. During the 1960s, 70s, and 80s, environmental policy was pushed along by a series of incidents that had the effect of keeping environmental issues on the front burner. The most important include the following:

- Santa Barbara oil spill, 1969
- Cuyahoga River in Cleveland catches fire, 1969
- *Amoco Cadiz* tanker wreck, 1978
- Love Canal toxic waste discovery, 1978
- Ixtoc I well blowout, Gulf of Mexico, 1979
- Three-Mile Island nuclear accident, 1979
- Times Beach dioxin spill, 1983
- Bhopal, India, toxic release, 1984
- Chernobyl nuclear accident, 1986
- *Exxon Valdez* oil spill, 1989

Since the *Exxon Valdez*, there have been no major pollution incidents that have captured wide public attention. Some people thought that the exceptionally hot summer of 1998 might help to move global warming onto the front burner, but this does not seem to have happened.

While it can seem successful in the short term for galvanizing political support, relying on environmental catastrophes to drive policy may not be effective in the long run. If environmental regulation is effective, then the galvanizing events that focus attention on the need to do something will presumably become fewer and fewer. Policy makers need to be able to make progress on environmental issues without being prodded by some catastrophe. To be effective over the long term and to focus on problems that the public and scientists believe to be most important, the environmental policy process must be proactive rather than simply crisis driven.

For events to trigger a response they need to be described and explained to people in a convincing way; this highlights the role of the media. In 1962 the publication of Rachel Carson's *Silent Spring*, which focused the spotlight on the effects of pesticides on wildlife, elevated the problem of chemical pollution into the public consciousness. The writings of E. O. Wilson have similarly drawn attention to the issue of conserving the world's biological diversity.[1]

Exhibit 3.1
Oil-Spill Politics: Getting the Problem on the Agenda

Vast amounts of petroleum and its products are transported on the world's oceans, bays, and harbors each year. Unfortunately, substantial amounts of it get spilled in tanker, barge, and terminal accidents. For decades national and state authorities have tried to put into place a set of regulations that would help to forestall future spills, and a process for cleaning up those spills that did happen. Oil-spill provisions were contained in Section 311 of the 1972 Clean Water Act. The Trans-Alaska Pipeline Authorization Act of 1973 established a cleanup fund for spills connected to that project. The Deepwater Port Act of 1973 provided liability limits and a cleanup fund for spills in ports. The Outer Continental Shelf Lands Act of 1978 had provisions applicable to offshore oil drilling operations.

What many people thought was needed was a comprehensive oil-spill liability, compensation, and response law that would cover the entire industry, which was growing rapidly in complexity and extent. But for many years political forces conspired against such an act. The petroleum transportation industry was largely against any new initiative. Many of the coastal states were also reluctant to support the effort because they did not want the federal government to preempt actions that states might want to implement. And many in the environmental community were focused more on general hazardous waste control, which they thought could readily be extended to deal with oil spills

Thus during the period from 1979 to 1989, those in Congress who wanted to form a comprehensive oil-spill program were unable to put together a coalition large enough to make it happen. This all changed in 1989, with the grounding of the *Exxon Valdez* in Alaskan waters and subsequent oil spill. With this single galvanizing event, the oil-spill problem was moved to the front burner (it achieved high saliency, in the language of the policy cycle), and in relatively short order the preemption issue was solved and Congress passed the Oil Pollution Act of 1990. This law provided for greatly increased penalties and liability provisions than did older laws, and gave the Chief Executive major new responsibilities in responding to oil spills.[a]

[a] For more information see Thomas A. Birkland, *After Disaster: Agenda Setting, Public Policy, and Focusing Events* (Washington, DC: Georgetown University Press, 1997).

But efforts like this are not necessarily easy, particularly when the environmental impacts being described are diffuse and subtle. For example, although there has been no specific, newsworthy calamity, many individuals and nations around the world are gradually being brought to the recognition of climate change as an important environmental priority. But this awareness is growing more slowly than the importance of the problem warrants. It is coming about largely through concentrated efforts on the part of scientists around the world to document rising temperatures and to link that with growing carbon emissions both theoretically (the "greenhouse effect") and empirically (through studies linking carbon emissions with temperature shifts.)

Environmental issues can achieve saliency also through strictly political means. In the early 1980s President Reagan's new appointees in the EPA clearly sought to roll back the regulatory activity of the agency. A public scandal developed over the expenditure of funds on the Superfund program. The press focused on the issue; it became front-page news and a prime source of bad publicity for the administration. The political heat rose to such a degree that major changes were made in the leadership of the EPA.

Formulating a Response

Once a problem is presented to decision makers, what then is to be done about it? Enact a new law containing an entirely new program? Tack a solution onto an existing program? Give it to the EPA? Pass it down to the states? Spend federal money directly? Regulate or otherwise compel better behavior?

There are hundreds of bills introduced each year by members of Congress, yet few of them get very far. Somehow, disparate ideas have to be shaped and harnessed into a response to the perceived problem. One way of doing this is by holding public hearings, at which people may make their views known and through which particular policy approaches can be emphasized. Congress frequently will commission studies by outside agencies, such as the National Academy of Sciences. The president often will try to work with legislative interests to promote certain ideas and policies. Within Congress, political/policy entrepreneurs will usually emerge around certain policy areas. In the early 1970s, for example, Maine's Senator Muskie became the chief environmental spokesperson and force within the U.S. Senate. These individuals try to achieve leadership positions in various areas, which allow them to influence how policy responses are shaped and adapted.

There are any number of private groups that will try to shape and influence new laws and regulations: interest groups, think tanks, scientific groups, foreign interests, and so on. They will work through one or more of the various routes through which such groups can exert influence.

Developing Political Support

It is natural for the proponents of any policy to maintain that it has wide popular and political support. But under normal circumstances advocates have to work hard to build enough support to get new laws enacted and implemented. This is done by putting together **coalitions** of groups and interests large enough to push through the desired policies.

With two major political parties in the United States, this process will often lead to the gradual building of coalitions around two competing proposals in Congress, one Republican and the other Democratic. If one party holds a majority in both the Senate and House as well as the presidency, then the majority party's proposals are the most viable politically, with the minority party attempting to advance its agenda through the media or by blocking opposing proposals in the Senate or through parliamentary means. Whether a proposal moves forward often hinges on the ability of participants to work out a compromise.

A good example of this is the attempt by Congress to develop a new statute for limiting airborne emissions from large power plants. The 1990 Clean Air Act incorporated a "cap-and-trade" program to reduce SO_2 emissions from large power plants in the United States. We will talk later about how a cap-and-trade program works and what it attempts to achieve.[2] The 1990 program has been judged by many people (though not necessarily by all) as a great success. Cap-and-trade programs also have been used to control other pollutants, especially in southern California and in the northeastern states.

There is now a major effort underway to expand the use of cap-and-trade programs in the country, to bring in more power plants under the SO_2 programs, and to have national programs for NO_x, mercury, and perhaps CO_2. Several years ago, bills were introduced into the Senate and House that would institute these programs, with an initial target date of 2007. Hearings have been held on the proposal and many environmental groups have come out in support of it. But for many Republicans, and especially President Bush, this proposal is too restrictive: target dates are too soon and target quantities of emissions are too low. They feel this is especially the case for carbon dioxide emissions. One of the first things President Bush did upon entering office was to repudiate the Kyoto Protocol and come out against any meaningful restrictions in U.S. emissions of CO_2.

The administration's response, therefore, was to introduce a bill containing its own program. It's called the "Clear Skies Initiative," and involves cap-and-trade programs for SO_2, NO_x, and mercury that are far less restrictive than the Senate's proposed "Clean Power Act" (see table 3.1). We have, then, two competing bills, with the advocates of each program trying to build enough support to get theirs enacted into law. Any ultimate action will depend on whether Republicans or Democrats remain in power in the House and Senate.

Enacting and Promulgating

The problem has moved to the front burner, new statutes have been developed, a reasonably broad coalition of interests has been put together. Now the job is to get the law passed and signed by the president, or governor if we are discussing action at the state level. There are constitutional requirements; for example, a bill must pass both houses of Congress, with the presi-

Table 3.1   Comparison of Clean Power Act and Clear Skies Initiative[a]

Total Allowable Emissions	Clean Power Act[b]	Clear Skies Initiative[c]
SO_2	2.25 mil. tons (2010)	4.5 mil. tons (2010)
		3.0 mil. tons (2018)
NO_x	1.51 mil. tons (2010)	2.1 mil. tons (2008)
		1.7 mil. tons (2018)
Mercury	5 tons (2009)	34 tons/year (2010)
	(no trading)	15 tons/year (2018)
CO_2	2.05 bil. tons (2010)	None

[a] As of 6/3/05.
[b] First introduced by Senator Jeffords in 1997.
[c] Introduced by the Bush administration in 2002.

Source: Resources for the Future, "Legislative Comparison of Multipollutant Proposals s. 150, s. 131, and s. 843, version 6/3/05" (www.rff.org/multipollutant).

dent's signature. There are also internal institutional requirements that Congress may impose; for example, during the high budget deficits of the late 1980s, Congress required that any new spending bills attach provisions for budget cuts in other areas so the net proposal was "budget neutral." After a bill is passed and becomes law, there is a continuing need to fund the program. Budget discussions are an annual event in Washington and many state capitals (some states have biennial budgets, where two-year budgets are passed every other year) and are the center of important political struggles. Besides budgetary matters, there will be pressure on agencies, such as EPA, to perform according to the sometimes vague language of the law itself. Regulatory agencies like EPA have to translate broad goals into concrete policy proposals—called **regulations**—that are the subject of intense political scrutiny.

Regulations must follow standards set forth in the Administrative Procedures Act, which requires appropriate notification of proposed regulations through the *Federal Register*, a response period so that interested parties can voice any concerns or support, and the requirement that the final regulation address the reasonable objections of those who comment through the regulatory process. Of course, the courts frequently are the final recourse for adjudicating disagreements over regulatory matters.

Implementing Policies

Often the heat and intensity of environmental conflicts appear to be centered on legislative activities and the enactment of new statutes. In reality, the arena in which most of the ongoing combat takes place is in writing rules and procedures to implement the statutes. This is where the general objectives listed in the laws are translated into specific standards and actions that will be applied to polluters and regulations. The **implementation process** itself can be depicted in terms of its own series of steps, as in figure 3.3. It involves pro-

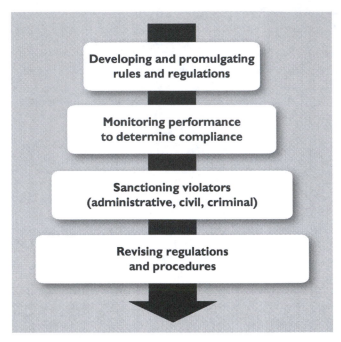

Figure 3.3   Stages in Implementation

mulgating rules and regulations, monitoring the performance of polluters, fining or otherwise punishing those who violate regulations, and adjusting and revising regulations as needed.

Evaluating and Revising

Environmental laws are updated frequently. The 1990 Clean Air Act was actually an amendment to the Clean Air Act of 1970, which also was amended in 1977. The Safe Drinking Water Act of 1996 is the last of a series of amendments made to the original SDWA of 1974. Many, if not most, environmental statutes are revisions of past laws. The policy cycle, in other words, is closed in the sense that as soon as a policy is put in place and experience starts to accumulate, forces and interests often start working toward change. Sometimes these changes can be relatively minor, although in other instances they can represent essentially new policy approaches.

A More Political View

The functional view is instructive in that it informs us about how environmental politics and policies move through stages and cycle through time. It isn't very informative, however, in telling us who the main actors are and how they influence these events, and about the political struggles that take place within and between these stages. For this we need to turn to a more explicitly political depiction of the policy process, or the **political model**.

In a democratic system, **politics** means a process in which individuals and groups contend for influence over public decisions that affect their interests and what they see as the public interest. In the context of the policy cycle mentioned earlier, we can think of all these interests and individuals struggling to shape what happens at various stages in the cycle. There are hundreds of ways of doing this: maneuver in the legislature to affect the content of new statutes; influence administrative agencies to implement new laws in desired directions; generate public support to get an issue on the table; work through the courts to amend the content of regulations; and so on.

One way of picturing this is shown in figure 3.4. At the core are the functions of the policy cycle, but now we have lots of different groups and interests arranged around the outside. Each is trying to gain influence over these functions, and this influence can be projected at many different points in the process. Perhaps the chief message of this view is that policy is not a one-person or one-group game. Consider environmental scientists, for example. Many people rightfully think that environmental policy should be solidly, and primarily, based on the scientific aspects of problems. But environmental sci-

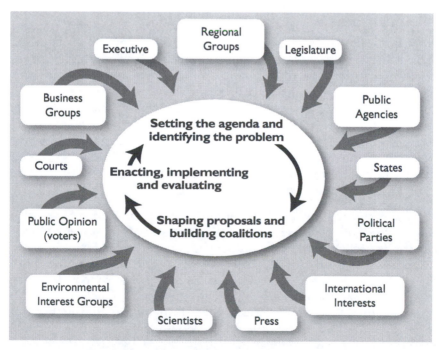

Figure 3.4   A Political View of Public Policy

entists are but one group of participants in the ongoing cycle of environmental policy and regulation; there are many others, some who may be in sync with the latest scientific results, others who may not. In addition, this rendition reveals groups who have influence that we may not have considered, for example the press, which is vital for opening up flows of information among different participants in the process.

Example: The Clean Air Act of 1990

The last major federal environmental law to be passed in the United States is the Clean Air Act Amendments of 1990. The original Clean Air Act was passed in 1955 and subsequently amended in 1963, 1970, and 1977. The 1970 amendments were fundamental in that they changed the very basis on which air pollution control was to be pursued in the future. Similar changes were subsequently made in federal water and land pollution control policies. In a later chapter we will discuss in some detail the content of the Clean Air Act; it applies to both stationary and nonstationary sources; it applies to standard emissions like SO_2 as well as emissions of toxic chemicals; it incorporates conventional technology-based approaches as well as newer incentive-based approaches. We can illustrate the open, contentious nature of the U.S. environmental policy process by looking briefly at events leading up to the passage of the 1990 act from the standpoint of the major groups and interests that were involved.

Public Attitudes. The rise of the Republicans in the early 1980s seemed to signal a lessening of public concern about environmental quality issues and a desire to reduce the burden of environmental regulations. At least that is how many people interpreted events at the time. But as the decade wore on, attitudes evolved in the other direction, leading to what many called a new "green mood" in the country. To some extent this was perhaps a reaction to the eight years of outright antagonism toward environmental issues emanating from the Republican administration. But other events of these years propelled environmental issues back into the public eye. The discovery of the ozone hole over Antarctica was getting wide publicity in 1987–88; in March 1989 the *Exxon Valdez* oil spill occurred in Alaska.

The Presidency. A key factor at this time was the change in the presidency, from Ronald Reagan to George H. W. Bush. The former had spent eight years beating back environmental policy initiatives and weakening federal environmental efforts, particularly those of the EPA. Bush took over at the beginning of 1989, asserting as he did so that he wanted to make a mark as an "environmental president." President Bush had apparently committed himself, during the presidential campaign, to putting forth a proposal for revising the Clean Air Act. Whereas in previous years the EPA had provided the initiative for new environmental legislation, in 1989 the White House took over this role, putting together a working group to develop ideas, write new legislation, and pursue the political networking required to build a successful support coalition.[3]

Congress. The Republican ascendancy in the 1980s was reflected also in Congress. Republicans formed the majority in the Senate from 1981 to 1986, though the House was still controlled by the Democrats. Environmental interests in the two bodies were seldom strong enough to overcome the opposition of individuals and regional groupings and push new laws through the labyrinthine legislative process. This was the case despite fairly widespread agreement that something new ought to be done with the Clean Air Act, last amended in 1977. The Senate Committee on Environment and Public Works reported out bills in 1982, 1984, and 1987, but these got nowhere in the full Senate. A major obstacle was Robert Byrd, a powerful senator from West Virginia, who blocked efforts to reduce SO_2 emissions from power plants as this would be disadvantageous to the coal-mining industry of his state.

In the House of Representatives, John Dingell, the long-time chairman of the House Energy and Commerce Committee, was effective at blocking action that might involve costly new emission standards on automobiles, a major industry in his state of Michigan. Of course, Rep. Dingle and other legislators argued that they were serving the broad national interest of protecting the important automobile industry.

Serious action in Congress, therefore, had to wait for the arrival of the Bush proposal in July 1989. The next 15 months was a time of intensive activity as supporters of the new law sought to build majority coalitions among the senators and representatives, each of whom was trying to protect the interests of his or her state or district. Exhibit 3.2 depicts just a small fraction of the bargaining that occurred as the law worked its way through the process.

The Senate finally passed a bill in 1989 and the House in May 1990. Lengthy negotiations were then needed to reconcile the two versions. Final votes in Congress occurred in October 1990, and the president signed the law in November.

Exhibit 3.2
Negotiations Leading Up to the Clean Air Act of 1990

Acid Rain

"The acid rain dispute pitted a small group of Midwesterners, who wanted some form of cost-sharing to help their utilities defray the costs of meeting acid rain controls, against a much larger group of 'clean state' members who did not want to pay.

"But the clean-state members had a problem of their own—the bill's tough cap on emissions meant they would have to buy pollution 'allowances,' most likely from Midwestern utilities, if they wanted to increase coal-burning utility capacity in the future. The Midwesterners sensed the possibility of a deal.

"Midwesterners Sharp of Indiana and Bruce and Republican Edward Madigan, both from Illinois, all pursued such a deal for months, but could not persuade their colleagues to budge. Part of the problem was that Sharp and the others wanted cash cost-sharing from an emissions fee on industrial sulfur dioxide (SO_2) emitters, a concept that violated Bush's no-new-taxes pledge and that many members found unacceptable.

"Some committee members suggested enhancing the bill's existing allowance trading system, which Cooper said was already a form of cost-sharing, since dirty, coal-fired utilities in the Midwest would be selling allowances to the rest of the country for cash. But Sharp distrusted the allowance scheme and worried about what the allowances would actually be worth.

"As with many clean air issues on both sides of Capitol Hill, resolution was possible only after staff and members had worked themselves to exhaustion. Dingell scheduled a meeting for 10 a.m. on April 4 to mark up an acid rain compromise. The committee, as it later turned out, would miss that deadline by 34 hours.

"Staff and members horse-traded throughout the day and into the night. At 2 a.m. on April 5, according to some accounts, 30 to 35 of the committee's 43 members were still on hand. Dingell had extended the committee meeting time, but only a little bit at a time, to keep members negotiating. Scores of lobbyists milled in the hallway outside the closed doors of the committee room, where a hand-lettered sign was intermittently updated by crossing out the previous meeting time and writing in a new one.

"Offers and counteroffers were made as late as 4:30 a.m. before members went home for a few hours, only to return to begin negotiating again.

"Negotiators finally reached a deal sometime in the afternoon of April 5. Markup convened about 8 p.m., and Sharp and others revealed that they had abandoned cash cost-sharing in favor of a system that manipulated the allowance trading scheme to give both the Midwest and the clean states extra allowances.

"Sharp lamented the loss of true cost-sharing, calling the compromise only 'a modest victory.' The committee approved it 39–4, with four Texans (Democrats Fields, Hall, and John Bryant and Republican Joe L. Barton) opposing it on the grounds that it did not do right by their state.

"Finally, the committee voted 42–1 to report the clean air bill, with William E. Dannemeyer, R-Calif., voting 'no' because he said the bill would be too costly."

Source: Excerpted from *Congressional Quarterly Almanac*, 101st Congress, 2nd Session, 1990, Volume 46 (Washington, DC, 1991):242. Copyright © 1991 CQ Press, a division of Congressional Quarterly, Inc.

Interest Groups.   As in all cases of complicated public policy, interest groups were arrayed on both sides of the issues brought up by the 1990 CAA amendments. The major split, of course, was between environmental groups on one side and business groups on the other. On both sides, umbrella organizations were formed to coordinate efforts and focus their influence. On the environmental side this was called the National Clean Air Coalition, while business interests were represented by the Clean Air Working Group. Another umbrella-type group to form was the Alliance for Acid Rain Control, a Washington-based coalition of governors, leaders of public interest groups, corporate executives, and others.

Environmental Scientists.   A major impetus behind the action on clean air policy was the accumulating scientific evidence on acid rain, its causes, and impacts. Acid rain had been an important issue in Europe since the 1960s, but in the United States the problem didn't gain attention until the late 1970s. President Carter tried to make it a priority, and began a massive publicly funded research program (the National Acid Precipitation Assessment Program, or NAPAP, started in 1980) to study the extent, causes, and impacts of acid deposition in the United States. The National Academy of Sciences weighed in with several reports in the 1980s recommending reductions in U.S. SO_2 emissions to reduce the impacts of acid rain.

While many scientists and scientific groups came out in favor of steps to reduce acid deposition by reducing SO_2 emissions, opponents also were able to mobilize scientific arguments. They pointed out that the final report of NAPAP did not attribute large-scale health or ecological damages to SO_2 related acidification. They mobilized a group of famous economists who took the position that the tighter regulations contemplated in the 1990 amendments would have a high economic cost, higher than the benefits they would produce. The sparring among scientists helped motivate the inclusion of a provision that the EPA conduct benefit-cost analyses of the Clean Air Act; the first study, covering the years 1970–1990, was finished in 1996.

Another path of scientific influence on the 1990 act was through an ad hoc group called Project 88. This was chaired by two U.S. senators, and it brought together many policy analysts from public and private sectors and agency administrators who were interested in environmental policy reform. Although their final report did not appear until 1991, their ideas were influential for several years prior to this. In particular, their recommendation that environmental policy be shifted away from command and control toward the use of incentive-based approaches was critical in shaping the transferable discharge permit program that was included in the 1990 act to control power-plant emissions of SO_2.

International Interests.   Throughout the 1980s, the United States and Canada worked to establish a program to combat acid rain. Canada was looking for reductions in U.S. SO_2 emissions, which it felt were largely responsible for acid deposition in the eastern part of that country. Negotiations were pursued, including the "Shamrock Summit" between President Reagan and Canadian Prime Minister Brian Mulroney, where the acid rain issue was on the agenda. The United States, however, was only willing to make a weak commitment to do more research on the issue. This changed with the shift of administrations in 1989.

Ideas about Influence and Power

The political model discussed above tells us much more than when we started, but it doesn't tell us some important things. We now know that the policy process involves many different institutions and participants, but we have said nothing yet about how these different interests sort themselves out in the political process, how they build and project influence on the issues of the day. It is one thing to note that there are multiple groups and parties involved in the policy game. It is another to determine which ones have the greatest influence on which particular issues, and how this influence is wielded. Naturally, multiple books could be, and have been, written on this topic. Here we will mention briefly some of the leading ideas.

Pluralism

One concept that has been put forward to describe an open system like this is **pluralism**. When there is a multiplicity of groups and interests that have formed around various issues, each with well-developed strategies and avenues of access, the outcome in terms of policy is usually some sort of compromise, or balancing, of these diverse groups and interests.[4] This has both a positive (this is the way it works) and a normative (this is the way it ought to work) dimension.

In its most benign interpretation, interest group pluralism views the various interests described above as representative of the different groups of citizens within the society. If Greenpeace has influence over policy making, it is because it represents the interests of many concerned voters and activists to which policy makers need to pay attention. The power accorded to any one group is a direct reflection of the resources and people behind it. Therefore, when interest groups fight it out to determine environmental policies, the product is the best possible representation of the interests of the nation's citizens, since they are represented indirectly by interest groups. Much as 60 million voters will prevail over 40 million in a national election, so too will larger interest groups prevail over smaller ones, and this will best represent the public interest from a pluralist perspective.

Interest group pluralism has received a strong challenge, articulated first in the work of Mancur Olson, and later popularized by Jonathan Rauch.[5] Rather than viewing interest groups as benign representatives of individual citizens' interests, Olson noted that interest groups only formed if there was a strong motivation for members to want to join in the first place. This was frequently a result of some financial advantage to banding together (business lobbies and unions are examples) or some other benefit (environmental groups are much more effective than individuals writing letters). Therefore, the interest groups that form may not necessarily represent the interests of all citizens equally, particularly broad and diffuse interests like climate change, but instead tend to represent narrower interests who are primarily concerned about their own benefits and costs.

Elite Theory

This suggests that among all the potential interest groups, some exercise much greater power in the policy process. An extreme version of this goes under the heading of **elite theory**. Elites are groups, sometimes but not always small, who have been able to gain control of the policy process and turn it to their advantage. While professing to be acting in the wider public interest, elites primarily act to maintain and extend their own positions and privileges. Even certain environmental groups, for example, have been charged with representing the interests of wealthy, largely white, patrons with greater concern for pandas and the tranquility of their own neighborhoods than for more significant environmental problems like substandard drinking water affecting millions of people worldwide.[6]

In an open, democratic system it is a fact of life that special interests will publicly proclaim that they are in fact acting in the wider public interest. This is political theater. More fundamental is whether special interest groups are able to cultivate positions that give them undue influence. In the political rhetoric of environmental policy and regulation, each side can normally be expected to accuse the other of being in that position.

Political Economy

Closely related to these ideas about how power and political access are distributed among groups is the perspective of **political economy**. The institutions, practices, and "outputs" of government are not to be thought of as independent factors, pursued according to some widespread notion of the "public interest." Rather, political/policy outcomes are to be regarded as largely influenced by, or a reflection of, the values and processes of the economic system itself. Political economy comes in many varieties. Those with a conservative outlook often stress the need to look at the policy process as one in which participants are not motivated by thoughts of the public interest but by the desire to advance their own private interests as much as possible. Among middle-of-the-road thinkers, a leading idea is that of "regulatory capture": regulatory agencies that are in effect so dominated by the industries they are supposed to regulate (for example, by appointing as agency leaders proponents of those industries) that they end up promoting the interests of that industry rather than the broader public interest. At the other end of the spectrum, political economy includes notions of corporate dominance, Marxist interpretations of economic dynamics, and the need for more democratic

economic and political institutions. In particular, the democratic tradition
views environmental policy as driven importantly by the way in which the
benefits and costs of that policy are distributed among the citizenry. Any policy or regulation entails both benefits and costs; one cannot have the first
without the second. Many struggles over environmental policy are not over
whether benefits exceed costs in an overall sense, but over who bears the costs
and who enjoys the benefits. Global warming is one such policy struggle. But
as long as positions of power are occupied by members of the "carbon sector"—those firms and individuals involved in producing carbon fuels and
who stand to lose with a vigorous carbon-control program—energetic action
to control carbon emissions is unlikely.

On Institutions and Ideas

These theories all view the political/policy process as a collision of interests, with outcomes determined by which interests are able to accumulate the
most influence. But it would be misleading to interpret the policy struggle
simply as a no-holds-barred cat fight among competing groups and interests.
Policy making involves collective decisions, which means that policies and
regulations are made and enforced within a particular institutional setting
and political culture. By **institutions** we mean the structure of organizations
and laws within which policy change takes place. In the United States, of
course, the governing framework is the Constitution. It sets basic ground
rules and limits, though these are subject to interpretations that can change
over time. We will discuss this at greater length in chapter 6.

By **political/policy culture** we mean those formal institutions together
with customs and habits that may never be explicitly identified in their constituent parts but exist nonetheless; it also includes the ethical norms that
affect what people feel is right and wrong, just or unjust, in political life. In
the United States, for example, it is part of our political culture that people
and organizations feel the right and the need to monitor closely the actions of
public agencies like the Environmental Protection Agency, and to intervene
actively if they think it necessary. In many other countries this type of attitude
and process are absent, or at least much weaker.[7] Another cultural/political
belief is that information should be widely shared, which leads to policies
such as "right to know" legislation and popular Web sites that show levels of
toxic emissions by ZIP code, the location of Superfund sites, and other information to inform citizen action.

States and communities also have their own policy institutions and cultures. By now all states have developed public agencies to administer environmental laws and regulations, though these vary greatly in terms of mission
and standard operating procedures. Likewise there are major differences
among states and regions in terms of the institutions and procedures of local
governments. In New England, local governments are still strong and the old-

fashioned town meeting is still conducted in many places. In many states county governments are a major locus of power and initiative.

Fundamental ideas about political morality and customs are clearly of great influence. But political and policy ideas are also important, especially when policy makers are casting about for ways of addressing a particular problem. Good ideas often will be influential, though it may take some time for this to happen. To take one example, economists had for years been pushing market-based emission control plans for reducing environmental pollutants such as sulfur dioxide, but it was not until the 1990 amendments to the Clean Air Act that a significant federal environmental law included a substantial market-based scheme. Ideas matter, but how they matter and under which circumstances can vary widely.

Summary

In this chapter we looked at some simple models of public policy making. The first was a simple rational-choice model in which policy makers are presented with a problem, consider alternative solutions, then choose and implement the one that will best secure their objectives. The second model was a functional one, in which the policy process is broken down into a series of steps arranged in a policy cycle. After that we considered a more political model, in which we recognized that there are a multiplicity of participants and interests on any given issue, and that policy is a result of the conflict and contention among these groups as they fight for influence and advantage. We also considered leading ideas that have been put forward to account for how these interests get mixed and arranged on any particular issue or set of issues. Finally, to counter somewhat the interest-group-centered model, we discussed the importance of institutions and ideas in the U.S. policy process.

Key Terms

alternative policy responses	political agenda
coalitions	political economy
elite theory	political model
functional model	political/policy culture
implementation process	politics
institutions	rational model
pluralism	regulations
policy cycle	

Questions for Further Discussion

1. Choose a recent environmental problem. How did it come to your attention? Which institutions, if any, reacted first? What was the nature of their reaction?

2. Which model of policy making best fits with your view of how policy making works?

3. Are there other important dimensions of the policy process that are omitted from these models?

4. How do *you* think environmental policies are formed? What is the role of citizens, interest groups, state and national institutions, and others?

5. Who wields the most power over policy making? Do you believe this has changed over time?

Web Sites

There are hundreds, if not thousands, of Web sites devoted to reporting on U.S. policy struggles. This includes the federal agencies themselves:
Environmental Protection Agency
www.epa.gov

Department of the Interior
www.doi.gov

Congressional Research Service
www.ncseonline.org/NLE/CRS/

There is an array of private companies who produce excellent policy-relevant material on all types of issues:
Congressional Quarterly
www.cq.com

National Journal
www.nationaljournal.com

A number of private organizations focus on environmental issues:
E&E Publishing
www.greenwire.com

Environmental Law Institute
www.eli.org

Additional Readings

Arnold, Craig Anthony, *Environmental Justice: Lessons Learned*, Environmental Law Institute Casebook Series (Washington, DC: ELI, 2004).

Bardach, Eugene, *A Practical Guide for Policy Analysis: The Eightfold Path to More Effective Problem Solving* (New York: Chatham House, 2000).

Baumgartner, Frank R., and Bryan D. Jones, *Agendas and Instability in American Politics* (Chicago: University of Chicago Press, 1993).

Birkland, Thomas A., *An Introduction to the Policy Process: Theories, Concepts and Models of Public Policy Making*, 2nd ed. (Cambridge: MIT Press, 2005).

Boyce, James K., *The Political Economy of the Environment* (Northampton, MA: Edward Elgar, 2001).

Davies, Clarence J., *The Politics of Pollution* (New York: Pegasus Press, 1970).

Dye, Thomas R., *Understanding Public Policy*, 9th ed. (Upper Saddle River, NJ: Prentice Hall, 1998).

Edelman, Murray, *The Symbolic Uses of Politics* (Urbana: University of Illinois Press, 1964).

Gerston, Larry N., *Public Policy Making: Process and Principles*, 2nd ed. (Armonk, NY: M. E. Sharpe, 2002).

Jones, Bryan D., *Reconceiving Decision-Making in Democratic Politics: Attention, Choice, and Public Policy* (Chicago: University of Chicago Press, 1994).

Kingdon, John, *Agendas, Alternatives, and Public Policies* (Boston: Little Brown, 1984).

Lowi, Theodore, *The End of Liberalism*, 2nd ed. (New York: W. W. Norton, 1979).

Majone, Giandomenico, *Evidence, Argument, and Persuasion in the Policy Process* (New Haven, CT: Yale University Press, 1989).

Peters, B. Guy, *American Public Policy: Promise and Performance*, 6th ed. (Chatham, NJ: Chatham House, 2003).

Riccucci, Norma M., *Unsung Heroes: Federal Execucrats Making a Difference* (Washington, DC: Georgetown University Press, 1995).

Rosenthal, Alan, *The Decline of Representative Democracy* (Washington, DC: Congressional Quarterly Press, 1998).

Sabatier, Paul A., ed., *Theories of the Policy Process* (Boulder, CO: Westview Press, 1999).

Schneider, Anne Larason and Helen Ingram, *Policy Design for Democracy* (Lawrence: University of Kansas Press, 1996).

Stone, Deborah, *The Policy Paradox: The Art of Political Decision-Making* (New York: W. W. Norton and Company, 1997).

Van Horn, Carl E., Donald C. Baumer, and William T. Gormley, Jr., *Politics and Public Policy*, 3rd ed. (Washington, DC: Congressional Quarterly Press, 2001).

Wolf, Michael Allan, *American Environment, Law and Politics: Studies in Reaction, Response, and Reform*, Environmental Law Institute Casebook Series (Washington, DC: ELI, 2004).

Notes

[1] Edward O. Wilson, *The Diversity of Life* (Cambridge, MA: Harvard University Press, 1992).

[2] In chapters 9 and 15.

[3] It did not hurt that a leading member of the team was John Sununu, the president's chief of staff. He was from New Hampshire, a state on the receiving end of the acid rain phenomenon. For more on this see Margaret E. Kriz, "Politics in the Air," *National Journal* 18 (May 6, 1989):1098–1102.

[4] A classic work in the application of a pluralist model to the study of American politics is David B. Truman, *The Governmental Process, Political Interests and Public Opinion* (New York: Knopf, 1971). A recent work that applies a modern pluralist model to environmental policy is Edward P. Weber, *Pluralism by the Rules: Conflict and Cooperation in Environmental Regulation* (Washington, DC: Georgetown University Press, 1998).

[5] Mancur Olson, *The Logic of Collective Action* (Cambridge: Harvard University Press, 1965); Jonathan Rauch, *Demosclerosis: The Silent Killer of American Government* (New York: Times Books, 1994).

[6] For a recent book that is based on an elite-theory approach, see George A. Gonzalez, *Corporate Power and the Environment: The Political Economy of U.S. Environmental Policy* (Lanham, MD: Rowman & Littlefield, 2001).

[7] For interesting discussions of cultural differences among countries in their environmental politics and policies see: Susan Rose-Ackerman, *Controlling Environmental Policy: The Limits of Public Law in Germany and the United States* (New Haven, CT: Yale University Press, 1995); Lennart J. Lundquist, *The Hare and the Tortoise: Clean Air Policies in the United States and Sweden* (Ann Arbor: University of Michigan Press, 1980); David Vogel, *National Styles of Regulation: Environmental Policy in Great Britain and the United States* (Ithaca, NY: Cornell University Press, 1986). We will discuss some of these ideas in chapter 19.

4

The Policy Front End

Public Opinion, Interest Groups, and Political Parties

In this chapter we look at what might be called the "front end" of public policy—public opinion and several of the main channels through which it gets expressed in the policy process. The essence of a democracy is to a large extent wrapped up in the notion that political and policy outcomes ought to reflect the interests and views of the citizenry. Of course this straightforward idea becomes more complicated in practice: How does one gauge public opinion? What if there are multiple publics? How does the system take an amorphous public opinion and shape it into a very specific configuration of political support on particular issues? How does it happen that public opinion can often be at odds with specific policies? To what degree is public opinion an independent force in the policy process, and to what extent is it actually a result of that process? These very interesting questions will help guide our discussion in this and the following chapters.

Public Opinion on the Environment

Basic civics says that in a democracy, government decisions are meant to be made in the interests of the citizenry at large. Thus of all the groups arrayed around the outside of figure 3.4, it is presumably the public, or public interest, that is or should be the prime driver in the process that produces public policy. The word "presumably" is used for several reasons, the main one being that on most issues there are actually many publics. **Public opinion** is not uniform, but divided into many diverse points of view according to the circumstances and attitudes of different parts of the population.

Beyond the fact of the heterogeneity of public opinion, it is also the case, as depicted in figure 3.4, that public attitudes are not the only source of opinions and viewpoints in the search for effective environmental policy. There is ongoing debate about how strong the connection is between public opinion and policy outcomes. Sometimes (e.g., gun control) clearly expressed majority public opinion does not seem to find expression in policy. Other times (e.g., any number of cases where special interests have been hard at work), laws can be enacted that seemingly have no significant support in public opinion, at least broadly considered. Nevertheless, it is undoubtedly true that a broadly supportive public opinion favoring the need for public action to protect environmental assets is an important resource for those who seek to move the political struggle in that direction.

There are two types of public opinion that are especially relevant here:

1. Generalized public opinion about environmental matters, both the overall state of the environment and the general status of environmental policy and regulation.

2. Public opinion on specific environmental issues, such as global warming, air pollution in one's region, or the preservation of a local wetland.

Generalized Public Opinion

It is not easy to gauge the overall state of generalized public opinion on environmental quality, even though the rise of polling organizations over the last fifty years has seemed to make public opinion a more tangible factor. Pollsters frequently ask questions to elicit the feelings of respondents about the general state of environmental policy and regulations. One problem is that none have asked the same question over an extended number of years. Table 4.1 pieces together some polling results obtained by various organizations over the period 1965 to 2004.

We can perhaps draw the following conclusions as regards the ebb and flow of general public opinion over the last 35 years or so.

1. The late 1960s and early 1970s saw a substantial growth in public opinion on environmental matters. To some extent this was because of the consciousness raising prompted by such books as Rachel Carson's *Silent Spring*.[1] To some extent it was an extension of the public concern and

Table 4.1 Trends in Selected Public Opinion Polls, 1965–2004[a]

				Percentage of Respondents				
	1965	1966	1968	1970	1972	1974	1976	1978
Opinion Research Corporation[b] Air/water pollution viewed as "very or somewhat serious" in the area:								
(a) air pollution	28	48	55	69				
(b) water pollution	35	49	58	74				
Louis Harris[c] Willing to pay $15/year more in taxes to finance air pollution control program		44 (1967)		54				
Michigan National Election Survey[d] Pollution, ecology, etc., volunteered as one of the country's "most important problems"			2	17	10			
Louis Harris[e] Pollution, ecology, etc., volunteered as one of "the two or three biggest problems facing people like yourself"				41	13	9		
Roper[f] More on the side of:								
(a) protecting the environment						39	44	38
(b) having adequate energy						41	33	43 (1979)
Roper[g] Environmental protection laws have gone:								
(a) not far enough						25	32	29
(b) too far						17	15	24 (1979)
NORC[h] U.S. spending on improving and protecting the environment:								
(a) too little						59	55	52
(b) too much						8	9	10 (1979)

(continued)

Table 4.1 Trends in Selected Public Opinion Polls, 1965–2004[a] *(continued)*

	1980	1982	1984	1986	1988	1990	1998	2002	2004
Roper[f] More on the side of:									
(a) protecting the environment	36								
(b) having adequate energy	45								
Roper[g] Environmental protection laws and regulations have gone:									
(a) not far enough	33								
(b) too far	25								
NORC[h] U.S. spending on improving and protecting the environment:									
(a) too little	48	50	58	58	65	71			
(b) too much	15	12	7	6	5	4			
Cambridge[i] Sacrifice environmental quality or sacrifice economic growth:									
(a) sacrifice economic growth		41	42	58	52	64			
(b) sacrifice environmental quality		31	27	19	19	15			
Gallup[j] Protection of the environment should be given top priority			61			71	68	54	49

[a] Sources: Specific sources are excerpted from material in: Riley E. Dunlap, "Trends in Opinions Toward Environmental Issues: 1965–1990," in *American Environmentalism: The U.S. Environmental Movement, 1970–1990*, edited by Riley E. Dunlap and Angela G. Mertig (New York: Taylor and Francis, 1992):89–116.

[b, c] H. Erskine, "The Polls: Pollution and Its Costs," *Public Opinion Quarterly* 36 (1972):120–135.

[d] K. E. Hornbeck, "Orbits of Opinion: The Role of Age in the Environmental Movement's Attentive Public," Unpublished Ph.D. Dissertation, Michigan State University (1974).

[e] R. C. Mitchell and J. C. Davies, III, "The United States Environmental Movement and Its Political Context: An Overview," Discussion Paper D-32 (Washington, DC: Resources for the Future, 1978).

[f, g] J. M. Gillroy and R. Y. Shapiro, "The Polls: Environmental Protection," *Public Opinion Quarterly* 50 (1986):270–279; and R. E. Dunlap, "Polls, Pollution and Politics Revisited: Public Opinion on the Environment in the Reagan Era," *Environment* 29 (July/August 1987):6–11, 32–37.

[h] National Opinion Research Center, General Social Surveys, 1972–1989: Cumulative Code Book (Chicago, 1989).

[i] *The Green Revolution and the Changing American Consumer* (Cambridge, MA: Cambridge Reports/Research International, 1990).

[j] Gallup Poll, www.gallup.com.

activism that had been mobilized during the 1960s on issues of civil rights and the war in Vietnam. It culminated in the first Earth Day (held on April 22, 1970, and estimated to have involved perhaps 20 million participants in one role or another).

2. A modest decline in general public opinion during the 1970s, though the level stayed higher than it had been before the early 1960s. To some extent this may be a reflection of an obverse relationship between policy outcomes and public opinion. The early 1970s saw a massive increase in federal statutes and regulations on various environmental problems. This may have produced in the minds of many people the idea that environmental issues were being addressed actively in Washington, so that public concern could now be safely directed at other issues.

3. Something of an upsurge in public opinion during the 1980s, again perhaps the result of public perceptions that the Reagan administration was threatening gains that had been made in environmental regulation in the 1970s.

4. Some erosion of public support in the late 1990s and early 2000s. Recent polls have suggested that this is not so much a diminishment of environmental concern, but instead reflects the rise of other issues that have tended to push environmental issues off the priority list of public concerns.[2]

What we are talking about in this evolution is generalized, or latent, public concern about the environment. The quality of the environment continues to be a reasonably strong background concern of the average citizen, though it is not in general the most important matter of concern. The continued presence of this latent concern for the environment has sometimes been overlooked. In 1994, when the Republicans won control of the U.S. House of Representatives, they put forth a radical antiregulatory program that would have weakened federal environmental regulations. One reason the initiative was eventually scuttled was the very negative public feedback that occurred, a testament to the latent opinion among a large segment of the public that environmental regulations were reasonable and appropriate. Exhibit 4.1 discusses how in 2001 the Bush administration struggled to come to terms with this background public opinion, which many people now think of as having become part of the continuing political/policy culture of the United States.

There is much more to be said about latent public opinion toward the environment. How broadly is it represented throughout society? (It has the reputation of being elitist, more concentrated among white middle-class folks than truly general across all segments of the population.) What are the best ways of nurturing it? (Is public opinion better mobilized by relying on the Chicken Little approach—"the sky is falling!!"—or by reasoned argument—"now let's consider the benefits and costs"?) How easily is it displaced by other concerns such as terrorism, crime, or the economy? And especially, how strongly felt is this favorable public attitude? (Lots of people express general concern, but when you ask them for real money to protect the environment, do other things turn out to be more important?) Let us discuss the last question.

Exhibit 4.1
The Art of Turning a Sow's Ear Into a Silk Purse

by Katharine Q. Seelye

This week the Bush administration moved closer to relaxing the rules for air-pollution controls on dirty power plants, and it moved in a California court to promote offshore oil drilling. It took an aggressive step forward for the nuclear power industry, declaring a Nevada mountain scientifically safe for the storage of nuclear waste. And it replaced a research program for auto fuel efficiency that was showing modest success for cars on the road with a more ambitious program that won't affect the car fleet for years, if ever, and in the meantime does nothing to cut gas consumption or promote efficiency.

These actions followed months of other pro-business regulatory actions that were hardly noticed in the post-September 11 world: allowing more roads and powerline construction on public lands, weakening rules over mining permits, delaying a ban on snowmobiles in national parks, letting developers build on wetlands without replacing them. The question is: Does anyone care? In a time of war and recession, is it politically safe to ignore the environment? The answer appears to be that it is not safe, and that this administration knows it.

Last year, when President Bush began making field trips to America's national parks, many in the environmental movement ridiculed what they saw as a cynical attempt by an anti-environmental administration to portray itself as "green" via photo ops.

This was the same administration, after all, that wanted to open the Arctic National Wildlife Refuge to oil drilling and that, in the person of Vice President Dick Cheney, had dismissed the idea that conservation could help reduce the nation's energy needs, contemptuously dismissing it as a mere "sign of personal virtue."

Nor was it only committed environmentalists who distrusted the Bush administration in these matters. Prior to September 11, polls showed that voters, particularly independents, suburbanites and women, saw the president as beholden to his like-minded friends in the extractive industries of oil, gas, coal, timber, and mining.

Mr. Bush and his advisers seemed finally to comprehend the depth of their problem when the public erupted over their pronouncements on arsenic. The administration seemed ready to allow a higher level of the poison in drinking water than the Clinton administration had recommended.

Mr. Bush later called this one of the biggest public relations disasters of his short tenure, and while the administration would continue to take actions that critics considered anti-environmental, it tempered those with moves calculated to placate voters. On September 10, the administration defused the issue by announcing that it would, after all, set the same level of arsenic as that recommended by the Clinton administration.

Even with a war on, the administration seems keenly aware that people still care about the environment. Notably, the administration went ahead last month and ordered General Electric, whose former head, Jack Welch, was a major Bush supporter, to clean up toxic chemicals from the Hudson River. The plan could cost the company half a billion dollars.

So, despite the anti-environmental stirrings by the administration, no one really argues these days that environmentalism is dead. Even much of corporate America recognizes that good environmental practices are good business. "The reward for good environmental performance is that your earnings go up," said Paul Tebo, a vice president for safety, health and environment for DuPont. Smarter use of raw materials, less waste, and cleaner-running equipment that is more energy efficient, he said, "are all benefits to the bottom line, big-time."

Charles M. McLean, president of the Denver Research Group, which advises big corporations on environmental policy, said that since September 11, he has seen no lessening of protests by environmentalists against various projects around the country.

"I'm surprised I haven't seen more deterioration in support for the environment since September 11, but environmentalism has become embedded in the culture," Mr. McLean said. "Of course, if we have five more major attacks and the economy tanks worse than it has now, all bets will be off. But at this point, it's still pretty solid."

Doug Honnold, an environmental lawyer in Bozeman, Montana, agreed. "In the national debate, the environment may not transcend terrorism and war," he said. "But I don't think the fire ever really dims. There was a psychic 'time out' after September 11, but I see us coming out of that now. It's now O.K. to say we can't just rubber stamp what the administration wants. The suburban demographic is particularly concerned about the environment and human health and recognizes that if we pollute the air, my kids are going to get asthma, and it doesn't matter if we are at war."

Public Opinion on Specific Issues

Environmental battles are usually fought over specific issues: a state law to require recycling; a proposal to build a chemical plant in a community; a plan to clean up the "x" river; a proposal to tighten restrictions on soot emissions from trucks. In such cases it is not generalized public opinion but rather attitudes toward a specific proposition that are likely to have real consequences in terms of both getting a cleaner environment and paying for it.

In 1992 Massachusetts voters were asked to pass judgment on a referendum proposal requiring that all packaging material used in the state contain a minimum content of recycled material. In the beginning, public opinion ran strongly in favor of the plan. As time went on, however, the battle between proponents and opponents increasingly focused on its estimated costs and benefits. As the public debate continued, public opinion also evolved and, when voters finally got to make a specific judgment, they rejected it.

Thus, when specific proposals are at issue and public opinion has to crystallize into attitudes about real consequences, outcomes can be problematic. Generalized feelings about environmental values do not automatically translate into action plans if the consequences of these plans are seen as being too costly.

There is a real question about the extent to which public opinion on an issue can actually be changed by concerted efforts of interest groups, political figures, and other opinion leaders. Something of a case study in this respect occurred in 1997, when President Clinton sought to elevate public consciousness and concern about the causes and consequences of global warming. He sponsored a White House Conference on Global Climate Change, and precipitated a major effort by the media to feature this problem. A study by several social psychologists suggests that the effort had little impact on public opinion overall, although there were some essentially offsetting shifts in public opinion among subgroups of society. Their study is summarized in exhibit 4.2.

Information Technology and the Public

Over the last 20 years we have seen a major change in telecommunications systems around the world. The introduction of the Internet—combining computers with ubiquitous connectivity—has established new, more flexible patterns of communication and made linkages possible that heretofore could not be imagined. How these new developments in **information technology (IT)** will impact the world of public policy in general, and environmental policy in particular, has yet to be fully determined. One probable impact is that regulatory agencies such as the EPA will be better able to gather the technical data they need to implement their programs and regulations.

Another significant impact of modern information technology is that it offers new channels for public opinions and concerns to be communicated into the policy process at various junctures. For example, the EPA, like many public agencies, has carried out standard notice-and-comment procedures. This involves issuing public notices about proposed procedures and regulations and inviting members of the public to offer comments and reactions. In 2001 the EPA conducted an online dialogue among almost 1,200 people to discuss the issue of public involvement in EPA decisions.[3] The program essentially allowed an ongoing conversation among participants, primarily members of the public and EPA staff, about matters of environmental regulation. It was an opportunity for not only public expressions of interest, but also for

EPA reaction and explanation. Expansion of the World Wide Web in years to come undoubtedly will increase opportunities for members of the public to access information and communicate their views on environmental issues.

Exhibit 4.2
American Opinion on Global Warming: The Impact of the Fall 1997 Debate

by Jon A. Krosnick, Penny S. Visser, and Allyson L. Holbrook

During the fall of 1997, the American media focused a great deal of new coverage on global climate change and the debate being waged over whether the phenomenon poses serious problems or even exists. Kicked off in early October by the White House Conference on Global Climate Change, the media barrage included hundreds of stories on global warming on television and radio and in newspapers and magazines. The surrounding debate about the issue and its implications received further amplification in advertisements, paid for by business and other advocacy groups, as well as radio talk shows and numerous Web sites. Coverage and debate continued until the United States and other nations met in Kyoto, Japan, in early December to sign a climate treaty. Afterward, the media turned away from global warming and attended to other issues.

Media focus on the environment at such a pitch has occurred rarely during the last thirty years. In only a few other instances has the concentration of coverage been comparable: in 1969, when both a blowout at an offshore oil-drilling platform in Santa Barbara and the first Earth Day heightened environmental consciousness, and then again in 1990, when the *Exxon Valdez* spilled millions of gallons of oil into Prince William Sound.

Did the 1997 media deluge and public debate have any impact on Americans' opinions on global warming?

Opinions in September–October 1997

Existence of global warming. Prior to the White House conference, substantial proportions of Americans said that they believed in the existence of global warming. A large majority of people (77 percent) said they thought the world's temperature probably had been rising during the last one hundred years, and 74 percent said the world's temperature will probably go up in the future if nothing is done to stop it.

A majority of Americans (61 percent) believed that global warming would be bad; 15 percent thought it would be good; and 22 percent thought it would be neither good nor bad.

When asked how much should be done to combat global warming, majorities of Americans advocated significant effort.

A large majority of Americans (80 percent) believed that reducing air pollution will reduce future global warming.

When asked whether they would be willing to pay any more money each month in higher utility bills in order to reduce the amount of air pollution resulting from some electricity generation, 77 percent of people said they would.

In sum, the American public largely shared the views put forward by President Clinton before the concentrated media coverage and related debate began in the fall of 1997. Majorities of people believed in the existence of global warming, believed it would be undesirable, felt efforts should be made to combat it, and supported federal legislation and personal sacrifice as mechanisms for doing so.

Opinion Change?

When examined on the surface, American public opinion seems to have remained largely unaltered. In December–February, 79 percent of people said global warming had been occurring; 75 percent said they thought it would occur in the future if nothing was done to stop it; 58 percent said it would be bad for people; 57 percent said the U.S. government should do a great deal or quite a bit to combat global warming; and 79 percent said they believed reducing air pollution would reduce global warming. These figures are not appreciably different than the comparable measurements made in September–October.

These changes in opinion distributions are not huge, leaving unchallenged the general conclusion that public opinion was largely stable. But political psychologists are always suspect of conclusions reached by such means, for a couple of reasons. First, when contentious debates between politicians and policy experts unfold as occurred on the issue of global warming, the public often takes its cues from the few political leaders they trust most. If different groups of citizens look to different leaders for cues, many people's opinions can move, but in opposite directions. These changes are masked when the public as a whole is examined. Second, all citizens are not equally likely to be moved by public debates of this sort. People with strong attitudes and beliefs will remain steadfast, while those with weak preferences and perceptions are most likely to look to trusted leaders for cues as to what to believe. So we must examine the attitudes of these latter citizens if we are to detect any changes.

As the media widely reported during the fall of 1997, President Clinton and Vice President Gore championed the notion that global warming was a potential problem that Americans need to address, while many prominent Republicans and conservatives expressed skepticism. Thus, Democratic/liberal citizens might be expected to have moved toward the administration's point of view at the same time that Republican/ conservative citizens moved away. And indeed, this is exactly what occurred. In September–October, the gap between self-identified strong Democrats and strong Republicans was relatively small, and it grew substantially by December–February.

Source: Excerpted with permission from Resources for the Future, *Resources* 133 (Fall 1998):5–9.

Environmental Interest Groups

There can be arguments about the extent and depth of environmental public opinion among the citizens of the United States. But there can be no disagreement about the existence of a broad and deep collection of private **environmental interest groups** in the country. Part of the "institutionalization" of the environmental movement in America is the huge corps of private citizen groups who are involved in environmental politics/policy at all levels of government.[4] Private groups of this type are a major feature of the open, conflictual style of the policy process in this country.

One might think, at least initially, that private interest groups are essential political conduits, communicating and representing the attitudes and opinions of the public on matters of policy. They certainly do this, though there can be questions of which particular public they represent. But interest representation ("lobbying") is only part of what they do. In fact, they are critical in maintaining and nurturing public opinion itself. We will discuss this below. First, a little history.

Historical Development of Environmental Groups

In the United States there are literally thousands of interest groups at work in the environmental arena. They can be classified along many dimensions: national vs. local (e.g., Sierra Club vs. Salem Sound[5]); membership vs. nonmembership (e.g., Audubon Society vs. the Environmental Policy Institute); traditional lobbying groups vs. direct action groups (Wilderness Society vs. Earth Action); broadly oriented vs. single-issue focus (e.g., Environmental Defense vs. Ducks Unlimited); and so on. Collectively they are the embodiment and voice of the environmental movement. One way to gain perspective on this diverse collection is to look at how these groups developed historically.

We can divide the history of environmental interest groups into three periods:

- starting in the Progressive Era, and continuing up to World War II
- post-World War II, the rise of environmentalism
- the last few decades, the rise of localism

The Progressive/Pre-World War II Period. The organized environmental movement usually traces its roots to the time known as the "Progressive Era" in U.S. history, the first two decades of the twentieth century. Progressivism arose in response to the perceived excesses of the previous few decades.[6] It involved a public outcry and backlash against the excesses of uncontrolled economic expansion: the rise of monopoly power in many important industries, conspicuous consumption by the rich, a burgeoning population of urban and rural poor, and overseas adventurism. One Progressive idea around which people organized was the conservation of natural resources. Conservation meant different things to different people; for example, wise use vs. no use. This was the time when many major national parks and national forests were created. It was also a time when new citizens' environmental organizations were started, particularly the Sierra Club (1892) and the National Audubon Society (1905). Some people call this the first generation of environmental activism, specifically focused on natural resource conservation. The groups formed during this period are now the "elder statesmen" among environmental groups, frequently criticized by liberals for being too bureaucratic and not sufficiently activist, and often criticized by conservatives for being too wedded to conventional policy approaches and not sufficiently supportive of new policy initiatives.[7]

This environmental movement continued during the interwar years (the 1920s and 1930s) and the early post-World War II years. Groups formed during these years included the Izaak Walton League (1922), the Wilderness Society, National Wildlife Federation (1935), Defenders of Wildlife (1947), and the Nature Conservancy (1951). The focus remained largely on conserving the nation's natural resources.

The Rise of Environmentalism. Environmentalism became an important public issue in the 1960s and early 1970s, and witnessed a major change in interest group formation and activity. During this second generation of resource and environmental activism, the focus turned to the control of the massive quantities of chemicals and other pollutants that were flowing from a rapidly expanding industrial economy. The traditional conservation organizations broadened their agendas, sought new sources of support, and added environmental issues to their expertise and policy concerns. This period also produced a number of interest groups focused specifically on environmental issues, such as Environmental Defense Fund, the League of Conservation Voters, the Natural Resources Defense Council, and Greenpeace.

Table 4.2 reveals membership trends for the major environmental groups from 1960 to 1995. The numbers show the very rapid increase of the 1960s, and then less rapid but positive growth during the 1970s. The 1980s again witnessed rapid membership increases in general. During the 1990s, some organizations had flat or slightly declining membership growth, while others continued to show moderate rates of increase.

The Rise of Localism. In the last decade or so we have seen what might be called the third generation of environmental interest group activity. This encompasses several developments. One is a major growth in local or "grassroots" organizations, organized around community environmental issues and pursuing activist roles in local and district settings. Local groups form around specific issues: to press for the cleanup of a particular hazardous waste site, to advocate cuts in pollution from a local factory, to block the construction of a new pollution-causing facility, to encourage recycling, to press for research into the impacts of some local environmental contaminant, and so on. Unlike the national environmental groups, local groups have had success in attracting African Americans, Native Americans, and Latinos, since community groups focus on particular issues that directly affect all members of the local population, such as the siting of hazardous waste dumps. Sometimes this is called **"place-based" environmentalism**.

Table 4.2   Membership Trends of Major National Environmental Groups, 1960–2000

Group	Year Founded	Number of Members (in thousands)				
		1960	1970	1980	1990	2000
Progressive Era, and up to World War II						
Sierra Club[a]	1892	15	113	181	630	642
National Audubon Society	1905	32	148	400	600	550
National Parks and Conservation Assoc.	1919	15	45	31	100	450
Izaak Walton League	1922	51	54	52	50	50
Wilderness Society	1935	10	54	45	350	200
National Wildlife Federation[b]	1936	NA	540	818	997	4000
Post-World War II: The Rise of Environmentalism						
Defenders of Wildlife	1947	NA	13	50	80	425
Nature Conservancy	1951	NA	22	NA	600	1029
World Wildlife Fund	1961		NA	NA	400	1200
Environmental Defense Fund	1967		11	46	200	300
Friends of the Earth[c]	1969		6	NA	9	10
Environmental Action	1970		10	20	23	0
League of Conservation Voters	1970		NA	NA	55	40
Natural Resources Defense Council	1970		NA	40	150	400
Greenpeace USA	1971		NA	NA	2350	350

[a] Does not include over 100,000 members of the Sierra Club Legal Defense Fund, the technically separate legal arm of the Sierra Club.
[b] Full members only. The Federation also counted affiliated memberships (e.g., schoolchildren) of around 4.4 million in 1995.
[c] Merged in 1990 with the 30,000 member Oceanic Society and the nonmember Environmental Policy Institute.
Note: Figures are rounded and in many cases are best-guess approximations based on conflicting data, definitions, or reporting dates. NA = not available.

Sources: Primary information taken from *Voices and Echoes for the Environment* by Ronald Shaiko. Copyright © 1999, Columbia University Press. Reprinted by permission of the publisher. Data for 1960 taken from Robert Cameron Mitchell, Angela G. Mertig, and Riley E. Dunlap, "Twenty Years of Environmental Mobilization, Trends Among National Environmental Organizations," chapter 2 in Riley E. Dunlap and Angela G. Mertig, eds., *American Environmentalism: The U.S. Environmental Movement, 1970–1990* (New York: Taylor and Francis, 1992):13.

A number of umbrella organizations and network groups have sprung up to help these local groups communicate among themselves; gain access to scientific, legal, and political help; and represent their interests at state and federal levels. Such groups as the Grass Roots Environmental Organization in New Jersey, the Citizens' Environmental Coalition in New York, the Citizens' Clearinghouse for Hazardous Wastes, the National Toxics Campaign, the Clean Water Network, the National Recycling Coalition, and the Citizens for a Better Environment in California are examples of this type of organization.

The NIMBY Phenomenon. Part and parcel of this trend toward local groups has been the rise of the NIMBY phenomenon. **NIMBY** stands for "not in my backyard" and refers to the mobilization of local groups to fight specific developments that are seen as threats to local environmental values. These may be housing developments, industrial plants, or public facilities like landfills or incinerators. It's not that people are opposed to these things, only that they should be put someplace else, not in their particular neighborhood. NIMBY groups tend to form quickly in response to perceived threats, act with great energy during the heat of battle, then disappear after the events have died down. In this way they are quite different from the long-lived environmental interest groups, which typically undertake more long-term agendas dealing with continuing issues. Of course these conventional interest groups often become embroiled in fights over specific community projects. But the NIMBY group is one whose primary purpose is to fight one community battle over a specific project.

NIMBY groups can be quite powerful. Their primary goals are to block action on proposals they see as threatening. The U.S. political system, at all levels, consists of institutions with legally specified operating procedures. These procedures usually have numerous points through which groups can gain access in order to slow down or stop a local project.

One can take different positions on NIMBY groups. They can be regarded as an expression of local democracy, in which citizens demonstrate solidarity in fighting against something they see as a threat to community life. They can be regarded as folks who are introducing local values and concerns into the siting process, in opposition to distant bureaucrats or planners who are trying to advance projects on purely technical grounds.

On the other side, NIMBY groups can be characterized as focusing only on the local costs of projects and not on benefits that will perhaps be widespread. A regional hazardous waste site, or incinerator, for example, will benefit people throughout the region. But its environmental cost will be registered primarily in the one community in which it is located. NIMBY groups, it is said, have too narrow a focus.

Environmental Justice

The concerns of the **environmental justice** movement are that the benefits and costs of environmental protection are not equitably distributed among the population. The main issue around which it largely was founded was the siting of hazardous waste facilities; the question was whether these are predominantly located in low-income communities and communities with relatively large populations of people of color. In recent years this movement has broadened somewhat to include the distributional impacts of other environmental regulations.

Most of the environmental justice groups are local (or statewide).[8] Some regional groups have formed, such as the Community Coalition for Environmental Justice, which is active in the Northwest. Most of the federal natural resource and environmental agencies have established environmental justice programs, as have many of the national environmental groups.

The International Focus

Recent developments have spurred another form of environmental group; that is, the international, or transnational, environmental group. Such groups, often called nongovernmental organizations (NGOs), focus on international issues like global warming, and on national or sub-national environmental and natural resource management issues. Although not governmental groups per se, in many countries they have achieved quasi-governmental roles, partnering with public agencies and political authorities to pursue environmental goals. The United Nations has given them associative (that is, participant) status in many of its organizations and meetings.[9]

Explaining the Growth

What accounts for the changes over time in the size and public popularity of the environmental interest groups? The first thing to observe is that, although there may have been some ups and downs over the last few decades, public membership in environmental organizations continues to be very strong. The only way to account for this is that, in general, environmental concerns continue to occupy an important place in the minds of a very large part of the citizenry of the country. Throughout history, it has frequently been the case that interest groups have appeared in response to particular social problems, lived a reasonably brief life as the politics and policy of these problems have been actively pursued, and then withered away as the issue becomes institutionalized, leaders became co-opted and/or tired, or as the public turned its attention to other problems.[10] This cycle does not seem applicable to environmentalism, at least as yet. Public interest has stayed strong enough that environmental interest groups have continued to thrive.

Another conclusion that can be gleaned from the experience of environmental interest groups is that membership changes are, to some degree, opposite to the perceived level and direction of federal activity toward environmental protection. The Reagan years, during which there was a great deal of open hostility in Washington toward environmental policy, witnessed rapid increases in group memberships. On the other hand, in the 1970s and early 1990s there was a feeling that environmental protection issues were being well represented in Washington, and thus memberships increased much more slowly. It appears that people are inclined to get more actively involved in environmentalism when environmental values and policies are felt to be under threat, and less involved when they feel that environmental issues are in good hands. Of course membership figures also reflect the energy with which groups pursue new members; they simply may have expended more energy during the Reagan administration and less in other periods.

Another important factor that affects the pace of activities of environmental interest groups is the flow of support funds. Much of the financial support for these groups, especially the membership groups, comes from individual contributions and dues. But in American political life, private foundations collectively control very large sums of money, most of it stemming from the philanthropic urges of people who have made lots of money in the business world. Many of these foundations have adopted environmental protection as a programmatic objective, which has moved them into funding, among other things, the activities of environmental interest groups. They also serve as a funding source for a considerable amount of scientific research on environmental matters, as we will discuss in chapter 7. Many environmental groups also receive funds from the corporate world.

What Environmental Interest Groups Do

Most directly, environmental groups are involved with traditional **lobbying**: working in the policy-making venues to influence outcomes in desirable directions. This means trying to influence those whose actions establish the policies and regulations: executives, legislators, administrators. There are many ways of doing this:

1. Networking with important policy makers to communicate views for or against particular proposals or laws.

2. Presenting position papers or analyses at public hearings (for example, staff members of Resources for the Future, a Washington environmental think tank, often present expert testimony at congressional hearings).

3. Providing legal expertise to help draft new proposals (for example, the Environmental Defense Fund was instrumental in drafting portions of the 1990 Clean Air Act Amendments).

4. Communicating with members and asking them to send letters or e-mails to policy makers on important environmental policy matters.

In general, the broader the group whose interests are being represented, the more effective the lobbying. Thus, another important tactic is:

5. Working to form coalitions among different groups in order to develop a united front on important issues. Several years ago a number of groups joined in sponsoring the National Resource Summit of America in an attempt to form common interests and joint actions among the "tree-hugger" and "hook and bullet" interest groups.[11] Early in the (second) Bush

administration, many environmental lobbying groups together formed the "Green Group" to forge common political strategies on various important policy issues. See also exhibit 4.3.

The efforts of environmental groups extend beyond traditional lobbying. For example:

6. Monitoring agency actions to ensure that regulations are enforced and laws are interpreted aggressively. An important and effective group in this activity is the Natural Resources Defense Council (NRDC). The NRDC devotes much of its efforts to pursuing legal action against public agencies that appear not to be pursuing environmental regulations with the vigor that Congress intended or which the agencies themselves are presumed to want, given their regulatory mandate.

Exhibit 4.3
Political Support from Unexpected Directions

It has been hard to get the business community to fully support steps to reduce greenhouse gas emissions. Some individual firms have done so, but for the most part the business sector has stressed the costs of doing so and the economic burden they feel this would create. One group of organizations that may be starting to see things differently is pension funds, both public and private companies that manage vast sums of financial assets earmarked to pay for pension benefits to future retirees.

Some in the industry argue that pension fund managers have a responsibility to take a longer view than firms and consumers typically take. They are concerned with the financial upheaval that significant global warming could produce in national and international financial markets. The effects of global warming can be expected to vary from location to location, but in addition to what seems like a modest increase in mean temperature, there could be substantial increases in weather variability, more extreme weather events, and major shifts in economic activity. One result of this could be more instability in financial markets, which could be very significant for those who manage huge pension funds.

Recently, therefore, a number of large fund managers met to form a coordinating group called the Investor Network on Climate Risk. The group will study the connection between global warming and financial markets, encourage pension managers to consider these connections and their reactions to it, and encourage Congress to take more aggressive steps to combat the phenomenon.

Source: Based on various sources, chiefly the article written by Barnaby J. Feder, "Pension Funds Plan to Press Global Warming as an Issue," *New York Times,* November 22, 2003.

7. Providing legal briefs and studies to courts that are working on environmental cases.

There are still other activities of importance. Lobbying is trying to influence decisions in Washington (or in state capitals). This appears to imply an information flow from the citizenry, or group members, into Washington. But there is an equally important flow of information in the reverse direction. It's hard for "outsiders" to know what is going on in the environmental policy struggle. Thus, one important task for environmental interest groups is:

8. Providing members and the public at large with news about what is happening on the policy front. Two important groups in this regard are Environmental Defense and the Environmental Working Group.[12] The best example of this in recent years is the flow of information made possible by the World Wide Web. All environmental groups now have Web sites where policy-relevant material is posted. In fact, there are so many of them that directory sites are now available (e.g., The Environment Web Directory, www.webdirectory.com; The Electronic Green Journal, http://egj.lib.uidaho.edu).

Many environmental groups also engage in direct action as a way of stimulating environmental awareness and propelling a response. Even direct action has many facets:

9. Engaging in sit-downs, picketing, or civil disobedience to highlight and disrupt environmentally destructive actions by businesses or governments. Examples include actions by Greenpeace, demonstrations by PIRGs, destructive acts such as those of the Earth Liberation Front, and the activities of Earth First!

10. Taking action within the "system" to protect particularly valuable parts of the natural environment. The main example here is the Nature Conservancy, a national organization that procures, either on the open market or through donations, areas of high ecological value. Others include the National Farmland Trust, and the many state and local groups that pursue the same type of direct action.

Opposition Groups

Of course, in the open-access system that is the U.S. policy process, opposition groups have the same opportunity to influence events in ways that are congenial to their views. This includes people from (1) the regulated community itself, especially businesses who regard environmental regulations as costly and economically debilitating, and (2) interest groups formed around opposition to the regulatory initiatives but not representing any particular firm or industry.

Regulated industries are in effect already organized in their capacity as ongoing businesses that have environmental impacts. So representatives of individual firms (oil companies, power companies, agricultural companies) frequently testify at public hearings, serve on advisory committees, run public information ads in newspapers, and so on to put forth their views. They also contribute to political campaigns to boost politicians who will represent these views in the policy struggle. Similarly, many industry groups have been formed to represent the perceived interests of firms in that sector. Some examples are the American Petroleum Institute, the National Mining Association, and the American Forest and Paper Association. At a more general level, there are business groups that work on behalf of large numbers of firms and associations from throughout the economy, such as the U.S. Chamber of Commerce, the National Association of Manufacturers, and the Business Roundtable.

Businesses often will form **coalitions** to focus on specific environmental problems. Examples are the Global Climate Coalition and the Clean Air Working Group. Occasionally business groups will form with the objective not to simply oppose regulations, but to encourage green activities among their members. Examples are the Global Environmental Management Initiative and the Energy Future Coalition. These groups promote the view that environmental pollution control can be good business, either because it is good for public relations purposes or because it can encourage firms to find operating efficiencies that will reduce costs as well as reduce emissions.

In the struggle for advantage, each side in the policy wars attributes excessive influence to the other side. The environmental community regards business groups as overly powerful; the regulated community thinks environmental groups have too much influence. Of course there are positive and normative aspects of this: how much influence a group actually has and how much it ought to have. It may be possible to sort out the former,[13] but there will always be contention over the latter.

There is another type of opposition group that, though not comprised of operating firms themselves, is financially supported by them and is a strong supporter of the antiregulation philosophy. Such groups might be thought of as a cross between lobbying groups and policy "think tanks." Policy think tanks, as we will discuss more fully in chapter 7, are groups who bring together policy analysts and decisions makers to study and make pronouncements on various issues related to public regulation. Examples are the Competitive Enterprise Institute, the American Enterprise Institute, and the Cato Institute.

There is one section of the business community that solidly favors stringent pollution-control standards. This is the envirotech sector, consisting of the many thousands of firms that provide compliance technology and information to polluters. The sector includes all kinds of firms: those that manufacture and install pollution-control equipment, those that help other firms actually carry out cleanup operations, consulting firms, legal firms, and so forth. In effect, the more stringent the pollution-control laws, the larger the market for firms in the envirotech sector.

The activities of environmental interest groups have become a major force in shaping environmental policy in the United States, as in other countries.

The range of action is wide, from the civil disobedience of Earth Liberation to the unobtrusive land-acquisition activities of the Nature Conservancy; from the strong antipolluter actions of the Public Interest Research Groups to the energetic but more conciliatory attitude of Environmental Defense; and from the solidly established track record of the old-line groups like the Sierra Club to feisty new NIMBY groups that have joined the battle in thousands of local settings around the country. These groups battle for a cleaner environment within the policy struggle, and just as importantly they act as keepers of the flame in terms of maintaining environmental awareness among the population at large.

Political Parties

Another important way that citizen interests and concerns get organized and articulated is through the activities of **political parties**. Virtually every democratic system around the world is characterized by the presence of political parties that recruit political leaders, contest elections, and try to shape policy outcomes in ways that are congenial to the interests and desires of their electoral supporters. Political parties are normally organized around political ideologies, which are deployed in an attempt to give policy positions a degree of social and political legitimacy.

In the United States the Republican Party normally presents itself as conservative in terms of social policy and oriented toward an economic system based on the unhindered operation of private markets. Democrats favor a more liberal position that encourages public regulation in cases where it is called for, and a greater concern for matters dealing with social and economic equity.

In the environmental arena, therefore, Democrats are usually thought to favor greater reliance on statutory pollution-control regulations as a way to improve environmental quality; Republicans are more inclined to stress the economic costs of pollution control and to tout the advantages of voluntary approaches to improving the environment. Some appreciation for the differences between the parties can be gained by looking at different positions taken in party platforms on a variety of environmental issues through the years. These are summarized in table 4.3.

Of course, while general party tendencies certainly exist, there are plenty of instances in the past where Republicans have taken what might be regarded as pro-environment steps, while some Democrats have done the opposite. President Nixon, a Republican, presided over some of the early 1970s environmental actions at the federal level, including the creation of the EPA. The first President Bush was instrumental in enacting the 1990 Clean Air Act. A long-time strong Senate supporter of environmental protection was Senator Chaffee, a Republican from Rhode Island. On the other hand, powerful Democrats in Congress have from time to time blocked action on environmental matters because they thought them adverse to the economic welfare of their states and districts.

Table 4.3   Key Elements of Positions on Environmental Issues in Party Platforms, 1976–1992

Democratic Party Platform	Year	Republican Party Platform
Environmental protection is necessary to achieve a more just society. Air and water pollution control are linked to health; economic impacts should be uniform across the country. Controls on strip mining endorsed.	1976	Clean air policy and land-use planning are the responsibility of state and local governments. Government regulation of coal mining should be minimal. Accelerate use of nuclear power.
Energy production and use linked to environmental protection. Energy conservation is high priority and nuclear waste disposal problem must be resolved.	1980	Clean Air Act regulations are too stringent and require reform. Benefits of environmental laws must justify the costs. Nation's energy supplies should be increased.
Superfund and other hazardous waste programs must be fully implemented. Clean Air and Water Acts should be strengthened. EPA's budget should be restored. Expansion of National Wilderness Preservation System is backed.	1984	Environmental protection must be balanced by economic growth to improve standard of living. More coal should be mined and more oil and natural gas developed. Increase number of nuclear power plants.
Offshore oil drilling strongly opposed. The U.S. should convene international summits to address depletion of ozone layer, global warming, and destruction of tropical forests. Promote energy conservation and the increased use of renewable energy sources; reduce reliance on nuclear power. More aggressive enforcement of environmental laws is necessary.	1988	Expand use of nuclear power but in an environmentally safe manner. Efforts to reduce air and water pollution, control hazardous waste disposal, protect the public lands, and prevent ocean dumping are supported. Takes credit for renewal of Superfund.
A genuine "no net loss" policy on wetlands is endorsed. Recommends establishment of a civilian youth conservation corps. Strongly opposes efforts by Republicans to weaken the 1990 Clean Air Act in the "guise" of competitiveness. Supports recycling, energy efficiency, and pollution prevention strategies. Nation's many critical environmental areas must be protected. All multilateral trade agreements (e.g., GATT, NAFTA) must address environmental concerns. U.S. must be a more aggressive world leader in addressing global warming, depletion of ozone layer, biodiversity, and explosive population growth.	1992	Will not tolerate obstruction of expansion of international trade. Property rights of farmers, ranchers, and foresters must be protected. Supports drilling in the Arctic National Wildlife Refuge and the Outer Continental Shelf. Public lands should be used for mining, oil and gas exploration, and lumber. Private ownership and economic growth is best security against environmental degradation. Takes credit for passage of the 1990 Clean Air Act. Defends President Bush's actions at the Rio Conference. Believes nation must protect its natural environment.

Source: Excerpted from Sheldon Kamieniecki, "Party Politics and Environmental Policy," in James P. Lester, ed., *Environmental Politics and Policy: Theories and Evidence*, 2nd ed. (Durham, NC: Duke University Press, 1995):153–154. Used with permission.

Evidence suggests that among the entire U.S. electorate, party affiliation has some, but not a particularly strong, relationship with how people feel about environmental regulations.[14] Party platforms can reveal tendencies and trends desired by party leaders, but their environmental planks are unlikely to play a very strong role in attracting voters.

A more important environmental role of the parties is in fostering the partisanship that has been increasingly roiling the affairs of Congress and the Executive Office. Partisanship, the identification of particular environmental policy positions with a political party, was muted in the 1970s but has been growing ever since. During the Reagan years the Republican Party saw itself as the vanguard of an antiregulation movement in the United States, and relaxing environmental regulation became part of the party's program for accomplishing this.[15] The Republican surge in Congress in the early 1990s exacerbated this trend. Then during the latter 1990s one occasionally heard rumblings from within the Republican Party about the need to back away from the strident antiregulatory positions of the early 1990s. The thought was that this might alienate middle-of-the-road voters who were reasonably comfortable with the current state of environmental regulation. But in the second Bush administration partisanship shows no sign of diminishing.

Green Parties

Green parties—that is, political parties with primarily an environmental agenda—have been active in many countries, particularly in Canada and Japan, as well as in Europe. While never large enough to seriously threaten the dominant political parties in these countries, they have been important catalysts for raising awareness, building coalitions, and generating publicity for environmental laws and their enforcement. By providing an organizing focus for environmentally concerned citizens, they sometimes have had an influence disproportionate to their actual size.

From time to time there have been efforts in the United States to organize or achieve power outside of the established parties, often by founding a green political party. Green motives were partially behind Ralph Nader's attempt to run as an independent candidate for president in 2000. Many years ago President Theodore Roosevelt tried to get reelected by founding a third party (called the Bull Moose party) that was based to some extent on a green position related to natural resource conservation. The Green Party USA was established in 1991. It has a number of local chapters and affiliated organizations around the country. The party has run candidates in many local elections and has been successful in some. The party has a broader perspective than just environmental issues; for example, it has devoted much time and energy to antiwar activities. In 1996 the Green Party of the United States was formed, also with a very broad social and economic agenda.

In American politics third parties have been notably unsuccessful at the national level, owing primarily to the system of voting that is used. In **plurality voting** systems such as that of the United States, the candidate with the most votes wins the election. All the other candidates receive nothing (i.e., it is a winner-take-all system). It is theoretically possible, for example, for a green party to take 49 percent of the votes for the U.S. Congress in every state and end up with zero representation in that Congress. Green parties have been more successful in some other countries where **proportional representation** is more common. In this system, seats in a legislature are allocated to each political party according to the percentage of votes the party receives in the general vote.

Summary

Environmentalism, as a public attitude, blossomed in the 1960s and led to the passage of many new environmental laws. Since then, public opinion on environmental issues has waxed and waned, but in general has stayed reasonably strong. There is a difference, however, between generalized, latent public opinion on the environment, which generally has been relegated to the back burner of public issues, and public opinion on specific issues. There are now thousands of environmental interest groups, working at all levels of government. While a major activity is lobbying on environmental laws and policy actions, interest groups engage in a broad range of other functions. In recent years there has been a substantial growth in the number of local groups, environmental justice groups, and groups focusing on the global environment. Because the United States employs a winner-take-all voting system, green parties have never been particularly successful in American elections unlike, for example, in Europe. Although the Democrats and Republicans have adopted positions on environmental issues that differ according to the ideological bases of the parties, these issues have never played a decisive role in national elections. This is not the case, however, for local-level elections.

Key Terms

coalitions	NIMBY
environmental interest groups	"place-based" environmentalism
environmental justice	plurality voting
green parties	proportional representation
information technology (IT)	public opinion
lobbying	regulated industries

Questions for Further Discussion

1. American citizens appear to be gradually becoming more conservative in their thinking. What does this imply about their environmental attitudes?

2. What do you think accounts for the fact that "environmentalism" has become deeply ingrained in American attitudes rather than faded away as many social movements have in the past?

3. Environmental interest groups range from those that employ a conservative, work-within-the-system approach to those that advocate a radical approach based on civil disobedience. Which types do you think are most effective?

4. Why have green political parties been so unsuccessful in American national elections?

5. Although environmental issues have not loomed large in federal and state election campaigns, they have much more significance at the local level. Why?

Web Sites

The main polling organizations have Web sites on which one can usually find information on environmental polls, though it may take some snooping around when environmental issues are not on, or near, the front burner. The major polling organizations are:

The Gallup Organization
www.gallup.com

Roper Center for Public Opinion Research
www.ropercenter.uconn.edu

The Harris Poll
www.louisharris.com

See also:
PollingReport.com

Public Agenda Online
www.publicagenda.org

Of course, the World Wide Web facilitates online polling, which is opening up new sources of data. Each of the organizations mentioned in this chapter can be found by consulting your favorite search engine. What appears to be a comprehensive list of environmental groups is available at the National Wildlife Federation Web site:

www.nwf.org/conservationdirectory/

See also the list of the National Council for Science and the Environment:
www.cnie.org/yellow/interests.htm

Environmental justice sites include:
People of Color Environmental Groups
www.ejrc.cau.edu/poc2000.htm

Environmental Justice Coalition
groups.msn.com/environmentaljusticecoalition

African American Environmentalist Association
www.aaenvironment.com

Many private foundations have established environmental programs to foster research and advocacy on environmental issues:

Rockefeller Family Fund, Environmental Integrity Project
www.rffund.org
Pew Charitable Trusts
www.pewtrusts.com

Additional Readings

Altman, I., and A. Wandersman, eds., *Neighborhood and Community Environments* (New York: Plenum Press, 1987).

Beierle, Thomas C., and Jerry Cayford, *Democracy in Practice, Public Participation in Environmental Decisions* (Washington, DC: Resources for the Future, 2002).

Bullard, R. D., ed., *Confronting Environmental Racism: Voices from the Grassroots* (Boston, MA: South End Press, 1993).

Bullard, Robert D., "Environmental Justice in the 21st Century." www.ejrc.cau.edu/ejinthe21century.htm.

Cigler, Allan J., and Burdett A. Loomis, eds., *Interest Group Politics*, 5th ed. (Washington, DC: Congressional Quarterly Books, 1998).

Dowie, Mark, *Losing Ground: American Environmentalism at the Close of the Twentieth Century* (Cambridge, MA: MIT Press, 1995).

Dunlap, Riley E., and Angela E. Mertig, eds., *American Environmentalism: The U.S. Environmental Movement, 1970–1990* (Washington, DC: Taylor and Francis, 1992).

Glave, Dianne D., and Mark Stoll, *To Love the Wind and the Rain: African Americans and Environmental History* (Pittsburgh: University Pittsburgh Press, 2006).

Gottlieb, Robert, *Forcing the Spring: The Transformation of the American Environmental Movement* (Washington, DC: Island Press, 1993).

Guber, Deborah L., *The Grassroots of Green Revolution: Polling America on the Environment* (Cambridge, MA: MIT Press, 2003).

Herrnson, Paul S., Ronald G. Shaiko, and Clyde Wilcox, eds., *The Interest Group Connection*, 2nd ed. (Washington, DC: Congressional Quarterly Press, 2004).

Hunter, Susan, and Kevin M. Leyden, "Beyond NIMBY: Explaining Opposition to Hazardous Waste Facilities," *Policy Studies Journal* 23 (Winter 1995):601–619.

Kempton, Willett, James S. Boster, and Jennifer A. Hartley, *Environmental Values in American Culture* (Cambridge, MA: MIT Press, 1996).

Petrace, Mark P., ed., *The Politics of Interests: Interest Groups Transformed* (Boulder, CO: Westview Press, 1992).

Piller, Charles, *The Fail-Safe Society: Community Defiance and the End of American Technological Optimism* (New York: Basic Books, 1991).

Rothman, Hal K., *The Greening of a Nation? Environmentalism in the United States Since 1945* (Orlando, FL: Harcourt Brace, 1998).

Shabecoff, Philip, *Earth Rising: American Environmentalism in the Twenty-first Century* (Washington, DC: Island Press, 2000).

Shutkin, William A., *The Land That Could Be: Environmentalism and Democracy in the Twenty-first Century* (Cambridge, MA: MIT Press, 2000).

Wenner, Lettie M., *U.S. Energy and Environmental Interest Groups: Institutional Profiles* (Westport, CT: Greenwood Press, 1990).

West, Darrell M., and Burdett A. Loomis, *The Sound of Money: How Political Interests Get What They Want* (New York: W.W. Norton, 1999).

Notes

[1] This book focused on damage to wildlife species from chemical residues in the environment. It was very influential in producing the ban on DDT in the United States.

[2] For example, a recent poll concludes that, while people still feel positive about the need for environmental policies, their willingness to sacrifice other goals for environmental protection has diminished. See Duke University News and Communications, "Survey: Why Pro-Environmental Views Don't Always Turn Into Votes," www.dukenews.duke.edu/2005/09/nicholaspoll.html.

[3] Called the National Dialogue on Public Involvement in EPA Decisions.

[4] By "private" interest groups we refer to groups composed of people who are not acting as government officials. There are, however, private groups consisting of government officials acting in nonofficial capacities.

[5] Salem Sound 2000 is a group in and around Salem, Massachusetts, devoted to fighting for cleaner water in that body of water.

[6] Called the "Gilded Age."

[7] For information about the conservation movement of this time, see the "American Memory" Web page of the Library of Congress: http://cweb2.loc.gov/ammem/amrvhtml/

[8] See the long list of local environmental justice groups listed at People of Color Environmental Groups Directory, www.ejrc.cau.edu/poc2000.htm. This is put together by the Environmental Justice Resource Center at Clark Atlanta University.

[9] For more on NGOs see the Duke University Non-Governmental Organizations Research Guide, www.lib.duke.edu/igo/guides/ngo.

[10] As one earlier researcher stated: "Judging from our expectations about the 'life-cycle' of such movements, and from the history of the earlier conservation movement, we might expect the demise of the current environmentalist movement within the decade." The decade referred to was that of the 1970s. Armand L. Mauss, *Social Problems as Social Movements* (New York: Lippincott, 1975).

[11] That is, environmental groups on the one hand, and hunting and fishing groups on the other.

[12] "Working group" is a common term for a group that is often pulled together from other groups to focus on some specific aspect of the environment, e.g., the Working Group on Environmental Justice.

[13] For a recent attempt to shed light on this see Sheldon Kamieniecki, *Corporate America and Environmental Policy: How Often Does Business Get Its Way?* (Stanford, CA: Stanford University Press, 2006).

[14] See Sheldon Kamieniecki, "Party Politics and Environmental Policy," in James P. Lester, ed., *Environmental Politics and Policy: Theories and Evidence*, 2nd ed. (Durham, NC: Duke University Press, 1995):146–167.

[15] As documented in Jerry W. Calvert, "Party Politics in Environmental Policy," in James P. Lester, ed., *Environmental Politics and Policy: Theories and Evidence* (Durham, NC: Duke University Press, 1989):158–178.

5

The Policy
Wheelhouse

Congress, the President,
and the EPA

At the end of the last chapter we discussed partisanship and the jousting of political parties over environmental policy and regulation. This chapter serves as a transition from thinking about the citizenry and the private environmental community to discussing the three prime federal institutions whose struggles determine the course of environmental policy. As an example of this struggle, consider the 2004 standoff in Washington over air pollution policy. President Bush proposed a new plan (called the Clear Skies plan), the effect of which would be to reduce the long-run stringency of some of the primary air pollution regulations.[1] Although Congress was controlled by the president's own party, there was enough opposition to stymie the proposal. Meanwhile, environmentally-minded members of Congress tried to rally support around a counterproposal. The EPA was split over the new plan; the top level, consisting of personnel appointed by the president, naturally leaned toward his proposal, while many of the career people in the agency were not enthusiastic about the plan. The result was a standoff among the three most powerful Washington institutions dealing with environmental policy: Congress, the president, and the EPA. Congress was unable to take action and has not done so as of mid-2006. In this chapter we will take a look at each of these groups, their basic makeup and operating procedures, as well as some of the traits that work against the making of aggressive and sound environmental policy and regulation.

The U.S. Congress

Congress is the archetypical institution of representative government: a collection of individuals democratically elected from diverse constituencies, whose job it is to produce authoritative judgment and action on the issues of the day. It is a place where shifting and colliding interests can be compromised and resolved, passions can be tempered and absorbed, coalitions can be patched together or split apart, and decisions can be made which, in appearance if not in reality, address the country's problems.

Congress and the Environment

It is fair to say that much of the impetus for the broad, new national environmental laws in the 1970s came from Congress. The Nixon administration was not particularly predisposed to lead the charge on these issues, but the groundswell of public concern about the environment and rising environmental activism in the country led to a response in Congress. Senator Muskie of Maine became prominent as the leading environmental statesman in Washington and rallied support in Congress for new environmental laws. The 91st Congress (1969–1970) enacted the National Environmental Policy Act and the 1970 Clean Air Act. The former set up machinery for conducting environmental impact studies of all major federal projects. The latter established a new federal command-and-control system for achieving federally mandated ambient air quality standards. The 92nd Congress passed, over President Nixon's veto, the Clean Water Act of 1972.

Congressional activity continued through the 1970s. Major amendments were made to the CAA and CWA, and a number of important new statutes were enacted on the management of toxic chemicals and hazardous materials. Congress worked with President Carter (1977–1980) to ramp up the staffing and budget of the Environmental Protection Agency.

All this changed in the 1980s. These were the Reagan years, when more conservative forces in Washington sought to dismantle the regulatory structure that the EPA was building. Environmental interests in Congress changed their focus somewhat from offense to defense; the main job was to fight off efforts to weaken environmental regulations, and to force the EPA, now controlled by Reagan appointees, to maintain implementation schedules of existing laws. Much of the dueling was over the amount of discretion that environmental laws gave the EPA. Antiregulation forces within the EPA tried to use this latitude to slow or stop federal action on environmental issues. In fights over new environmental laws (the 1990 Clean Air Act was notable in this respect), congressional environmental interests sought to write more detailed laws that would force EPA to act.

In the 1990s Congress had become more conservative. The 104th Congress (1995–1996), in which the Republicans gained control of both Senate and House, targeted federal environmental regulation for an aggressive rollback. Although they were effectively beaten back by pro-environmental forces in Congress and the Clinton administration, efforts have continued. The administration of George W. Bush has witnessed a substantial stalemate in Congress, making it difficult to move forward with new laws such as the Bush-proposed bills on energy and air pollution, which are being fought by congressional environmental forces.

How Congress Works

Before discussing the political factors affecting Congress, it's useful to review some of the more formal aspects of this body. The U.S. Congress is a **bicameral legislative body** made up of representatives elected in the states and districts of the country. The House of Representatives has 435 members and the Senate has 100 members. Congresses are numbered according to their years of existence, thus the 108th Congress served in 2003 and 2004. The constitutional responsibilities of Congress include originating new public policies and appropriating the funds necessary to implement them.

The two bodies of Congress are each organized by whichever political party has a majority in that body. The majority party, in other words, appoints the leaders of the body and the chairpersons of the many committees and subcommittees that are established to pursue the business of the House and Senate. Table 5.1 gives some information on recent Congresses.

Much of the work of Congress is done in the committees and subcommittees of the two houses. It is here where much of the political pushing and shoving occurs regarding the directions in which policy will go and the precise form it will take. Bills[2] are taken under consideration, perhaps pushed forward if there is enough support, or buried if there isn't. Public hearings often are held to allow supporters and opponents of bills to offer their input. Compromises can be hammered out in executive sessions. If a bill is successfully negotiated through the gauntlet of political and procedural steps, it is then sent to the full House or Senate to be debated and voted on. Table 5.2 gives a brief outline of the steps through which a proposal becomes a statute.[3] Table 5.3 lists the standing committees[4] of Congress that have some jurisdiction over environmental issues.

Congress does more than pass new laws and appropriate funds. Another important role is monitoring agency performance with respect to laws already on the books. This can be done through formal committee hearings, or simply by individual members of Congress who have lines of communication into the agency. Another major activity is constituency service, a job that takes up substantial amounts of time for the typical member of Congress. In the case of environmental regulation, this often means contacting the EPA on behalf of a constituent, be it polluter or pollutee, to recommend actions favorable to these interests.

Table 5.1   Recent U.S. Congresses

Number	Years	Organized by: Senate	House	Major Environmental Laws
I	1789–1790			
91	1969–1970	D	D	NEPA, CAA
92	1971–1972	D	D	CWA
93	1973–1974	D	D	
94	1975–1976	D	D	RCRA, TSCA
95	1977–1978	D	D	CAA, CWA
96	1979–1980	D	D	CERCLA
97	1981–1982	R	D	
98	1983–1984	R	D	
99	1985–1986	R	D	SARA, EPCRA
100	1987–1988	D	D	
101	1989–1990	D	D	CAA
102	1991–1992	D	D	
103	1993–1994	D	D	
104	1995–1996	R	R	
105	1997–1998	R	R	
106	1999–2000	R	R	
107	2001–2002	D	R	
108	2003–2004	R	R	

Key:
NEPA: National Environmental Policy Act
CAA: Clean Air Act
CWA: Clean Water Act
RCRA: Resource Conservation and Recovery Act
TSCA: Toxic Substances Control Act
CERCLA: Comprehensive Environmental Response, Compensation and Liability Act (Superfund)
EPCRA: Emergency Planning and Community Right to Know Act
SARA: Superfund Amendments and Reauthorization Act

Factors Impacting Congressional Effectiveness

Congress has always been subject to criticism, even outright derision.[5]
Yet surveys have shown consistently that most voters think their own senators
and congresspeople do a good job of representing their interests. In their
views, unified action to further these interests (which in their mind is usually
thought of as the "public interest") is thwarted by narrow-minded politicians
from other states and districts. When Congress pulls itself together and passes
a law dealing with one of the nation's problems—say a law on air pollution
control—they are praised by those members of the citizenry who advocate

Table 5.2   General Procedures for New Laws

Proposed laws (bills) are introduced by members of Congress.	Bills can be introduced on their own initiative, or on behalf of the president.
Bills are sent to the appropriate committee and subcommittee for consideration.	Committees may hold hearings, invite comments or reports; many bills get buried here in the sense that no action is taken; substantial revisions can be made to the original proposals.
Proposed statutes are voted on in committee and, if approved, are sent to the full House or Senate for consideration.	The two bodies have their own rules about when and how a proposal will come before the full membership and be voted upon.
A bill approved by one body is then sent to the other one, which can accept it, reject it, or pass its own version.	
If different bills are approved by House and Senate, a conference committee is set up to work out a compromise; this is then sent back to the two bodies for approval.	
After passage by both houses, the bill is sent to the president for signature.	If the president signs the bill, it becomes a law; if he refuses to sign it and sends it back to Congress, this constitutes a veto. If the president retains the bill for ten days (Sundays excluded) without signing, it becomes law, but if Congress has adjourned during that ten days, the bill automatically fails; this is called a pocket veto.
A vetoed bill can be considered by Congress; if it receives less than two-thirds vote, it goes no further; if it receives more than two-thirds vote, the president's veto is overridden and the bill becomes a law.	

the action, and berated by those who oppose it. When it takes no action, the attitudes of these two segments are reversed. A number of explanations have been advanced to explain why Congress seems so rarely to be able to act with common purpose and stately bearing on the important issues of the day.

There is no more common criticism of Congress than that it is fragmented and uncoordinated, seemingly unable to pass environmental laws that are comprehensive, consistent among their many parts, and forward-

**Table 5.3   Congressional Committees and Subcommittees Having
Some Jurisdiction over Environmental Issues, 107th Congress**

House of Representatives

House Committee on Agriculture
Subcommittee on Department Operations, Oversight, Nutrition, and Forestry
Subcommittee on Conservation, Credit, Rural Development, and Research

House Committee on Appropriations
Subcommittee on Energy and Water Development
Subcommittee on Interior
Subcommittee on the Department of Veterans Affairs, Housing and Urban Development, and Independent Agencies (includes EPA)

House Committee on Energy and Commerce
Subcommittee on Energy and Air Quality
Subcommittee on Environment and Hazardous Materials

House Committee on Resources
Subcommittee on National Parks, Recreation, and Public Lands
Subcommittee on Fisheries Conservation, Wildlife, and Oceans
Subcommittee on Forests and Forest Health
Subcommittee on Water and Power

House Committee on Science
Subcommittee on Energy
Subcommittee on Environment, Technology, and Standards

House Committee on Transportation and Infrastructure
Subcommittee on Water Resources and Environment

House Committee on Government Reform
Subcommittee on Energy Policy, Natural Resources, and Regulatory Affairs

Senate

Senate Committee on Agriculture, Nutrition, and Forestry
Subcommittee on Forestry, Conservation, and Rural Revitalization
Subcommittee on Research, Nutrition, and General Legislation

Senate Committee on Appropriations
Subcommittee on Veterans Affairs, HUD, and Independent Agencies

Senate Committee on Commerce, Science, and Transportation
Subcommittee on Surface Transportation and Merchant Marine
Subcommittee on Oceans, Atmosphere, and Fisheries
Subcommittee on Science, Technology, and Space

Senate Committee on Energy and Natural Resources
Subcommittee on Energy
Subcommittee on Public Lands and Forests
Subcommittee on National Parks
Subcommittee on Water and Power

Senate Committee on Environment and Public Works
  Subcommittee on Transportation, Infrastructure, and Nuclear Safety
  Subcommittee on Superfund, Toxics, Risk, and Waste Management
  Subcommittee on Clean Air, Wetlands, and Climate Change
  Subcommittee on Fisheries, Wildlife, and Water

Senate Committee on Government Affairs
  Subcommittee on Oversight of Government Management, Restructuring, and the
    District of Columbia

Total number of committees with jurisdiction over EPA: 13
Total number of subcommittees with jurisdiction over EPA: 30

Source: National Academy of Public Administration, *Setting Priorities, Getting Results: A New Direction for EPA* (Washington, DC: National Academy of Public Administration, 1995):124–125.

---

looking. When crises arise (e.g., the Santa Barbara oil spill, the *Exxon Valdez*), they can produce in Congress a sense of urgency sufficient to get a reasonably quick response. The need and desire for action will prompt a greater willingness to compromise and move forward. Not all action is necessarily substantive action, however. National politics, of which Congress is a major part, has a large component of **political theater.** Appearances can often be as important as reality, and much of what happens in Congress is done with eyes solidly on public image.

Some of the specific reasons for congressional inaction are the following.

The Committee Structure.   Many people have pointed to the structure of congressional committees as partially to blame for the difficulty Congress has in dealing with environmental issues in an integrated and consistent fashion. Congress is called upon to address a vast range of issues; it is logical, then, to create a structure where issues are divided up and parceled out to subgroups whose members specialize in that particular topic. But there are at least two major problems with this system. First, there is a complicated set of jurisdictions assigned to each subcommittee. Creating jurisdictional borders means that problems often are approached from a perspective that is too narrow. A subcommittee on air pollution deals with regulations for controlling emissions; a different subcommittee deals with transportation issues. But transportation planning has important air pollution consequences.

Second, a complicated committee structure also means a multiplicity of power centers within the houses of Congress. Each subcommittee and committee has a chairperson, who exercises substantial influence over the activities of the group and the decisions it makes. Multiple power centers mean multiple opportunities for action to be blocked and integrated policy decisions to be frustrated. The difficulty of putting together a substantial coalition in this milieu means that most bills never see the light of day. Table 5.4 contains a selection of environmental bills that were at least considered in subcommittee (the first step) in the three-year period from 1993–1996. Of the

Table 5.4   Selected Efforts in Environmental Legislation, 1994–96

Legislation	Title and Content	Results
H.R. 4771 / S. 993	Federal Mandate Accountability and Reform Act of 1994. Would have required the Congressional Budget Office (CBO) to estimate costs of federal mandates to state, local and tribal governments, compelled agencies to analyze benefits and costs of new federal mandates.	Referred to committee in House and Senate, no floor action taken.
H.R. 3948 / S. 2093	Water Quality Act of 1994 / Water Pollution Prevention and Control Act of 1994. Reauthorization legislation for Clean Water Act; considered making CWA more flexible, less prescriptive regarding non-point source regulation, municipal stormwater regulation, wetlands designation, and permitting.	Reported in Senate, introduced in House, no floor action taken.
H.R. 4329 / S. 2050	FIFRA Amendments of 1994. Would have directed EPA administrator to develop criteria for designation of "reduced risk pesticides," required coordination between USDA and EPA on environmental risk reduction.	Referred to committee in House and Senate, no floor action taken.
H.R. 3392 / S. 2019	SDWA FY95 Authorization Bill / SDWA Amendments of 1994. S. 2019 would have required EPA to rank pollution sources based on risk. H.R. 3392 would have required EPA to consider risk reduction benefits and costs in setting standards. Both would have eliminated 1986 requirement that EPA regulate 25 more contaminants every 3 years.	Passed Senate and House. No Conference Committee convened.
H.R. 4306	Risk Assessment Improvement Act of 1994. Would have established EPA program to develop risk assessment guidelines, oversee implementation, require scientific peer review, etc.	Reported in House.
H.R. 2099	Rider to FY 1996 VA-HUD Independent Agencies appropriations bill. The House approved 17 major riders that would have prohibited EPA from spending FY 1996 funds on a number of regulatory and enforcement activities.	Passed House and Senate, vetoed by Clinton.
S. 1316	Safe Drinking Water Act Amendments of 1996. Requires EPA to determine whether the benefits of all new drinking water maximum contaminant levels (MCLs) justify the costs. Revokes mandate that EPA regulate 25 new contaminants every 3 years.	P.L. 104-182.

H.R. 961	Clean Water Act Amendments of 1995. Would have made CWA less prescriptive, amending standards, regulatory requirements, and wetlands dredge and fill permitting.	Passed House, no action taken in Senate.
H.R. 1627	Food Quality Protection Act of 1996. Amends FIFRA and the Federal Food, Drug and Cosmetic Act. Removes pesticide residues on processed food from the list of Delaney "zero-risk standard" substances.	P.L. 104-170.

Source: Excerpted from Sheila M. Cavanagh, Robert W. Hahn, and Robert N. Stavins, "National Environmental Policy During the Clinton Years," in Jeffrey A. Frankel and Peter R. Orszag, eds., *American Economic Policy in the 1990s* (Cambridge, MA: MIT Press, 2002). Permission granted by the MIT Press.

nine proposals listed, only two got all the way to final passage: amendments to the Safe Drinking Water Act and the Food Quality Protection Act of 1996.

"All Politics Are Local." This famous expression was uttered by Congressman Tip O'Neil of Massachusetts, Speaker of the House of Representatives from 1977 to 1987. What he meant is that the overriding concern of individual members of Congress is their state or district; their constituents elected them, thus it is the interests of those constituents that are uppermost in the minds of legislators. When members of Congress consider a piece of proposed legislation, they are not so much thinking "how will this impact the country" but rather "how will this affect the interests of my state or district and my political position there." The local political battles that were fought to get elected to Congress continue to be the primary context in which they make their decisions and pursue their agendas.

Localism of this sort doesn't make it impossible to pursue policy that is in the national interest, but it does make it harder. It means that policies normally are a patchwork of provisions that have been bargained and horse-traded to produce support sufficient for their passage.

The Election Cycle. Compounding the problem of localism is the fact that members of Congress must devote a large amount of time to getting reelected. For a member of the House elections come every two years, for Senate members every six years. With these short cycles, the overarching concern is not so much "will this proposal be in the long-run interests of the country?" but "how will this proposal affect my next campaign?" which in effect is probably already underway. A short-term perspective like this makes people much more prone to consider programs that appear to offer visible short-run results rather than solutions that will be effective in the long run. It produces an incentive to take quick action that provides good material for use in the next campaign, when legislators actually should be concerned with long-run consequences. Short-term appearances trump long-term reality.

Scientific Uncertainty. When public concern surfaces about an environmental issue, there may be very sparse scientific evidence to support one solution over another. Congress must act, but Congress does not consist of scientists who can sift through technical studies and design appropriate public policies in the face of large uncertainty. Most members of Congress are lawyers and so are prone to focus on legal issues, together with whatever they can discern about potential impacts on their home states and districts. We will discuss the question of science and policy at greater length in chapter 7. Suffice it to say here that scientific uncertainty is one of the main reasons Congress often hesitates to act and why, when it does act, Congress often passes much of the initiative to the EPA and other agencies, who are better equipped to deal with scientific issues.

The President

The president is the chief executive of the nation, supposedly representative of the entire citizenry. As such, he or she is obviously a focal point in the political struggle that culminates in environmental policy and regulation. Presidents may or may not come into office with well-thought-out views about how environmental policy and regulation should be pursued. Whether or not they have a focused environmental agenda, in actuality they are just one of the many players in the policy struggle. What presidents can accomplish depends on the degree to which they want to make the environment an issue and the strategies and tactical possibilities available to them at the time.

Recent Presidents and the Environment

The early post-World War II presidents had little to say about the environment. For Presidents Truman, Eisenhower, Kennedy, and Johnson, attention was focused on other matters, and issues of pollution and environmental quality were not yet visibly a part of the public agenda at the national level. This is not to say that there was no action at all on environmental issues. In fact, a number of laws were passed, and the realization was growing that environmental pollution was becoming a more important problem.[6] But up until the late 1960s the prevailing attitude was that environmental problems could be handled by the individual states, with some degree of backstopping by the federal government.

President Nixon (1969–1974) was the first modern president to be faced with significant demands in environmental policy. Nixon was a conservative Republican but did not have the strong antiregulatory outlook that would characterize some later Republican leaders. He did understand, however, that environmental concerns were becoming a much more important issue at the national level, and sought to some extent to co-opt them. He presided over the creation of the Environmental Protection Agency in 1970, and both the 1970 Clean Air Act[7] and 1972 Federal Water Pollution Control Act were enacted during his administration. These were the seminal laws by which the federal government sought to take the initiative in pollution-control policy. They established the command-and-control approach that would characterize most pollution-control policy over the next several decades. The initiative and pressure for these laws came primarily from Congress rather than the president. In fact, the 1972 Federal Water Pollution Control Act actually was passed over Nixon's veto.

Following President Nixon's resignation, his remaining term was filled by President Ford (1974–1976), who had too little time to develop a reputation or track record on any particular issue. Nevertheless, during his administration two significant federal environmental laws were enacted: the Resource Conservation and Recovery Act of 1976, applicable to the control of hazardous waste, and the Toxic Substances Control Act of 1976, applying to the use of toxic materials in production (we will discuss these in chapter 11).

Ford was succeeded by President Carter (1977–1980), a traditional Democrat who was substantially more inclined than his immediate predecessors to deploy federal regulatory powers in the name of environmental pollution control. He ramped up the resources available to the EPA and worked to pass the Comprehensive Environmental Response, Compensation and Liability Act of 1980 (known more familiarly as Superfund).

The environmental initiatives of the Carter administration came to an abrupt halt with the election of a Republican president in 1980. President Reagan came into office with a strong antiregulation agenda, and pursued that in the EPA by reducing its budgets and appointing top personnel who sought to diminish its regulatory activism. As we learned earlier, environmental policy leadership in Washington shifted into Congress, and the 1980s were marked by an ongoing struggle between the Reagan administration, the Reagan EPA, and congressional groups who were interested in moving ahead on various policy issues.

President George H. W. Bush (1989–1992) succeeded Reagan. Although a Republican and, therefore, presenting himself as a conservative, he nevertheless was far more inclined than his predecessor to address environmental issues. In fact, during his campaign in the fall of 1988, he sought to run as an environmental candidate, portraying his opponent as a backslider in this respect. He was instrumental in gaining passage of the Clean Air Act of 1990, the last major piece of environmental legislation enacted by the U.S. Congress. On the other hand, Bush's vice president, Dan Quayle, achieved some notoriety by leading, within the Executive Office, the Council on Competitiveness, a watchdog group that aggressively worked against both new and existing regulations on the grounds, as its named implied, that they weakened the competitive positions of U.S. businesses.

President Clinton (1993–2000) came into office with the expectation that he would pursue environmental protection actions more actively than his predecessors. Moreover, his vice president, Al Gore, had authored a book[8] recommending more aggressive action for environmental protection. Clinton undertook a number of initiatives,[9] but it is fair to say that environmental protection never achieved a central role during his administration, at least in terms of fighting for new environmental laws. Clinton did, however, appoint an active EPA administrator who sought to advance the environmental protection agenda by buttressing and tightening existing regulations.

George W. Bush (2001–) succeeded Clinton, bringing with him conservative credentials, a conservative administrative team, and a strong association with the business community. These translated into a strong antiregulation stance and an attempt in his first year to weaken both existing environmental regulations and proposals made earlier by President Clinton.[10] Since September 11, 2001, attention in Washington has been substantially refocused on the fight against terrorism, which has preempted other policy concerns.

Thus over the last three decades there has been substantial differences among presidents in terms of their inclination to pursue an environmental agenda and push for stronger statutes and regulations. No doubt this will continue in the future, which has a couple of implications. One is that progress toward more effective environmental policies will always be a back-and-forth tussle; regulations made during one administration will be relaxed by the next, which will be reinstated by the next, and so on. This is frustrating for those who support continued evolution and improvement in environmental regulations. No doubt it also frustrates the people who seek change in the other direction. Another implication is that long-term environmental improvement will depend on establishing a more or less automatic system of environmental management, not one that is subject to the whims of high-stakes presidential politicking.

Presidential Powers and Roles

The formal powers of the president are specified in the U.S. Constitution. They include the following:

> 1. to ". . . nominate, and by and with the advice and consent of the Senate, shall appoint ambassadors, other public ministers and consuls, judges of the Supreme Court, and all other officers of the United States . . ." (Article II, Section 2).

This power of appointment means, for example, that the president appoints the head of the EPA and many other top officials of that agency. Thus each president may populate the agency with people whose outlooks on policy and regulation are congenial to his or her own.

> 2. to ". . . recommend to their (i.e., Congress') consideration such measures as he shall judge necessary and expedient . . ." (Article II, Section 3).

The president can recommend to Congress specific laws for their consideration and, perhaps, approval. The president is not the only person who can originate new statutes; in this he or she must compete with members of Congress themselves. But the president is in a position to develop new statutes that incorporate the inevitable compromises and provisions that have a chance of commanding majorities in Congress. A good example of this occurred with the Clean Air Act of 1990. Congress had been considering this issue for a number of years, trying to produce a new law amidst all the pushing and shoving taking place within Congress on the issues involved. President George H. W. Bush was able to craft a proposal that crystallized the issues and satisfied the diverse interests sufficiently to secure its passage. Not all presidential proposals end up like this. President Clinton, in the first year of his administration, sent to Congress a proposal to introduce a carbon tax on fuels to address problems of air pollution. The proposal was never seriously considered by Congress.

> 3. to "... take care that the laws be faithfully executed ..." (Article II, Section 3).

Laws are of little consequence unless they are implemented. This means creating the regulations that give life to the statutes, and then enforcing the regulations. This process also works in the opposite direction. If a president is interested in weakening existing environmental regulations, he or she can pull back resources from implementation and use the discretionary latitude that implementation requires to delay enforcement, thus effectively reducing the impact of these regulations.

The institutional apparatus for carrying out this function has developed over the years. Today it is in the form of large implementing agencies, such as the Environmental Protection Agency. In his or her capacity as chief executive, the president can direct the EPA: setting priorities, sponsoring certain programmatic initiatives, setting funding levels, and so on.

> 4. to "... veto power of the President ..." (Article I, Section 7).

The president has the unique power to withhold his or her signature from legislation enacted by Congress. This veto power effectively stops a measure from becoming law unless overridden by two-thirds votes in the House and Senate. The threat of a veto can substantially increase a president's influence over the content of new statutes.

Apart from these powers specified in the Constitution, there are other means by which presidents can influence the policy process. One is through the use of executive orders. An **executive order** is a directive issued by the president which in effect has the force of law, at least until it is cancelled or contravened by another executive order. Executive orders do not have to be approved by Congress, and for this reason have been controversial through the years. Exhibit 5.1 contains an executive order issued by President Bush in 2002. It was an order establishing a procedure for expediting reviews, especially environmental reviews, of "critical" transportation infrastructure projects supported by the Department of Transportation. This order, like many of them, was controversial. Critics saw it as an attempt by the administration to let highway projects proceed without thorough environmental

Exhibit 5.1
Executive Order

For Immediate Release
Office of the Press Secretary
September 18, 2002

Executive Order: Environmental Stewardship and
Transportation Infrastructure Project Reviews

By the authority vested in me as President by the Constitution and the laws of the United States of America, and to enhance environmental stewardship and streamline the environmental review and development of transportation infrastructure projects, it is hereby ordered as follows:

Section 1. Policy. The development and implementation of transportation infrastructure projects in an efficient and environmentally sound manner is essential to the well-being of the American people and a strong American economy. Executive departments and agencies (agencies) shall take appropriate actions, to the extent consistent with applicable law and available resources, to promote environmental stewardship in the Nation's transportation system and expedite environmental reviews of high-priority transportation infrastructure projects.

Section 2. Actions. (a) For transportation infrastructure projects, agencies shall, in support of the Department of Transportation, formulate and implement administrative, policy, and procedural mechanisms that enable each agency required by law to conduct environmental reviews (reviews) with respect to such projects to ensure completion of such reviews in a timely and environmentally responsible manner.

(b) In furtherance of the policy set forth in section 1 of this order, the Secretary of Transportation, in coordination with agencies as appropriate, shall advance environmental stewardship through cooperative actions with project sponsors to promote protection and enhancement of the natural and human environment in the planning, development, operation, and maintenance of transportation facilities and services.

(c) The Secretary of Transportation shall designate for the purposes of this order a list of high-priority transportation infrastructure projects that should receive expedited agency reviews and shall amend such list from time to time as the Secretary deems appropriate. For projects on the Secretary's list, agencies shall to the maximum extent practicable expedite their reviews for relevant permits or other approvals, and take related actions as necessary, consistent with available resources and applicable laws, including those relating to safety, public health, and environmental protection.

Section 3. Interagency Task Force. (a) **Establishment.** There is established, within the Department of Transportation for administrative purposes, the interagency "Transportation Infrastructure Streamlining Task Force" (Task Force) to: (i) monitor and assist agencies in their efforts to expedite a review of transportation infrastructure projects and issue permits or similar actions, as necessary; (ii) review projects, at least quarterly, on the list of priority projects pursuant to section 2(c) of this order; and (iii) identify and promote policies that can effectively streamline the process required to provide approvals for transportation infrastructure projects, in compliance with applicable law, while maintaining safety, public health, and environmental protection.

GEORGE W. BUSH
THE WHITE HOUSE,
September 18, 2002.

Source: http://www.whitehouse.gov/news/releases/2002/09/20020918-14.html.

reviews. Proponents, of course, defended it as a way to reduce the environmental "red tape" that unduly slows (they say) necessary highway projects. Executive orders are just one way for presidents to stamp their influence on the policy process and its outcomes.

A major, but informal, power that a president has is the ability to command center stage in the public discourse on policy matters. Teddy Roosevelt called this the **bully pulpit**, the power to have one's views and pronouncements covered by the media and widely disseminated.[11] It doesn't mean that everybody will agree with the ideas, or even take them seriously in all cases. But the fact that these opinions come from the president gives them a potential status and weightiness that other political leaders find hard to duplicate. Of course, this power can be overused. If a president takes on too many issues and frequently makes public pronouncements about them, he or she is very likely to see the public's interest wane. Everyone with a stake in public policy wants to see the president embrace their cause and give it public exposure. But presidents should resist the temptation to overuse the bully pulpit, otherwise their influence may become too diffused.

Closely related to this is the notion of "political capital." In economics, "capital" refers to accumulated wealth; this wealth can be converted to consumption through a variety of means. Presidential **political capital** is the accumulated political leverage and goodwill a president acquires as a result of his or her actions. It builds from mundane activities like doing political favors for others, and also encompasses the status a president has as chief executive of the country. Political capital gets expended when the president tries to push events in a desired direction or has to deal with unforeseen problems. Those with specific policy interests want the president to spend some of his or her political capital to further that interest. This is perhaps one source of some of the disappointment expressed by environmental groups with the Clinton/Gore administration. President Clinton saw his political capital erode during his eight years in the White House, and after the first few years was unwilling to expend it in the direction of environmental policy. George W. Bush experienced an erosion of his political capital in his second term as a consequence of his choice to take the country into a war in Iraq.

Participants in the policy struggle try to instill in the general public a perception of problems and solutions that is congenial to their own objectives and ideologies. In recent years the political buzzword for this is **framing**; that is, the process through which a simple, defining component of an issue is communicated enough to give it widespread currency in the minds of the public. The Bush administration was quite successful in framing the terms of the debate on environmental regulation as primarily a matter of cost. The costs of environmental regulation became the primary, sometime exclusive, criterion for evaluating action, and extreme sensitivity to cost became the dominant mode of framing environmental policy issues. The president has a major role to play in this phenomenon because he, or she, has the greatest ability to command public attention.

Environmental Protection Agency

Environmental laws, once enacted, have to be implemented, or administered, if they are to have any impact on pollution levels. This is the primary job of the public administrative agencies (often called, usually pejoratively, bureaucracies) that marshal the necessary legal, scientific, and administrative resources to pursue this activity. The prime federal agency in environmental policy is the Environmental Protection Agency (EPA). Other federal agencies with important responsibilities in environmental quality programs are listed in table 5.5.

Each state also has administrative agencies to translate state laws into action and enforcement and to help in implementing federal laws. Within the tens of thousands of local communities there are diverse public bodies and officials whose mandate it is to enforce the ordinances of these local areas.

Growth of the EPA

For more than three decades the preeminent implementing agency in the United States has been the EPA. The EPA was established by executive order in 1970. Before that, environmental actions were spread among a number of agencies (air in the Department of Health, Education and Welfare; water in the Department of the Interior, etc.). By executive order these were all brought together into the new agency. Figure 5.1 shows the growth of the

Table 5.5   Federal Agencies Having Important Environmental Responsibilities

Agency	2004 Budget ($ millions)
Environmental Protection Agency (EPA)	$7,832
U.S. Department of Agriculture (USDA)	
U.S. Forest Service (FS)	1,711
Natural Resource Conservation Service (NRCS)	785
Department of Defense	
Deputy Undersecretary of Defense (Installations and Environment)	241
Department of Energy (DOE)	
Office of Environmental Management (OEM)	5,638
Nuclear Regulatory Commission (NRE)	615
Department of the Interior (DI)	
Fish and Wildlife Service (F&WS)	1,085
Bureau of Reclamation (BR)	563
National Park Service (NPS)	1,578
Bureau of Land Management (BLM)	1,123
Office of Surface Mining Reclamation and Enforcement	105

Source: Budget of the United States Government, Fiscal Year 2006, Appendix (www.whitehouse.gov/omb/budget/fy2006).

EPA in terms of personnel and budget. Both grew rapidly in the 1970s, and both were decreased substantially in the early 1980s. Since then the workforce has gradually grown, to about 17,000 people in recent years. The budget, after a sharp drop in the mid 1990s, seems to have stabilized in the vicinity of $1.5 billion.[12] The EPA has its central headquarters in Washington, DC, and 10 regional offices around the country.[13]

Actions of the EPA

Because the EPA's job (and that of other administrative agencies) is implementation, it occupies a critical and contentious spot in the whole process of environmental pollution control. Environmental interests want the EPA to pursue its implementation duties with diligence and vigor; the business community usually wants it to proceed slowly and with caution; Congress wants it to act in a manner that will redound to the benefit of its members and their constituencies; the president wants it to proceed in ways consistent with the presidential agenda, and so on. Over the years the EPA has been charged by its critics with having virtually every pathology that public bureaucracies have ever displayed: myopia, inconsistency, incompetence, elitism, being unconstitutional, being unscientific, etc. It also has been lavishly praised for having a committed staff, responding well to the virtually impossible dictates of Congress and the president, spearheading new initiatives, and so on.

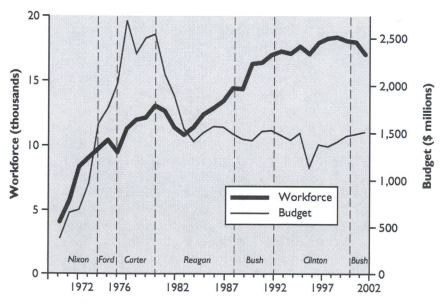

Source: U.S. Environmental Protection Agency, "EPA's Budget and Workforce, 1970–2002" (www.epa.gov/history/org/resources/budget.htm).

Figure 5.1   EPA's Budget and Workforce, 1970–2002

The two most important functions of the EPA are rule making and enforcement. It also has direct action responsibilities, particularly in cleaning up old hazardous waste sites. In addition, it has a critical role to play in carrying out, and sponsoring, the scientific research that underlies environmental policy.

Rule Making. The first step in implementation is to establish the regulations, or rules, required to apply the relevant statutes. Statutes can never be so precise that they specify exactly what polluters will have to do (e.g., what records they will have to keep, what reports they will have to make to pollution-control authorities, what specific actions will trigger penalties, etc.) and how regulators will have to pursue their activities. The job of filling in the details is the job of **rule making**.

Rules can be of various types. One very general "rule" is an ambient standard. An ambient standard is meant to be a never-exceed level, or target, for some pollutant in the environment, for example, a limit of 0.4 parts per million (ppm) of sulfur dioxide (SO_2) in the air, on average, over a specified time period. Some types of rules are definitional findings, like the rule that mercury is to be regarded legally as a hazardous material. Ambient standards are normally set without reference to the actual means that will be adopted to achieve them. Other types of rules specify actions that polluters are to take: These may be simply emission standards, e.g., to emit no more than a certain tonnage of SO_2 each year or per each kilowatt-hour of electricity generated. Sometimes the rules will specify that certain procedures or technical means be adopted, e.g., that certain types of treatment technology be installed. When we look at the different types of policies to address specific environmental concerns (chapters 8 to 13), we will discuss in more detail the many types of regulations that have been put in place over the years.

Twice a year the EPA (and other regulatory agencies) publishes a regulatory agenda, delineating recently completed regulatory actions as well as those being contemplated. The agenda is published in the *Federal Register*, and also made available on the Internet (www.epa.gov/epahome/rules.html). Different parts of this document explain the regulatory process, contain a statement of the EPA's policies and priorities, and detail the specific rules that are proposed.

To create a regulation, the EPA issues a **notice of proposed rule making (NOPR)**. When published in the *Federal Register*, the NOPR will indicate the EPA's reasoning in terms of what it is trying to accomplish with the rule, why this particular option was chosen, what public participation options are available, and so on. The NOPR also contains the specific language of the proposed rule, and a section on how the EPA proposes to get public feedback on the proposal. On the basis of public comment, the agency will revise the rule and then issue it as a final rule. The preamble of the final rule will explain EPA's reactions to the public comments made on the proposed rule. Once the regulation has been printed in the *Federal Register*, it is published in the *Code of Federal Regulations* and has the force of law. At various points along this path the EPA will have to get approval by officials in the Executive Office.

Looking just at the formal steps of rule making can give the impression that it is largely a technical exercise undertaken to fill in the details of new statutes. This, of course, is not the case. Politics follows the statutes into the EPA, where every decision will have its backers and detractors. In our open political system, contention and conflict continue as people and groups use their influence and access to shape the way the rules are written. See, for example, exhibit 5.2.

Exhibit 5.2
Jousting over Administrative Discretion

The EPA is expected to develop rules to implement the statutes enacted by Congress. But these statutes can be written in such a way as to allow the EPA great latitude in doing this, or so as to restrict their rule-making latitude. This variability sometimes brings these two bodies into sharp conflict.

An example of this is the conflict surrounding RCRA, the Resource Conservation and Recovery Act of 1976. RCRA covers the handling and disposal of hazardous chemicals, chemicals that comprise the waste streams of the thousands of industrial, manufacturing, and commercial operations in the country.[a] When RCRA was first enacted, Congress gave the EPA great latitude and flexibility in designing a program for managing hazardous waste. This was a time when the EPA, in its early years, was being asked to gear up rapidly and develop many challenging new pollution-control programs. The late 1970s was also a time when the EPA was being led by people with strong environmental credentials, people on whom congressional interests could rely to act aggressively to put an effective RCRA program in place.

All of this changed when President Reagan succeeded President Carter. The leadership of the EPA shifted dramatically in the new appointments. Administrators pursuing the antiregulation agenda of the Reagan administration could now use the built-in discretionary latitude of the original RCRA law to slow down the development of the RCRA program. Congress responded in 1984 with the Hazardous and Solid Waste Amendments. It sought in this law to take the RCRA process into its own hands by specifying detailed regulatory requirements that the EPA was to put in place, and by specifying exact timetables that were to be followed.

To some extent this type of conflict has dissipated in more recent years as rules and procedures have become more institutionalized and routinized. As we shall see, however, these conflicts continue to surface in other areas of environmental policy.

[a] We will discuss RCRA in Chapter 11.
For a discussion of these events see James J. Florio, "Congress as Reluctant Regulator: Hazardous Waste Policy in the 1980s," *Yale Journal of Regulation* 3, no. 2 (1986):351–382.

Enforcement.   Rules and regulations have little impact unless they are actually enforced. Enforcement is a matter of **monitoring** polluters and gathering information on compliance, then pursuing some type of **enforcement** action against those sources judged to be in violation of regulations.

Information gathering can take a number of forms. Sources may be required to monitor their operations and emissions and keep records that can be accessed by public officials; on-site inspections can be undertaken to determine compliance, for example compliance with required operating procedures or technical standards; in some recent programs (e.g., the cap-and-trade programs) polluters are required to self-monitor and transmit the data to the EPA via the Internet; citizen complaints also are a means of obtaining information on potential violators.

Different types of pollution call for different types of monitoring. Measuring the number of tons of sulfur coming out of a power plant stack calls for different procedures than monitoring the disposal of drums of chemicals by a hazardous waste handler.

To move against violators, or apparent violators, EPA has a number of options. It may proceed somewhat informally, sending a notice of violation and inviting the party to discuss steps it might take to come into compliance. It might proceed with an administrative order to a polluter, requiring certain changes in operations and perhaps involving a fine or penalty. Should the polluter wish to challenge the order or object to some of its provisions, an administrative law process is available within the EPA. We will discuss this at greater length in the next chapter. The agency may decide to go all the way and refer the case to the Department of Justice for civil or criminal action. We will also discuss this procedure in the next chapter.

The EPA and Direct Action.   To some extent the EPA is also involved in direct action as well as in regulatory activities. The Superfund program, aimed at cleaning up old hazardous waste sites, allows the EPA to use money from the fund to engage directly in cleaning up sites. It then attempts to recover as much as possible of these expenditures from the companies who put the material in the sites in the first place.

The EPA as Scientific Agency.   An important role of the EPA is fostering the advance of environmental science and nurturing the science/policy interface. We are going to discuss this activity at greater length in chapter 7, but it's worth reviewing some of its important features. Most environmental policy controversies and initiatives have scientific roots; they stem from conditions requiring scientific description (e.g., global warming, pesticide impacts); their solutions require new scientific discoveries (e.g., substitutes for ozone-depleting chemicals, methods for better soil remediation at hazardous waste sites); or controversies surrounding them hinge importantly on scientific relationships (e.g., the health impacts of fine particulate matter, the effects of meteorological conditions on air pollution transport). EPA is a major player in environmental science, both in terms of research done by EPA scientists as well as research elsewhere that is funded by the agency.

Factors Impacting EPA Effectiveness

The EPA is staffed with thousands of people who are committed to the cause of environmental improvement and work hard to bring it about. Throughout the agency there are competencies that have been developed which, along with a strong sense of public responsibility, make the EPA the preeminent regulatory agency in the world as regards environmental matters. From time to time the EPA has undertaken important internal initiatives to increase its ability to grapple effectively with the issues of the day and those of the future. Nevertheless, there are a number of factors that diminish the EPA's effectiveness in terms of public regulation.

The Sway of Politics. There are countries in the world where environmental agencies are expected, and trusted, to act responsibly and in the public interest without a great deal of public oversight. Not in the United States, however. The tradition in this country allows and expects interested groups to exercise influence within the EPA on issues related to rule making and implementation. And decisions on these issues are inherently political, because they are pushed and pulled between those who want tighter regulation and those who want less restrictive regulation. All of which means that political sensitivities and influence are facts of life for the EPA; although one might wish that the agency make its decisions purely on rational scientific and economic bases, political considerations will always be present.

The Legal/Engineering Culture of the EPA. Any large public (or indeed private) organization has a dominant culture, or character, that shapes its behavior and decisions. The dominant culture historically at the EPA has been what one might call a legal/engineering one. Pollution control, according to this culture, is best accomplished by having the EPA identify the best methods and procedures for different sectors of the economy to achieve pollution control, then enforcing these with standard institutions of law enforcement: inspectors, courts, fines, and so on. This ethic is encouraged by many in the environmental community who see pollution as essentially the result of illegal activities. This philosophy has tended to produce a huge collection of very fine-grained statutory and regulatory fiats. As we have mentioned a number of times before (and below), this is the command-and-control mentality in pollution control.

Congressional Mandates. Congress usually wants to appear decisive and responsive to environmental problems that rise to the level of public awareness. It often does this by drawing up explicit and detailed action mandates that give the appearance, at least, of resolute action. It is left to the EPA to find the means to carry them out, or at least accommodate them with the rest of its workload. The Clean Air Act of 1990 requires the EPA to develop, according to a specific timetable, standards for 189 named toxic air pollutants. The 1996 Safe Drinking Water Act Amendments require the EPA to develop a list of unregulated contaminants and analyze these substances every five years. The Food Quality Act of 1996 required the EPA to assess thousands of pesticide tolerance levels within ten years. It also required the EPA to examine up to 600,000 chemicals, identify those that might be endocrine disrupters, conduct tests on their toxicity, and report the results to Congress within two years.

Summary

What we refer to as the federal policy "wheelhouse" consists of Congress, the president, and the EPA. These are the preeminent Washington institutions whose actions, reactions, and interactions shape the directions of federal environmental policies and regulations. Congress is a highly diverse group of legislators, each with a home constituency, with an organization and set of operating procedures that lead to a great deal of political theater and some substantial policy outputs. The president and his or her administration, with a national political constituency, may or may not have strong views on environmental policy but nevertheless has to fit this action area into the full array of political and policy problems on which they are called upon to expend their political capital. The EPA is a complex mixture of political and career personnel whose mission requires them to balance all the political, scientific, and legal factors that environmental policy brings into play. It is also the focal point for the continuing struggle between those in society who wish to see more vigorous environmental regulation, and those who do not.

Key Terms

bicameral legislative body	monitoring
bully pulpit	notice of proposed
enforcement	rule making (NOPR)
executive order	political capital
framing	political theater

Questions for Further Discussion

1. Presidents must expend political capital to push through environmental policies in the face of opposition. Where does he or she get this capital?
2. Discuss ways in which the internal "culture" of the EPA could have an impact on the status of environmental quality in the United States.
3. How is environmental policy likely to be impacted by the continued partisan bickering in Congress?
4. How does the complicated committee structure of Congress impact environmental policy and regulation?
5. What are the different ways a president can influence the course of environmental policy?

6. What are the long-term implications for environmental regulation of the change in upper levels of EPA personnel after each presidential election cycle?

Web Sites

The White House and the EPA both have their own major Web sites: **www.whitehouse.gov** and **www.epa.gov**

Each house of Congress has its own Web site: **www.house.gov** and **www.senate.gov**

There are many other Web sites providing information on major policy participants:

Congress

http://Thomas.loc.gov

www.c-span.org/congress

www.firstgov.gov (the U.S. government's "official" Web portal)

www.lcv.org (the League of Conservation Voters)

www.cq.com (*Congressional Quarterly*)

President

www.thepresidency.org (Center for the Study of the Presidency)

www.pbs.org (Public Broadcasting Service)

EPA

See the Web sites of the regional EPA offices, for example:

www.epa.gov/region1

www.regulations.gov

Additional Readings

Land, Mark K., Marc J. Roberts, and Stephen R. Thomas, *The Environmental Protection Agency*, expanded edition (New York: Oxford University Press, 1994).

Lutter, Randall, and Jason F. Shogren, eds., *Painting the White House Green: Rationalizing Environmental Policy Inside the Executive Office of the President* (Washington, DC: Resources for the Future Press, 2004).

Mintz, Joel A., *Enforcement at the EPA: High Stakes and Hard Choices* (Austin: University of Texas Press, 1995).

Morgan, M. Granger, and Jon Peha, *Science and Technology Advice for Congress* (Washington, DC: Resources for the Future, 2003).

Shanley, Robert A., *Presidential Influence and Environmental Policy* (Westport, CT: Greenwood Press, 1992).

Soden, Dennis L., ed., *The Environmental Presidency* (Albany: State University of New York Press, 1999).

Wilson, James Q., ed., *The Politics of Regulation* (New York: Basic Books, 1980).

Notes

[1] We will look at these in chapter 9.

[2] A "bill" is a proposed law; once a bill has been approved by Congress and the president it becomes a statute.

[3] A more complete discussion of the legislative process can be found on several Web sites, for example: http://thomas.loc.gov/; click on "How Congress Makes Laws."

[4] From time to time Congress will also organize temporary committees to deal with specific issues.

[5] As Mark Twain is supposed to have said: "Congress could do great things if they just had more adult supervision."

[6] For a list of these early laws see Dennis L. Soden and Brent S. Steel, "Evaluating the Environmental Presidency," in Dennis L. Soden, ed., *The Environmental Presidency* (Albany: State University of New York Press, 1999):315–317.

[7] This act was actually a set of amendments to the Clean Air Act of 1963.

[8] *Earth in the Balance: Ecology and the Human Spirit* (Boston: Houghton Mifflin, 1992).

[9] For example, a carbon tax and revisions of the Clean Water Act and the Superfund program.

[10] Bush has sought, among other things, to disassociate the U.S. from the Kyoto agreement, reverse Clinton's decision to tighten maximum arsenic levels in drinking water, encourage oil drilling in the Alaskan wildlife refuge, delay a ban on snowmobiles in national parks, and ease requirements for building on wetlands.

[11] "Teddy" Roosevelt was president from 1901 to 1908 and pursued an aggressive effort to promote natural resource conservation and other goals of the "Progressive Era."

[12] This is $1.5 billion in 1970 dollars. The actual budget (in current dollars) in 2004 was $7.8 billion.

[13] The ten EPA regions are: Region 1 (Connecticut, Maine, Massachusetts, New Hampshire, Rhode Island, and Vermont); Region 2 (New Jersey, New York, Puerto Rico, and the U.S. Virgin Islands); Region 3 (Delaware, Maryland, Pennsylvania, Virginia, West Virginia, and the District of Columbia); Region 4 (Alabama, Florida, Georgia, Kentucky, Mississippi, North Carolina, South Carolina, and Tennessee); Region 5 (Illinois, Indiana, Michigan, Minnesota, Ohio, and Wisconsin); Region 6 (Arkansas, Louisiana, New Mexico, Oklahoma, and Texas); Region 7 (Iowa, Kansas, Missouri, and Nebraska); Region 8 (Colorado, Montana, North Dakota, South Dakota, Utah, and Wyoming); Region 9 (Arizona, California, Hawaii, Nevada, Guam, and American Samoa); and Region 10 (Alaska, Idaho, Oregon, and Washington).

6

The Policy Fulcrum

Law and the Courts

Environmental policy making is contentious and competitive. These conflicts take place throughout the system: congressional hearing rooms, administrative offices, the White House, and elsewhere. There must be an ultimate venue for settling conflicts authoritatively. That venue is the **court system**—the judges, juries, rules, and traditions that comprise the legal apparatus of the country. It is here that adversaries meet, present their cases, and have their differences resolved in a definitive way. In the United States this process is primarily an adversarial one; the burden is on the parties involved to present evidence supporting their point of view, and it's the role of judges and juries to consider the evidence and adjudicate the cases; that is, to set the terms of the resolution.

The U.S. Court System

The United States is organized as a federal system; political authority is exercised at two levels, that of the state and that of the federal government. In a later chapter[1] we will discuss the implications of this system in terms of taking regulatory initiative in environmental matters. Here we focus on courts and the resolution of environmental conflicts.

Not surprisingly, our national system has two court systems, state and federal. And each of these systems contains two types of courts, trial courts and appeals courts. Cases are usually first heard in the trial court; decisions made there may then be appealed in the appellate courts. Each state has its own terminology for designating the courts in its system: in Florida, for example, trial courts are called county courts and there are actually three layers of appeals courts: circuit courts (where each circuit contains a number of counties), district courts (where each district contains several circuits), and the state supreme court. In the federal court system there are 96 district courts corresponding to trial courts, 12 circuit courts of appeals (where each circuit contains a number of districts), and one Supreme Court.

In terms of jurisdiction, state trial courts normally handle issues related to state environmental regulations. They also preside over private cases involving environmental damages inflicted by one person, or business, on another. A few types of cases (e.g., bankruptcy and patent questions) may be heard only in federal courts; others may be heard in either state or federal courts. Most federal environmental statutes grant exclusive jurisdiction to the federal courts.

Common-Law Approaches to Environmental Management

One way of classifying law is to distinguish common law from **statutory law**. The latter refers to statutes passed by a legislature (and signed by a president or governor) and regulations promulgated by a regulatory agency. They contain provisions applying to a complete category of actors: all power plants, all dry-cleaning establishments, and so on. **Common law** refers to cases where an individual (or a company) inflicts harm on others. In environmental cases the harm is through the effects of pollution. In common law the legal doctrines that have developed over time to govern these kinds of cases include nuisance, trespass, liability, punitive damages, and so on. Common law is sometimes called "judge-made law," because it has been developed over time as the result of actual cases being decided by judges and juries; these past decisions become precedents for future cases.

Common law can apply to cases involving either individuals or groups. If one neighbor dumps trash over a fence onto another's property, that person may undertake a private suit in common law to gain some redress in the form of a cease-and-desist order, an order to clean up past dumpings, and/or some compensation related to the damages suffered. An example of a common-law environmental case involving a group would be a firm polluting a river that damages a number of people who live downstream. In this case the group would sue the polluter to gain some sort of relief.

In theory, common law could provide a substantial part of society's effort to address the problems of modern environmental pollution. Polluters would be held responsible for the damages they cause in the sense that they would be required to make amends in some fashion. Questions of fact and the determination of who was responsible and the amount of the damages would be ascertained through classic adversary proceedings in the courts. The fact that decisions are made on the basis of precedent would signal to would-be polluters that they need to take these potential damages into account before they occur; ideally, it would lead them to incorporate environmental impacts into their decision making, without the need for the massive regulatory apparatus that has evolved to address environmental problems.

Many federal and state laws limit the rights of individuals to recover damages for personal injuries or property damage resulting from the environmental impacts of regulated activities. Consequently, if individuals are going to be able to get compensation for these damages, they must do so through the complicated common-law doctrines of trespass, nuisance, and strict liability. Thus, each year in the United States there are many cases filed involving application of common-law doctrines to instances of local pollution. And these are not necessarily small cases; much of the legal activity surrounding the *Exxon Valdez* oil spill, for example, relied on the common law. There are, however, very substantial impediments to using the common law as the primary weapon in the fight against environmental pollution.

> In a common-law suit, a party suffering an environmental injury must shoulder a heavy burden of proof and produce factual evidence that is often beyond that party's practical reach. In a toxic tort action, for example, a plaintiff must generally show that the defendant acted in an unreasonable fashion or caused the release of polluting substances onto the plaintiff's property and that the defendant's activities, and not those of a third party, caused injury to the plaintiff's health or property. The plaintiff must also prove the extent of damages it suffered and show the actual, as opposed to speculative, monetary value of the damages. Collecting this kind of evidence can be prohibitively expensive, particularly where more than one possible source of pollution must be traced in order to determine which is responsible for the plaintiff's injury. Proving that the defendant's activities directly contributed to an illness such as cancer can be enormously difficult if other environmental or genetic factors may also have played a role. Furthermore, such injuries to health may not appear until many years after exposure, when responsible parties, such as corporate defendants, may no longer be financially viable or extant.[2]

These problems were evident in the well-known case of groundwater contamination in Woburn, Massachusetts (see exhibit 6.1). Despite these limitations, there are many who believe that the role of common law in pollution control should be enhanced. The main reason for this is that

> . . . the common law relies principally on private ordering, whereas the administrative state, with its command-and-control mindset, seeks to order vast swaths of human activity through public power. The common law provides rules for dealing with externalities but otherwise leaves decisions about whether to control pollution, and how, up to private persons.[3]

Exhibit 6.1
A Civil Action

One of the most well-known legal battles over a case of environmental contamination was the one that took place in Woburn, Massachusetts, in the early 1990s. It was dramatically described in a best-selling book[a] and dramatized again in a popular film.[b] In the 1980s Woburn was the site of a cluster of leukemia cases, most involving children. When clusters like this happen, people naturally look for causes. In this case the residents of Woburn thought that it could be related to their drinking water. Water coming from their taps was widely considered unsightly and ill-tasting, and subsequent testing found that it had been contaminated with certain industrial chemicals. Some of the townspeople got together and sued the party they thought was responsible, a large U.S. chemical corporation that had handled chemicals in the vicinity of some of the town's water wells. The suit was originally undertaken in a state trial court, but subsequently moved to the federal district court in Boston. The main person on whom the outcome hinged was the presiding judge of that court.

The case illustrates the problems in trying to use standard common-law doctrines of trespass, negligence, and damage compensation in cases where the end points (the handling of the chemicals and the leukemia outbreak) are readily apparent, but the causal linkages between them are not. Major questions were raised about this linkage: what chemicals were involved, how they might have migrated in the soil and groundwater, whether these chemicals actually caused the cases of leukemia, and so on.

At the end of the trial, which received national attention, the jury presented a verdict that was not particularly strong for either side in the conflict. The case was appealed to the federal circuit court of appeals, which bounced it back to the district court for additional work. Ultimately, there was a settlement, but controversy persisted over lawyers' motives, the compensation going to the plaintiffs, and other aspects of the case. The site itself became a Superfund site at which the EPA launched a major cleanup.

[a] Jonathan Hare, *A Civil Action* (New York: Random House, 1995).
[b] "A Civil Action," starring John Travolta, Kathleen Quinlan, and Robert Duvall.

Nobody should be surprised that there are differences of opinion on this matter, as there are in most facets of environmental policy. Perhaps it is reasonable to agree that common law may be the best approach when there are few people involved, the wealth and political status of the participants are roughly equal, causal connections are reasonably clear, and damages are easy to assess. But because these conditions do not exist in all cases, a comprehensive program of statutory law and public regulation is necessary to govern the natural environment.

Statutory Law: The Constitutional Basis

The U.S. Constitution is the fundamental law of the land; it establishes the responsibilities of the various governmental bodies and sets limits on their actions. A critical function of the federal courts is to act as a final arbiter on whether specific actions undertaken by policy makers are constitutional. If such actions are determined to be constitutional, they may go forward; if not they must be abandoned.

The public law of pollution control hinges for the most part on regulation, establishing and enforcing rules that polluters would not voluntarily undertake. A major task of **constitutional law** is, therefore, determining what public statutory and regulatory actions are constitutionally admissible. We will briefly discuss some of the sections of the Constitution that apply.

The Interstate Commerce Clause

The Constitution empowers Congress (in Article I) to pass laws to ". . . regulate Commerce with foreign Nations, and among the several states, and with the Indian Tribes." The **interstate commerce clause** is the primary constitutional justification for federal environmental laws. Environmental laws affect business; virtually all businesses in the United States engage in interstate commerce, thus environmental laws impact interstate commerce, thus Congress has the right to enact comprehensive pollution-control laws for the country. As we shall see in later chapters (see especially chapter 17), this does not necessarily resolve all of the problems regarding how pollution-control authority is, or ought to be, distributed among federal authorities, states, and communities. Can California pass laws requiring the sale of low-emission vehicles in that state? (Apparently yes, but this point is still in play in the federal courts.) Can individual states limit the quantities of trash brought in from other states? (No, says the U.S. Supreme Court, since this would constitute interference with interstate commerce, in this case commerce in trash.)

Constitutional Prescription of Unreasonable Searches

The Fourth Amendment to the Constitution guarantees to individuals the right not to be subject to unreasonable searches and seizures of their persons, houses, papers, and effects. How does this apply to environmental regulations? To implement these regulations polluters must be monitored to determine if emissions exceed allowable levels, or if prescribed procedures and technologies are being properly used. But this requires some degree of intrusion and inspection of private operations; these are covered by the Fourth Amendment. Thus, a whole body of law has developed through court decisions as to what constitutes "reasonable" environmental inspections; for example, what records must be kept, whether inspections must be pre-announced, whether the inspectors must have probable cause, and so on. As monitoring technology improves (e.g., automatic recording of auto emissions as cars pass a remote device), questions may arise as to whether it violates this constitutional limitation.

The Equal Protection Clause

The Fourteenth Amendment to the Constitution states that no state ". . . shall deny to any person within this jurisdiction the equal protection of the laws." Thus, environmental laws and regulations must be equally applied to everybody. In the last several decades some real questions have been raised as to whether this is the case. In particular, there is substantial evidence that people in poor communities and people of color have been less vigorously protected under environmental laws than others. This issue has come to be known as **environmental justice**, or "environmental equity."

Evidence clearly shows that hazardous waste sites around the United States are not randomly distributed, but are more likely to be located in poor African-American communities. In addition, cleanup records show that sites in these communities tend to get cleaned up more slowly and less thoroughly than sites elsewhere. There are various ways of interpreting this situation, but certainly one conclusion is that siting decisions involve discrimination and racism, which is a violation of the Fourteenth Amendment.

The Takings Clause

The Fifth Amendment to the Constitution states ". . . nor shall private property be taken for public use without just compensation." If land is physically taken for a public use (a highway, a public park), its owners must receive just compensation. But what if a regulation has the effect of reducing the value of a person's land, though it does not involve a physical appropriation? For example, suppose a community passes an ordinance barring any development of acreage that is designated as a wetland. Might this not be a **taking** in effect that would require compensation of wetland owners who wanted to build houses? The interpretations by the federal courts about what constitutes a taking and what doesn't have gone back and forth over the years in response to the changing weight of opinion on federal panels as older judges retire and new ones are appointed.

The Nondelegation Doctrine

The Constitution gives the U.S. Congress the power and responsibility to make the laws governing U.S. citizens. Over the years the U.S. Supreme Court has been called upon to determine exactly what this responsibility encompasses. One of the determinations is the **nondelegation doctrine**. In making the laws, Congress may delegate to administrative agencies the power to make rules and regulations that are needed to implement these statutes. This delegation will not be regarded as an unconstitutional shifting of legislative power, as long as Congress gives the agencies some degree of guidance (the requirement is "an intelligible principle") as to how they (the agencies) are supposed to make their decisions.

In the case of environmental laws some degree of delegation is normally a necessity. The scientific and technical details associated with, for example, setting requirements for an acceptable hazardous waste landfill would be impossible to work out and incorporate in a law passed by Congress; the law can set out the general criteria and principles, but thousands of details have to be left to the EPA. The degree of delegation is not necessarily the same in every law. Congress itself set the numerical tailpipe emission standards that cars have had to meet over the last three decades, while it left to the EPA the decision on what the exact ambient air quality standards will be. But it has become part of settled doctrine that the delegation of these types of actions to agencies like the EPA is not a violation of the U.S. Constitution.

Recently, however, that accepted doctrine was questioned. The case involved the delegation to the EPA of the power to set these ambient air quality standards. Exhibit 6.2 discusses the case and the outcome. Had that outcome been different it could have jeopardized a substantial amount of the regulatory activity of the EPA. It remains to be seen if this case heralds the beginning of a gradual evolution away from a liberal interpretation of nondelegation toward a more restrictive one that requires Congress to work out the details before it hands laws to the EPA for implementation.

Exhibit 6.2
The Constitutionality of Ambient Air Quality Standards Set by the EPA

One of the major features of the Clean Air Act (CAA) is the establishment of National Ambient Air Quality Standards for a number of important air pollutants. These are never-exceed levels that states and municipalities are supposed to achieve by a variety of means (we will study these in more detail in chapter 9). In 1997 the EPA promulgated tightened standards for ozone and particulate matter. Not surprisingly, this action was challenged by a number of interests. The primary case was a lawsuit by the American Trucking Association, whose concern was the added cost to truck owners that the new standards would entail. Pursuant to the CAA, this suit was filed in the U.S. Court of Appeals for the District of Columbia Circuit, where challenges to government regulation are frequently filed. The three-judge panel ruled (on a 2–1 vote) in favor of the plaintiff. The challengers had based their claim on a constitutional issue known as the nondelegation doctrine.

This separation-of-powers doctrine derives from Article I of the Constitution, which vests "[a]ll legislative Powers" in Congress. Not surprisingly, the Supreme Court reads this vesting provision loosely, recognizing that Congress routinely delegates quasi-legislative powers to non-Article I bodies. In particular, Congress frequently commits to the specialized expertise of executive-branch agencies the task of rulemaking in technical areas—such as air pollution control. The nondelegation doctrine says that such delegations pass constitutional muster only if Congress gives the agency an *intelligible principle* to guide its exercise of that authority.

The majority opinion below found that EPA had construed CAA section 109 so loosely as to render it an unconstitutional delegation. The court agreed with the *factors* used by the agency to assess the public health threat posed by air pollutants. But, it said, EPA had articulated no intelligible principle for translating the factors into a particular NAAQS, nor is one apparent from the statute. Given that both ozone and particulates are non-threshold pollutants (adverse health effects occur at any concentration above zero), *some* public health threat has to be tolerated if EPA is to avoid shutting down entire industries. The agency, in the court's view, had articulated no standard for determining *how much*.[a]

The EPA appealed the case to the U.S. Supreme Court, and that group of judges reversed the lower court decision, saying that the responsibility given by Congress to the EPA to establish ambient standards was "... well within the outer limits of our nondelegation precedents." Had the Supreme Court upheld the circuit court, it would have derailed a major part of the CAA machinery and thrown the whole process into disarray. The Supreme Court ruling was fundamental to the continued fight for cleaner air in the country.

[a] Robert Meltz and James E. McCarthy, "The Supreme Court Upholds EPA Standard Setting Under the Clean Air Act: Whitman vs. American Trucking Association," Congressional Research Service, RS30860 (March 28, 2001):2.

A Constitutional Guarantee of a Clean Environment?

There is nothing in the U.S. Constitution that explicitly mentions pollution or the maintenance of the natural environment, though we have already mentioned several instances where it clearly applies. This brings up the question of whether there ought to be another amendment (it would be the 28th) explicitly guaranteeing to everyone the right to a clean and healthy natural environment.

There are countries around the world that have adopted constitutional provisions of this type, as have several states within the United States. There are arguments for and against the desirability of this proposal, not to mention its feasibility in the U.S. political system. On one side are those who believe it would enhance the status of environmental values and perhaps make it easier to justify more stringent policies. It might be especially useful for people who are exposed to environmental damage to argue for relief. Those on the other side of the proposition question its practicality and whether it would be an improvement over the present situation, where public agencies and courts are called upon to define and establish environmental standards.

Actions of the Courts

On the statutory/regulatory side, courts are called upon to perform a number of functions. One of the most direct is to enforce existing regulations. But there are a number of others, including interpreting laws, deciding whether regulators have acted in a lawful fashion, and determining whether the laws are being adequately enforced.

Adjudication within the EPA

We normally think of the formal court system, state courts and federal courts, as being the primary venue for the airing and resolution of legal disputes. But a substantial amount of this type of activity takes place within the EPA itself. Many contested decisions (e.g., a permit that is denied; an emission violation that is alleged; a technical standard that allegedly has been violated) will be resolved, or at least initially considered, within the agency itself, using administrative procedures designed for this purpose.

Generally, cases that are handled administratively are those that are less contentious and relatively easy to sort out. They are heard before an **administrative law** judge, whose decisions may be appealed to higher EPA officials[4] or into the federal court system. In this way the EPA performs an adjudication function similar to that of the courts. It may seem contradictory for the EPA to be both setting the regulations and then acting as judge on questions of their violation. But as explained by several legal scholars:

> At first blush, it would appear patently unfair and even absurd that an official of the agency bringing a legal action is responsible for ruling on the merits of the case. However, administrative hearing officers are protected from undue influence by fellow agency officials by fairly stringent bureaucratic mechanisms. Agencies usually cultivate the independence and neutrality of their hearing officers in order to maintain the integrity of a process that benefits the agencies by providing a relatively expeditious means of penalizing and rectifying violations. Agency officials are aware that if the administrative hearing process appears to be biased or corrupt, legislators may repeal the statutory authorization for them, which would deprive their agency of the more expeditious adjudicative tools the administrative forums provide. Thus the long-term benefits of maintaining the integrity of administrative hearing processes usually outweigh any short-term benefits that might be achieved by unfairly influencing administrative hearings. Likewise, administrative hearing officers themselves have a significant institutional stake in the fairness and integrity of the administrative hearing process.[5]

Administrative actions of this type frequently end with judges issuing compliance orders, an example of which appears in exhibit 6.3.

The Office of Administrative Law Judges, the main office within the EPA that organizes these administrative actions, also offers mediation services to involved parties. This entails discussions with the parties (EPA officials and alleged polluters) to try to hammer out agreements before proceeding to litigation before the administrative law judges. In recent years there has been increasing emphasis on getting parties to accept mediation efforts.

Exhibit 6.3
A Typical Administrative Law Order

VI. Order

_____, Incorporated, is held to have violated Section 301(a) of the Clean Water Act, 33 U.S.C. § 1311(a), by discharging fill material into navigable waters of the United States without a permit issued under Section 404 of the Act, 33 U.S.C. § 1344. Pursuant to Section 309(g) of the Clean Water Act, 33 U.S.C. § 1319(g), respondent is ordered to pay a civil penalty of $65,000 within 60 days of the date of this order.[a]

Unless an appeal is taken to the Environmental Appeals Board pursuant to 40 C.F.R. 22.30, this decision shall become a Final Order as provided in 40 C.F.R. 22.27(c).

_____
Administrative Law Judge

[a] Payment is to be made by certified or cashier's check, payable to "Treasurer of the United States of America," The First National Bank of Chicago, EPA Region 5 (Regional Hearing Clerk), P.O. Box 70753, Chicago, Illinois, 60673.

Source: www.epa.gov/aljhomep/orders/bricks-id.pdf.

Enforcing Regulations

Of course, a primary goal of EPA is enforcement, which means monitoring polluters and taking legal action if they appear to be in violation of the relevant regulations. We saw above how this can be done to some extent "in-house," using administrative law judges within the EPA. Alternatively, violators can be pursued by taking action in the federal courts. This can be a civil action, in which polluters can be fined or required to make amends of some type; or a criminal action, where polluters can actually be sent to jail. These cases are normally pursued through the environmental crimes section of the U.S. Department of Justice, acting on behalf of the EPA. Table 6.1 contains recent data on federal environmental enforcement actions and penalties, illustrating the variety of ways that laws may be enforced.

Table 6.1   Data on Federal Environmental Enforcement Actions and Penalties in Recent Years

	1998	1999	2000	2001	2002
EPA inspections	23,237	21,847	20,417	17,560	17,668
Civil referrals to DJ[a]	411	403	368	327	342
Civil judicial settlements	253	215	219	221	216
Value of injunctive relief[b] ($ mil)	1,978	3,424	1,562	4,453	3,932
Judicial penalties ($ mil)	64	141	55	101	55
Administrative penalties ($ mil)	28	25	29	24	26
Value of supplemental projects[c] ($ mil)	91	237	56	89	56
Criminal referrals to DJ	266	241	236	256	250
Criminal penalties ($ mil)	93	62	122	95	62

[a] Department of Justice.
[b] Value of injunctive relief is the cost to violators of performing according to the injunctions specified by the courts.
[c] Projects that a violator agrees to undertake to reduce pollution beyond what is required.

Source: Reprinted with permission from *Environment Reporter* 34, no. 6 (February 7, 2003):334. Copyright 2003 by The Bureau of National Affairs, Inc. http://www.bna.com.

Through the years there has been a substantial ebb and flow in the priority, energy, and resources the EPA has devoted to **enforcement** through actions in the courts. In the early years of the agency when it first encountered many new problems, EPA tried to deal with enforcement cases for the most part with administrative procedures, relying on negotiations and the judgments of administrative officials. During the Carter administration (1977–1980) this changed, and litigation in the courts was pursued much more aggressively. This changed again in the Reagan years, and so on.

One of the primary results of this type of case is a **consent decree**, in which the polluter against whom action has been taken agrees to undertake steps to rectify its behavior and bring it into line with regulations. It can involve reducing emissions and/or remedial action, and can be accompanied by fines. Exhibit 6.4 shows a recent consent decree between the EPA, the Department of Justice, and Chevron USA, Inc.

What is the Law?

In the 1970s the EPA was busy trying to implement the new Clean Air Act of 1970 and its 1977 amendments. As we shall see in chapter 9, these laws had a major impact, especially on what are called **nonattainment areas**,

Exhibit 6.4
Consent Decree Involving the EPA, the Justice Department, and a Major Petroleum Refiner

Chevron USA Clean Air Act Settlement

The U.S. Justice Department, the Environmental Protection Agency (EPA), and the U.S. Attorney, San Francisco, announced a comprehensive Clean Air Act settlement with Chevron U.S.A. Inc. The settlement is expected to reduce harmful air emissions by almost 10,000 tons per year from five U.S. petroleum refineries that represent more than five percent of the total refining capacity in the United States.

The states of Hawaii, Mississippi, and Utah, and the Bay Area Air Quality Management District in California are joining the settlement, which is part of EPA's national effort to reduce air emissions from refineries.

A consent decree filed October 16, 2003 in U.S. District Court in San Francisco, Calif., will require Chevron to spend an estimated $275 million to install and implement innovative control technologies to reduce emissions at its refineries. Chevron's actions under this agreement will reduce annual emissions of nitrogen oxides (NO_x) by more than 3,300 tons and sulfur dioxide (SO_2) by nearly 6,300 tons. The air pollutants addressed by today's agreements can cause serious respiratory problems and exacerbate cases of childhood asthma.

"The emissions reductions required by this settlement will lead to cleaner air and significant environmental and public health benefits," said Assistant Attorney General Thomas L. Sansonetti. "We expect to continue our strong enforcement efforts and see to it that other refiners will follow suit by improving environmental controls to reduce harmful emissions."

To meet obligations under EPA's New Source Review program, Chevron will cut emissions significantly from its largest emitting units through the use of innovative technologies. In addition, under the negotiated settlement, Chevron will upgrade its leak detection and repair practices, implement programs to minimize flaring of hazardous gases, reduce emissions from its sulfur recovery plants, and adopt strategies to ensure the proper handling of hazardous benzene wastes at each refinery. The affected Chevron refineries are located in Richmond and El Segundo, Calif., Pascagoula, Miss., Salt Lake City, Utah, and Kapolei, Hawaii.

Chevron also will pay a $3.5 million civil penalty and spend more than $4 million on further emissions controls and other environmental projects in communities around the company's refineries. Part of the penalty is to resolve claims for hazardous substance release reporting violations at its El Segundo, Calif., refinery. The states of Hawaii, Mississippi, and Utah, and the Bay Area Air Quality Management District will share in the cash penalties and the benefits of the environmental projects to be performed by Chevron.

Source: www.epa.gov/compliance/resources/cases/civil/caa/chevron.html.

portions of the country in violation of the National Ambient Air Quality Standards. The EPA was attempting to set up an implementation system that would require substantial cutbacks in emissions in these regions without causing serious economic dislocation. One of the ideas it came up with was the "bubble" concept, where all the separate sources (e.g., smokestacks) of a given company could be treated in the aggregate as a single source. This would allow firms with multiple sources to shift emissions around so as to achieve cost-effective overall emission reductions.

The Natural Resource Defense Council (NRDC), an environmental group emphasizing legal action, brought suit against the EPA. The NRDC maintained that the Clean Air Act did not explicitly mention this type of approach, so the EPA could not by law put it into effect. Thus, the courts were called upon to determine whether or not the language of the law allowed the EPA to employ the bubble concept in its implementation program. The Circuit Court for the District of Columbia ruled against the EPA, but the case was appealed to the Supreme Court, which upheld the agency. As it turned out, there were many officials within the agency who were not enamored of the bubble concept, so its effective implementation was postponed until the end of the 1970s. This case illustrates one critical question answered by the courts: What does the language of the statute as enacted by Congress say, either explicitly or implicitly, about the regulations that the EPA will be allowed to use in implementing the law?

This type of case is very common in environmental policy, given the regulatory controversies that are inherent in the performance of the EPA. Members of the regulated community often argue that a particular statute doesn't permit the types of regulations the EPA is trying to use. Members of the environmental community usually seek to convince the courts that the statutes allow or require more stringent regulations. Exhibit 6.5 discusses another recent case.

The courts may be called upon not just to interpret the laws passed by Congress but to fill in important details omitted by Congress. Often this happens because members of Congress couldn't agree among themselves on how to address a problem, so tossed the job to the courts. The Comprehensive Environmental Response, Compensation and Liability Act of 1980 (CERCLA, usually known as Superfund) authorizes the EPA to clean up old hazardous waste dump sites and recover the costs of doing so from the businesses that disposed of the material in the sites. But Congress, because of internal political divisions, did not indicate in the law the details of the liability standards to which polluters would be held. This was left up to the federal courts to determine in a series of cases. Their decision was based on what they could discern about the intent of the majority in Congress, which was that firms could be held to a standard of **strict, joint, and several liability**. Strict, in the sense that they could be held liable for cleanup costs even though dumping at the time might have been legal. Joint and several, in that one firm could be held liable for the entire cost of cleanup even though it had not dumped all of the material at the site. We will return to this issue in chapter 11.

Exhibit 6.5
Role of the Courts: What Is the Law?

All over the country thousands of water conveyance structures have been built to perform a variety of functions: flood control, diversion of irrigation water, regulating in-stream flows, etc. In many cases these conveyances have the effect of moving water from one river basin to another (a river basin is a defined drainage area connected to a particular river). In addition, the water may be contaminated to some extent. For example, agricultural runoff may have high nitrogen content from fertilizer, or in-stream water may be contaminated by industrial discharges. If this water is subsequently diverted to another river basin, it may introduce contaminated water into that new basin. A legal question arises: Does this act of diverting contaminated water constitute a "discharge" under the Clean Water Act? If it does, the diverters will have to get a permit for the diversion; if it doesn't, no permit will be required.

In a recent case, the Eleventh Circuit Court of Appeals ruled that a diversion of contaminated water into the Everglades (for controlling floods in southeastern Florida residential areas) did indeed constitute a discharge, so the diverters, who had nothing to do with the original contamination of the water with phosphorus, were nevertheless required to obtain a discharge permit from water pollution control authorities. In similar cases before this, other federal courts had ruled that such diversions did not constitute discharge under the CWA. The Eleventh Circuit decision, if it holds up, promises to have a major impact on similar practices in other parts of the country. The case was appealed to the U.S. Supreme Court, which in 2004 sent it back to the circuit court for further work. As of yet the problem has not been resolved, but this case highlights the critical role of the courts in determining the applicability of a statute.

Did the EPA Follow Acceptable Procedures?

Sometimes it is not the substance of the rules but rather the EPA's procedures in devising the rule that sparks controversy. The U.S. Administrative Procedures Act of 1946 and its amendments specify the procedures that agencies must follow if the regulation that ensues is to be legally enforceable. The act also covers the procedures for the administrative adjudication function discussed above. Thus, another strategy that either side can pursue in a regulatory controversy is to take the EPA to court on grounds that it did not follow legal procedures in setting a regulation. It is then up to the courts to decide whether or not this is the case.

Is the Law Being Enforced?

Enforcement is critical to law making, and one of the continuing concerns of the environmental community is that the EPA be vigorous in its enforcement actions. If its judgment is that EPA is not doing this, members of that community can take legal action against the agency. This means that the courts will be asked to decide whether the EPA is acting according to the law with respect to enforcement.

Citizen Suits

Most of the major environmental laws incorporate the rights of **citizen suits**, or more technically the provision for private attorneys general. What this means is that private individuals, including organizations, have been given the power to initiate legal action directly against polluters on the grounds that they are in violation of pollution-control laws. Individuals have always had the right to sue agencies like the EPA for not implementing pollution-control laws to their satisfaction, and they have always had the common-law right to sue a polluter who is damaging them directly. The power to proceed with citizen suits goes beyond this, and in a sense allows a private citizen to act to some extent like an enforcing agency, bringing suit, as an agency would, against polluters who are (allegedly) violating a pollution-control law.

The outcome of a citizen suit depends very much on the "standing" question. Legal standing means essentially that a person or group has a legally recognized right to pursue the suit and seek some sort of redress for the environmental problem at issue. For an individual to have standing he or she must show that the environmental problem had a direct impact (e.g., made the stream next to his or her house unsightly or smelly or unhealthy). For a group to have standing it must show that one or more of its members has been impacted. Thus, an environmental group with no members in the region of the environmental problem normally would lack standing to sue over that particular problem.

Standing requires that plaintiffs actually be impacted, but what does "impact" mean? Does it require some physical connection between pollution and pollutee? Can it be based on aesthetic factors? Is it sufficient simply that the people within range of the environmental problem express concern or a negative assessment of the situation?

Actions at the State Level

Though we have featured federal courts in the discussion so far, we should also note that a great deal of analogous activity goes on in state courts. Every state in the union has environmental laws unique to it; we will look at the issue of policy decentralization in a later chapter.[6] Thus, state courts have the same role to play for state policies and regulations as the federal courts do for federal policy. For example:

1. In Minnesota, the Court of Appeals directed the state pollution-control agency to reconsider its decision on the granting of wastewater discharge

permits to two municipalities. A Minnesota environmental group (the Minnesota Center for Environmental Advocacy) objected to the permits on the grounds that they did not include limits on phosphorus emissions.[7]

2. In California, the San Diego Superior Court reviewed a decision of the Los Angeles Regional Water Quality Control Board to set a total maximum daily load (TMDL) for trash in the Los Angeles River of zero. The court decided that the Board had erred in not doing a benefit-cost analysis on which to base its decision.[8]

3. A state court in California approved a consent decree by which the City of Los Angeles would undertake steps to offset the expected increases in pollution to be expected from a new 174-acre container complex at the port of Los Angeles.[9]

4. In Massachusetts, a state court worked out a civil settlement in which a company making analytical instruments would pay $6.5 million to settle charges that it violated certain state environmental laws.[10]

5. A Connecticut court sentenced two people to jail for three years and ordered them to pay $498,000 in fines for violating state laws applying to underground storage tanks.[11]

The Courts and Politics

Resort to the courts is regarded as a basic political right by all Americans, so there is no question that state and federal courts will continue to be called upon to resolve hard-fought disputes in environmental policy and regulation. And although we rely on the courts to render reasoned decisions, we can be sure that political and economic factors will continue to influence these decisions.

Environmental decisions normally have major scientific dimensions. But judges are not scientists, nor are they necessarily experts on environmental policy matters. This, and the adversarial nature of most legal cases, would appear to work against the goal of making objective decisions based on the best available scientific information. How much should judges defer to the presumably more knowledgeable views of the EPA and Congress, and how much should they try to make their own way through the issues that are involved in adjudicating environmental cases? There is no definitive answer to this question, which assures that it will continue to be controversial in the ebb and flow of environmental cases in the future.

Presidents have the responsibility of appointing federal judges, to be confirmed by the Senate. So appointed, the judges have lifetime tenure. The indirect influence of a president on court decisions can therefore be considerable, and the shadow of this influence can persist long after the president's term. Presidents clearly are going to appoint judges congenial to their own views, ideological and otherwise. Thus, conservative presidents appoint conservative judges, who lean more toward business interests; judges appointed by liberal presidents are more prone to lean toward environmental interests.

Federal judges in the Northeast and West Coast have tended to favor environmental litigants. Those in the Southwest and mountain states have tended to favor economic interests.[12] And so on. Major fights have occurred in the Senate over court nominations, and these will no doubt continue in the future.

Summary

There is very little activity within the realm of environmental policy/regulations that is not contentious. The environmental community and the regulated community stand on opposite sides of most decisions. The place where these conflicts are resolved is in the court system, according to the laws and procedures governing this institution. In the United States the system consists of state courts and federal courts. Issues with respect to federal laws and federal agencies are normally taken up in the federal court system. The governing document applicable to environmental decisions by public bodies is the U.S. Constitution, which establishes the rationale, and limits, of federal actions.

Actions in federal courts serve several functions. A substantial amount of adjudication on environmental cases, especially the enforcement of regulations, is done within the administrative courts of the EPA itself. Formal legal proceedings initiated against polluters by the EPA, in conjunction with the U.S. Department of Justice, are undertaken in civil or criminal cases before the federal courts. These judges also are called upon to decide cases involving uncertainties over what statutes actually say, whether the EPA has followed lawful procedures in establishing specific regulations, and whether it is enforcing environmental regulations with sufficient vigor.

Key Terms

administrative law	environmental justice
citizen suits	interstate commerce clause
common law	nonattainment areas
consent decree	nondelegation doctrine
constitutional law	strict, joint, and several liability
court system	taking
enforcement	

Questions for Further Discussion

1. Suppose there is a medium-sized corporation that operates a dozen plants at various locations. Suppose the manager of one of these plants illegally disposes of some leftover chemicals, unbeknownst to the chief executive officer (CEO) of the overall firm. Should the CEO nevertheless be held criminally responsible for this action? (See the Supreme Court case, *United States vs. Park*, 1975.)

2. Suppose a firm conducts an environmental audit of its operations and finds that over the last few years a low-level manager has been illegally dumping waste into a nearby stream. The company immediately stops the dumping and notifies the EPA of what has happened. Should the company be penalized for its past behavior? (See the EPA's Final Policy on Penalty Reductions, 1995.)

3. A president can indirectly influence the tone and direction of environmental policy and regulation long after his or her term of office has ended. How?

4. What is the relevance for environmental policy of the "takings" clause of the U.S. Constitution?

5. Discuss the different types of environmental policy and regulation cases that the federal courts may be called upon to adjudicate.

Web Sites

A major source for material on environmental law is the Environmental Law Institute:

www.eli.org

Environmental Law Net is a site put together to assist corporate environmental managers:

www.environmentallawnet.com

There are a number of law journals that specialize in environmental law:

Journal of Land, Resources and Environmental Law
http://www.law.utah.edu/programs/journals/jlrel/index.html

Missouri Environmental Law and Policy Review
www.law.missouri.edu/melpr/

Boston College Environmental Affairs Law Review
www.bc.edu/schools/law/lawreviews/environmental/

Columbia Journal of Environmental Law
www.columbia.edu/cu/cjel/

Ecology Law Quarterly
www.law.berkeley.edu/journals/elq/

Environmental Law (of the Northwestern School of Law of Lewis and Clark College)
http://law.lclark.edu/org/envtl/

Georgetown International Environmental Law Review
www.law.georgetown.edu/journals/gielr/

Harvard Environmental Law Review
www.law.harvard.edu/students/orgs/elr/

Florida State Journal of Land Use and Environmental Law
gort.ucsd.edu/newjour/j/msg02686.html

The Buffalo Environmental Law Journal
wings.buffalo.edu/law/belj/

Southeastern Environmental Law Journal
www.law.sc.edu/

Duke Environmental Law and Policy Forum
www.law.duke.edu/journals/delpf/

Tulane Environmental Law Journal
www.law.tulane.edu/tuexp/journals/enviro/current.html

Virginia Environmental Law Journal
www.velj.org/

Additional Readings

Abbott, E., "When the Plain Meaning of a Statute Is Not So Plain," *Villanova Environmental Law Journal* 6(2), 1995. http://vls.law.vill.edu/students/orgs/elj/vol06/abbott.htm.

Kubasek, Nancy K., and Gary S. Silverman, *Environmental Law,* 3rd ed. (Englewood Cliffs, NJ: Prentice-Hall, 2000).

Meiners, Roger E., and Andrew P. Morriss, eds., *The Common Law and the Environment: Rethinking the Statutory Basis for Modern Environmental Law* (Lanham, MD: Rowman and Littlefield, 2000).

O'Leary, Rosemary, *Environmental Change, Federal Courts and the EPA* (Philadelphia: Temple University Press, 1993).

Percival, Robert V. et al., *Environmental Regulation: Law, Science, and Policy* (Gaithersburg, MD: Aspen Law and Business, 2000).

Powell, Frona M., *Law and the Environment* (St. Paul, MN: West Educational Publishing, 1998).

Revesz, Richard L., *Environmental Law and Policy, Statutory and Regulatory Supplement, 2003–2004 Edition* (New York: Foundation Press, August 2003).

Revesz, Richard L., *Foundations of Environmental Law and Policy* (New York: Foundation Press, 1997).

Salzman, James, and Barton H. Thompson, Jr., *Concepts and Insights in Environmental Law* (New York: Foundation Press, 2003).

Valente, Christina M., and William D. Valente, *Introduction to Environmental Law and Policy* (St. Paul, MN: West Publishing, 1995).

Wenz, Peter, *Environmental Justice* (Albany: State University of New York Press, 1988).

Notes

[1] See chapter 17.

[2] Christina M. Valente and William D. Valente, *Introduction to Environmental Law and Policy* (St. Paul, MN: West Publishing Company, 1995):45–46.

[3] David Schoenbrod, "Protecting the Environment in the Spirit of the Common Law," in Roger E. Meiners and Andrew P. Morriss, eds., *The Common Law and the Environment* (Lanham, MD: Rowman and Littlefield, 2000):18.

[4] Within the EPA an Environmental Appeals Board consisting of three-judge panels has been established to consider appeals from administrative law decisions. See www.epa.gov/eab.

[5] Christina M. Valente and William D. Valente, *Introduction to Environmental Law and Policy* (St. Paul, MN: West Publishing Company, 1995):37.

[6] See chapter 17.

[7] *Environment Reporter* (Jan. 16, 2004):143.

[8] *Environment Reporter* (Jan. 9, 2004):86.

[9] *Environment Reporter* (March 14, 2003):618.

[10] *Environment Reporter* (July 18, 2003):1615.

[11] *Environment Reporter* (Aug. 15, 2003):1845.

[12] Lettie McSpadden, "Environmental Policy in the Courts," in *Environmental Policy*, 4th ed., Norman J. Vig and Michael E. Kraft, eds. (Washington, DC: Congressional Quarterly Press, 2000):154.

7

Environmental Science and Environmental Policy

The impacts that human beings have on the natural environment depend both on how humans behave and how the environment actually functions in all its physical, chemical, and biological complexity. Likewise, the way the environment affects the welfare of humans and nonhuman organisms involves an enormous number of complicated relationships between environmental factors, human health, production processes, ecosystem variables, and so on. Since environmental policy seeks to regulate the relationship between humans and the natural environment, it obviously has to have a strong foundation in the sciences that explore all these linkages and relationships. These efforts collectively are called the **environmental sciences**.

Everyone can agree that environmental science ought to have an important role in policy. The call for "sound science" as a basis for policy is often heard. It is certainly true that more and better science can usually help alleviate the conflicts and controversies surrounding environmental policy decisions. But it is not true that with more science we can take the politics and social values out of environmental issues and turn them into problems for which simple scientific solutions will satisfy all parties. In fact, the calls for sound science come from both proponents and opponents of more aggressive environmental policy.

In this chapter we will discuss the manifold interconnections between environmental science and environmental policy. We will see that these are not necessarily simple and straightforward; there is no "linear" model by which value-free science produces results that are communicated to decision makers in a largely apolitical way, and the latter make better decisions as a result. There is instead a complex interweaving of science, political institutions, and policy makers that evolves and changes over time.

Environmental Science

Environmental science is an applied science. It takes the models and concepts of basic science and applies them to the study of the reciprocal relationship of humans and the environment: the impacts of human activities on the manifold elements of the natural environment, and the impacts of the environment on the health and welfare of humans and nonhuman organisms.

Range of Disciplines

Environmental science encompasses a broad range of scientific activities, including the following:

Health Sciences. These studies examine the impacts of environmental factors on human health and are based heavily on toxicology and epidemiology (e.g., the effects of lead exposure, or noise, on human health).

Earth Sciences. These disciplines examine the impacts of pollution on earth processes; they are based primarily on geology and hydrology/hydrogeology (e.g., the geochemistry of contaminated land).

Agricultural Sciences. The agricultural sciences study the effects of environmental factors on agricultural productivity; they also examine agricultural pollution (e.g., the effects of pesticide and fertilizer use on water quality).

Marine Sciences. Exploration of human impacts on marine resources is the realm of the marine sciences, which include marine biology and oceanography (e.g., pollution of coastal waters, the role of the oceans in global warming).

Engineering Sciences. These fields apply engineering and advanced technology to environmental issues (e.g., sanitary engineering, water quality engineering, development of less polluting industrial and consumer technology).

Ecological Sciences. These sciences explore whole ecosystems in terms of their interrelated parts, with particular emphasis on human impacts.

Climate Sciences (Climatology). These involve studies of local and global climate processes, especially in relation to the activities of humans. Climate sciences are based on meteorology, atmospheric chemistry, and wind science (e.g., study of the processes leading to global warming).

Social Sciences. The social sciences study human behavior, including reactions to polluted environments as well as decision making that leads to pollution. They are based particularly on economics, but include sociology, psychology, and others (e.g., studies of the value people place on cleaner environments and of the principles that underlie the design of more effective pollution control policies and regulations).

Organizational Elements

We can usefully distinguish three primary dimensions of the environmental science enterprise: the "bench" scientists, scientific communicators, and the funders of environmental science.

Bench Scientists. The ultimate source of the scientific information that affects policy to a greater or lesser extent are the scientists who conduct the studies, analyze the data, and write the research reports. They may work in a laboratory, in an office with a computer, or in the field collecting data. They are sometimes referred to as "bench scientists" because they are the ones who actually conduct the research, as opposed to others in the chain of communication between them and policy makers.

The majority of these working scientists pursue their efforts in the **research universities** that are spread throughout the country. They may be individual scientists attached to an academic department, or more likely a team that is following a particular research agenda. They are likely to be involved with environmental science/environmental studies programs in the academic curricula. Most universities also organize special institutes or centers to manage and focus the scientific work on particular environmental problems. These scientists are critical both for doing the research and for training new environmental scientists.

Public agencies often employ scientists. The Environmental Protection Agency has a number of scientists located in the many research labs and offices of the EPA, or in the technical division of the various program offices. Many of these are in the Office of Research and Development (ORD). Table 7.1 outlines scientific efforts ongoing in other federal agencies.

Most environmental science **research institutes** are affiliated with universities, but there are some that are not. The **National Laboratories** are funded by the federal government and do research on, among other things, topics in environmental science.[1]

Substantial amounts of research are done by private corporations. Chemical companies, for example, are required to provide test data to the EPA in order to get chemicals and pesticides cleared for use. These data are generated by scientists working for these firms, either directly or as independent contrac-

Table 7.1   Federal Agencies Involved in Environmental Research and Development (R&D)

National Aeronautics and Space Administration (NASA). NASA supports environmental R&D through its Earth Science Enterprise, most of which is included within the U.S. Global Change Research Program. This research centers on developing and deploying satellite-based experiments that monitor a wide range of radiation, atmospheric, terrestrial, and oceanic phenomena.

Department of Energy (DOE). The mission of DOE science programs is the "development of the scientific basis for advanced energy technologies and the understanding of environmental effects of energy production." DOE's Environmental Management R&D addresses the agency's unique cleanup problems, mostly related to past development of nuclear weapons.

National Science Foundation (NSF). NSF programs are largely organized along disciplinary lines (e.g., Geosciences, Biological Sciences, Mathematical and Physical Sciences, Engineering), but the agency continues to strengthen its support for multidisciplinary environmental science through integrative initiatives, such as Biocomplexity in the Environment, and other mechanisms. NSF is unique among federal agencies for the diversity of the research it supports and for its nearly exclusive use of competitively awarded grants to support basic research. Almost all of NSF funding goes to researchers at universities, colleges, and other nonprofit institutions; less than 5 percent of its funding is expended for administration and other internal purposes.

Environmental Protection Agency (EPA). EPA conducts R&D in support of its responsibility to administer more than a dozen major environmental laws. Most of EPA's R&D budget is targeted at its strategic goals in the areas of Clean Air, Clean and Safe Water, Safe Food, Preventing Pollution, Waste Management and Contaminated Waste Sites, Global Change and Cross-Border Environmental Risks, Information and Sound Science.

Department of Defense (DOD). DOD's environmental R&D is directed principally to remove or reduce environmental impediments to its operations and to ameliorate the impacts of past and future operations on the environment. This includes clean up of hazardous wastes, compliance with environmental laws, pollution prevention, and environmental stewardship and management of natural resources.

National Oceanic and Atmospheric Administration (NOAA). NOAA is charged with monitoring, managing, and conserving the nation's marine and coastal resources and with describing and predicting changes in the earth's environment, particularly the weather. Its R&D programs address a broad range of fisheries issues through the National Marine Fisheries Service and of global climate issues through the program for Oceanic and Atmospheric Research. NOAA's other major research programs are administered by the National Ocean Service and the National Weather Service. NOAA works closely with NASA regarding the satellite-based observations of the earth.

Department of the Interior. The Department of the Interior supports environmental R&D through five bureaus: U.S. Geological Survey (USGS), National Park Service, Bureau of Land Management, Minerals Management Service, and Bureau of Reclamation. The USGS is responsible for 85 percent of the Interior Department's environmental R&D.

Department of Agriculture (USDA). The Agricultural Research Service largely supports intramural R&D. The Cooperative State Research, Education, and Extension Service largely supports extramural R&D through its Formula-Funded Programs to particular schools and a Competitive Grants Program.

U.S. Global Change Research Program (USGCRP). The USGCRP is the largest interagency R&D initiative in the environmental sciences. It supports research on the interactions of natural and human-induced changes in the global environment and their implications for society.

Source: National Council for Science and the Environment, *Handbook of Federal Funding for Environmental R&D:FY 2002* (www.ncseonline.org/Affiliates/handbook/).

---

tors. The enviro-tech industry, consisting of firms that provide new technologies for pollution control as well as those that offer services like benefit-cost analysis of new policy initiatives, also employ large scientific staffs.

Science Communicators. The bench scientists are actually at one end of a long science/policy chain. At the other end are the upper-level decision makers who ultimately have the authority to set the policies and regulations. In between these two groups is a substantial layer of people and organizations who function as scientific intermediaries, or communicators. A partial list of these includes the following:

1. **Scientific publications** designed to be comprehensible to nonscientists (e.g., *Scientific American*).

2. Nonscientific public media: newspapers, television, etc.

3. **Scientific advisory groups** put together by the EPA or other agencies to offer scientific advice to decision makers. In addition, many of the scientists employed by agencies such as the EPA actually perform the role of aggregators and communicators of scientific information to policy decision makers.

4. Public institutions, such as the **National Academy of Sciences** and the **National Research Council**, who are called upon by decision makers to review the state of the science on a wide range of topics. Formerly included in this category was the **Office of Technology Assessment**, recently eliminated by Congress.

5. Private groups who seek to collect scientific expertise and scientific knowledge and project these into the policy process, for example the **Union of Concerned Scientists**, the **Physicians for Social Responsibility**, and the **National Council for Science and the Environment**.

6. Public institutions whose main focus is providing public funding for scientists and communicating the results of their efforts. For example, the **National Institute of Environmental Health Sciences**[2] **(NIEHS)** publishes a journal called *Environmental Health Perspectives* that reports on new scientific findings in the health impacts of environmental pollution.

While these institutions are within the realm of the science communication process, they do not all function in similar ways. In fact, the way in which science is communicated can have its own influence on how that information is understood and the impacts it has on policy events. Exhibit 7.1 discusses a study that dealt with this phenomenon.

The Science Funders.   The third leg in the environmental science enterprise is obviously critical; it's the flow of funding that supports the other two legs, the bench scientists and the communicators of scientific results. The major source for environmental science funding is the federal government.

The EPA is by no means the only, or even the leading, source of funds for environmental research. Table 7.2 shows the environmental research and development (R&D) figures for federal agencies involved in this activity; these data include both intramural (within the agency) and extramural R&D expenditures.

Exhibit 7.1
On Communicating Environmental Risks to the Public

Over the last several decades there have been many occasions where major alarm has spread throughout the population concerning some substance or practice in widespread use. These cases involved such issues as contaminated cranberries, asbestos, thalidomide, mercury in tuna, medical x-rays, DDT, Alar, electromagnetic radiation, and cyclamate. Often these alarms were based on initial studies undertaken by scientists, and propagated by the press and political and policy decision makers. In short, the channels of scientific communication mentioned in the text were active and instrumental in spreading the alarms. Many of these initial alarms turned out to be true (e.g., asbestos); others turned out to be false (e.g., Alar).

Allan Mazur has studied numerous such cases, looking particularly at what factors led more readily to false alarms, and what factors produced true warnings. His conclusions are:

- True warnings are more likely than false alarms to reach the news media from reputable scientific sources operating in conventional scientific ways.

- False alarms are more likely than true warnings to have sponsors with biases against the producer of the alleged hazard.

- Hyped media coverage is more likely to indicate a false alarm than a true warning.

- A "derivative warning"—one arising from a popular social issue—is more likely to indicate a false alarm than a true warning.

Source: Allan Mazur, *True Warnings and False Alarms: Evaluating Fears about Health Risks of Technology, 1948–1971* (Washington, DC: Resources for the Future, 2004):5–6.

**Table 7.2	Federal Environmental Research and Development (R&D) Fiscal Years 2000–2004 ($ millions)**

	Fiscal Year				
	2000	2001	2002	2003	2004
NASA	1,690	1,762	1,628	1,717	1,608
Department of Energy	1,499	1,743	1,840	1,581	1,589
National Science Foundation	829	935	1,004	1,111	1,145
Environmental Protection Agency	537	574	592	567	662
Department of Defense	399	431	400	490	539
Department of Commerce—NOAA	643	561	677	663	621
Department of the Interior	618	621	623	643	627
U.S. Department of Agriculture	405	466	482	532	553
National Institutes of Health	60	63	81	84	78
Department of Transportation	39	44	68	76	53
Smithsonian Institution	14	31	31	33	31
Corps of Engineers	48	27	27	21	21
Marine Mammal Commission	1	2	2	3	1
Total	6,782	7,260	7,455	7,521	7,528

Source: National Council for Science and the Environment, *Handbook of Federal Funding for Environmental R&D—FY 2006*, table 2-1 (www.ncseonline.org/Affiliates/handbook/). Used with permission.

There are many nonfederal sources of funding, though it is hard to gauge their extent in quantitative terms. State governments, universities, foundations, and private companies are all significant contributors to research on topics within the category of environmental science.

Public funding of scientific research brings with it a host of problems: the level of the funding; how much of it should go to permanent contractors rather than applicants who must compete for funds; how much to basic research and how much to applied, issue-oriented research; how much to spend on different topics within the environmental spectrum (air, water, land, local, global, etc.); and so on.

Private funding brings with it many of these problems as well as some unique concerns. Research supported by private companies usually prompts questions of whether it is biased in favor of the profit-making activities and opportunities of these firms. Research funded by private foundations is often seen as arising from the particular political/policy agenda of these groups.

The Science–Policy Interface

The scientific world is one of inquiry and explanation; the policy world is one of conflict and decision. The interface between them is not a clear and unambiguous linkage but rather a relationship of substantial complexity, one that involves a two-way flow of information.

Science Impacting Public Policy

For the most part we think of scientific results playing a direct role in the actual decisions made by policy makers at the point policy and regulatory alternatives are being assessed and compared. But reality is more complicated, and interesting, than this. Think back to the policy cycle discussed in chapter 3. At any point in this cycle it is possible for the input of scientists to have an impact on the direction and speed of the cycle.

Scientific results, when reasonably clear and unambiguous, can help define the policy agenda, in effect bumping an issue higher on the priority list so that it is more likely to be addressed. The scientific discovery of actual stratospheric ozone depletion, as opposed to the theoretical possibility that it might happen, was instrumental in moving this issue to the front burner. Similarly, ongoing scientific work can lead authorities to revise past policy decisions.

In thinking about the impact of science we might envision a direct line linking science to policies. Scientists do the necessary studies to clarify an environmental impact; these results get communicated unambiguously to decision makers; and decisions are shaped accordingly. But the process is not as simple as this. Real-world policy issues are almost always characterized by scientific uncertainty, evolving information, multiple agency involvement, major time lags, political sensitivities, and so on. Introducing scientific information into this complex process is not necessarily straightforward.

One can appreciate the truth of this by looking at a typical institutional time line on a specific measure. Table 7.3 shows the sequence of steps through which the EPA moved toward revising the ambient particulate matter (PM) standard under the Clean Air Act. Starting with initial research in 1974, the new standard was finally issued in 1987. Within this period there was a complex sequence of report writing and revision, public hearings, the appearance of new scientific results, and the formal procedure for issuing new regulations. Contributions were made by outside scientists, various scientific advisory committees, internal scientists, EPA program offices, and others. There are many opportunities during a process like this to introduce new scientific results; there are just as many opportunities for scientific findings to be relegated to the file cabinet and given little consideration.

Policy Impacting Science

Not only does science affect policy, but the reverse is true: policy decisions affect science. We discussed earlier the issue of funding environmental science. Most of this funding is public, so political decisions in this arena obviously will affect the rate at which scientific work can move ahead.

In addition, specific environmental policy initiatives, and the resources they command, produce incentives for new directions and effort in environmental science. For example, the information needs of the "Superfund" law aimed at cleaning up past hazardous waste sites has led to major increases in the efforts of scientists to understand such phenomena as the migration of pollutants in soils.

Table 7.3 Time Line for the 1987 Particulate Matter NAAQS Revision

1974   EPA air program begins investigating fine-particle standard.

1979   EPA announces that it is in the process of revising the criteria document for particulate matter (and sulfur oxides), and reviewing existing air quality standards for possible revisions.

1980   April 11: Draft 1 of revised particulate matter/sulfur oxides criteria document (CD), prepared by the Environmental Criteria and Assessment Office (ECAO), made available for external review.

       August 20–22: Clean Air Science Advisory Committee (CASAC) public meeting to review Draft 1 of CD. The committee recommends five additional public meetings be held at EPA to discuss the draft. Meetings held: November 7, 1980; November 20, 1980; November 25, 1980; December 4, 1980; January 7, 1981.

1981   January 29: CD Draft 2 released.

       Spring: Draft 1 of staff paper (SP) prepared by the Office of Air Quality Planning and Standards.

       July 7–9: CASAC public meeting to review Draft 2 of CD, Draft 1 of SP.

       October 28: CD Draft 3 released.

       November 16–18: CASAC public meeting to review Draft 3 of CD and Draft 2 of SP.

       December: Final draft of CD completed.

1982   January: CASAC closure memorandum endorses CD and SP. Final draft of SP released.

       December: Final draft of CD released.

1983   EPA Administrator Anne Gorsuch-Burford resigns.

1984   February: EPA releases regulatory impact analysis.

       March: Environmental Criteria and Assessment Office issues revised CD.

       March 20: Notice of proposed rule making (NPRM) proposes replacing TSP with PM-10, and a primary standard with a 24-hour level in the range of 150 to 250 $\mu g/m^3$ and an annual level in the range of 50 to 65 $\mu g/m^3$.

1985   December 16–17: CASAC meets to discuss relevance of new scientific studies on health effects of PM that emerged since the committee completed its review of the CD and SP in January 1982. The committee recommends that the agency prepare separate addenda to the CD and SP.

1986   May 22–23: Peer-review workshop at EPA (Research Triangle Park) to review first draft of CD addendum.

       July 3: External review draft of CD addendum available.

       September 16: External review draft of SP addendum available.

       October 15–16: CASAC public meeting to review draft CD and SP addenda. The SP and CASAC float reduced lower ends of the proposed ranges for the daily and annual levels (140 $\mu g/m^3$ and 40 $\mu g/m^3$, respectively).

       December: CASAC sends closure memorandum on CD and SP addenda to Administrator. Final CD and SP addenda released.

1987   July 1: EPA promulgates final rule replacing TSP with PM-10 and setting primary NAAQS levels at 150 $\mu g/m^3$ (daily) and 50 $\mu g/m^3$ (annual).

Source: Mark R. Powell, *Science at EPA: Information in the Regulatory Process* (Washington, DC: Resources for the Future Press, 1999):246–247.

The way in which environmental policy is designed also can affect the incentives to engage in pollution-control R&D. For example, policies that specify pollution-control techniques that polluters must adopt reduce the incentives for trying to find even better pollution-control technologies and procedures. Conversely, incentive-based policies encourage scientists and engineers to develop more sophisticated means of monitoring environmental performance, especially emission levels.

Science and Politics

Good science is supposed to be value-free. It is a search for an understanding about how humans are related to the natural environment. Politics is anything but value-free. It is about people projecting influence and trying to shift outcomes toward the particular values they wish to represent. In effect there is a cultural gap between scientists and policy makers. Science operates in a culture that is infused with the precepts of the **scientific method**:

- identify a problem
- develop a hypothesis based on theory
- collect data
- test the hypothesis
- accept, reject, revise the hypothesis

This is a patterned course of action that guides scientists in organizing and pursuing their work with a marked deliberateness. It doesn't mean that scientists don't sometimes cut corners, proceed on the basis of hunches, or misinterpret results. But the method does provide a strong framework for action that affects the way scientists think about their work. In particular, most scientific results are probabilistic and "suggestive" rather than definitive and conclusive. The interrelationships of humans and nature are so complicated that it is extremely hard to understand them with complete clarity. So scientists normally couch their results in terms of tendencies, probabilities, and ambiguities, and lay plans for the next study to reduce these uncertainties.

The world of the policy maker is entirely different. It tends to be a legal culture that bases action on simple rules, on unambiguous notions of cause and effect, and on the need always to look for the political implications of decisions. Furthermore, the ethos of science is to proceed with value-free premises, while the very essence of policy decision making is to ascribe social values to all the different causes and consequences of alternative actions.

Given these differences it is no surprise that there is ongoing tension between the scientific community and the political policy process. Where there is scientific uncertainty (a very normal state of affairs), there is opportunity for political maneuvering, as exhibit 7.2 illustrates. When there are different cultural languages, there are great opportunities for distorted communications.

Exhibit 7.2
Scientific Uncertainty = Political Opportunity: What is the Ozone Background Level?

The EPA is charged with establishing an ambient standard for ozone (produced by emissions of NO_x and VOCs). In 1997 EPA set a standard of 84 ppb, which is now being implemented. But efforts are underway to have this standard reduced, to perhaps 40 ppb. The critical question is, what is the "normal" ozone background level? EPA naturally feels that it is not appropriate to set a standard below this level. But here is where scientific results are not clear. A recent report by scientists at Harvard University concludes that in the United States normal background ozone is 15 to 35 ppb. But other scientific reports put it at something more than this, perhaps 50 to 60 ppb. What is difficult, of course, is trying to determine, in any ozone measurement, how much was caused by human activity and how much is natural background. The scientific answer will depend on the particular meteorological model used. Of course, this creates space for political maneuvering. Those who favor less stringent ozone standards gain support from scientists who believe the background level is 50–60 ppb, because this implies a lesser need for EPA to cut back the ambient standard; those political interests favoring more stringent cutbacks point to science that suggests a 15–35 ppb background. This is not a case of scientists necessarily being co-opted by policy makers, but of rival decision makers taking advantage of the real scientific uncertainty that exists on this issue.

Drawing Science into the Political Fray

As political groupings in Congress and elsewhere try to gain advantage and influence, science can get drawn into the battle. Science and scientists become not objective, reasoned participants in the process of making public policy, but rather weaponry with which the two (or more) sides in political squabbles can seek political gain over one another. Dueling political groups look for ways of bringing in dueling scientists.

In 1993 the 104th Congress took office. This was a Republican-dominated Congress with many new, young, conservative members who were convinced that, among other things, environmental scientists had been enlisted (co-opted) into helping advance a radical regulatory agenda by the environmental community. These lawmakers sponsored, through the House Committee on Science, a series of hearings meant to focus on the alleged abuses of science that had been committed in recent years by advocates of environmental regulation. They focused especially on scientific background related to:

- regulations phasing out CFCs to help preserve the earth's ozone layer
- efforts to get action to reduce greenhouse gases, especially CO_2
- restrictions on the use of the chemical dioxin

In each case they sought to bring in scientists and policy makers who would take views contrary to the prevailing scientific evidence on these issues (that CFCs were destroying the ozone layer, that CO_2 emissions were leading to global warming, and that dioxin caused health damages in humans). The hearings were published with great fanfare.[3]

This effort was answered by those in Congress who agreed with and sought to publicize conventional scientific results and thinking on these issues. Hearings were held, rebuttals were fashioned, and reports also were published with fanfare.[4]

In addition to the "dueling scientists" phenomenon, there is the more straightforward tactic in which powerful political forces attempt to reduce the prominence of scientists and/or scientific results that are counter to their perceived interests. This can happen at the individual level, where government scientists are subject to pressure and influence by political forces.[5] It can happen at the agency level, where agency officials exert pressure to filter out scientific information that does not conform to political positions.[6] It can happen at the institutional level, when political interests exert influence on the rise and decline of science agencies; exhibit 7.3 discusses the case of the demise of the Office of Technology Assessment.

The Limits of Science

Even though we recognize how important it is to have good scientific information on which to base environmental policy, we have to recognize also that science has its limits. Controversies in environmental policies are related to differences in value, in policy judgments, and in distributional impacts; and science alone, no matter how powerful, can not "solve" these conflicts. A good example is the controversy over the development of a site in which to store high-level nuclear waste.

Nuclear power plants and government nuclear weapons programs produce large amounts of high-level radioactive waste. At present this waste is stored in nearly 100 sites scattered around the country. In 1987 Congress decreed that a large repository for these wastes be developed at Yucca Mountain, near Las Vegas, Nevada. Although geologically quite inert, there is nevertheless a good probability that airborne radioactivity release, groundwater contamination, and human exposure will occur sometime during the million years that the material will retain some radioactivity. The goal at Yucca Mountain was to design a repository that would hold this expected level of human impact below some threshold level.

EPA sought for many years to devise this threshold, or standard, level, but the job was surrounded with great controversy. Then in 1992, Congress passed the Energy Policy Act, one part of which was directed at trying to find a scientifically sound level for this standard. It did this by asking the National Academy of Sciences, through the National Research Council (NRC), to

---

Exhibit 7.3
The Saga of the Office of Technology Assessment

As an object lesson in science and politics, the ill-fated Office of Technology Assessment (OTA) stands out. The OTA originated in 1972. It was organized by Congress as the result of a growing sense that technological changes were happening with increasing strength and speed, thereby increasing the potential for disruptive social and political impacts. Many in Congress felt the need for better and more independent information on these potential impacts. Thus, they organized the Office of Technology Assessment, an organization that could bring to bear technical and scientific expertise to examine these technical changes and report to Congress on their findings. OTA was set up to be accountable to Congress, and as much as possible to avoid duplicating the efforts of other public scientific agencies (such as the National Academy of Sciences).

Over the next several decades the OTA turned out a number of impressive studies on the technological challenges of the day. Its first study was on the viability of generic drugs. It did controversial studies of the feasibility of the Supersonic Transport and the Anti-Ballistic Missile proposal. It studied a number of environmental issues, including the potential impacts of offshore drilling. It functioned with a Director, a Board of Directors drawn from members of Congress, and an Advisory Board composed of experts from outside government.

The OTA was meant to do technological assessment, not policy analysis; and to assess long-term impacts, not short-term results. But many of its reports were controversial, and there was almost continuous conflict within Congress over who should direct OTA's activities. Conservative members of Congress, in particular, argued that the OTA was being used to further the agenda of liberal members. Many of its reports were, in fact, oriented more toward policy than toward hard-core technology assessment. The OTA increasingly became a conservative target during the 1980s, and when the Republicans finally won both the House and Senate in the 104th Congress, one of their first acts was to stop funding for the agency. The OTA closed its doors in 1995, testimony to the extraordinary difficulty of separating science from advocacy from policy from politics.

These studies and much more concerning the OTA can be found at www.wws.princeton.edu/~ota/.

evaluate the scientific basis for a Yucca Mountain standard, and directed the EPA to establish a standard in accordance with these NRC findings. Congress hoped, in other words, to call on science and scientists to solve a problem that was causing continuing political conflict.

To establish a standard it is necessary to specify what level of protection is to be achieved, who is to be protected, and over what time period. Clearly these questions are policy questions, not scientific; they clarify what we should do in terms of human protection, rather than elicit information on how the repository might perform over time.

Once the standard is established, however, it would seem to be a straightforward scientific question as to whether the Yucca repository would meet it. But even here science is unable to provide all the answers. The extent to which human exposure may occur in the future depends not only on the geology of the area, but also on the decisions made by humans themselves, for example, how many people might choose to locate somewhere near the repository over the next million years, and how likely is it that humans would intrude on the repository during that time (e.g., looking for oil or water). Trying to predict how people will behave in the very distant future is a task that is beyond the best social science of today.

Thus while it is possible to perhaps set some limits on expected human exposures, it is not possible to predict these very accurately, even though scientists know a great deal about the actual geology of the site. As one member of the NRC committee concluded: "The chief lesson is that the soundest science rarely provides black-and-white answers to regulatory decision making; it only brightens a bit the familiar gray space in which decisions are made."[7]

The Role of the Popular Press

Most scientists aspire to publish their work in scientific journals and reports that are not normally read by either the general public or policy makers. An important route by which scientific results are conveyed to these audiences is through the scientific press: people who write science-based stories to appear in the popular media: newspapers, magazines, and TV. These writers must be knowledgeable about the purely scientific issues involved and must be able to package the material in ways that will be interesting and comprehensible to the lay public. This is not necessarily an easy balance to achieve. Inevitably it means simplifying what are likely to be complicated scientific hypotheses and findings, so writers lay themselves open to charges of oversimplification, inaccuracy, and shallow reporting. Even when scientists themselves write for the popular press, they often are criticized on the same grounds.

Another problem in reporting scientific information via the popular press is that writers have to give their articles enough dramatic quality to entice the average reader to read the story. This runs against the normal scientific attitude, which is to proceed cautiously from formulating a hypothesis to testing it, and to avoid drawing overly dramatic conclusions. Thus, science writers risk being accused of over-hyping the scientific findings they write about when they are simply trying to generate interest in their work.

But perhaps the most difficult problem in conveying scientific results to a general audience is acknowledging the issue of scientific uncertainty. Science progresses by gradually revealing the nature of things, especially the nature of connections among diverse events (causes and effects, such as the connection between using chlorofluorocarbons and their impact on atmospheric ozone and the earth's radiation balance). But these connections are usually never known with certainty, and the more scientifically complicated the connection, the less certainty that exists. This has two effects on scientific communication. One is that popular scientific stories will often make things appear to be much more certain than they are in fact; uncertainty doesn't have much attention-grabbing appeal when it comes to writing for the general public.

The other impact is more dramatic. Policy decisions based on scientific understanding are often politically controversial. The uncertainty of many scientific questions can play into this political conflict, because different sides in that conflict can cite different scientists with divergent views on the underlying scientific question. Nothing illustrates this more clearly than the controversy over doing something to avert global warming. Although there is a growing scientific consensus on global warming as a phenomenon of importance, there are still some scientists (and perhaps a few pseudoscientists) who disbelieve. Popular scientific writing based on the thinking of the skeptics can create confusion about the whole phenomenon in the mind of the public. The same can be said about such phenomena as pollution-related health outcomes. The presence of scientific uncertainty can make it very hard for scientific writers to convey accurate and convincing understandings to the public.

Scientific Information on the World Wide Web

The Internet has become part of the lives of most people in the developed world, and even many in the developing countries. The World Wide Web offers an extremely easy way for producers of information to make it available, and searchers of information to find it. The Web has become, therefore, a major battleground in the policy struggle. One aspect of that battle is what one might call "dueling information" posted on the Web by policy adversaries. As an experiment, log onto a major search engine such as Google and conduct a search on some current policy issue (e.g., the Clear Skies air-pollution control proposal of the Bush administration). You will find dozens of sites containing information posted by supporters and adversaries of the plan, some strident, others trying for some degree of balance. The information is posted there by government agencies, interest groups, research organizations, academics, and others. Few of these are likely to be disinterested observers; most have a particular point of view, and readers will be hard pressed in most cases to evaluate the essential quality of the information.

Summary

The primary role of environmental science is to reveal the interrelationships between humans and the natural environment: human impacts on the environment, and environmental impacts on humans. Virtually everybody agrees that environmental science should play a major part in fashioning policies and regulations, though it is impossible to reduce all environmental policy issues to questions of science. Environmental scientists are located throughout public agencies, universities, scientific institutes, and private companies. In addition to the "bench scientists," who actually conduct the scientific studies, there is a large sector of scientific communicators, people and groups whose major job is to channel scientific results into the policy process. The relationship between science and the policy process is reciprocal: scientific results impact policy, and policy affects science through funding and through the incentives for scientists to work on particular problems.

There will always be a certain amount of conflict between the scientific community and policy makers. Science is meant to be value free; policy is the aggressive pursuit of influence to advance particular values. The different cultural languages of scientists and policy makers create gaps that are difficult to bridge. And the inherent uncertainty surrounding most scientific results creates opportunities for political maneuvering.

Key Terms

environmental sciences	Office of Technology Assessment
National Academy of Sciences	Physicians for Social Responsibility
National Council for Science and the Environment	research institutes
	research universities
National Institute of Environmental Health Sciences	scientific advisory groups
	scientific method
National Laboratories	scientific publications
National Research Council	Union of Concerned Scientists

Questions for Further Discussion

1. When members of the 104th Congress came to Washington in 1994, they promised to institute a more "science-based" environmental policy. What did they mean by this?

2. Given the answer to question 1, what is, or should be, the role of science in resolving policy disputes?

3. Discuss the importance of the public media (newspapers, television, etc.) in establishing public recognition of the scientific aspects of environmental issues.

Web Sites

There are numerous Web sites whose goal is to provide a link between environmental science and the policy process, for example:

Union of Concerned Scientists
www.ucsusa.org

Physicians for Social Responsibility
www.psr.org

Among government agencies:

Center for Environmental Information and Statistics (an EPA site)
www.epa.gov/eq/

National Climatic Center Online Library
www.ncdc.noaa.gov

U.S. Geological Survey
http://waterdata.usgs.gov/nwis

National Council for Science and the Environment
www.ncseonline.org

The National Research Council, a part of the National Academy of Sciences, publishes numerous lengthy science-based reports on environmental topics:
http://books.nap.edu/v3/makepage.phtml?val1=subject&val2=ev

A very useful site for links to environmental science sites is:
www.educationindex.com/environ

See also the Web site of the Insightful Corporation:
www.probstatinfo.com/esfsp.htm

Among the important "think tank" sites are:

Resources for the Future
www.rff.org

Institute for Policy Studies
www.ips-dc.org

Some other relevant sites are:

Center for Science in the Public Interest
www.cspinet.org

American Association for the Advancement of Science
www.aaas.org

Environmental Literacy Council
www.enviroliteracy.org

Additional Readings

Fumento, M., *Science under Siege: Balancing Technology and the Environment* (New York: William Morrow and Company, 1993).

Harrison, Neil E., and Gary C. Bryner, eds., *Science and Politics in the International Environment* (Lanham, MD: Rowman and Littlefield, December 2003).

Jasanoff, S., *The Fifth Branch: Science Advisors as Policymakers* (Cambridge, MA: Harvard University Press, 1990).

Krimsky, Sheldon, *Science in the Private Interest* (Lanham, MD: Rowman and Littlefield, 2003).

Landy, M., M. Roberts, and S. Thomas, *The Environmental Protection Agency: Asking the Wrong Questions* (New York: Oxford University Press, 1994).

Lemons, J., ed., *Scientific Uncertainty and Environmental Problem Solving* (Cambridge, MA: Blackwell Science, 1995).

Morgan, M. Granger, and Jon M. Peha, eds., *Science and Technology Advice for Congress* (Washington, DC: Resources for the Future, 2003).

National Academy of Public Administration, *Setting Priorities, Getting Results: A New Direction for EPA*, a NAPA Report to Congress (Washington, DC: NAPA, April 1995).

National Research Council, *Science and Judgment in Risk Assessment* (Washington, DC: National Academy Press, 1994).

National Research Council, *Interim Report of the Committee on Research and Peer Review in EPA* (Washington, DC: National Academy Press, March 1995).

National Research Council, *Linking Science and Technology to Society's Environmental Goals* (Washington, DC: National Academy Press, 1996).

National Research Council, Committee on Research and Peer Review in EPA, *Strengthening Science at the U.S. Environmental Protection Agency* (Washington, DC: National Academy Press, 2000).

Powell, Mark R., *Science at EPA: Information in the Regulatory Process* (Washington, DC: Resources for the Future, 1999).

Smith, B., *The Advisers: Scientists in the Policy Process* (Washington, DC: Brookings Institution, 1992).

Tickner, Joel A., ed., *Precaution, Environmental Science and Preventive Public Policy* (Washington, DC: Island Press, 2003).

Uman, M., ed., *Keeping Pace with Science and Engineering: Case Studies in Environmental Regulation* (Washington, DC: National Academy Press, 1993).

U.S. Environmental Protection Agency, *Innovations in Research at EPA*, Office of Research and Development, EPA 600/F-03/006, May 2003, www.epa.gov/ord.

U.S. Environmental Protection Agency, *Safeguarding the Future: Credible Science, Credible Decisions*, Report of the Expert Panel on the Role of Science at EPA (Washington, DC: EPA, March 1992).

Notes

[1] The National Laboratories were founded around the time of WW II, primarily to work on issues related to nuclear weapons. Since then many have branched out into scientific work on other matters. Some have undertaken substantial programs of research in environmental science. Some of the most well-known national labs doing environmental research are the Oak Ridge National Lab in Tennessee, the Brookhaven National Lab in New York, and the Argonne National Lab in Illinois and Idaho.

[2] The National Institutes of Health are a group of several dozen agencies, funded by Congress, each of which supports health-related research in a particular field. Included are NIEHS and the National Institute of Occupational Safety and Health.

[3] Scientific Integrity and the Public Trust: The Science Behind Federal Policies and Mandates: Case Study 1—Stratospheric Ozone: Myths and Realities, Hearings before the Subcommittee on Energy and Environment of the House Committee on Science, 104th Congress, September 20, 1995; Case Study 2—Climate Models and Projections of Potential Impacts of Global Climate Change, November 16, 1995; Case Study 3—EPA's Dioxin Risk Assessment, December 13, 1995.

[4] George F. Brown, Jr., "Environmental Science Under Siege: Fringe Science and the 104th Congress," A Report to the Democratic Caucus of the House Committee on Science (October 23, 1996).

[5] In 1989 there was a brief political flap over actions by the Office of Management and Budget in the Bush administration to change the testimony of a NASA scientist. His original statement suggested that there was already sufficient evidence of global warming to justify action. When his testimony appeared in public this conclusion had been substantially watered down. There was an outcry in the environmental community over the attempts by politicians to tamper with scientific judgments. See "Opposition to Global Warming Convention," *Environmental Policy and Law* 19:3/4 (July 1989):116.

[6] See the discussion by Mark Powell of political influence on science within the EPA during the 1980s: Mark R. Powell, *Science at the EPA: Information in the Regulatory Process* (Washington, DC: Resources for the Future, 1999):285–300.

[7] Quote taken from and discussion based on Robert W. Fri, "Using Science Soundly: The Yucca Mountain Standard," *Resources* 120 (Summer 1995):15–18.

SECTION III
THE POLICIES

Having discussed the rudiments of the policy process and the forces that shape environmental policy, we now turn to a discussion of what is contained in these policies. The next section contains six chapters from this perspective. Chapter 8 discusses the wide range of policy instruments available to public authorities. Chapters 9 through 13 each cover a substantive area of federal environmental policy. It needs to be kept in mind that in the real world each of these policy areas is extremely complex, with its own concepts, vocabulary, and a detailed structure that has evolved through time. We have space here for a discussion only of the general outlines of each policy area. But even these general discussions will demonstrate that each area of pollution control has its distinct set of problems and potentials for future environmental improvement.

8

The Wide Range of Policy Instruments

Environmental policy is sometimes described as consisting of just two things: regulations and the police. There is some historical truth in this. Public regulations in the name of environmental quality first appeared at the community level, as exercises of community police power to improve public health and welfare. As we shall see over the next six chapters, this command-and-control approach continues to be the mainstay of environmental policy at the national level. But before discussing this approach it is useful to first discuss briefly the full variety of public policy options that are available. Situations evolve, environmental conditions change, politicians come and go—this dynamic status of the policy arena has produced a diverse array of policy options. It is useful to keep in mind, as we look at real policy experiences, that there are many policy/regulatory alternatives and that each alternative has its strengths and weaknesses.

Policy Diversity

Table 8.1 contains a catalogue of different public sector means for improving environmental quality. It is divided into two parts, one dealing with the different political/administrative actions that are available, and the other with the different policy types that may be used.

Diversity in Political/Administrative Actions

Policy actions mean actions by policy makers, who are distributed throughout the political and administrative institutions of public action. There are many places within the system where initiatives can be pursued.

Statutory Changes. The major environmental statutes set priorities, directions, and primary modes of action for the nation's environmental problems. Most of the major federal enactments took place decades ago; the last one was the Clean Air Act (CAA) Amendments of 1990. These were epi-

---

Table 8.1   The Diversity of Collective Action

Diversity of Political Actions	Diversity of Policy Types
Statutes	***Standards***
New statutes (e.g., Superfund law)	Technology standards (e.g., requiring certain
Amended statutes (e.g., 1990 Clean Air	types of pollution-control equipment)
Act Amendments)	Performance standards (e.g., maximum
Funding (e.g., changing annual appropria-	emission quantities or rates)
tions for EPA)	Ambient standards (e.g., max SO_2 concen-
Regulations	tration in the air)
Issue or change regulations (e.g., new rules	***Incentive-Based***
governing new-source compliance)	Taxes or subsidies (e.g., tax on SO_2 emis-
Develop new programs under existing	sions, bottle laws)
statutes (e.g., Brownfields programs	Cap and trade (e.g., 1990 SO_2 program)
under RCRA)	***Product Bans or Limitations*** (e.g., ban on
Enforcement changes (e.g., reduce the	DDT or CFCs)
number of inspections of polluters or	***Liability and Insurance Rules*** (e.g., hold-
increase litigation against polluters)	ing shipping companies liable for oil spill
Presidential Orders (e.g., orders to do ben-	damage; requiring hazardous waste
efit-cost analyses or use recycled paper)	handlers to have insurance)
Institutional	***Moral Suasion*** (e.g., "pitch-in" to control
Appointments to public agencies (e.g.,	trash)
administrators of EPA appointed by the	***Information-Based Programs***
president)	Research funding (e.g., the climate pro-
Change agency organization (e.g., make	gram of the NSF)
EPA less mediacentric)	Making information public (e.g., TRI)
Change Executive Office organization (e.g.,	Publicizing environmental issues (e.g., Pres-
downgrading of Council on Environ-	ident Clinton's effort to publicize cli-
mental Quality)	mate change)
Organize public advisory committees	Voluntary actions (e.g., voluntary recycling,
Private Initiative	voluntary emission cutbacks)
Actions of a voluntary nature that do not	
involve formal government institutions	

sodes that witnessed great political negotiations and battles. These were the times when the media was attentive, interest groups on all sides were highly charged, and public attention was probably at its height. Given the political maneuvering and coalition building required to pass a major law, it is not surprising that it happens infrequently. For the last several years a congressional battle has been simmering over a major rewrite of the CAA. For many years environmental supporters in and out of Congress have tried to fashion a major revision of the Clean Water Act, but so far this has not come to pass.

Regulatory Changes.   One of the most famous observations on the actual workings of the U.S. policy process was by Congressman Dingell of Michigan: "You write the laws and I'll write the procedures and I'll screw you every time." This quote reinforces a point we made in chapter 3; statutes don't implement themselves, specific **regulations** have to be written and promulgated to bring them to life, and the regulations will determine if and how this happens. Regulations can be written with greater or lesser stringency and yet stay within the bounds of the original statutes. Of course the courts often are called upon to adjudicate issues of this type: Is this regulation consistent with the law or with apparent congressional intent when it passed the law?

Of course regulations, once promulgated, have to be enforced if they are to have an impact. Examples can be found throughout the world of environmental laws and regulations that are not enforced or not enforced strictly. Enforcement takes real resources and can be highly controversial, so one way of altering the effective content of environmental policy, without having to change the laws themselves, is to change the level of enforcement. Sometimes this is simply a matter of scarce resources spread too thinly. If laws are passed without sufficient consideration for the means to enforce them, then available resources can not keep up with the enforcement requirements. Sometimes it is a matter of policy preferences. If a new administration takes office and is less committed to environmental matters (the George W. Bush administration in comparison to the Clinton administration, for example), reduced enforcement can be a policy choice.

Executive Orders.   Presidents (and governors) have the authority to issue **executive orders**. These have the force of law, while circumventing the need for congressional action. They have been used to set aside land reservations (e.g., national parks), require certain agency behavior (e.g., requiring the evaluation of policy options), establish new public initiatives (e.g., to promote the development of alternative fuels), and many other purposes. Executive orders often provoke controversy because they sidestep Congress and the normal give and take that occurs there.[1] Furthermore, an order made by one president can be reversed by a later one. President George W. Bush, for example, has used executive orders to attenuate efforts to introduce environmental considerations into other agency decisions, for example into transportation planning. The courts may step in and declare invalid any executive order that goes beyond some bound, though what that is in particular circumstances is often unclear. Thus, it is unlikely that this technique could be used to begin a major new policy initiative.

Institutional Changes.   By "institutional changes" we mean primarily changes in the organizational structure of the policy process. It could involve setting up new citizen or scientist advisory committees to offer advice to politicians and/or administrators. It might be establishing some new agency within the Executive Office of the president to oversee decisions made in, say, the Environmental Protection Agency. It might mean establishing a new committee structure by a newly elected Congress. Or it could involve changes in the way the EPA is organized in terms of its Washington office and/or its regional offices.

The impact of organizational changes can be hard to predict. Policy outcomes are to a large extent a matter of which interests have the most effective avenues of access and which ideas get the greatest representation. By changing an organization's structure or introducing a new component, these avenues and ideas can be altered, sometimes subtly, sometimes with great effect.

Private, Voluntary Actions.   Private action to control pollution can be seen as an alternative to formal government programs, or as a complement to them. Private activity can be discussed under two headings: private action among polluters and pollutees to regulate their affairs through recourse to common-law remedies, and private collective action, where people get together voluntarily to help address perceived environmental problems.

Private legal remedies work through a system in which those damaged by pollution may sue those who have caused it, seeking compensation and cease-and-desist orders as determined by the courts according to established common-law precedents. Theoretically, this should work to make polluters responsible for damages, giving them a direct incentive to reduce emissions to escape the resulting liability. In cases where damage is clear, responsibility easily established, and the number of parties reasonably small, this approach can be an effective alternative to passing laws and setting standards. In the modern world, however, none of these factors may be particularly strong, making strictly private recourse to the courts an ineffective way of tackling large-scale pollution problems.[2]

Voluntary collective actions to reduce pollution play an important role. For example, voluntary recycling programs have capitalized on the desire of many people who want to contribute to reducing the stream of MSW that needs disposal. The payoff in this case is both the improved environmental quality as well as the civic pride enjoyed by those who see themselves as making a positive contribution.

Private companies will often adopt voluntary emission reduction programs to develop and polish a green image. The payoff here may be largely the perceived commercial (public relations) advantages of the greener reputation. What are called **pollution prevention (P2)** actions are voluntary efforts by businesses to reduce waste leftovers that have to be handled (recycled or discharged); the incentive here is often the cost savings from generating less pollution that requires disposal. Voluntary pollution-reduction contracts are another tactic, as discussed in exhibit 8.1.

Diversity of Policy Types

By policy types we mean the specific forms that policies take, including their objectives, the behavioral actions that polluters will be required to undertake, and the management and enforcement actions that administrators will be expected to take. These are sometimes called **policy instruments**.

Exhibit 8.1
Command and Covenant

Imagine you run a manufacturing company that is part of an industry composed of many similar firms. To control a pollution problem emanating from firms in the industry, you get together and negotiate an agreement to reduce your emissions, to which each firm in the industry pledges its compliance. Alternatively, firms in your industry meet under the auspices of the EPA and each pledge to cut back emissions somewhat more than is required under any existing law. These are examples of environmental contracts, pollution-control agreements (or covenants, hence the reference to command and covenant, as distinguished from command and control) to which polluters voluntarily commit themselves.

Contractual agreements of this type are quite popular in some European countries, particularly Belgium, France, Germany, and the Netherlands. They have been used on a limited basis in the United States. One example is the EPA's 33/50 program, to which a number of firms pledged a 33 percent reduction in certain chemical emissions by 1992, and a 50 percent reduction by 1995.

The effectiveness of programs like this is a matter of some doubt. The contracts they produce are usually the result of some degree of bargaining among participants. Polluters normally have to be given inducements to join the agreements, either carrots or sticks. Questions arise over whether firms are committing to more in the way of environmental performance than they would have done anyway. Moreover, if firms do not live up to their stated commitments, there is little recourse. The likelihood of getting negative publicity if they go back on their commitments may compel some firms to adhere to the covenants. But the lack of legal enforceability, especially in the U.S. system, where courts are resorted to on a daily basis to enforce laws, is a substantial detriment to the effectiveness of voluntary agreements.

For more information see Eric W. Orts and Kurt R. Deketelaere, eds., *Environmental Contracts: Comparative Approaches to Regulatory Innovation in the United States and Europe* (London: Kluwer Law International, 2001).

Command and Control.   "Command and control" refers to statutory/regulatory action that establishes pollution-control standards, which are then enforced through the threat of sanctions should they be violated by polluters. Standards can be of various types. A **technology standard** requires polluters to adopt certain approved types of technical means or operational procedures. A **performance standard** establishes a never-exceed level, whether for total emissions or perhaps emissions per unit of output or input. In some cases a legal standard on emissions can become an effective standard on technology (as in the case, for example, of catalytic converters on cars).

Pollution-control standards historically have been the mainstay of environmental policy. Sometimes the standards have been set in laws enacted by Congress or state legislatures; sometimes they are set in specific terms by agencies like the EPA. The standards-based systems of U.S. environmental policies have become enormously complicated over time; tens of thousands of detailed regulations have been promulgated in an effort to get polluters to meet various pollution-control requirements, and major political battles have been waged over the stringency of the standards.

Incentive-Based.   Incentive-based policies are designed to take advantage of the **information asymmetries** inherent in public regulations. Polluters generally (though not always) know more about the technological options available to them to reduce emissions than do public regulators. Incentive-based policies are designed to take advantage of this, to give polluters an incentive to employ cost-effective means to reduce emissions. We will discuss this in greater detail in chapter 15.

There are essentially two types of incentive-based policies: **emission charges** (and subsidies, which can often be thought of as reverse charges), and market-based programs. Charges (often called taxes) serve to discourage certain types of behavior (e.g., higher gasoline taxes discourage gasoline consumption), while subsidies serve to encourage behavior (e.g., subsidies for developing energy alternatives promote research and development of renewable energy sources). In addition, taxes raise revenues for governments while subsidies cost money. Economists and others have for years advocated greater use of taxes to promote environmental protection because they focus directly on the pollution itself and can be adjusted over time to optimally control pollution. In many European countries emission charges have been widely used. In the United States they are little used. Part of the problem is constitutional in that all taxes are supposed to originate in Congress. Another factor is their effectiveness: setting them too high will create economic burdens, too low and they will have little impact on pollution. But mostly the hesitation to use emission charges is political, the natural aversion to taxes that appears to run deep in the American political consciousness.

The most common type of market-based policy is called "cap and trade." Authorities set an overall cap on total emissions, then distribute emission permits to participants in the program, usually the polluters. Each permit corresponds to a unit of emissions, for example one ton of SO_2 emissions. The permits awarded to each polluter represent their base, from which they can now buy or sell permits to increase or decrease their emission allowance. Regulations specify that a source cannot emit more emissions than they have permits in their possession. So trading tends to redistribute the total emissions, which are capped, among the sources participating in the program.

We will discuss this type of program more fully in chapter 15. Suffice it to say here that cap-and-trade programs are becoming quite popular in the United States. The 1990 Clean Air Act instituted a cap-and-trade program for controlling SO_2 emissions from large power plants in the country; it has been judged to have been very successful. Other national programs have been put into place for controlling NO_x emissions. Proposals to establish a cap-and-trade program for mercury emissions have been advanced. There is great controversy at the present time about the desirability of a cap-and-trade program to reduce CO_2 emissions.

Information-Based Policies. An information-based policy works by trying to increase the available information on which the public, and policy makers, can base their judgments. Programs to increase scientific results and understanding come under this heading; in chapter 7 we discussed the links between environmental policy and environmental science.

One of the first of the federal initiatives of the 1970s was a combined information/science type program. This was the National Environmental Policy Act (NEPA), signed by President Nixon on January 1, 1970. NEPA mandated that federal agencies undertake detailed assessments of the environmental impacts of major federal actions. Forcing agencies to do environmental impact assessments was a way of trying to generate the type of information necessary for agencies to make decisions that were more environmentally sensitive. NEPA is a procedural requirement; it requires agencies to do environmental impact studies. It does not require that agencies actually make decisions incorporating particular environmental criteria. Nevertheless, actions on environmental impact statements became a new tool for people and groups in the environmental community to challenge projects they felt would be environmentally disruptive.

Other important programs under this heading include the public release of environmental information. Sometimes this is simply hard to find information; for example the EPA has recently undertaken an effort to inform the general public more fully about the state of the nation's environment and changes in it. The program is called the Environmental Indicators Initiative, and its first report was the Draft Report on the Environment 2003.[3] It is meant to provide baseline data that can be used by policy makers and the public to assess future progress of our efforts to improve the environment.[4]

Another information-based program provides for the collection and release of data that would otherwise be inaccessible. The Toxic Release Inventory is this type of program and provides data that is relevant to people's judgments and actions with respect to their immediate environments. Under the Emergency Planning and Community Right to Know Act of 1986, data on releases of toxic materials must be reported to the EPA; these are then made available to the public. Thus, people in a particular town or neighborhood have access to data showing quantities of materials released in their location. The theory is that this provides the basis for community action if residents believe these local releases are too high.

Among other types of public information policies are laws which require that certain consumer goods (cars, refrigerators, light bulbs) have labels showing energy costs; presumably consumers are now better able to make informed choices. Companies may release environmental performance data voluntarily on the theory that this will give a boost to their public image. Information may also be supplied directly by public agencies. The EPA, as well as many state agencies, routinely provides technical and policy information on such things as how to set up recycling programs, how to handle potentially hazardous wastes, and how to examine your operations to find ways of reducing wastes.

Voluntary Programs. Beyond programs that simply provide information as a basis for action, there are programs in which polluters are asked voluntarily to take overt steps to reduce their impacts on the environment. The inducement for this may be feelings of civic virtue that voluntary action can produce (especially if it's publicized), a desire to escape the perceived heavy hand of formal public regulators, or perhaps the publicity value a polluter may garner among patrons by adopting a greener image. Several well-known recent programs of this type include:

- *Green Lights.* A program started in 1991 to get businesses voluntarily to install more energy-efficient lighting technologies.
- *33/50.* In 1991 EPA asked industries to voluntarily reduce their emissions of 17 high-priority chemicals by 33 percent by the end of 1992 and 50 percent by the end of 1995.
- *Project XL.* A voluntary program started in 1995 whereby the EPA relieves polluters from certain regulatory requirements in exchange for emission cutbacks that are deeper than standard regulations require.

It has been difficult to evaluate the success of voluntary programs, in particular the extent to which they motivate behavior that polluters might not have otherwise engaged in. Naturally, those who favor more aggressive pollution-control regulations usually do not express great enthusiasm for voluntary programs; those who favor such programs often turn out to be those who are looking for ways to relieve the pressure for stricter controls.

On Considering Alternative Policies

As discussed in chapter 1, public policy can be studied from two different perspectives: positive and normative. From a positive standpoint, we ask questions such as: How have particular policies and regulations been shaped in the past? What political and environmental forces have been influential? What impacts have the policies had on environmental quality? From a normative perspective we ask questions such as: Have the policies been the right ones? Have they been effective? How should we try to shape, or reshape, policies and regulations in the future?

Positive Analysis

In the next five chapters we are going to be engaged primarily in positive discussion of the major federal environmental policies of the United States. Our goal is to determine what these policies consist of; that is, what processes and procedures they try to put in place to reduce environmental pollution. This is actually more complicated than it may sound. Back in the early 1970s environmental laws put on the books by Congress were relatively small in terms of number of pages, as was the number of environmental regulations in effect. All that has now changed. Environmental laws are long and complex, containing hundreds of sections and subsections. Regulations run into the tens of thousands. So just gaining an awareness of what laws are in effect is a major task. In our reviews of the major policy areas we will be limited to looking at the main features of each area. You should keep in mind that within each area there is a vast depth of detail that we will not be able to survey.

Normative Analysis

From a normative perspective the job is to choose the most desirable policies from among the alternatives. Doing this requires some sort of criteria in order to identify the preferred choices. There are, in fact, many such criteria. One, for example, is political feasibility. A policy that is not politically feasible, that is unable to command enough support to get adopted, may be theoretically interesting but not especially practical.

But political practicability is clearly not the only relevant consideration, or ought not to be. One major reason is that this factor can change markedly over time. Not only do policy makers change, bringing with them new interests and ideologies, but circumstances also change. What is politically acceptable today may not have been ten years ago or even two years ago. It is true that many politicians, especially at the national level, are given to grandstanding and posturing, and are as concerned about the political appearance of advancing environmental policy as they are about its substance. But ultimately, environmental policy is enacted in the name of environmental improvements, so incorporating criteria beyond strictly political considerations is critical.

One such criterion is whether the stated objectives of the policy make sense. The Clean Water Act of 1972 stated as an objective the complete elimination of all waterborne waste discharges as of 1984. It's not clear how many people back then actually thought this was a reasonable goal, but of course it was, and is, completely impractical. Even if it were possible, it probably wouldn't be desirable.

Another consideration is whether the procedures undertaken under the policy are reasonably cost-effective. Each year the United States spends hundreds of billions of dollars on pollution control. It probably isn't enough, compared to how much money is spent on other programs. But whatever the amount, we should all be able to agree that we should be getting the biggest pollution-control bang for the buck. Part of the cost-effectiveness criterion is whether the policies/regulations can be enforced without enormous cost.

Policy makers also need to consider whether the policy is fair. Are the people who get the benefits the same as those who pay the costs? Should they be? Does a policy (e.g., policies and procedures for siting hazardous waste landfills) create special hardships for certain people? Does a policy create special advantages for certain people (e.g., the makers of MTBE and/or ethanol gasoline additives)?

Another criterion for assessing policy alternatives is whether a particular policy/regulation leads to desirable technical advances. The creation of new pollution-control technologies and procedures is a vital part of the long-run effort to reduce the impacts of our modern economy on the environment. We want policies that will give polluters and others strong incentives to search for and develop these new technologies. One of the main criticisms of current environmental policy is that it tends to be too specific about what pollution-control technologies are acceptable. In this and other ways it substantially weakens the incentives for people to create and adopt less-polluting technologies.

As we work through the next five chapters, we will encounter all types of policies and regulations that have been put in place to address different kinds of environmental problems. For the most part we know that they passed a rudimentary political test; they must have been politically feasible, at least at some point in time. But how do they stack up against these other criteria? Much of the following discussion will necessarily focus on determining the actual content of these policies; from time to time we will also strive to learn how they rate against these other policy criteria.

Summary

Before getting into discussions of the specific federal environmental laws, as we shall do in the next five chapters, we have reviewed the major forms that collective action can take. Actions along the political dimension vary from private, voluntary efforts to statutory and regulatory actions, to presidential orders, to institutional and organizational changes. In terms of policy types, the approaches vary from different types of command-and-control/standard-setting policies, to incentive-based programs, to information-based plans. We will find all of these forms represented in U.S. federal environmental policy.

Realizing that there is a diversity of policy types raises the issue of distinguishing among them. We briefly looked at some of the criteria one might use to evaluate policies, including political feasibility, adequately formed objectives, cost-effectiveness, fairness, and advancement of pollution-control technology.

Key Terms

command and control	performance standard
emission charges	policy instruments
executive orders	pollution prevention (P2)
incentive-based policies	regulations
information asymmetries	technology standard
information-based policies	

Questions For Further Discussion

1. What are the pros and cons of using "political feasibility" as a criterion for evaluating the desirability of a given environmental policy?

2. Cost-effectiveness and fairness often are in conflict when it comes to evaluating a particular policy. How might these criteria be reconciled?

3. What factors might influence the extent to which public information programs might be effective in promoting environmental improvement?

4. "You write the law and I'll write the procedures and I'll screw you every time." What is this a reference to?

5. Under what conditions might private, voluntary actions be expected to be an effective substitute for statutory action to address an environmental problem?

Web Sites

The Organization for Economic Cooperation and Development (OECD) puts out lots of material describing and comparing the effectiveness of different types of environmental policies, or policy instruments:
www.oecd.org/topic/0,2686,en_2649_34281_1_1_1_1_37425,00.html
See also the World Bank site on "new ideas in pollution regulation":
www.worldbank.org.nipr/index.htm
As regards information-type instruments, the EPA has a Web site designed to give people information about their local environment:
www.epa.gov/enviro/wme/

Additional Readings

Anderson, Terry L., and Donald R. Leal, *Free Market Environmentalism* (Boulder, CO: Westview Press, 1991).

Arora, S., and T. N. Cason, "A Voluntary Approach to Environmental Regulation: The 33/50 Program," *Resources* (Washington, DC: Resources for the Future, Summer 1994).

Blodgett, John E., *Environmental Protection: New Approaches*, RL 30760 (Washington, DC: Congressional Research Service, December 11, 2000).

Boyd, James, *Searching for the Profit in Pollution Prevention: Case Studies in the Corporate Evaluation of Environmental Opportunities*, EPA 742-R-98-005 (Washington, DC: EPA, 1998).

Commoner, Barry, "Pollution Prevention: Putting Comparative Risk Assessment in Its Place," in *Worst Things First? The Debate over Risk-Based National Environmental Priorities*, edited by Adam Finkel and Dominic Golding (Washington, DC: Resources for the Future, 1994).

Dale, Virginia, and Mary R. English, *Tools to Aid Environmental Decision Making* (New York: Springer Verlag, 1998).

Dietz, Thomas, and Paul C. Stern, eds., *New Tools for Environmental Protection, Education, Information and Voluntary Measures*, National Research Council (Washington, DC: National Academy Press, 2002).

Government Institutes, *Environmental Law Handbook*, 17th ed. (May 2003).

Koontz, Tomas M., Toddi A. Steelman, JoAnn Carmin, Katrina Smith Korfmacher, Cassandra Moseley, and Craig W. Thomas, *Collaborative Environmental Management: What Roles for Government?* (Washington, DC: Resources for the Future, August 2004).

Koplow, Douglas, *Federal Energy Subsidies: Energy, Environmental, and Fiscal Impacts* (Washington, DC: Alliance to Save Energy, 1993).

Marcus, Alfred A., Donald A. Geffen, and Ken Sexton, *Reinventing Environmental Regulation, Lessons from Project XL* (Washington, DC: Resources for the Future, 2002).

Organization for Economic Cooperation and Development, *Improving the Environment Through Reducing Subsidies* (Paris: OECD, 1998).

Rietbergen-McCracken, Jennifer, and Hussein Abaza, eds., *Economic Instruments for Environmental Management: A Worldwide Compendium of Case Studies* (London: Earthscan, June 2000).

Sterner, Thomas, *Policy Instruments for Environmental and Natural Resource Management* (Washington, DC: Resources for the Future, 2002).

tenBrink, P., *Voluntary Environmental Agreements: Process, Practice and Future Use* (Sheffield, England: Greenleaf Publishing, 2002).

Notes

[1] In one of the most famous executive orders, President Truman desegregated the U.S. military.

[2] See chapter 6.

[3] Available at www.epa.gov/indicators.

[4] In terms of this and future reports on the environment, we should keep in mind the political ramifications and sensitivities of this type of information, a problem we discussed in chapter 2.

9

Air Pollution Control Policy

Air is essential to humans. We breathe it and use it as an important input into our industrial system. In using it, we affect its quality, which in turn impacts our health and welfare. The same can be said about nonhuman, terrestrial animals and plants; the health of these organisms is directly linked to the quality of the air in which they exist.

Air quality problems are not new. For as long as people have burned fossil fuels for warmth, they have had to worry about the resulting smoke and soot. Today the problems of air pollution include many more substances, and range in extent from the quality of the air in the room (or space) in which you are sitting to the composition of the entire global atmosphere.

The first public responses to air pollution in the United States were at the local level. A city ordinance was passed in Pittsburgh in the late 1860s prohibiting the use of bituminous coal or wood in locomotives. Cincinnati and Chicago adopted laws in the 1890s to control smoke and soot emissions from factories and locomotives.[1] Initially the individual cities and towns did not have an effective legal framework on which to base their laws. For this they looked to their state governments to put enabling laws in place so the localities could act. But the states were ill-equipped to do this. One of their biggest problems was being able to convincingly demonstrate the connection between diminished air quality and ill health. The states needed data and research on the effects of air pollution, and for this they turned to the federal government.

At the federal level the first air pollution law (one-and-a-half pages long!) was enacted in 1955. The law authorized the federal government to help states train air pollution control managers and technicians, and to finance research on the impacts of air pollution. During the 1960s no less than five other federal air pollution laws were passed, structured for the most part along the same lines: federal aid to the states to help them develop air pollution control laws (see table 9.1). The 1963 law was called the Clean Air Act (CAA), and amendments to this statute have been the prime (though not the only) vehicle for federal action in air pollution control. Significant amendments to the CAA were made in 1970, 1977, and 1990. Since 1990 numerous efforts have been made to amend the CAA in a variety of ways, but none has been successful.

Table 9.1 Major Federal Air Pollution Laws

Legislation	Content
Air Pollution Control Act (APCA) of 1955	Authorized the Secretary of Health, Education, and Welfare to spend up to $5 million a year to do research and to help the states with training and technical assistance on matters of air pollution. Extended in 1959 and 1962.
Motor Vehicle Exhaust Study Act of 1960	Directed the Secretary of HEW to do a study on "Motor Vehicles, Air Pollution and Health" within two years.
Clean Air Act (CAA) of 1963	Authorized federal grants to states to develop state and local air pollution control programs; established a conference system to deal with problems of interstate air pollution; extended authorization for federal research on air pollution.
Motor Vehicle Air Pollution Control Act of 1965	Authorized the Secretary of HEW to set *emission standards* for new cars (but no deadline was established); dealt with international air pollution and called for more research.
CAA Extension of 1966	Extended the CAA of 1963 and added authority to make grants to states to support air pollution control programs.
Air Quality Act (AQA) of 1967	Provided for additional grants to states to plan air pollution control programs; provided for interstate air pollution control agencies; expanded research on fuels and vehicles; required HEW to establish air-quality regions of the country; published air-quality criteria and control technology reports for the common pollutants; required states to establish ambient air-quality standards for the "criteria" pollutants and develop attainment programs; authorized HEW to give finan-

	cial assistance to states to establish motor-vehicle inspection programs.
CAA Amendments of 1970	Established *national* ambient air-quality standards (NAAQSs) for criteria pollutants; required the establishment of new-car emission standards along with certification programs; EPA was to establish emission standards for major toxic or hazardous pollutants; EPA was to establish technology-based emission standards for all *new sources* (NSPS) of the common air pollutants; required state implementation plans (SIPs) to control existing stationary sources of air pollutants.
CAA Amendments of 1977	Established the goal of "prevention of serious deterioration" (PSD) in areas already cleaner than the national standards; established three classes of already-clean areas:
	Class I areas: no additional air-quality deterioration permitted (includes national parks, etc.)
	Class II areas: some air-quality deterioration to be permitted (includes most PSD regions)
	Class III areas: air quality to be allowed to deteriorate to level of NAAQSs
	Established a technology standard known as "lowest achievable emission rate" (LAER) for new sources in nonattainment areas, and "best available control technologies" (BACT) for new sources in PSD regions.
CAA Amendments of 1990	Established tougher tailpipe standards for new cars, with longer warranty period; mandated pilot program of "clean" cars in some cities; reformulated fuels in some cities; Phase II pumps at gas stations; onboard fume canisters on cars; streamlined stationary-source permitting procedures; provided for reduction of 189 toxic airborne emissions through TBES ("maximum achievable control technology," MACT); provided for stricter local plans to reduce ozone, carbon monoxide, and particulates in the worst cities; further rules for phasing out of CFCs; provided for a system of transferable discharge permits among power plants to reduce sulfur dioxide emissions.

Sources: Arthur C. Stern, "History of Air Pollution Legislation in the United States," *Journal of Air Pollution Control Association* 32, 1 (January 1982):44–61; Paul R. Portney, "Air Pollution Policy," in Paul R. Portney, ed., *Public Policies for Environmental Protection* (Washington, DC: Resources for the Future, 1990), chapter 3; *EPA Journal* (January/February 1991):8–9.

The Politics of Air Pollution Control

The political struggle over air pollution control has been protracted and vigorous; it will undoubtedly continue to be so for the indefinite future. The contending parties have fought for influence and the advancement of their interests. What has resulted is not so much a comprehensive and rational attack on a significant environmental problem, but a patchwork of programs and initiatives that is gradually evolving as a function of the diverse environmental and political forces that are at work.

At the federal level much of the political heat on air pollution control is generated in Congress. In the Senate, air pollution policy is handled by the Subcommittee on Clean Air, Climate Change and Nuclear Safety of the Committee on Environment and Public Works. In the House, air pollution control is handled by the Subcommittee on Energy and Air Quality of the Committee on Energy and Commerce.[2] These are the committees on which legislators seek to serve if they are passionate, in one direction or the other, on air pollution matters. Over the years, strong personalities of committee members have shaped their performance and output. For many years Michigan Representative Dingell was chairman of the House Committee on Energy and Commerce, and he saw to it that the interests of the auto industry were well represented. Representative Waxman from California was a strong voice for tougher air pollution control in the 1970s and 1980s. On the Senate side, Senator Byrd from West Virginia, through his position as majority leader, was able to block certain types of actions that he deemed detrimental to the coal miners of his state and the electric utilities of the Midwest who used that coal.

A major collection of players in air pollution politics is the regulated industries themselves. Chief among these are the motor vehicle, electric power, petrochemical, and heavy industrial sectors such as steel producers. These groups are capable of generating enormous political pressure not only because they have money to spend and know how to spend it, but also because they tend to represent another side of the equation—employment and the prospects, real or imagined, of lost jobs. These considerations resonate strongly with many members of Congress.

Another important set of players in air pollution policy consists of the specialized air pollution divisions within the federal and state environmental agencies. In the U.S. Environmental Protection Agency, air pollution matters are handled by the Office of Air and Radiation, under an assistant administrator. This is where expertise exists for shaping new programs, developing new regulations, and putting enforcement procedures into place (in conjunction with the EPA's office of Enforcement and Compliance Assurance). Most state environmental protection agencies also have bureaus or divisions that specialize in air pollution control.

One important cleavage in air pollution control politics is that between federal authorities and the states. The first serious attempts to control motor-vehicle emissions were made in California, starting in the late 1950s. Because of the topography and meteorology of the Los Angeles Basin, airborne emissions tend to get trapped by the surrounding mountain ranges and accumulate in the local atmosphere. It was here that the term *smog* (a combination of the words smoke and fog) was invented, to refer to the thick, eye-burning haze that comes largely from vehicle exhaust. The Clean Air Act specifically allows California to set emission standards for that state that are stricter than national standards. Over the years other states have won the right to set standards similar to those in California. Yet there continue to be important questions about what actions states may legally take and what actions are effectively preempted by the federal government. In recent years some states have sought to take the initiative in pushing for more aggressive air pollution control actions, having perceived that the Republican administration in Washington is less likely than previous administrations to push in this direction.

As we will discuss in later chapters, air pollution control has now become a global concern, primarily because of two issues: protection of the earth's ozone layer and the phenomenon called global warming. This means that air pollution politics now has a strong international dimension, which implies the involvement of groups like the United Nations and hundreds of private, international NGOs (nongovernment organizations); the negotiation of international treaties;[3] and the general intertwining of domestic and foreign policy issues.

The Federal Clean Air Act

In this section we will discuss the principal features of the federal Clean Air Act (CAA) as it currently exists. We stress the word principal. The CAA is a long, complex law that covers hundreds of situations and contains thousands of detailed provisions. Multiple books could be written on its various sections.[4] This chapter will discuss the CAA's major provisions to get an idea of the general approach taken in the United States to control air pollutants from stationary and mobile sources. Keep in mind that we are at a point in time when major changes are under consideration.

Types of Air Pollution and Sources

In a modern economy there are hundreds of different types of substances that get into the air, and millions of sources from which these materials are emitted. The major categories of airborne pollutants are the following.

Criteria Pollutants. These are the six major air pollutants for which controls were first developed. They are called "criteria" pollutants because of the early federal laws that required agencies to develop decision criteria for the states to use in controlling these pollutants. They are carbon monoxide (CO), sulfur dioxide (SO_2), nitrogen oxides (NO_x), ozone (O_3), lead, and particulate matter (PM).

Hazardous Air Pollutants (HAPs).   These are substances emitted into the air that are known to have toxic effects on people and other components of the ecosystem. Examples are benzene, dioxin, asbestos, and methylene chloride.

Ozone-Depleting Substances.   This is a group of widely used chemicals whose release into the air has been shown to degrade the earth's stratospheric ozone layer. They include chlorofluorocarbons, halons, carbon tetrachloride, and methylchloroform. Some of these are also included under HAPs.[5]

Greenhouse Gases.   These are substances that contribute to global warming.[6] The most common is carbon dioxide. Also included in this category are methane, nitrous oxide, hydrofluorocarbons, perfluorocarbons, and sulfur hexafluoride.

Indoor Air Pollutants.   This is a set of pollutants, some also listed under previous categories, that are common inside homes, offices, and buildings. These pollutants include carbon monoxide, cigarette smoke, radon, molds, and a variety of household products.

Radiation.   This includes emissions of ionizing (damaging) radiation from a variety of sources, including nuclear power plants, nuclear weapons sites, medical equipment, and many industrial sites.[7]

The two major types of sources addressed in air pollution control laws are:

Stationary Sources.   Large and small sources associated with power plants, industrial establishments, homes, and offices.

Mobile Sources.   These are the many sources that normally move around, presenting unique pollution-control challenges. Mobile sources include cars and trucks, buses, trains, airplanes, recreation vehicles, lawn and garden equipment, and tractors.

National Ambient Air Quality Standards (NAAQSs)

The 1970 CAA directs the administrator of the EPA to establish **National Ambient Air Quality Standards** for the country. They are national because they are meant to apply to all regions of the country; they are ambient because they apply to the outside air (not to air inside buildings and houses); and they are standards in the sense that they specify never-exceed levels for the criteria pollutants (though, of course, setting the standards is not the same as attaining them). The NAAQSs incorporate **primary standards**, which are aimed at protecting human health, and **secondary standards**, which are meant to protect public welfare; that is, nonhealth factors that relate to human welfare, such as impacts on crops or other organisms. Table 9.2 lists the current NAAQSs.

The CAA gives the EPA the power and responsibility to set NAAQSs, but Congress put language in the statute that is meant to specify the basis for doing this. For the primary standards the relevant clause is the following:

> National primary ambient air quality standards . . . shall be ambient air quality standards the attainment and maintenance of which in the judgment of the Administrator, based on such criteria and allowing an adequate margin of safety, are requisite to protect the public health. (Sec. 109, (b) (1) of the 1970 CAA)

Thus the two criteria that are to be followed in setting the NAAQSs are (1) they must protect public health and (2) they must contain an adequate margin of safety. Both of these clearly require interpretation, judgment, and political balancing on the part of the EPA.

In recent years the procedures used by the EPA to set NAAQSs has come under significant attack. In 1996 it proposed new and tighter standards for ozone and particulate matters. The ozone standard was to be set at 0.08 ppm measured over 8 hours, which was more stringent than the existing standard of 0.12 ppm over 1 hour. For particulate matter the EPA proposed to create a new standard for "fine particulates," defined as material less than 2.5 microns

Table 9.2   Current Ambient Air Quality Standards[a]

Pollutant	Standard Value[b]		Standard Type
Carbon Monoxide (CO)			
8-hour average	9 ppm	(10 mg/m^3)	Primary
1-hour average	35 ppm	(40 mg/m^3)	Primary
Nitrogen Dioxide (NO$_2$)			
Annual arithmetic mean	0.053 ppm	(100 µg/m^3)	Primary and secondary
Ozone (O$_3$)			
1-hour average	0.12 ppm	(235 µg/m^3)	Primary and secondary
8-hour average[c]	0.08 ppm	(157 µg/m^3)	Primary and secondary
Lead (Pb)			
Quarterly average	1.5 µg/m^3		Primary and secondary
Particulate (PM 10)	_Particles with diameters of 10 micrometers or less_		
Annual arithmetic mean	50 µg/m^3		Primary and secondary
24-hour average	150 µg/m^3		Primary and secondary
Particulate (PM 2.5)	_Particles with diameters of 2.5 micrometers or less_		
Annual arithmetic mean[c]	15 µg/m^3		Primary and secondary
24-hour average[c]	65 µg/m^3		Primary and secondary
Sulfur Dioxide (SO$_2$)			
Annual arithmetic mean	0.03 ppm	(80 µg/m^3)	Primary
24-hour average	0.14 ppm	(365 µg/m^3)	Primary
3-hour average	0.50 ppm	(1300 µg/m^3)	Secondary

[a] As of June 2006.
[b] Parenthetical value is an approximately equivalent concentration.
[c] The ozone 8-hour standard and the PM 2.5 standard were challenged in court and ultimately (Feb. 2001) upheld by the U.S. Supreme Court. Full implementation has been delayed pending actions by both the U.S. Court of Appeals and the EPA.

in diameter. For this material it established an annual limit of 15 μg/m^3 and a 24-hour standard of 65 μg/m^3. These proposed standards were opposed by industry representatives, who initiated lawsuits to keep EPA from putting them into effect.

In May 1999 the U.S. Court of Appeals for the D.C. Circuit ruled (in a split 2–1 decision) that the EPA had unconstitutionally usurped legislative powers. The court said:

> Although the factors EPA uses in determining the degree of public health concern associated with different levels of ozone and PM are reasonable, EPA appears to have articulated no intelligible principle to channel its application of these factors, nor is one apparent from the statute.

The EPA appealed this decision to the U.S. Supreme Court, which handed down its opinion in February 2001. The Supreme Court upheld the EPA's procedure in setting ambient standards, saying these did not violate the U.S. Constitution as regards the delegation of power by Congress to agencies such as the EPA. The Court also reaffirmed that the language of the CAA essentially barred the EPA from considering costs in setting the standards.

Having established ambient air quality standards, the next challenge is to reduce emissions of material that pollutes the air. Air pollution control is typically divided into two main parts: the control of emissions from stationary sources and the control of emissions from mobile sources.

Stationary Source Emission Control

Technology-Based Effluent Standards.   Suppose you and some fellow citizens lived in a community whose air quality was degraded by the emissions of a number of upwind industrial firms. In consultation with your neighbors, you might proceed by first coming to some agreement about the level of air quality you would like to have in your community. Then, using your understanding about how air quality is affected by the emissions of the various upwind enterprises, you would translate your air quality objectives into specific plans for reducing the emissions of different plants by varying amounts depending on the costs of doing this together with the degree to which each plant's emissions affect air-quality parameters. If you proceeded in this way, you would be following an ambient-based approach to pollution control: Determine the ambient level of pollution you want, then determine how much the emissions of the various polluters have to be reduced to achieve these targets.

Now change the situation. Suppose you know nothing about the quantity of emissions coming from each source (you have no way of monitoring emissions, for example), nothing about how much it would cost each source to reduce emissions, and nothing about how the emissions of each one affects air quality. Suppose you also believe that the firms would resist any attempt on your part to apportion among them some plan for reducing their emissions. You might then be tempted to switch to a technology-based emission control strategy. Employing this strategy you, in the form of a regulatory agency, would require each of the polluters to adopt certain kinds of pollution-control technologies. Then, to assure compliance, you would have to confirm that the different technologies had indeed been installed and were operating.

This switch, from an ambient-based to a technology-based approach, is essentially what happened in the early 1970s in federal pollution-control policy. The CAA of 1970 was the first major federal law to incorporate this approach. It gave the EPA the authority and responsibility to establish emission standards that would, in effect, specify the technologies that polluters would have to install and operate to reduce emissions.

Note that we said emission standards. Emission standards are never-exceed levels for the emissions of various pollutants coming from industrial sources. In theory, an emission level could be established while leaving the polluter free to figure out the best way (presumably the cheapest way) to achieve the standard. But that is not the way the 1970 CAA was written. The relevant language is the following:

> (1) The term "standard of performance" means a standard for emissions of air pollutants which reflects the degree of emission limitation achievable through the application of the best system of emission reduction which (taking into account the cost of achieving such reduction and any nonair quality health and environmental impact and energy requirements) the Administrator determines has been adequately demonstrated.[8]

This is indeed an emission standard, but it is tied to a technology. In other words, the standard has to "reflect" the control achievable through a system that is in some sense the "best" one available. In this case the criterion seems to be technology that has been "adequately demonstrated." In other cases the EPA was instructed to set emission standards based on other criteria, as we will discuss below.

What initially might have sounded like a straightforward emissions standard (lower your emissions to the standard level using whatever means you want) in practice turned into a technology standard; the EPA identified acceptable technologies and provided incentives for firms to adopt these particular technologies. Firms treated these EPA-designated technologies as technology standards primarily because of monitoring difficulties. If a firm thought it could reduce emissions using some other means but didn't have any practicable way of proving this, it would have to adopt the EPA-approved technology in order to ensure it would be held in compliance. In this way the emission standards, which are called technology-based effluent standards, essentially work like technology standards.

One of the implications of the CAA was that as soon as it was signed, the EPA was committed to studying every industry in the United States that was emitting air pollutants, identifying the different pollution-control technologies available to these industries and evaluating them in terms of costs and emission performance, and then choosing the best technology on which to base the emission standards for the industry. This was, and continues to be, an immense task and is one reason why the EPA has moved more slowly over the years than many would have liked. But the CAA was consistent with the spirit of the times; in the 1970s and 1980s the general thinking was that it was necessary to take the initiative and responsibility for adopting more aggressive pollution-control technology away from the polluters and shift it to the EPA.

Differentiated Control. The 1970 CAA reinforced the tradition in pollution-control programs of treating certain types of sources differently than others in terms of pollution-control requirements. Several different classes of sources were created in the law: old or existing sources vs. new sources; and sources in areas where the ambient air quality is worse than the NAAQSs vs. sources in regions where ambient quality is better than that specified in the NAAQSs.

Virtually all environmental laws make a distinction between new and existing sources. New sources are almost invariably subject to more restrictive rules than existing sources. There are good political reasons for this and perhaps some economic justification. Politically, it is always easier to require more stringent controls on future sources, which are not presently at the political bargaining table, than on currently operating sources, which are at the table and actively pursuing weaker restrictions. Economically, one can argue that it is usually cheaper to build in pollution-control measures as an integral part of a new factory than to retrofit older plants with add-on pollution-control devices. Whatever the truth of the matter, it is an undisputed fact that virtually all pollution-control laws have this type of differentiated control between new and old pollution sources.

The 1970 CAA incorporated this tradition by specifying **new source performance standards (NSPS)** for new and modified stationary sources, while leaving much of the regulation of existing sources to the discretion of the states. In the 1977 amendments a new wrinkle was added: **new source review (NSR)**. NSR required new or modified sources to get a permit before building or changing, with the permit to be given only if the sources adopted the approved technology.

Differentiated control was also introduced into the Clean Air Act by distinguishing sources in different regions. The 1970 act created ambient air quality standards that were supposed to be applied to all parts of the country. This immediately created a problem. In places where the air quality was already worse than the standards (called **nonattainment areas**), the law called for efforts to rectify the situation. There was a serious question, however, about those areas where the air quality was already better than the NAAQSs. Would increased emissions be freely allowed in these areas until the air quality deteriorated to the level of the national standards, or would something be done to preserve the status quo there? The 1970 CAA was essentially silent in this regard. What happened to move this issue toward resolution was a lawsuit initiated by the Sierra Club. It claimed that the CAA required reducing emissions in nonattainment areas and protecting existing air quality in the areas that were currently better than the NAAQSs. The result was a set of amendments to the CAA in 1977, among which was the designation of **PSD regions** (prevention of significant deterioration), in which the technology-based effluent standards would be different from those in nonattainment regions.

For criteria pollutants, the technology-based effluent standards that were in effect after the 1977 CAA amendments can be summarized as follows:

	Nonattainment Regions	**PSD Regions**
Existing sources	RACT (reasonably available control technology)	none
New sources	LAER (lowest achievable emission rate)	BACT (best available control technology)

Note that these are meant to be criteria for identifying specific technologies and the emission standards associated with them. For example, the state implementation plans (SIPs) require that existing sources emitting in nonattainment regions reduce their emissions consistent with what is called **reasonably available control technology (RACT)**. In the early days of the CAA, the EPA took the lead in specifying for each industry what technology would constitute the RACT for firms in that industry. To do this, it had to become knowledgeable about the different technical options that were available to the firms in each industry, then use data on emissions performance and costs of these alternatives to choose the RACT for that industry. More recently these effluent standards are determined more at the state level on a case-by-case basis.[9]

The Clean Air Act also specifies technology-based effluent standards for hazardous air pollutants. The applicable standard is **maximum achievable control technology (MACT)**, defined as the average level of control attained by the best performing 12 percent of the relevant sources.

The implication of pursuing pollution control in this way should be clear. In effect, it shifts the initiative for finding the most appropriate pollution-control technology from the polluters to the government. An alternative approach would have been for the EPA to establish and announce emission reduction targets, then leave it to the polluters themselves to find the best way of achieving these goals. This would have provided incentives to polluters to use their own initiative, resourcefulness, and knowledge of the industry to select the best pollution-control technology. Of course, this approach would require some public oversight to ensure that pollution reductions in one direction were not achieved at the expense of increases in another.[10] At any rate, this was not the approach chosen. Instead, Congress called for technology-based effluent standards and put the burden for figuring out the most appropriate technologies on the EPA.

State Implementation Plans.   While the CAA asserted federal power over new or modified sources to a substantial degree, it also tried to give the states more power over existing sources. This was done by instituting the system of **state implementation plans (SIPs)**. Each state is supposed to analyze emissions in its region and their contribution to ambient air quality conditions. When ambient standards are expected to be violated (called exceedances, in the language of air pollution control), the SIP is supposed to lay out the steps the state will undertake to bring the region into compliance.

Although the SIPs give the states substantial responsibility for achieving improved air quality, the federal government specifies many conditions that the plans must meet. One is in effect a criterion for technology-based effluent standards to be applied to existing sources in nonattainment regions. The criterion is that these sources must adopt, "as expeditiously as possible," reasonably available control technology (RACT) for reducing emissions.

As one would expect, SIPs have been the subject of enormous contention and controversy over the years. While the federal government, through the EPA, has created the requirements and specified the conditions, it has been the states that have had to undertake the political and economic pushing and shoving to develop and enforce the necessary pollution-control measures. There has been a continuing problem with states enforcing pollution-control measures with enough vigor to achieve air quality goals. The federal government has employed various "carrots" and "sticks" to motivate states, significantly the threat to withhold federal highway funds from states that have not submitted, or implemented, adequate SIPs.

If pollution-control measures are going to be enforceable, some legal structure has to be put in place so that violations can be identified and penalties levied. In air pollution control (and in water, which is the subject of the next chapter) this is done through permit systems. A **permit system** is simply a requirement that polluters, in order to operate legally, must have in their possession a permit issued by the relevant regulatory agency. The permit can be simple or complicated. A driver's license is a very simple permit. A permit to emit certain types and quantities of pollutants is much more complicated because it will normally specify terms and conditions for a large number of practices, procedures, equipment, and so on. Permits are popular in environmental regulation because they provide a ready means of enforcement; permits can be made specific enough that violations can be relatively easy to detect. This does not by any means imply that violators will in fact be identified and sanctioned. Whether or not this is done, or the extent to which it is done, depends on the resources devoted to the task. But the permit system essentially creates a means by which provisions of the CAA can be enforced.

The CAA allows states to take over the permitting process. In the first two decades of the law, about 30 states did so, but with mixed results. There was great variation among the states in terms of specific procedures and the comprehensiveness of their permitting coverage. Thus the 1990 amendments introduced more standardized procedures for permitting programs, which all of the states are now approved to operate.

Incentive-Based Programs. Regulation of air pollution under the CAA has been based primarily on getting polluters to adopt specific pollution-control technologies. Efforts to introduce incentive-based approaches have continued through the years, however. These culminated in the cap-and-trade program in the 1990 CAA, and currently the momentum is shifting strongly in the direction of expanding these types of programs.

Incentive-based programs are designed to take advantage of polluters' normal incentives to minimize the costs of achieving pollution control. Their goal is to achieve cost-effective pollution control, or pollution control that gets the maximum reduction in pollution for the money spent. There are two types of incentive-based approaches.

1. *Emission charges.* Authorities levy a charge, or tax, for each unit (ton, pound, etc.) of a pollutant introduced into the environment. By essentially putting a price on what was formerly used for free, namely the pollution-disposal capacity of the environment, firms would be motivated to use less of those services. The higher the price, the lower the use of the environment for waste disposal. Firms would have substantial flexibility to choose the least costly methods of reducing emissions.

2. *Cap-and-trade programs.* Authorities set a maximum cap on the total emissions of some pollutant, distribute permits for this total amount among polluters responsible for the discharges, then let the polluters buy and sell the permits among themselves. Also, cap-and-trade programs normally make it possible for nonpolluters to buy and sell emission permits. This means environmental groups can buy and retire permits, thereby reducing the total number of outstanding permits.

As with all environmental policy initiatives, political concerns have produced supporters and detractors. Many in the environmental community have been against incentive-based programs on the basis that they leave too much latitude to polluters. The ethos of technology-based command and control is strong in the history of pollution control. Many people believe that public authorities can best determine what polluters need to do to reduce emissions, specify these actions in regulations, then send out inspectors to ensure compliance. A contributing factor is that in the early days of pollution control there were few good ways of monitoring emissions accurately; this control was best exercised by specifying the technologies to be used in production and pollution control.

In the early 1970s, when the major revision of the CAA was being developed, there was considerable interest in using pollution charges to control emissions. The discipline of environmental economics had emerged in the 1960s, and these folks were vocal in recommending this technique. A number of members of Congress sought to include emission charges in the pollution-control laws of the 1970s. President Nixon actually proposed legislation that included emission taxes on three things: parking surcharges, lead additives in gasoline, and sulfur oxide emissions. These proposals never went very far, however. Not only were many in Congress opposed to pollution charges on various grounds, the business community was adamantly opposed. Pollution charges would mean paying for something they had been getting free.

On the other hand, cap-and-trade programs normally begin by distributing to firms in the polluting community valuable property rights, i.e., permits to emit pollutants. They are valuable because they may be bought and sold. Thus, for polluters the financial aspects of pollution control with cap-and-trade programs are very different from that of emission charges.

The Mobile-Source Program

Mobile sources are sources that move around under normal conditions of use. They are usually divided into on-road and off-road. The former includes cars, trucks, buses, and motorcycles; the latter includes trains, airplanes, ships, snowmobiles, lawnmowers, and construction equipment. For some pollutants, such as carbon monoxide, nitrogen oxides, and hydrocarbon compounds, mobile sources account for half or more of total U.S. emissions. Mobile sources are the prime (though not the sole) cause of that modern-day scourge: smog, which infects many of the urban areas of the country and can even drift into nonurban areas.[11]

There are millions of autos and trucks, but only a small handful of auto and truck manufacturing companies. Thus, the early thrust of federal efforts to control pollution from mobile sources considered placing requirements on manufacturers, not users. Furthermore, in the 1960s California had started to forge ahead with mobile source controls, and it dawned on the manufacturers themselves that it would be far better to put in place a set of federal standards applicable in all states rather than let individual states potentially establish 50 sets of requirements. The result was to some extent a convergence of interests supporting federal emission standards for motor vehicles. In 1965 Congress passed the Motor Vehicle Air Pollution Control Act permitting, but not requiring, the federal secretary of Health, Education, and Welfare to establish emission standards for new motor vehicles. Of course, there was no consensus on how stringent these should be; environmentalists wanted substantial reductions in emissions, manufacturers wanted less restrictive rules.

The upshot was that the 1970 Clean Air Act incorporated mandatory tailpipe standards applying to new cars, covering carbon monoxide (CO), nitrogen oxides (NO_x), and volatile organic compounds (VOCs). The standards (i.e., never-exceed levels) were expressed in terms of maximum allowable grams per mile of vehicle operation; they have been gradually tightened over the years; in the 1990s particulate-matter standards were added, and in future years they will also include formaldehyde (HCHO) (see table 9.3).

The enforcement of these standards was pursued in two directions:

1. *New car certification.* Manufacturers would have to certify that their new cars met the emission requirements; penalties were specified if they did not meet the standards.

2. *Inspection and maintenance (I&M).* To assure that vehicles, as they aged, continued to meet the standards, states were required to establish I&M pro-

grams. This would presumably allow them to detect cars whose emissions fell below the standards and require them to be fixed.

The difference between stationary and mobile source controls should be noted. With stationary sources, Congress set the criteria and let the EPA determine the exact emission standards, but with mobile sources Congress itself set the exact emission limits that new cars would have to meet. The difference reflects the attitudes and political situation that existed at the time. Many members of Congress, and most of the environmental community, felt that auto manufacturers should be required to meet a detailed, stringent emission-reduction schedule. The schedule would be set so that the companies would be forced to develop new technology for reducing new car emissions at reasonable cost; this became known as a "technology forcing" approach. There are three ways to reduce auto emissions: switch to different fuel; change the way the engine operates; and/or introduce an add-on that will treat the residual stream. Auto manufacturers, with the cooperation of EPA, chose the last one, with the introduction of catalytic converters in the 1970s.

Table 9.3   Automobile Emission Standards Established in Federal Law, 1974–2004

	VOCs	CO	NO$_X$	PM	HCHO
	Grams per mile				
Uncontrolled emissions (c. 1970)	8.7	87.0	3.5		
Federal standards:					
1974	3.0	28.0	3.1	n/a	n/a
1978	1.5	15.0	2.0	n/a	n/a
1980	0.41	7.0	2.0	n/a	n/a
1990	0.41	3.4	1.0	n/a	n/a
1994[a]					
Cars (< 3,751 lbs.)	0.25	3.4	0.4	0.08	n/a
Trucks (3,751–5,750 lbs.)	0.32	4.4	0.7	0.08	n/a
Trucks (> 5,750 lbs.)	0.39	5.0	1.1	n/a	n/a
2004[b]					
All vehicles[c]	0.09	4.2	0.07	0.01	0.18

Key:
VOCs: volatile organic compounds, now called "nonmethane organic gas"; CO: carbon monoxide; NO$_X$: nitrogen oxides; PM: particulate matter; HCHO: formaldehyde.
[a] To be met by 40 percent of all light vehicles manufactured in 1994, 80 percent in 1995, and 100 percent in 1996 and beyond.
[b] This is the year in which the new standards began to be phased in; the final standards will not be reached until 2009.
[c] These are the "full useful life standards," that is, the standards that cars are expected to meet after 120,000 miles. The standards for new cars are slightly more restrictive. The standards for VOCs, CO, PM, and HCHO may vary slightly from the numbers shown because manufacturers are allowed some flexibility to certify cars with varying profiles of emission standards, as long as the fleet average for NO$_x$ is less than .07 grams per mile.

Until recently, converters have been the prime technical means of reducing auto emissions. In addition, a national program to phase out leaded gasoline was completed by the end of 1995.

By 1990, average vehicle emissions were much lower than they were in 1970.[12] But with many more cars on the road, and the average car being driven more miles per year, aggregate emissions from mobile sources actually went up during this period. The 1990 CAA amendments contained a plethora of new command-and-control type requirements, including the following:

1. The mandated introduction of vapor-recovery systems at gas stations in heavily polluted areas.

2. A requirement to switch to cleaner gasoline (gas with a higher oxygen content) in certain cities at certain times of the year.

3. More rigorous inspection and maintenance programs in certain states.

4. A requirement that companies and institutions with large numbers of employees force them into, or compensate them for, carpooling.

5. For California, the right to require car manufacturers to supply a certain number of zero-emission vehicles in that state.

6. Reduced allowable tailpipe emissions and lengthened the mandated warranty period for pollution-control equipment.

The mobile-source emission control program is a massive collection of command-and-control requirements, not all of them consistent and not all of them well understood in terms of their ultimate effects. The main focus in recent years has been in two areas: trying to get trucks and SUVs covered under the same emission standards as sedans, and trying to encourage the development of alternatives to the classic internal combustion engine.

California has long courted the idea of electric cars. Its desire to compel the production of these cars has been in conflict with the practical drawbacks of the technology, leaving the idea in limbo. More recently, much attention has been focused on hybrid cars (small fossil-fueled engines driving electric motors, which in turn drive the car). Many in the environmental community are also hopeful that research will progress on hydrogen-fueled cars whose only emissions would be water vapor.

The mobile-source pollution control program is a classic example of a technology approach to a behavioral problem. Policy makers are reluctant to interfere in the romance that Americans have with their cars and the freedom they provide. The result is a near-total focus on technological factors, with little emphasis on behavioral changes in how, where, and when people drive their cars.

Current Issues in Air Pollution Control

In this section we discuss some of the current issues in U.S. air pollution control policy. Most of these problems are inherent in the way the CAA is designed, especially as regulators seek to apply it in conditions of demographic and economic growth. At the same time, forces are evolving to make very substantial changes in the basic design of air pollution control statutes.

Setting Ambient Standards

How strict must an ambient standard be in order to "protect" the public health? And what is an "adequate margin of safety"? One way to think about these is in terms of a **damage function**, which is a function showing how damages increase as the quantity of pollutants in the ambient air increases. Two hypothetical damage functions are shown in figure 9.1. The horizontal axis shows parts per millions of SO_2 in the region under consideration, beginning at zero and increasing to the right. The vertical axis shows an index of health outcomes. Health outcomes can obviously be measured in a variety of ways (number of excess deaths, number of days sick, etc.); here it is indexed as the number of excess hospital admissions attributable to SO_2 in the air.

There are two plausible damage functions pictured in the figure. The one marked (a) begins at the origin and extends linearly up to the right; damage in this case is depicted as increasing in constant proportion to the increase in ambient SO_2. Damage function (b), on the other hand, starts from point x_1 on the horizontal axis; to the left of this point damages are zero, and they go up nonlinearly from x_1. This function, in other words, has a **threshold** at x_1 below which there are no damages.

In the early days of ambient standard setting, the general presumption among policy makers was that the damage functions for most pollutants were like (b); below some threshold level people would not be affected by pollut-

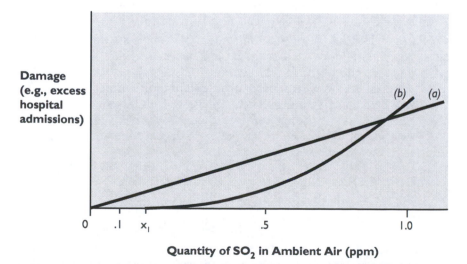

Figure 9.1   Hypothetical Damage Functions

ants such as SO_2. In this case, setting the standard to protect the public health would imply setting it no higher than point x_1; introducing an "adequate margin of safety" might actually lead us to set it somewhat lower than x_1.

But suppose the typical damage function does not have a threshold. Research since the 1970s suggests that in many cases there are no thresholds. For example, although the average person might not be affected with pollution below some level, there are likely to be some people who are affected even at very low levels, such as those with asthma. This either comes about strictly by chance, or because certain people may be particularly sensitive to the pollutant in question. In this case we are dealing with a damage function like (a) in figure 9.1, and now it is no longer obvious at what level the standard should be set to satisfy the language of the CAA. If we interpret the act literally, we would have to set the standard at zero. But doing this would have enormous consequences; in fact, the only real way of doing it would be to shut down all the facilities that produce SO_2 emissions, which would mean, among other things, shutting down all the fossil-fueled power plants in the country. It may be quite feasible to reduce power consumption in the United States by a significant fraction, and it certainly is possible to encourage a shift toward nonfossil power generation (e.g., renewables), but a complete and immediate shutdown of the fossil-fuel power system is simply not feasible.

This creates a quandary. If the damage function has no threshold, and it's impossible to reduce to emission level to zero, where does the EPA set the standard? Notice one other extremely important feature of the criteria established in the CAA: They say nothing about the costs of achieving reductions in ambient pollution levels. In fact, the language of the CAA seems specifically to enjoin the EPA from taking costs into account in setting the standards. This is a reflection of the philosophy that prevailed at the time the CAA was passed; in those days the general spirit was "never mind the cost, let's just get on with the task of reducing air pollution."

So how does the EPA establish standards in this situation? Clearly, it must take costs into account, despite the language of the CAA. One approach it is to interpret the words "adequate margin of safety" as meaning that the standards must achieve a reasonably high level of health protection, not that there need be literally zero health consequences. Thus, a standard might be regarded as adequate in these terms even though some people in the population are negatively affected by the air pollutant in question. And, in fact, this seems to be the way the EPA has proceeded.

The Battle Over New Source Review (NSR)

The Clean Air Act of 1970 makes a distinction between existing sources and new sources. Regulations are stricter on the latter than the former. In effect, many existing stationary sources were grandfathered, allowing them to continue operating as long as they made no substantial changes in their production practices. In 1977 a provision called new source review was added to the CAA. Firms contemplating alterations or upgrading of their plants must undertake a review of their plans to see if the changes would qualify them as a new source. Some power plant companies in the Midwest and South have been able to avoid controlling emissions by simply continuing to operate their older coal-fired plants. Critics maintain that many of the companies have actually changed and upgraded their operations over time, which should have triggered the new source review procedures of the Clean Air Act. According to them, the EPA should have initiated these reviews when operating changes were made, and potentially applied more restrictive pollution-control regulations to the upgraded plants (in effect regulating them as "new" plants). The companies maintain that they have engaged in "routine maintenance" only, and thus do not qualify for new source review and the tighter regulations this might trigger.

The main protagonists on the side of new source review have been environmental groups (the Natural Resources Defense Council has been especially active) and many of the northeastern states, whose air quality is diminished by these older coal-fired plants. The opposing side is composed of the companies themselves, together with the organizations they have established to defend their interests, such as the Electric Reliability Coordinating Council. Lawsuits against the companies have been initiated, and court decisions have impacted the fight in various directions. The outcomes primarily have hinged on how courts interpret the "maintenance" practices of these companies as constituting either routine work or significant alterations in their operations. The EPA played dual roles in this combat. During the Clinton years (1993–2000) it usually sided with the northeastern states, even pursuing its own legal challenges to these companies. Even so, it was criticized for not being more aggressive in its actions.

During the Bush administration (2001–   ), power companies gained the advantage. As substantial contributors to Republican election campaigns, power companies were able to find many people in the administration who were sympathetic to their views. The Bush EPA relaxed the rules on new source review, essentially making it possible for power companies to substantially upgrade their facilities without triggering NSR. Furthermore, they withdrew court challenges to previous actions by the plants which may have been illegal under the old rules. These actions took the EPA out of the legal battle to force power plants to adopt more aggressive pollution-control measures (on the grounds that their past actions in effect made them subject to NSR), and left the states and the environmental community to proceed on their own. Without EPA support, the states will have a much harder time. As one former EPA official said: "When it comes to suing big, powerful energy companies, you're going to do battle with some of the toughest law firms in the U.S. You really need the federal government on your side."[13]

In early 2003, with the support of the Bush administration, Congress attached to an appropriations bill a rider that had the effect of dismantling NSR. Legal sparring is still going on (as of mid-2006), however, between proponents and opponents of NSR. The issue may very well end up in the Supreme Court.

The Spread of Cap and Trade

Whether ending new source review will result in more or less pollution remains to be seen. The battle now shifts to the cap part of the cap-and-trade programs. The historic objective of NSR, to make existing plants upgrade their pollution-control equipment, can be achieved more cost effectively simply by applying smaller overall caps to the industries responsible for the pollutants being controlled. New proposals, from both sides of the environmental struggle, incorporate cap-and-trade plans for a wider set of pollutants and sources. In the current lexicon these new proposals have come to be called "multipollutant" laws. The differences among the cap-and-trade programs presented by different interests lie in the stringency of the caps, in terms of their emission level and time line for compliance, and the pollutants to which they will apply. Environmentalists, for example, want a rigorous cap-and-trade program applied to, among other things, carbon dioxide emissions; the Bush administration is opposed to this, in keeping with its opposition to the provisions of the Kyoto Protocol.

Cap-and-trade programs, although becoming more common, are still widely misunderstood.[14] They are incentive-based programs in the sense that they take advantage of economic incentives (the incentives that normal commercial enterprises have to keep costs at a minimum) to reduce emissions cost effectively. They require authorities to set the overall cap, establish rules for trading emission permits, and monitor both emissions and trading so that violators can be identified and sanctioned.

Interstate Air Pollution

The logic of the Clean Air Act of 1970 and the 1977 amendments was that ambient air standards would be set by the EPA; states with nonattainment regions[15] would then develop implementation plans to control the sources that were causing noncompliance. This approach is well suited to regions like the Los Angeles basin, or the Denver metro area, where diminished air quality is a function solely of the emissions originating within those areas. But it soon became apparent that in many places ambient air quality is a function not only of local emissions but of emissions that originate in other regions. In the northeastern United States, for example, it is apparent that air pollution indices are affected not only by emissions from sources in that area, but also by emissions originating in the Midwest that are transported by the prevailing winds to the Northeast.

The original CAA amendments had no effective means of addressing this problem. Particles of air pollution do not come affixed with labels showing their region of origin, and it is very hard scientifically to account for these interstate movements of various pollutants. In addition, each state has an incentive to claim that much of its air pollution originates elsewhere, so as to shift as much as possible the cost of bringing the state into compliance.

To address this problem Congress included a new provision in the 1990 CAA amendments. Section 176A of that statute permits the EPA, on its own or by petition from any state, to establish transport regions, which are multi-state regions in which there is a problem stemming from the interregional movement of emissions. For each transport region the EPA would establish a commission of EPA and state officials who would study the problem and make policy recommendations to the EPA. Based on these recommendations, the EPA would have the power to require the states to revise their SIPs.

The 1990 amendments also created one of these transport regions statutorily, the Ozone Transport Region for the northeastern United States. The Ozone Transport Assessment Group (OTAG), consisting of representatives of the EPA, the 37 easternmost states of the country, the District of Columbia, industry, and environmental groups, was formed to address the problems associated with this transport region. In 1998 OTAG issued a very complex final report of its findings about the interstate transport of ozone precursor emissions (nitrogen oxides and volatile organic compounds), and a set of very complex recommendations about emission reductions to be required of electric utilities and other stationary sources in order to reach compliance with the NAAQS. It also split off some states from the original OTAG group, recommending that Iowa work with Wisconsin to develop an implementation plan for southwestern Wisconsin, that Kansas and Missouri work jointly to address the problem in Kansas City, and that Oklahoma, Texas, Arkansas, and Louisiana coordinate their actions.

In 2005 the EPA issued the Clean Air Interstate Rule, providing for the establishment of cap-and-trade programs for SO_2 and NO_x in 28 eastern states and the District of Columbia. The plan is integrated with the SO_2 cap-and-trade program of the 1990 CAA. With Congress in a stalemate over different statutory plans for SO_2 and NO_x cap-and-trade programs, the interstate rule represents EPA's attempt to accomplish the same goals through administrative action alone. Some environmental groups regard this as a positive, though incomplete, step while others think of it as a retreat from the technology goals of the original Clean Air Act.

Summary

The primary federal acts governing air pollution control are the Clean Air Acts of 1970, 1977, and 1990. The major components of these acts are: ambient air quality standards set by the EPA; technology-based emission standards for stationary sources; and a mobile-source program that includes new car emission standards and inspection and maintenance programs. An important part of the program is state implementation plans (SIPs), which generally are highly complex plans detailing the steps to be taken by the states to bring noncompliant areas into compliance with the ambient standards. Major problems still exist in deciding at what level to set ambient standards, interstate transport of air pollutants, and the many perverse incentives that are inherent in the command-and-control structure of the program. One innovation in the 1990 law was a cap-and-trade program for controlling SO_2 emissions from large power plants. Cap-and-trade programs are likely to be used increasingly for the control of stationary-source air pollutants.

Key Terms

cap-and-trade programs
criteria pollutants
damage function
emission charges
greenhouse gases
hazardous air pollutants (HAPs)
indoor air pollutants
maximum achievable
   control technology (MACT)
mobile sources
National Ambient Air Quality
   Standards (NAAQS)
nonattainment areas

ozone-depleting substances
permit system
primary standards
PSD regions
radiation
reasonably available
   control technology (RACT)
secondary standards
state implementation plans (SIPs)
stationary sources
technology-based effluent standard
threshold

Questions for Further Discussion

1. Why do air pollution laws, as well as most other types of pollution-control laws, incorporate differentiated control?

2. Discuss the importance of whether damage functions have thresholds, and what this implies for establishing ambient air quality standards.

3. If we were to do away with the new source review provision in the CAA, what might we put in its place to address the problem?

4. How might it be possible to design a cap-and-trade program to address mobile-source air pollution?

5. Discuss the difference between an ambient-based approach to pollution control and a technology-based approach.

Web Sites

There are hundreds of Web sites devoted to air pollution. A good place to start is the EPA's site on the subject:

www.epa.gov/epahome/airpgram.htm

Naturally there are many advocacy and business Web sites with information on air pollution. Several of the former are:

The Clean Air Trust
www.cleanairtrust.org/

The American Lung Association
www.lungusa.org

Clean Air Action
www.cleanairaction.org

For business sites see, for example, that of the American Petroleum Institute:
http://api-ep.api.org/environment/index

and the site of the Electric Power Research Institute:
www.epri.com/corporate/products_services/project_opps/ index_env.html

There are numerous centers and institutes that deal with technical aspects of air pollution, such as the National Center for Vehicle Emissions Control and Safety at Colorado State University:
www.colostate.edu/Depts/NCVECS/

For issues related to interstate air transport, see the Web page of the Ozone Transport Assessment Group:
http://capita.wustl/edu/OTAG

For a site dealing with cap-and-trade control programs, see the Clean Air Conservancy:
www.cleanairconservancy.org

The regulated community has sponsored sites that take a more optimistic view toward past progress and conservative policy proposals, for example:

The Foundation for Clean Air Progress (conservative)
www.cleanairprogress.org

Center for the Study of Carbon Dioxide and Global Change
www.co2science.org

There are a number of good regional agencies with informative Web sites, for example:

Northeast States for Coordinated Air Use Management
www.NESCAUM.org

South Coast Air Quality Management District
www.aqmd.gov

Useful technical information is available at the Web site of the Institute of Clean Air Companies, comprised of producers of control technology:
www.icac.com

For a good discussion of the very complex issue of tailpipe emission standards, see the site of the Union of Concerned Scientists:
www.ucsusa.org/clean_vehicles/cars_and_suvs

Additional Reading

Bryner, Gary C., *Blue Skies, Green Politics: The Clean Air Act of 1990* (Washington, DC: Congressional Quarterly Press, 1993).

Cohen, Robert, *Washington at Work: Back Rooms and Clean Air*, 2nd ed. (Needham Heights, MA: Allyn and Bacon, 1995).

Cook, Brian J., *Bureaucratic Politics and Regulatory Reform: The EPA and Emissions Trading* (New York: Greenwood Press, 1988).

Crandall, Robert W., Howard K. Gruenspecht, Theodore E. Keeler, and Lester B. Lave, *Regulating the Automobile* (Washington, DC: The Brookings Institution, 1986).

Goklany, Indur, *Clearing the Air: The Real Story of the War on Air Pollution* (Washington, DC: Cato Institute, 1999).

Jones, Charles O., *Clean Air: The Policies and Politics of Pollution Control* (Pittsburgh: University of Pittsburgh Press, 1975).

Morgenstern, Richard D., and Paul R. Portney, eds., *New Approaches on Energy and the Environment: Policy Advice for the President* (Washington, DC: Resources for the Future, November 2004).

National Research Council, *Evaluating Vehicle Emissions Inspection and Maintenance Programs*, Committee on Vehicle Emission Inspection and Maintenance Programs, Board on Environmental Studies and Toxicology, Transportation Research Board (2001).

Organization for Economic Cooperation and Development, *Automotive Fuels for the Future: The Search for Alternatives* (Paris: OECD, 1999).

Stern, Arthur C., "History of Air Pollution Legislation in the United States," *Journal of the Air Pollution Control Association* 32, no. 1 (1982):44–61.

U.S. Environmental Protection Agency, *The Benefits and Costs of the Clean Air Act Amendments of 1990*, EPA 410-R-99-001 (Washington, DC: EPA, 1999).

U.S. Environmental Protection Agency, *The Benefits and Costs of the Clean Air Act, 1970 to 1990* (Washington, DC: EPA, 1997).

Notes

[1] For discussions of the early history of air pollution control in the United States, see the works by Jones and Stern listed at the end of the chapter.

[2] The names of the committees change from time to time; these are the names as of this printing in 2006.

[3] In chapter 18 we will look especially at two of these: the Montreal Protocol (aimed at reducing threats to the ozone layer) and the Kyoto Protocol (aimed at global warming).

[4] Several are listed at the end of the chapter.

[5] We will discuss this issue in chapter 18.

[6] Also to be discussed in chapter 18.

[7] We will discuss these in chapter 13.

[8] This comes from Section III(a)(1) of the Clean Air Act.

[9] The EPA maintains a clearinghouse of information from the states regarding their decisions in technology-based effluent standards. See www.epa.gov/ttncatc1.

[10] For example, reducing the amount of pollutants emitted via a smokestack by increasing the amount emitted into the water (though in some cases this may be justified if total damages are reduced).

[11] Nitrogen oxides and hydrocarbons from mobile and other sources produce, in the presence of sunlight, ozone, which, mixed with particulate matter from mobile and stationary sources, leads to smog.

[12] For VOCs and CO the average car emitted about 95% less per mile in 1990 than in 1970; for NO_x the reduction was about 70%.

[13] Comments of Eric V. Schaeffer in "States Planning Their Own Suits on Power Plants," *New York Times* (November 9, 2003):24.

[14] In chapter 13 we will explain in some detail how cap-and-trade programs are designed to work.

[15] Regions whose pollution levels exceeded the NAAQSs.

10

Water Pollution Control Policy

The water resources of the United States are a huge collection of diverse bodies of water, from huge lakes to tiny pools; immense main stem rivers to local, seasonal rivulets; surface water and ground water; fresh water and salt water. Our uses of these resources are equally diverse: water for drinking, cooking, and cleaning; water for operating sanitary sewer systems; water for crop irrigation, industrial processes, and food production; water for any number of recreational activities, for scenic pleasures, and for a large number of ecological services such as flood control, erosion control, and temperature and climate regulation.

A Brief History of Federal
Water Pollution Control Policy

Throughout much of U.S. history our primary, if not sole, concern with our water resources was in terms of their quantity: large-scale sources of water needed as inputs in industrial projects; water needed to charge rivers and canals so they would support navigation; water that could be impounded and used to generate hydroelectricity; water that would support large-scale crop irrigation; new sources of water needed to support a population that was growing in terms of both numbers and affluence.

Some early concerns with the qualitative dimensions of water resources did occur. In 1899 Congress passed the Refuse Act, making it unlawful for anyone to ". . . throw, discharge, or deposit . . . any refuse of any kind . . . into the navigable waters of the United States."[1] The target in this case was the increasing quantities of bulk waste, such as sawdust and industrial trash, that could sometimes clog navigable waterways. In 1914, as part of the Progressive Era focus on food quality, Congress passed the first of what would become a long line of statutory standards governing the quality of water in public water supply systems.

Widespread concern with water quality and water pollution control began to grow more rapidly after World War II. In 1948 Congress passed the Federal Water Pollution Control Act, which authorized federal grants to states and localities for sewage treatment plants, and authorized the surgeon general of the Public Health Service (PHS) to help the states develop water pollution control programs. Additional federal statutes were enacted in 1956 and 1965 (see table 10.1). The 1965 law in particular is important because it envisaged an **ambient-based system** for water pollution control. States were required to establish water quality standards (ambient standards) for interstate waters, together with plans for allocating emission reductions among sources sufficient to achieve the ambient standards. Essentially this required authorities to follow three steps: (1) determine water quality goals for particular bodies of water, (2) determine where the pollution was coming from that contributed to the impairment of water quality, and then (3) establish and enforce effluent limitations on the appropriate sources. Steps (2) and (3) were very difficult; (2) because it required close monitoring and analysis to link particular emissions with particular levels of water quality, and (3) because assigning emission reductions to particular sources involved a vigorous political game as individual firms and sources sought to shift the burden to others. States made only modest progress on this over the next few years.

Table 10.1   History of U.S. Water Pollution Control Laws

Legislation	Content
Refuse Act of 1899	U.S. Army Corps of Engineers authorized to operate a permit system applying to dischargers of refuse matter into navigable waterways.
Federal Water Pollution Control Act of 1948	Authorized the federal government to engage in research, investigations, and surveys on water pollution; also authorized federal authorities to lend money to localities to construct wastewater treatment plants; did not contain any power for federal authorities to set water quality goals or standards or regulate waterborne pollution discharges.

Water Pollution Control Act of 1956	Authorized federal grants to communities to construct waste treatment facilities; established enforcement conferences that would bring together state and federal authorities, polluters, and others to develop voluntary pollution control programs for specific bodies of water.
Federal Water Pollution Control Act Amendments of 1961	Increased funds for treatment plant program, vested administration of water pollution programs in the Department of Health, Education, and Welfare; several other minor changes.
Water Quality Act of 1965	Mandated that states establish minimum water quality standards for portions of interstate waters within their borders; required the states to determine maximum pollutant (emission) loads for particular water bodies and divide these among the major dischargers into those bodies.
Clean Water Restoration Act of 1966	Increased funding for treatment works grant program.
Water Quality Improvement Act of 1970	Increased petroleum company liability for offshore oil spills.
Federal Water Pollution Control Act of 1972	Authorized the EPA to establish a system of technology-based effluent standards, to be enforced by a permit system; substantially increased the funds available for supporting the construction of wastewater treatment facilities; established a goal of fishable/swimmable waters throughout the United States by 1983, and a deadline of 1985 for the elimination of all pollutants into navigable waterways.
Clean Water Act of 1977	Postponed some of the deadlines contained in the 1972 statute, and expanded the program to cover toxics; authorized an additional $25.5 billion over 6 years for POTW grant program.
Municipal Wastewater Treatment Construction Grant Amendments, 1981	Reduced the federal role and resources going to the municipal sewage treatment program.
Water Quality Act of 1987	Postponed deadlines for technology-based effluent standards, and changed the municipal wastewater treatment program from grants to federal contributions to state revolving-fund programs.

Source: Adapted from A. Myrick Freeman III, "Water Pollution Policy," in Paul R. Portney and Robert N. Stavins, eds., *Public Policies for Environmental Protection*, 2nd ed. (Washington, DC: Resources for the Future, 2000):172–173, with additional material from the author.

The main problem at this time was that there existed no good statutory means at the federal level for establishing and implementing abatement requirements for industrial sources whose emissions were contributing to diminished water quality. In casting around for a way to do this, some policy makers first hit on the idea of trying to resuscitate the 1899 Refuse Act, which applied to navigable waters. The newly established EPA developed a Refuse Act Permit Program (RAPP), requiring all facilities discharging into public waterways to get a permit from the U.S. Army Corps of Engineers, the agency responsible for overseeing inland navigation in the United States. RAPP was mandated by executive order in 1970, but a year later was invalidated by the Federal District Court of Ohio. The court held that abatement requirements of the RAPP were essentially arbitrary. This effectively threw the issue into the lap of Congress.

Congress responded by enacting the Federal Water Pollution Control Act of 1972, which left much of the ambient-based machinery in the law but added a significant new **technology-based approach**. The precedent for this had been established in the 1970 Clean Air Act. A technology-based program simply requires all sources to meet specified abatement-reduction standards. As in the air pollution law, the standards in the water program were (and still are) technology-based effluent standards. That is, they are standards (i.e., never-exceed levels) for emissions, but these are based on the abatement performance of specific pollution-reduction technologies available to the firms in different industries. The technology standards established in the 1972 law were as follows:

1. *For existing industrial sources:*

   Best practicable control technology currently available (BPT), by July 1, 1977. This was defined by the EPA as the average of the best existing performance by well-operated plants in each industry sector.

   Best available technology economically achievable (BAT), by July 1, 1983. Defined as the best performance that has been, or is capable of being, achieved by existing plants.

2. *For new industrial sources:*

   New source performance standards: Best available technology within 90 days of start-up.

The other major component of the 1972 law was the municipal wastewater treatment facility construction grant program. This program was authorized in earlier laws, but the 1972 law substantially increased the federal funding for that program. In fact, it was the fight over this funding level that provided much of the political drama leading up to its passage. President Nixon had expressed a preference for a funding level of $6 billion, but the bill sent to him by Congress called for $18 billion. Nixon vetoed the bill, largely for this reason. Congress then passed the bill over the president's veto. The law established a target date of July 1, 1977, for all waste treatment facilities to have at least secondary treatment.

The 1972 statute, like most of the laws enacted at this time, reflected the substantial environmental idealism that prevailed at the time. For example, it set a goal for the complete elimination of all discharges into navigable waterways by 1985. It also assumed, as in the air pollution law, that the EPA could gear up and establish technology-based effluent standards for all U.S. industries quickly enough so that they could be adopted and operating within five years. Neither of these goals was remotely possible in the real world.

In 1977 Congress made what might be thought of as a mid-course correction; it passed the Clean Water Act, which was essentially a set of amendments to the earlier law. This law pushed back the deadline for compliance to 1984, and introduced a new technology standard, called Best Conventional Pollution Control Technology (BCT). This law also introduced into water pollution control a new categorization of pollutants: conventional pollutants, nonconventional pollutants, and toxic, or priority, pollutants. The 1977 law established a BAT standard for toxic and nonconventional pollutants.

Since 1977 there have been two significant federal laws affecting water pollution. In 1981, with conservative President Reagan in the White House, Congress passed the Municipal Wastewater Treatment Construction Grants Amendment. This changed the wastewater treatment program from one of federal grants to one of federally subsidized **state revolving fund** programs. With initial federal help, states could establish a fund to help finance the construction of local treatment works. The localities were to pay these loans back into the state fund, which could then be used to finance additional treatment works in other towns. The next significant law was the Water Quality Act of 1987. This law postponed compliance deadlines again, this time to 1989. It also developed new programs for nonpoint source discharges and for waterborne discharges of toxic materials. Since 1987 there have been no significant changes in federal laws governing water pollution. As we shall learn, however, there are substantial proposed changes currently being debated within the context of existing laws.

Current Water Pollution Control Policies

Although no new major water pollution control statutes have been enacted at the federal level, implementation of the existing laws continues to evolve, and of course new controversies continue to appear. This is what one would expect because, though the law may be unchanged, the country continues to change economically, technologically, politically, demographically, and internationally. Before looking at these developments, let's review some of the basic terminology of water pollution control law.

Water Pollution Control Terminology

Point Source.   A discrete conveyance such as a pipe or ditch, or other structure, through which wastewater is emitted.

Nonpoint Source. A type of emission that is diffuse and relatively unchanneled, so that exact quantities are difficult or impossible to monitor. This includes, for example, runoff from agriculture, urban streets, and construction sites.

Conventional Pollutants. These include BOD_5, or five-day biochemical oxygen demand, which is the amount of oxygen required over a five-day period to break down organic pollutants into constituent elements; total suspended solids (TSS); pH; fecal coliform; and oil and grease.

Toxic Pollutants. This category contains a collection (currently numbering 126) of toxic pollutants sometimes called priority pollutants.

Nonconventional Pollutants. These include certain substances, such as chlorine, that are listed neither as conventional nor toxic pollutants.

Direct Pollutants. Those pollutants that are discharged directly into a water body.

Indirect Pollutants. Those pollutants that are discharged initially into a publicly owned treatment work (POTW).

Point Sources: Technology-Based Effluent Standards

The heart of the current water pollution control program is the establishment and implementation of the technology-based effluent standards according to the criteria expressed in the 1972 law. Congress initially gave the EPA just five years to establish the standards throughout the economy. To develop emission standards for a single industry required a thorough study of the firms in that industry to establish current emissions and how much emissions might be reduced with the various technological options available. Cost estimates had to be developed for each option, and then judgment exercised to select what would be regarded as the best practicable or best available technologies. All this had to be worked out in a contentious atmosphere with the industry that was to be regulated, which also was the primary source of the data needed to develop the standards. To do this for all U.S. industries with the resources and time available was an impossible mandate for the EPA.

One response was to fall back on informal procedures in an effort to expedite standard setting. These procedures became known as best professional judgment (BPJ). "Instead of a corps of professionals combining their expertise to set national limits for an industry, a single permit writer developed discharge limits based on knowledge of the industry and the specific discharge."[2] About 70 percent of the standards in these early years of standard setting were accomplished under BPJ. This is a very good illustration of how an implementing agency copes with a congressional mandate that provides insufficient resources and impracticable completion deadlines. Another response, as noted above, was to postpone the timetable for establishing the standards.

Implementing the Standards: The National Pollutant Discharge Elimination System. The actual implementation of the Clean Water Act is through the National Pollutant Discharge Elimination System (NPDES). The NPDES is a permit program; any source that discharges pollutants into waters of the United States must, if its discharges are to be legal, have a permit issued by the appropriate authorities. This applies to industrial, commercial, and some municipal sources only, not to individual homeowners, farmers, or certain public facilities such as military bases.

Application for, and approval of, a permit is a reasonably lengthy process. In fact through the years efforts have been made to streamline the permitting process. A permit will normally contain the following:

1. *Effluent limits.* These are based on the appropriate standards written in the applicable law.

2. *Monitoring and reporting requirements.* These generate data that determine compliance, total waste streams entering a water body at different points, and so on.

3. *Additional permit conditions.* These spell out such factors as the legal status of the permits, special procedures that must be followed, and so forth.

The permit programs under the Clean Water Act are actually administered by the states. Enforcement is in terms of permit violations; sources found to be in violation of the terms of their permits can be penalized through fines or other means. Penalties can be invoked not only for discharging pollutants over their limits, but also for violating other permit conditions, such as reporting requirements.

Nonpoint Sources

The first efforts at water pollution control were directed at point source emissions. It has now become clear that a very substantial amount of water pollution stems from nonpoint sources. This includes farm runoff, septic tanks, and urban storm water runoff. Nonpoint sources are harder to come to grips with because by definition they are widely dispersed and do not offer obvious control points. In addition, they tend to be localized and somewhat unique in terms of their causes and consequences. The result is that it has not been feasible to enact a comprehensive federal law dealing with nonpoint sources of pollution throughout the country. Thus, much of the federal effort at addressing nonpoint source water pollution has been to employ various carrots and sticks to motivate the states to take on the issue.

The 1987 Water Quality Act authorizes the EPA to offer grants to the states to assist in developing nonpoint source control programs. One aspect of these state programs is to identify best management practices (BMPs) that might be used to control different types of nonpoint source pollution. In 1990 Congress passed an amendment to the Coastal Zone Management Act of 1972, requiring the 29 coastal states to develop programs to address problems of nonpoint source pollution in coastal waters. The EPA helps identify the best available, economically achievable measures for achieving control of coastal nonpoint source pollution, as well as the policy measures that might be used to achieve them.

Within the states there is a wide variety of grants subsidies and financial support to localities for nonpoint source control. The states also rely on a huge array of enforceable laws and regulations that they have put into place to combat this problem. This includes land-use controls, laws on discharges, requirements for using specific pollution control technologies (such as BMPs), monitoring requirements, and "bad-actor" laws (allowing authorities to regulate only those operators who have already committed, or are about to commit, "bad acts" in terms of pollution) and laws permitting emission trading by nonpoint sources.

The POTW Program

A substantial part of the water quality problem in the United States comes not from corporate sources but from individuals and public bodies. A major point source in this respect is public sewage disposal systems for the handling of human wastes.[3]

In earlier times, when human populations were mostly dispersed and rural, the disposal system for human wastes was a solid waste system, based on the outhouse. But since the invention and adoption of indoor plumbing, the sanitary waste system is a water-based system, in which a stream of water is used to collect and convey the wastes. Water that comes into a house as a high-quality, unpolluted stream leaves as polluted wastewater. In the early years of public sewer systems the waste streams from individual houses were aggregated through a system of collector pipes, and eventually introduced into a river, large lake, or ocean. As long as the wastewater streams were reasonably small, the natural assimilative capacities of the receiving waters could be relied upon to render the waste inoffensive, to break the waste into constituent elements so that actual pollution was confined to a small area and perhaps for a brief time period.

But as city populations and waste loadings grew, these natural assimilative capacities were basically overpowered, leading to wider pollution problems. This is the situation America found itself in right after the World War II: burgeoning urban populations and inadequate public waste treatment systems.

Sanitary waste systems consist of a (1) collection system to transport the waste from point of origin to a (2) treatment facility, which will transform the waste stream to some extent based on the technology used, and a (3) disposal system, which takes the treated waste streams and introduces them into the environment. There are two important waste streams—the **wastewater** and the **biosolids** (sometimes called sludge) that have been extracted from the incoming waste stream.

Wastewater Treatment Technology. Domestic sewage is primarily organic matter which, when placed in water containing oxygen, will be degraded, or converted into its constituent elements. The quantity of incoming pollutant is usually measured in terms of the quantity of oxygen-consuming organic matter in the incoming waste stream, indexed as the quantity of **biochemical oxygen demand (BOD)**. There are several types of BOD: for example, BOD_5 is carbonaceous BOD, or oxygen demand from the decomposition of organic carbon; BOD_u includes the former together with the oxygen demand from the decomposition of ammonia and organic nitrogen.

It is customary to describe wastewater treatment technology in terms of a three-stage technical capacity.

1. *Primary treatment.* This is primarily a procedure of screening and settling that can remove 50–60 percent of the incoming organic and inorganic material.

2. *Secondary treatment.* This treatment uses the bacteria in the sewage sludge itself to break down the sewage further; with additional sedimentation and disinfection, up to 85 percent of the incoming organic matter can be removed.

3. *Tertiary treatment.* This technology involves additional chemical processes and can remove up to 98–99 percent of the original organic material.

Naturally, the costs of sewage treatment increase as one goes from primary to secondary to tertiary treatment. The Clean Water Act of 1970 contained as a goal that all public sewage facilities would have at least secondary treatment by 1977 (later extended to 1988).

Federal Actions. Congress initially responded to the municipal sanitary waste problem in 1948. In the Water Pollution Control Act of 1948 it authorized federal grants to municipalities for the purpose of constructing (but not operating) wastewater treatment facilities. These facilities have come to be called **publicly owned treatment works, or POTWs.** The original spirit behind this program was that the municipalities themselves would know what had to be done to protect water quality, and that all they lacked was a source of money to do it. What happened then was what has often happened before and since: Congress proclaimed the goal and the program, but failed to appropriate any money to fund it. That had to wait until the Water Pollution Control Act of 1956. In 1972 Congress substantially increased (to $18 billion over 3 years) the money available for federal financing of POTWs, and this was increased again in the 1977 Clean Water Act. The feds were authorized in these statutes to cover up to 75 percent of the total construction cost of a plant. Operation and maintenance costs, on the other hand, had to be covered completely by the municipalities involved.

The POTW program has some important subprograms. Two of these are the pretreatment program and the sludge management program. Industrial sources of water pollutants may discharge in one of two ways: direct discharge into water bodies, or indirect discharge through a POTW. Direct discharges are handled with the permit system discussed earlier. Indirect discharges are those going to POTWs, where they become part of the influent stream with which the treatment plants must deal. Industrial emissions, unlike domestic sewage, can contain a variety of substances, including toxic chemicals. Many have the potential to damage the operation of the typical POTW by corroding sewer pipes and equipment or by interfering with biological treatment processes. The **pretreatment program** consists of regulations that must be followed by indirect dischargers to avoid overloading or otherwise damaging the processes of the POTW.

The objective of the **sewage sludge program** is to dispose of the vast quantities of solid or semisolid material that is left over at the end of the typical POTW treatment process. Each year many millions of tons of this material is generated and must be dealt with. Some portion of it is incinerated; the rest is treated (to become biosolids) and recycled as fertilizer or landfilled. The EPA program consists of regulations applicable to various stages of this process, especially regulations to reduce potential public exposure to chemicals that might be contained in the biosolids.

In the 1981 Municipal Wastewater Treatment Construction Grant Amendments Act, Congress reduced to $2.4 billion (over 4 years) the amount of federal authorization for the POTW program. It also lowered the federal cost-sharing rate to 55 percent of total construction cost. The 1987 Water quality Act substantially changed the program. Though Congress extended the federal grant program until 1990, at that time it would be replaced by a federally supported state revolving-fund (SRF) system. In this system federal grants are made to states to help them establish funds that are used to make loans to municipalities. These loans are supposed to be paid back into the state fund so that the money can be used to make loans to other localities. The 1987 law was vetoed by President Reagan on grounds that, among other things, it involved too much federal money. It was subsequently passed over his veto.

Program Accomplishments. From 1970 to 1995 the EPA distributed $61.1 billion in grants for the construction of POTWs capable of secondary treatment or better. Since 1988, upwards of $20 billion has been given to the states to establish water quality improvement revolving funds, which can be used for constructing POTWs as well as for some other purposes. There are now about 16,000 POTWs operating in the United States, servicing about 190 million people.[4] Has the program been a success?

There can be no question that the average level of treatment of the municipal wastewater stream has been increased substantially since the program went into effect. For example, in 1968 the total flow of influent BOD into all the POTWs of the country was 35,000 metric tons per day and 39 percent of it was removed by treatment. In 1996 the daily inflow was 47,500 metric tons and 65 percent was removed through treatment. And there can be no doubt that federally supported treatment plants are performing the bulk of the treatment. By this token it may be judged a success, as the EPA definitely does.[5] Nevertheless, the program has come in for its share of criticism, as discussed below. Critics have asked whether the amount of money invested in the program produced the maximum results in terms of improved water quality.

Issues with the Federal POTW Grant Program. There are several legitimate points that can be raised, one of which is the substitution effect. If we look only at the federal money going into the POTW program, we get the impression that it added large sums to the overall effort to control water pollution from this source. But one common result with federal programs of this type is that they displace funds that would have been spent by states and municipalities themselves to address the problem. Thus, the net addition of funds was probably substantially less than indicated simply by the federal grant numbers. It is impossible to know just how much state and local money would have been allocated for wastewater treatment if the federal program had not been developed, but it may have been substantial.

Other concerns center on the allocation of funds. The objective of the federal POTW grant program was to improve the quality of the nation's waters. But with such large sums of money allocated to the program, inevitably political interests intervene and have the potential to substantially reduce the effectiveness of the funds in achieving the objective. Members of Congress seized the opportunity to increase their local political support by taking credit for bringing federally funded projects into their states and districts. Thus, the political pressure on EPA authorities sometimes resulted in local projects that were not the most efficient use of program resources. So the nation's waters got cleaner, but perhaps not to the extent that would have occurred if the money had been allocated with the sole objective of improving environmental quality.[6]

Another criticism of the POTW program was that it distorted local incentives. When grants or subsidies are made available by federal (or state) authorities to localities, the terms under which the grants are given can distort the incentives of local officials. For example, there are two important cost elements in a wastewater treatment plant: construction costs and operating and maintenance (O&M) costs. The federal POTW program offered grants to cover a large portion of the construction costs, but did not cover O&M costs. The incentives of the municipalities were, then, to plan for relatively large plants, so they could justify applying for large grants. But large treatment plants usually imply large O&M costs. This meant that cities would end up with large, ongoing O&M costs.

In addition, the program offered the temptation for cities to build large POTWs and then offer the services of the facility to developers and businesses at a very low cost in order to attract new firms to their cities. The federal subsidy, in other words, could get passed on to private parties in the form of below-cost wastewater treatment services. The federal pretreatment program was designed to address this. Indirect dischargers do not have to meet the normal BCT and BAT technology-based effluent standards; instead they must meet certain categorical standards governing the quality of the effluent they send to the POTWs. These categorical standards cover both conventional and nonconventional water pollutants.

Continuing Issues in the New SRF Programs. The move from direct grants to state revolving funds also has raised questions.

1. Allocation of funds has always been a problem in the federal POTW program, and will continue to be one with the SRF program. How do municipalities qualify for a loan, and are the loans made to the places where water quality problems are the worst?

2. A community that currently has an adequate POTW may use loan funds to address certain other waste problems, such as nonpoint source water pollution. If funds are used in this way, they may sometimes be used to support private operators, while if the loans are used for wastewater treatment facilities, these facilities must be publicly owned.

3. Who ultimately will pay for the facilities? Many different loan repayment arrangements are possible. For example, municipalities may sell bonds, which ultimately will be paid off by taxpayers; they may assess user charges on people and businesses using the treatment facility; or they may impose fees on various groups or individuals, such as developers or recreationists.

Current Issues in Water Pollution Control Policy

As we have mentioned a number of times, the 1972 Water Pollution Control Act introduced a technology-based approach implemented through a permit system. Since that time, the technology/permit system has been developed and adopted throughout the country and has become an established component of our environmental policy/regulation system. At the same time, however, economic growth has occurred, as has population growth and redistribution. Thus, although individual point sources have adapted to the permit system, the growing number of sources coupled with increasing nonpoint source emissions mean that many water bodies remain polluted. In other words, many waters may still be polluted despite the fact that all point sources have adopted the pollution-control technologies specified in the laws.

The Shift Back to an Ambient System

This has led pollution-control authorities to move in the direction of reestablishing an ambient-based approach to the problem. The water pollution statutes still contain language that seems to allow an ambient-based approach; the 1972 law simply added the technology plan to it. Section 303(d) of the Water Pollution Control Act requires states to list the waters within their boundaries for which the technology-based standards required by the law are not sufficient to achieve water quality goals. These are called **impaired waters**. In 2000 the EPA issued more detailed regulations requiring that states determine, for each of their impaired waters, the **total maximum daily loads (TMDLs)** of pollutants that could be introduced into them without violating water quality standards. Once a TMDL is established for a body of water, the state would be required to distribute this load among the relevant pollution sources, which would imply, for many of them, emission reductions in excess of what has been required under the technology/permit program. The last sentence reads "would be required," because the TMDL program has been the subject of much legal action and controversy, and is currently being vigorously contested (see exhibit 10.1).

The steps that have to be taken under a successful TMDL program are filled with scientific and political difficulties.

1. Developing an accurate notion of whether a body of water is impaired requires an appropriately specified objective (fishable, swimmable, wadable, lookable, etc.), criteria for determining whether this objective has been attained, accurate monitoring to collect water quality data, and then somebody to interpret the data and make the overall decision about impairment.

2. Determining the TMDL for the impaired body of water requires a thorough scientific/engineering analysis of the sources of incoming pollutants, how each source affects water quality at various points, and how specific

Exhibit 10.1
The Struggle Over TMDL

"Section 303(d) of the Clean Water Act requires states to identify pollutant-impaired water segments and develop 'total maximum daily loads' (TMDLs) that set the maximum amount of pollution that a water body can receive without violating water quality standards. If a state fails to do so, EPA is required to develop a priority list for the state and make its own TMDL determination. Most states have lacked the resources to do TMDL analyses, which involve complex assessment of point and nonpoint sources and mathematical modeling, and EPA has both been reluctant to override states and has also lacked resources to do the analyses. Thus, for many years there was little implementation of the provision that Congress enacted in 1972. In recent years, national and local environmental groups have filed more than 40 lawsuits in 38 states against EPA and states for failure to fulfill requirements of the Act. Of the suits tried or settled to date, 22 have resulted in court orders requiring EPA to develop TMDLs expeditiously. EPA and state officials have been concerned about diverting resources from other high-priority water quality activities in order to meet the courts' orders. In 1996, EPA created an advisory committee to solicit advice on the TMDL problem. Recommendations from the advisory committee formed the basis of program changes that EPA proposed in August 1999. The 1999 proposal set forth criteria for states, territories, and authorized Indian tribes to identify impaired waters and establish all TMDLs within 15 years. It would require more comprehensive assessments of waterways, detailed cleanup plans, and timetables for implementation.

"The 1999 proposal was highly controversial because of issues such as burdens on states to implement a revised TMDL program and potential impacts on some agriculture and forestry sources which are not now subject to CWA regulations. The controversies also have drawn congressional attention, and 13 congressional hearings were held during the 106th Congress by four separate House and Senate committees. Public and congressional pressure on EPA to revise or withdraw the TMDL proposal entirely was great.

"TMDL issues also were addressed in FY 2001 appropriations bills. Before the July 4, 2000 congressional recess, the House and Senate approved a FY 2001 Military Construction and emergency supplemental appropriations bills (H.R. 4425, H. Rept. 106-710) that included a provision to prevent EPA from spending any funds in FY 2000 or FY 2001 to finalize or implement new TMDL rules. President Clinton signed the bill on July 13, 2000, in spite of the TMDL restriction, which the Administration opposed (P.L. 106-246). However, the EPA Administrator signed the new rules on July 11 but delayed the effective date until October 2001, when the limitation in P.L. 106-246 would expire.

"The FY 2001 appropriations act providing funds for EPA, P.L. 106-377, included report language mandating studies by the National Academy of Sciences (NAS) and EPA on the scientific basis of the TMDL program and on the potential costs for states and businesses of implementing the revised TMDL rules. The NAS report, examining the role of science in the TMDL program, was issued June 15, 2001. . . . The NAS panel concluded that scientific knowledge exists to move forward with the TMDL program and recommended that EPA and states use adaptive implementation for TMDL development. . . . In August 2001, EPA issued a draft report on costs of the 2000 TMDL program. It estimates that average annual costs to states and EPA of developing TMDLs could be $63–$69 million, while implementation costs for pollutant sources could be between $900 million and $4.3 billion per year, depending on states' actions.

"The Bush Administration announced in October 2001 that it would delay the effective date of the 2000 rule until April 30, 2003, to allow for further review. That announcement came after a federal court granted the Administration's request for a similar 18-month suspension of litigation which is challenging the regulation (nearly a dozen interest groups sued EPA over various parts of the TMDL rule). In the interim, current program requirements under existing regulations issued in 1992 and court-sanctioned TMDL schedules remain in place."

Source: Excerpted from U.S. Congressional Research Service, *Water Quality: Implementing the Clean Water Act* (CRS IB89102, August 27, 2003):4–5.

reductions from each source would produce specific increases in water quality in various parts of the body of water.

3. Allocating the TMDL among different point sources and nonpoint sources means placing responsibility for emission reduction on sources, many of which will regard themselves as already in compliance with pollution-control laws, and individually will be motivated to shift more of the responsibility away from themselves and onto others.

Given these difficulties it is no wonder that the TMDL program has produced a lot of controversy. Most environmental groups would like to see it pursued with vigor; industrial sources of water pollutants would like to see it disappear; some nonpoint sources, such as those in agriculture, are afraid they would be subject to new restrictions; states are concerned that inadequate resources are available to do the necessary studies; and of course the political atmosphere at the EPA (as well as in the state environmental agencies) changes from election to election.

Cap-and-Trade Programs for Water Pollution Programs

Cap-and-trade programs are becoming a popular way to control airborne emissions. It is only natural that policy makers consider them for wider use in water pollution control. A few such programs have been developed so far, but the question is whether they ought to be adapted for greater use. Water pollution problems are different from air pollution in several important respects. One of the most important is that water pollution problems tend to be more localized. Waterborne emissions enter a water body and diminish the quality of the water therein, but this diminishment may be localized, both because of the limited extent of the water body itself, and because the water will tend to degrade and dilute the pollutants it receives. This means, among other things, that the geographical extent of the trading networks in the case of water pollution will have to be limited in size. A power plant in Illinois may trade SO_2 permits with a plant in Tennessee because their emissions contribute to the same air pollution problem in the northeastern United States. But a plant on one river ought not to trade permits with a plant in another watershed, even if it is relatively nearby, because they are contributing to different water pollution problems.

A number of emission-trading programs have been established or planned around the country in recent years. These include:

- nitrogen trading among municipal wastewater treatment plants discharging into Long Island Sound
- phosphorus trading among sources discharging into the Cherry Creek area of Colorado
- phosphorus trading among a number of point and nonpoint sources in the Lower Boise River of Idaho
- nitrogen and phosphorus trading among sources discharging into the Tar-Pamlico basin in North Carolina

- heavy metal trading among a number of indirect industrial dischargers to the POTW of the Passaic Valley Sewage Commission

In early 2003 the EPA issued a new policy statement on the prospects of using cap-and-trade programs in water pollution control.[7] It estimates that the national cost of the TMDL program could be cut by almost $1 billion annually if trading is allowed under that program. It encourages states, regions, and tribes to implement trading programs, and discusses some of the technical problems that will be encountered, such as:

- defining the pollutants and units that may be traded
- establishing a system for verifying trades and emission charges consistent with the permit trading
- establishing baselines from which trading may take place
- establishing an appropriate agency with the legal authority to establish rules and manage the programs

Time will tell whether these problems can be solved to the extent that cap-and-trade programs become widely popular in water pollution control.

Drinking Water Policy

Approximately 90 percent of the population of the United States obtains its drinking water from public water supply systems; the rest obtain theirs from individual systems, largely wells.[8] People are naturally concerned about the quality of water coming out of their taps. Public water systems presumably require some type of public oversight to regulate this quality dimension. The history of public policies governing the quality of drinking water has been influenced by a number of factors:

1. The evolution of science on water testing and the understanding of connections between water quality and human health.
2. Advancements in engineering knowledge about water treatment.
3. The push and pull among political authorities and other interested parties over who (communities, states, feds) would take the initiative and responsibility for regulating the systems, who would get credit for so doing, and who would pay for it.

The first federal drinking water standards were put into effect in 1914, an outgrowth of Progressive Era concerns about the quality of the food system. These applied only to water moving in interstate commerce, and included standards only for bacteria. Over the next half century these standards were revised a number of times (see table 10.2), but the prevailing political view was that public water supply systems were primarily local responsibilities, requiring local initiative and action. This responsibility was shifted to federal authorities with the 1974 Safe Drinking Water Act, which decisively moved the federal government into the position of regulating local water supplies.

Table 10.2   History of Federal Actions Governing the Quality of Drinking Water

Date	Action
1914	First federal standards issued for drinking water, administered by the U.S. Public Health Service (PHS), applicable only to water systems that could be regarded as involved in interstate commerce. The standards applied to coliform bacteria (no more than 2 coliforms/100 milliliters of water) and to total bacteria (a maximum of 100/milliliter).
1925	Revised standards issued, with the inclusion of three inorganic substances (lead, copper, zinc).
1942	Revised standards, 10 more inorganics added.
1946	Revised standards, with added language that they apply to "all water supplies in the United States."
1962	Revised standards.
1974	Safe Drinking Water Act. Required the EPA to establish maximum contaminant levels (MCLs) for substances thought to have adverse health effects; established primary standards based on health and secondary standards based on taste, odor and appearance; established a program of federal subsidies to states and localities for drinking water quality improvement; established an EPA enforcement procedure.
1986	SDWA Amendments. Enumerated 83 specific contaminants requiring standards within 3 years, based on best available technology; increased penalties for failure to comply, increased funding for federal grants, included groundwater quality.
1996	SDWA Amendments. Created a new $9.6 billion fund to help upgrade local systems; established state revolving-fund system; gave EPA more flexibility in identifying substances that represent the greatest potential risk.

Setting MCLs

The SDWA requires the EPA to set maximum contaminant levels (MCLs) for each recognized contaminant, of which there are currently about 100 that have been identified. MCLs are in effect never-exceed levels, and determining where they should be set is difficult. For each substance EPA must set a **maximum contaminant level goal (MCLG)**, ". . . at a level at which no known anticipated adverse health effects occur and that allows for an adequate margin of safety."[9] For carcinogens and microbes the MCLGs must be set at zero. These health-based goals are established on the basis of presumed health impacts without regard to whether it is actually feasible for public water supplies to meet them. Figure 10.1 depicts this relationship. It shows an assumed damage function, relating levels of some contaminant in the water to health impacts. It rises to the right: the higher the contaminant level the greater the health effects. It is shown with a "threshold," a level of contaminant below which there is no apparent damage.[10] The MCLG might

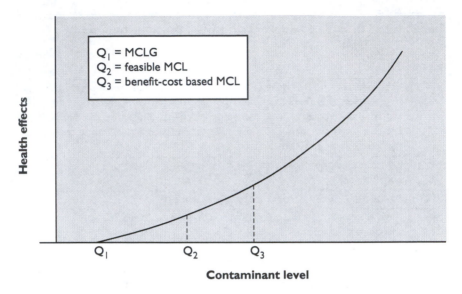

**Figure 10.1   Establishing Standards for Contaminants in Drinking
                 Water Supplies**

be set at the point of this threshold, labeled Q_1 in the diagram. But to establish an enforceable maximum contaminant level (MCL) the EPA is permitted to take into account the feasibility of achieving lower contaminant levels, considering the technologies available to do so and the costs involved. Thus, the EPA might establish the MCL at the level designated Q_2 in the figure.

In the 1996 amendments to the SDWA there was some concern expressed that feasible MCLs for large, better financed systems might not be feasible for small communities where costs might loom larger and potential benefits smaller. Thus, language was incorporated in the law allowing the EPA to establish standards that were less stringent than the feasible levels shown as Q_2, basing them on a comparison of both the benefits and costs of the standard. Such a "benefit-cost" based MCL might be located in a position such as Q_3 in figure 10.1.

In setting standards under the SDWA, the EPA may identify goals based solely on health impacts, but set enforceable standards at a less stringent level based on an analysis of both the benefits and costs of achieving them. The latter approach often goes under the heading of "balancing," and is controversial in its application to environmental regulations. Environmental groups, in particular, are skeptical of balancing because they think it gives undue weight to the costs of achieving pollution reduction. Others support balancing as a way to achieve greater cost effectiveness in pollution-control programs. We shall discuss this at greater length in chapter 16.

Since this statute was enacted, it has generated considerable political debate revolving primarily around the following:

The Pace at which EPA Has Identified Water Supply Contaminants. By the mid-1980s the EPA had identified only a handful of new contaminants, and critics charged that authorities were dragging their feet in this effort. As a result the 1986 amendments listed 83 new substances that EPA was to study, and tried to set up a timetable for establishing MCLs for these. But in later years the EPA argued that the 1986 law took away the flexibility it needed to identify and regulate the most damaging substances. Thus, the 1996 amendments allowed the EPA to establish priorities and focus more on the substances that were potentially most harmful.

Controversy over Unfunded Mandates. The SDWA requires the EPA to set MCLs, but then requires local water supply systems to take whatever steps are necessary to meet these standards. Local officials continue to argue that this saddles them with the high cost of meeting the standards without giving them adequate financial resources for doing so. This controversy has produced two results: (1) a provision in the 1996 amendments establishing a relatively large financial program to help local systems defray their costs of coming into compliance, and (2) a provision in the law that allows local systems some flexibility if they can demonstrate that in their particular circumstances compliance costs would be very high.

The National Politics of a Local Issue

What types of environmental quality problems should be handled by the federal government, and what kinds are better addressed by local authorities? There are several ways of looking at this question. One of the most straightforward might be the following: If the origins of an environmental problem and the damages it causes are largely local in extent, limited to the population of a community or a few neighboring communities, that problem should rightfully be addressed by the local population. They are the ones confronted with all the various implications of the problem, who can presumably sort out the pros and cons of different responses and choose the one they find most congenial to their circumstances, values, and budget.

On these grounds, the quality of local drinking water should be, for the most part, a matter for local initiative. Its effects are limited largely to the local population. Supply systems—reservoirs, wells, etc.—are limited in extent, except for the large cities. Yet the U.S. Congress has become a major player in the politics of drinking water quality. Why?

In some cases local water supplies are threatened by pollution from very large industrial firms or public agencies (as in, for example, the case of Rocky Flats; see chapter 13). In such cases federal involvement may be necessary to achieve a more balanced distribution of power between the local population and the perpetrators of the pollution.

Another explanation for congressional involvement lies in the way the American political system works. As Tip O'Neill, ex-speaker of the House of Representatives, pronounced: "All politics are local." Although Congress is our national legislature, the nature of the system means that the incentives of those elected derive from what's happening in their districts and states. The way to win reelection is to be, or at least appear to be, responsive to the problems and concerns of local constituencies. Surveys have consistently shown that drinking water quality is a major concern of the average citizen. Thus, incentives exist for members of Congress to use the issue to demonstrate their concern. Which is why large majorities in the House and Senate, both Republicans and Democrats, voted in favor of the Safe Drinking Water Act and its amendments.

Finally, the costs of achieve high-quality drinking water are prohibitive to many local governments, and large sums of federal money have not been sent to the states in these laws. As mentioned above, MCLs are mandated by the EPA, but local governments bear the cost of trying to meet them. In an attempt to address this problem, Congress in 1996 established a **state revolving-fund program (SRF)** by which federal money would be used to establish state loan programs to help local communities upgrade their public water systems. This is analogous to the federal POTW program discussed earlier. It provides a vehicle through which national politicians can bring home federal money to fund local community projects.

Funding Improvements in Water Supply Systems

As with the need to invest in wastewater treatment facilities, so with the infrastructure needs of the drinking water system. EPA officials have performed a gap analysis of future funding needs to upgrade drinking water supply systems. They estimated a gap of $45 billion over a 20-year period from 2000 to 2019.[11] On the other hand, the Water Infrastructure Network estimated a need for additional investments of $23 billion annually more than current expenditure levels in water supply infrastructure.[12]

There is controversy over who should provide these investment funds. On one side are those who believe that federal sources, and to some extent state sources, should be the primary supplier of these funds. They are anxious to publicize the problem and move it up on the funding priority list for these public budgets.

There is another point of view that stresses water pricing as a source of these funds. In most countries of the world drinking water systems are to some extent subsidized. This means that the full costs of the systems are not borne by water consumers; they are supported to some extent by general tax revenues. If prices were set so that systems became more nearly self-supporting, more money might be available for improvements. There are substantial political implications of water pricing, however, not the least of which is access to safe drinking water by the poor.

Summary

Federal water pollution control policy began in 1948, and over the next two decades a number of statutes were passed, the primary objective being to help the states set water quality targets and establish emission-control programs to achieve them. In 1972 the federal program shifted its emphasis to a technology-based system. Each industrial plant discharging into a water body is required to meet certain technology-based emission standards, a requirement that is implemented through a permit program. In addition, Congress funded a major program of federal grants to municipalities for public wastewater treatment facilities. In more recent years greater emphasis has been placed on trying to control nonpoint source pollutants and nonconventional pollutants.

In the 1990s the Clinton administration, under pressure from court decisions resulting from cases brought by environmental groups, sought to resuscitate an ambient-based approach to water pollution control. This led to the TMDL (total maximum daily load) program, in which states would identify waters with impaired quality, determine a total maximum daily load that would be possible to meet water quality targets, and distribute this load among polluters. This is a controversial program that the subsequent Bush administration was substantially less willing to pursue with vigor. In recent years there also has been an effort to introduce cap-and-trade programs into water pollution control policy.

Key Terms

ambient-based system	nonpoint source
biochemical oxygen	point source
demand (BOD)	publicly owned treatment
biosolids	works (POTWs)
conventional pollutants	pretreatment program
direct pollutants	sewage sludge program
impaired waters	state revolving fund
indirect pollutants	technology-based approach
maximum contaminant	total maximum daily load (TMDL)
level goal (MCLG)	toxic pollutants
nonconventional pollutants	wastewater

Questions for Further Discussion

1. Distinguish between an ambient approach and a technology approach to water pollution control. Why is it politically more difficult to implement the former than the latter?

2. What is the primary mechanism with which the Safe Drinking Water Act is implemented? What is the relationship of this program to the issue of "unfunded mandates"?

3. Why is the Clean Water Act so different in how it treats industrial polluters (technology-based effluent standards) and municipal polluters (federal grants to construct treatment plants)?

4. What are likely to be some of the main problems in adopting cap-and-trade programs for water pollution control?

Web Sites

Of course the EPA site has a major water quality page:
www.epa.gov/ow/

See its *Introduction to the Clean Water Act:*
www.epa.gov/watertrain/cwa

Other government agencies involved with water issues are:
U.S. Geological Survey
www.usgs.gov

National Oceanographic and Atmospheric Administration
www.noaa.gov

At the state level there is the:
Association of State and Interstate Water Pollution Control Administrators
www.asiwpca.org

At the regional level there are organizations like:
The Great Lakes Commission
www.glc.org

The Chesapeake Bay Program
www.chesapeakebay.org

New England Interstate Water Pollution Control Commission
www.neiwpcc.org

There are many groups devoted particularly to water pollution policy; at the national level there is:
Clean Water Action
www.cleanwateraction.org

A number of universities have formed research institutes that specialize in water issues:
National Institutes for Water Resources
http://niwr.montana.edu/

Iowa State Water Resources Research Institute
www.water.iastate.edu

See also the Universities Council on Water Resources
www.ucowr.siu.edu

The World Resources Institute has established a site to encourage nutrient trading within watersheds:

www.nutrientnet.org

For material on trading water quality permits:

www.epa.gov/owow/watershed/trading.htm

Additional Readings

Adler, R. W., J. C. Landman, and D. M. Cameron, *The Clean Water Act: 20 Years Later* (Washington, DC: Island Press, 1993).

Copeland, Claudia, *Clean Water Act: A Summary of the Law*, Congressional Research Service Report for Congress, January 20, 1999 (www.cnie.org/nle/crsreports/water/h20-32.cfm).

Craig, Robin K., *The Clean Water Act and the Constitution* (Environmental Law Institute Casebook Series, 2004).

El-Ashry, Mohamed T., and Diana C. Gibbons, *Troubled Waters: New Policies for Managing Water in the American West* (Washington, DC: World Resources Institute, 1986).

Environomics, "A Summary of U.S. Effluent Trading and Offset Projects," Report to the EPA (November 1999).

General Accounting Office, *Water Quality: Inconsistent State Approaches Complicate Nation's Efforts to Identify Its Most Polluted Waters*, FAO-02-186 (Washington, DC: GAO, January 2002).

Hay, Bruce L., Robert N. Stavins, and Richard H. K. Vietor, eds., *Environmental Protection and the Social Responsibility of Firms: Perspectives from Law, Economics, and Business* (Washington, DC: Resources for the Future, January 2005).

Houck, Oliver A., "The Regulation of Toxic Pollutants Under the Clean Water Act," *Environmental Law Reporter* 21 (September 1991):10528–10560.

Houck, Oliver A., *The Clean Water Act TMDL Program: Law, Policy, and Implementation*, 2nd ed. (Washington, DC: Environmental Law Institute, 2002).

Knopman, D. S., and R. A. Smith, "Twenty Years of the Clean Water Act: Has U.S. Water Quality Improved?" *Environment* 35, no. 1 (1993):17–41.

Kovalic, J. M., *The Clean Water Act of 1987*, 2nd ed. (Alexandria, VA: The Water Pollution Control Federation, 1987).

National Research Council, Water Science and Technology Board, *Assessing the TMDL Approach to Water Quality Management* (Washington, DC: National Academy Press, 2001).

Northwestern School of Law, Lewis and Clark College, "The Clean Water Act Turns 30, Celebrating Its Past, Predicting Its Future," Symposium, *Environmental Law* (Winter 2003).

Patrick, R., F. Douglass, D. M. Palavage, and P. M. Stewart, *Surface Water Quality: Have the Laws Been Successful?* (Princeton, NJ: Princeton University Press, July 1992).

Schultz, Martin T., and Mitchell J. Small, "Integrating Performance in the Design of a Water Pollution Trading Program," in Paul S. Fischbeck and R. Scott Farrow, eds., *Improving Regulation: Cases in Environment, Health and Safety* (Washington, DC: Resources for the Future, 2001):380–404.

U.S. Environmental Protection Agency, *National Pollutant Discharge Elimination System Permit Program* (http://cfpub.epa.gov/npdes/).

U.S. Environmental Protection Agency, *Progress in Water Quality: An Evaluation of the National Investment in Municipal Wastewater Treatment* (Washington, DC: EPA, 2000).

U.S. Environmental Protection Agency, *The Quality of Our Nation's Waters,* Office of Water 841-5-00-001 (Washington, DC: EPA, June 2000).

U.S. Environmental Protection Agency, *U.S. EPA NPDES Permit Writers' Manual,* EPA-833-B-96-003, Office of Water (Washington, DC: EPA, December 1996):1–28.

Notes

[1] Quoted by A. Myrick Freeman III in "Water Pollution Policy," chapter 6 of Paul R. Portney and Robert N. Stavins, eds., *Public Policies for Environmental Protection,* 2nd ed. (Washington, DC: Resources for the Future, 2000):170.

[2] U.S. Environmental Protection Agency, Office of Water, National Pollutant Discharge Elimination System Permit Program, Office of Wastewater Management (www.cfpub.epa.gov/npdes/), p. 3.

[3] A substantial amount of human waste is treated and released from individual septic tanks, which makes this essentially a nonpoint source problem.

[4] The total inflow per day to these facilities is about 32 billion gallons, which means that these facilities handle about 170 gallons of wastewater per person per day.

[5] See *Progress in Water Quality: An Evaluation of the National Investment in Municipal Wastewater Treatment,* U.S. EPA, n.d. (www.epa.gov/owm/wquality/index.htm).

[6] My first university teaching job, in the 1960s, was at George Washington University in Washington, DC. While there I was retained as a consultant by the Department of Health, Education and Welfare, which at the time (before the EPA was formed) was responsible for allocating modest amounts of federal money to municipalities for waste treatment plants. The work project was to do an analytical paper that would suggest various criteria for allocating grant money. The aim was to develop these criteria so as to reduce the influence of solely political criteria in making these funding decisions.

[7] See www.epa.gov/owow/watershed/trading/finalpolicy2003.pdf.

[8] The dividing line between individual wells and public systems is not as clear as one might think. A single well that serves several households is still regarded as a nonpublic system. At present any system that supplies water to either 25 people or 15 homes and businesses falls under the purview of the EPA.

[9] Mary Tiemann, *Safe Drinking Water Act: Implementation and Issues,* Congressional Research Service, Report IB10118 (August 20, 2003):3.

[10] It is the job of environmental scientists—biologists, epidemiologists, etc.—to determine the shape of damage functions such as this. Given the normal difficulties of scientific work, we are unlikely ever to know these functions with complete certainty, which of course complicates the task of setting MCLs.

[11] U.S. Environmental Protection Agency, *The Clean Water and Drinking Water Infrastructure Gap Analysis,* EPA-816-R-02-020, Washington, DC (Sept. 2002) (www.epa.gov/owm/gapreport.pdf)

[12] The Water Infrastructure Network is a broad coalition of groups (local elected officials, wastewater and water supply system administrators at local and state levels, environmental groups, and others) whose major activity is to push for greater funding, from federal, state, and local sources, to cover the costs of maintaining, replacing, and expanding the water infrastructure. See its report *Future Investment in Drinking Water and Wastewater Infrastructure.*

11

Toxic Materials and Hazardous Waste

In the twentieth century, especially during the second half, there developed what can be called a "chemical society." Hundreds of thousands of new chemicals have been developed on the basis of advances in chemistry and chemical technology. Each year thousands of new chemicals are introduced. People today have an uneasy relationship with chemicals. Nobody can deny the vast benefits that chemicals provide; modern medicine would be impossible without modern chemicals, as would most other aspects of the contemporary economy. It is also true, however, that chemicals have permeated throughout the environment such that human chemical exposure has become extremely complex in terms both of its extent and the nature of its impacts. One of the precipitating events of the modern environmental movement was a book about chemical exposure and its ecological impacts.[1] Among other things this book made clear is that it is not just short-term acute exposure to chemicals that is damaging, but also long-term, low-level exposures where impacts are less easy to identify and assess.

While a few people would argue that we should revert to a pre-chemical economy, and others would advance the products of the chemical industry without limitation, social reality lies somewhere between the extremes. The relevant questions are how to decide which chemicals will be allowed, and how to safely and effectively manage those in use.

The entire chain of chemical production, use, and disposal is complex. There are several hundred firms that produce basic chemicals, thousands of other firms that take these basic chemicals and turn them into intermediate and finished chemicals, and tens of thousands of firms that use these chemicals directly or indirectly in producing their outputs of goods and services. We can classify these chemicals in many ways; for example, organic and inorganic chemicals, the former based on carbon-containing substances and the latter not; medicinal and botanical chemicals used in the pharmaceutical sector; fertilizers and pesticides used in agriculture; and many other sector-specific collections of chemicals.

The difficulty with managing chemical use and preventing potential damage to humans and nonhuman organisms is due to (1) the extraordinary variety of chemicals and (2) the vast number of ways that chemicals enter and move throughout the environment, i.e., large and small streams of chemicals as they are dispersed throughout the economic system, among and between firms, households, vehicles, agencies, and all the other entities and technologies of the modern world.

For purposes of discussing the various public policy issues related to chemical toxics, it is useful to divide them into three categories:

1. Managing exposure to toxics during production and consumption; in particular, exposures in the workplace and in consumer products.

2. Managing toxic emissions from industrial, commercial, and domestic sources.

3. Managing hazardous waste disposal.

Table 11.1 lists the major federal laws governing toxic chemicals under these three categories. Each law has its own statutory specification, modus operandi, regulatory apparatus, and ongoing political life. It isn't possible here to describe in detail each of these laws. Instead we will discuss the major laws within each of the three categories listed above.

Policies on Chemical Use in Production and Consumption

Chemicals used in production and consumption have two potential avenues to affect humans adversely: by exposure in the workplace and through consumer products. In either setting they also can impact the surrounding nonhuman environment. Major laws in this category are:

- Federal Insecticide, Fungicide, and Rodenticide Act (FIFRA) for pesticides

- Toxic Substance Control Act (TSCA) for industrial chemicals

Table 11.1   Federal Laws Dealing with Toxic and Hazardous Substances

Policy and Statute	Responsible Agency	Coverage
Policies on Chemicals Used in Production and Consumer Products		
Federal Insecticide, Fungicide, and Rodenticide Act (1972)	EPA	Pesticides
Food, Drug, and Cosmetic Act (1938)	FDA	Basic coverage of food, drugs, cosmetics
Food additives amendment	FDA	Food additives
Color additives amendments	FDA	Color additives
New drug amendments	FDA	Drugs
New animal drug amendments	FDA	Animal drugs and feed additives
Medical device amendments	FDA	Medical devices
Section 346(a) of the Food, Drug, and Cosmetic Act	EPA	Tolerances for pesticide residues in human food and animal feeds
Federal Hazardous Substances Act (1960)	CPSC	"Toxic" household products (equivalent to consumer products)
Consumer Product Safety Act (1972)	CPSC	Dangerous consumer products
Poison Prevention Packaging Act (1970)	CPSC	Packaging of dangerous children's products
Lead-Based Paint Poison Prevention Act (1991)	CPSC	Use of lead paint in federally assisted housing
Federal Meat Inspection Act (1907)	USDA	Food, feed, and color additives and pesticide residues in meat and poultry products
Poultry Products Inspection Act (1957)	USDA	Poultry products
Egg Products Inspection Act (1970)	USDA	Egg products
Federal Mine Safety and Health Act (1977)	MSHA	Coal mines or other mines
Toxic Substances Control Act (1976)	EPA	Requires premanufacture evaluation of all new chemicals (other than food, food additives, drugs, pesticides, alcohol, tobacco); allows EPA to regulate existing chemical hazards
Occupational Safety and Health Act (1970)	OSHA	Workplace toxic chemicals
Food Quality Protection Act of 1996	EPA	Pesticides in food

(continued)

Table 11.1 *(continued)*

Policy and Statute	Responsible Agency	Coverage
Policies on Chemical Emissions		
Clean Air Act (amended 1970)	EPA	Hazardous air pollutants
Clean Water Act (amended 1972)	EPA	Toxic water pollutants
Safe Drinking Water Act (1974)	EPA	Drinking water contaminants
Policies on Handling, Storage, Transportation, Treatment, and Disposal of Hazardous Wastes		
Resource Conservation and Recovery Act (1976)	EPA	Hazardous wastes
Maritime Protection, Research, and Sanctuaries Act (1972)	EPA	Ocean dumping
Comprehensive Environmental Response, Compensation, and Liability Act (1980)	EPA	Hazardous waste sites
Hazardous Materials Transportation Act (1975)	DOT	Transportation of toxic substances generally
Federal Railroad Safety Act (1970)	DOT	Railroad safety
Ports and Waterways Safety Act (1972)	DOT	Shipment of toxic materials by water
Dangerous Cargo Act (1871)	DOT	Shipment of toxic materials by water

Key:
EPA = Environmental Protection Agency; FDA = Food and Drug Administration; OSHA = Occupational Safety and Health Administration; CPSC = Consumer Product Safety Commission; DOT = Department of Transportation; USDA = United States Department of Agriculture; MSHA = Mine Safety and Health Administration.

Sources: Michael Shapiro, "Toxic Substances Policy," in Paul R. Portney, ed., *Public Policies for Environmental Protection* (Washington, DC: Resources for the Future, 1990):198–199; original sources are: Toxic Substances Strategy Committee, *Toxic Chemicals and Public Protection* (Washington, DC, 1980) and Council of Environmental Quality, *Environmental Quality—1982* (Washington, DC, 1982).

- Occupational Safety and Health Act (OSHA) for workplace standards
- Food, Drug, and Cosmetic Act (FDCA) for chemicals in food

Pesticide Regulation

Annual pesticide use in the United States increased from about 650 million pounds (in terms of active ingredient) in 1965 to about 900 million pounds by the end of the century. Most of this (about 70 percent) is used in agriculture; the rest is split fairly evenly between industry and household use.[2] While there are hundreds of different pesticides available on the market, about two-thirds of the total is accounted for by the 25 most commonly used pesticide active ingredients.

Pesticides are regulated under FIFRA, the Federal Insecticide, Fungicide, and Rodenticide Act. The first federal pesticide control statute was passed early in the twentieth century.[3] But it had nothing to do with environmental protection. Instead it was primarily to assure farmers that pesticides they purchased were as effective as advertised. The environmental implications of pesticide use were first addressed in 1947. Later amendments to FIFRA (in 1970, 1972, and 1988) transformed it into its current form.

Under FIFRA, the EPA carries out four main tasks:

- registration of new pesticides
- reregistration of old pesticides
- testing pesticides that are already in use
- implementing a licensing program for pesticide applicators

In order for a pesticide to be legally used it must be registered with the EPA. Manufacturers who wish to introduce new pesticides (i.e., one not in use as of 1972) are required to provide information to the EPA on the efficacy and the potential environmental impacts of the material. EPA will issue a **pesticide registration** if:

1. The pesticide's composition warrants the proposed claims for it.
2. Its labeling complies with the act.
3. The pesticide will perform its intended function without unreasonable risks to people and the environment (taking into account economic, social, and environmental costs and benefits of the pesticide).
4. When used in accordance with commonly used practice, the pesticide will not cause unreasonable risk to the environment.[4]

As implied in item 3 above, FIFRA incorporates a **balancing** approach: In considering whether to register a pesticide the EPA may weigh benefits and costs. The balancing problem is depicted in figure 11.1.[5] The benefit is the pest control the substance provides; the costs are its full social costs, including the conventional costs of production, distribution, and application, and also the environmental costs in terms of potential human health impacts or ecological effects.

To register new pesticides manufacturers must provide the EPA with sufficient data to allow a registration decision. In this case there is substantial burden on the applicants to show that the material's benefits exceed its costs. The EPA can reject the application if the data are insufficient.[6]

For existing pesticides (i.e., those in use prior to 1972) the burden of proof is quite different. In 1972 there were about 50,000 pesticides grandfathered in under old registrations. For these the EPA has been burdened with doing the appropriate testing and analysis to determine if these registrations should be revoked. In addition, the law sometimes requires that producers be

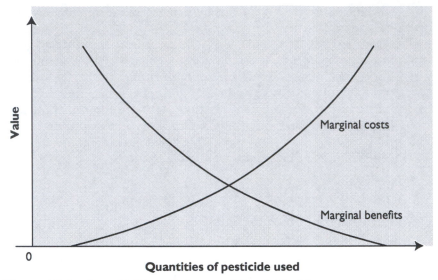

Figure 11.1   Benefit/Cost Balance of Pesticide Use

compensated for lost value in cases where a pesticide registration has been revoked. All of this means that the EPA has been hard pressed to move ahead with evaluating and reregistering the older pesticides in a timely manner. Congress has continually tried to prod the agency along, establishing deadlines for completion of these reregistrations, but EPA has never been able to meet any of the deadlines.

In 1988 Congress passed a revision of FIFRA to accelerate the rate at which EPA reviewed and reregistered old chemicals. In 1992 the EPA established the Worker Protection Standard Program. This involves a series of regulations designed to protect workers who handle pesticides; for example, a regulation requiring that pesticide labels contain instructions to workers to wear protective eyeglasses when handling the material.

Industrial Chemicals

As we saw in table 11.1, there are many statutes that address the toxic chemical problem. We just discussed FIFRA, applicable to pesticides. Later in this chapter we will look at the Clean Air and Clean Water Acts as they apply to toxic emissions. The Food and Drug Act applies to chemicals in food, and there are major laws dealing with leftover chemical wastes. In the mid-1970s Congress felt that there was a major flow of industrial chemicals not well addressed by these laws, and sought a program to bring that flow under some kind of regulatory control. The result was the Toxic Substances Control Act (TSCA) enacted in 1976.

The aim of TSCA was to give the EPA a statutory means by which it could identify industrial chemicals whose actual or prospective use was likely to be damaging to humans, and then regulate their use. The enormity of this task can be appreciated by the fact that, when TSCA was passed, there were already about 60,000 chemicals in use, with thousands more being introduced every year.

TSCA contains the following provisions:

1. For new chemicals, a **premanufacturing** (or pre-importing) **notice** at least 60 days prior to production, whereby the producer or importer firm informs the EPA of its plans. The notice is supposed to contain known information about the chemical, proposed uses, estimated future production data, and estimated exposure information.

2. For existing chemicals, a procedure for the EPA to compile information on a chemical's effects and exposures, and to require industry testing if it finds that the substance presents an unreasonable risk or may result in significant human or environmental exposure.

3. Authorization for the EPA to regulate the use of any chemical that it judges would present an unreasonable risk; these regulations may include outright prohibition, restrictions on use, labeling, record keeping, restrictions on disposal, or other means; the requirement being that the EPA choose the "least burdensome means" for accomplishing the goal.

4. Authorization for citizen suits against anyone judged to be in violation of TSCA.

5. Requirement for the EPA to maintain a Chemical Substance Inventory, containing all the chemicals (of which there are currently about 75,000) that are presently in use and therefore considered as "existing chemicals" under the law. This includes the chemicals that were in existence in 1976, plus those that have been approved since then.

TSCA provisions embody such concepts as "unreasonable risk" and "significant exposure." These have been interpreted to mean that TSCA, like FIFRA, must balance competing concerns. The EPA is required to consider both the benefits and the costs of any regulatory decisions it makes under the law. One route by which these decisions can be challenged, therefore, is on the basis of an inadequate benefit-cost analysis. A case of this type is discussed in exhibit 11.1.

TSCA has been extended to permit its application to the products of the biotechnology industry. By an EPA rule, any organism that has been created with genes from more than one taxonomic genera (a so-called intergeneric microorganism) is considered a new chemical, and thus comes under the TSCA process.

TSCA would seem to give the EPA sufficient power to develop an aggressive testing and toxics control program. In fact, however, it does not. It clearly was written to be minimally disruptive of the ongoing process of chemical production and use in the country. For example, the premanufacturing notice does not require that companies do toxicity testing and make

---

Exhibit 11.1
TSCA Follies: Politics Trumps Science?

The toxic effects of asbestos have been known for many years. Asbestos-related illness and death is a significant concern among miners, ship workers, cement workers, insulation workers, and others exposed to the substance through their occupations. Beginning in the early 1970s, plaintiffs in "toxic tort" cases began to have some success in recovering damages from occupational asbestos-related diseases. In 1979, the EPA announced its intention to seek a complete ban on asbestos production and importation under TSCA. Over the next ten years it amassed a huge amount of scientific information linking exposure to atmospheric asbestos fibers with human disease. In 1986 the Occupational Safety and Health Administration established a workplace standard for asbestos exposure, stating that ". . . OSHA is aware of no instance in which exposure to a toxic substance has more clearly demonstrated detrimental health effects on humans than has asbestos exposure."[a]

In 1989 the EPA issued its asbestos ban and phaseout rule. This move, of course, was immediately challenged in the courts, and in 1991 the U.S. Fifth Circuit Court of Appeals invalidated most of the ban. Despite the clear evidence on the health effects of asbestos, the court ruled that the EPA had not performed its analysis in keeping with the requirements specified in TSCA. Specifically, the court found that EPA had not proposed the least burdensome regulatory approach, and had not completed a reasonably accurate benefit-cost analysis of the rule.

Meanwhile, the European Union banned the importation, manufacture, marketing, and use of asbestos, effective in 2005. Though the U.S. government has banned the use of asbestos in some consumer products and in home-construction materials, "consumers cannot always assume that products they buy are asbestos-free . . . in the U.S., asbestos-containing products are not legally required to be labeled as such . . ."[b]

[a] Cited in Mark R. Powell, *Science at EPA: Information in the Regulatory Process* (Washington, DC: Resources for the Future, 1999):303.
[b] Anne Nadakavukaren, *Our Global Environment: A Health Perspective*, 6th ed. (Long Grove, IL: Waveland Press, 2006):218.

---

the results available to the EPA. In addition, if the agency undertakes to require testing of an existing chemical, it must follow a complicated and easily challenged procedure for documenting that testing is necessary. Thus, evaluations of progress under TSCA conducted by outside groups not connected to the chemical industry have concluded that progress has been extremely slow.[7]

Occupational Safety and Health Act (OSHA)

OSHA requires the Occupational Safety and Health Administration[8] to establish workplace standards for exposure to toxic materials. The standards are known as **permissible exposure levels (PELs)**, and are regulatory limits on the amounts or concentration of hazardous substances in workplace air. There are 8-hour weighted average limits, ceiling (never-exceed) limits, and very short-term exposure limits. There are currently about 500 PELs in effect in the United States, with OSHA under pressure to issue more and to reevaluate existing standards to keep them up to date with current research on the impacts of toxic chemicals on humans.

Food, Drug, and Cosmetic Act (FDCA)

The history of efforts by public authorities to ensure the quality of food and drugs dates back to the nineteenth century. These early actions focused on stopping people from adulterating food (e.g., putting water in milk) and medicine (e.g., making fake drugs). Initially, such efforts originated in the states, many of which passed laws dealing with their particular circumstances. The first federal law, the 1906 Food and Drug Act, was fought vigorously by the makers of liquor and patent medicines. In 1938 the (6-page) Food, Drug, and Cosmetic Act was passed, prohibiting the interstate commerce of adulterated or misbranded foods. The law is implemented by the Food and Drug Administration (FDA), an agency within the Department of Health and Human Services. The EPA establishes chemical tolerance levels for chemicals in food. These are essentially maximum amounts (for example, maximum levels in terms of parts per million or per billion) of a chemical that are permitted in both fresh and processed foods. The primary target of these tolerances are the pesticides that are used in commercial food production.

The Food Quality Protection Act (FQPA) of 1996 changed the criterion for establishing these tolerances. The goal was to unify a very complicated and inconsistent area of regulation. The FQPA requires the EPA to set all pesticide tolerances in food at that level for which there is a "reasonable certainty of no harm" from the exposure allowed by the tolerance.[9]

What Is "Reasonable Risk"

Most of the laws currently used to manage toxic materials have language that requires the implementing agencies to assess the levels of risk that are, or would be, associated with their use. Thus, TSCA incorporates the notion of "unreasonable risk." FIFRA has "unreasonable adverse effects on the environment," and the Food Quality Protection Act of 1996 (a revision of the Federal Food, Drug, and Cosmetic Act) establishes "a reasonable certainty of no harm" as the general safety standard under the law. All of these require administrators to develop a criterion for defining a **reasonable risk**. Under most circumstances reasonable risk does not mean zero risk, but of course it is a matter of controversy. The environmental community pushes for a more stringent notion of "reasonable risk," while the regulated community urges a less restrictive definition. We will encounter this again in chapter 16.

Policies for Controlling Toxic Emissions

Each year millions of tons of toxic chemicals are released into the nation's water and air. Developing appropriate controls over these emissions has been an ongoing policy struggle. Both the Clean Air Act and the Clean Water Act have sections dealing with toxic emissions. In addition, this is one area where an information-based policy appears to have been very successful.

Control of Toxic Airborne Emissions

The 1970 Clean Air Act focused primarily on criteria pollutants. As regards emissions of toxic chemicals (often called hazardous air pollutants or HAPs), the responsibility was given almost completely to the EPA to address the problem. The agency was instructed to mount a program that would identify all toxic pollutants that caused "serious and irreversible illness or death," and then develop standards to reduce emissions sufficiently to provide an "ample margin of safety" to the public. Given the enormity of this task alone, not to mention all the other environmental issues with which the EPA was dealing, the problem of airborne HAPs was not addressed with great vigor. Between 1970 and 1990 the EPA regulated only seven airborne toxics (asbestos, benzene, beryllium, inorganic arsenic, mercury, radionuclides, and vinyl choloride).

Congressional (and public) frustration with this slow progress led to a renewed effort as part of the Clean Air Act of 1990. In this law Congress specifically enumerated 188 substances, and established a timetable for the EPA to develop control strategies for them. Over the next 10 years, regulations were adopted for 45 air toxics on the 1990 list (though not without great controversy, of course, as exhibit 11.2 details for the case of mercury).

The standard for regulating air toxics is **maximum achievable control technology (MACT)**. This is a technology-based standard, defined in the following way:

1. *For existing sources.* The average emissions performance of the 12 percent of best-performing (in terms of emissions, expressed either as percentage reduction or concentration limit) sources in the same industry.

2. *For new sources.* Emissions equal to the emissions performance of the best-performing source in the same industry.

These MACT specifications are actually minimum reductions, or in the language of the air toxics program, the "MACT floor." The MACT standard may be set more restrictively if this is deemed necessary.[10]

Exhibit 11.2
Sparring Over MACT for Mercury

To control toxic airborne releases the Clean Air Act directs the EPA to establish minimum technology-based emission standards according to the criterion of maximum achievable control technology (MACT). The agency has defined MACT as the emissions attained by the average of the 12 percent of best-performing sources. This may sound straightforward, but it isn't, as illustrated by the case of mercury. Mercury is an important toxic, and about 40 percent of airborne mercury emissions in the United States comes from large coal-fired power plants. Mercury is one of the specific toxics identified in the 1990 CAA for which the EPA was to proceed expeditiously to develop emission standards. After spending much of the 1990s studying the situation, EPA issued in 1998 a report called *Study of Hazardous Air Pollutants from Electric Utility Steam Generating Units*, Final Report to Congress.[a] While recognizing in the report that mercury emission control was justified, the EPA put off specifying explicit MACT standards for the future.

This prompted a lawsuit brought by environmental groups. In the ensuing settlement agreement, EPA promised, among other things, to issue a "regulatory finding" by December 15, 2000; a proposed regulation by December 15, 2003; and a final regulation by December 15, 2004. The regulatory finding was duly issued in December 2000, stating that power plant mercury emissions were sufficiently damaging to warrant regulation. Over the next few years environmental groups and utility companies sparred vigorously over how stringent the EPA would make the MACT standards. Environmental groups wanted a standard that reflected up to a 90 percent reduction in mercury emissions from the source. They cited in particular the presence of emerging new and cheaper technologies for controlling mercury emissions, the adoption of which would be encouraged with strict standards. Utility companies wanted far less stringent emissions, citing issues of cost and scientific uncertainty. The EPA's advisory committee recommended the larger cutbacks. The Bush administration leaned strongly toward less restrictive standards.

On December 15, 2003, EPA issued a proposed rule, specifying new MACT standards, but also giving states an option to control power plant mercury with cap-and-trade programs. On March 16, 2004, the EPA published a supplemental statement proposing that mercury emissions be controlled uniquely through cap and trade, thus essentially sidestepping the whole MACT apparatus in this case.

[a] EPA 453/R-98-004a.

Control of Waterborne Toxics

The Clean Water ACT (CWA) of 1977 identifies toxic pollutants as a special category of waterborne emissions. It requires that sources emitting such pollutants adopt the **best available technology (BAT)** for their control. This includes both direct dischargers and those who discharge into public sewer systems. BAT standards apply also to nonconventional pollutants. BAT is defined as the ". . . best existing performance of treatment technologies that are economically achievable within an industrial point source category or subcategory."[11] Of course, the term "economically achievable" introduces an important qualification. What is economically achievable? This was originally defined somewhat loosely: "The very best control and treatment measures that have been or are capable of being achieved."[12]

The Toxic Release Inventory

In 1984 a cloud of methyl isocyanate released accidentally from a local chemical plant killed thousands of people in Bhopal, India. Shortly after, there was a serious chemical release at a plant in West Virginia. In both cases there was surprise and outrage on the part of many local residents that they had been living in proximity to these plants without knowing the underlying danger. This prompted Congress to address the issue of how residents of communities could be provided with better information about ongoing toxic releases in their community or the presence of stored chemicals that could be accidentally released. The result was the Emergency Planning and Community Right to Know Act (EPCRA) of 1986.[13]

The law has three main provisions:

1. Section 311 requires businesses to report to state and local governments quantities of chemicals stored on site.
2. Section 312 requires businesses to report chemical releases to air and water and transfers to other locations.
3. Section 313 requires the EPA to collect data on releases and transfers and make it available to the public on the **Toxic Release Inventory (TRI)**.

By most measures the TRI has been a very successful law. Publication of the data has made it possible for people to learn more about chemicals in their community environment. The theory is that this is the first step in empowering them to do something about it if conditions warrant. There are examples of communities organizing to take action as a result of TRI data. The Internet has made it possible for people easily to access TRI data.[14]

The principles underlying the TRI may be challenged by the new emphasis on secrecy born out of our concern about domestic terrorism. TRI is based on the notion that providing citizens with complete information will help create awareness of situations that ought to be dealt with; chemical releases that were once made in secrecy or without being recorded are now tallied and published. But the war on terrorism has promoted the idea that access to public data ought to be restricted. And chemical polluters are likely to try to take advantage of this and seek to restrict information on chemical releases.

Policies to Manage Hazardous Waste

We come now to the problem of chemical leftovers. The entire solid waste stream[15] is subdivided into two parts: hazardous waste and nonhazardous waste. The latter includes what is called municipal solid waste (i.e., trash) and will be discussed in the next chapter. Here we will cover that portion of the solid waste stream that consists of hazardous material, which is primarily, but not entirely, leftover chemicals.

Table 11.2 shows the major routes for the disposition of hazardous wastes in the United States. It may come as a surprise to learn that the vast majority of this material is disposed of by underground injection into deep wells or salt caverns. The EPA has an injection well program applicable to all types of wells into which hazardous wastes are put.[16] They distinguish five types of wells. Class I wells are very deep, usually drilled wells that go below groundwater layers. Most of these are on the premises of, and used by, individual companies to dispose of their own hazardous leftovers. A few are commercial wells that accept and dispose of waste from many companies. Type I

Table 11.2   Summary of Hazardous Waste Management Methods with 2003 Quantities

Management Method	Quantity (million tons)	Percent of Total
Disposal		
Landfills and surface impoundments	1.7	4.0
Underground injection (injected into deep wells or salt caverns)	14.5	34.4
Other	3.3	7.8
Treatment		
Chemical treatment	7.7	18.3
Incineration	1.2	2.9
Stabilization (solidified or immobilized)	.7	1.7
Sludge treatment	.6	1.4
Other treatment	7.7	18.3
Recycling and reuse		
Metals recovery	1.2	2.8
Energy recovery	1.4	3.3
Other	2.1	5.0
Total	42.1	100.0

Source: U.S. EPA, *The National Biennial RCRA Hazardous Waste Report* (based on 2003 data). (www.epa.gov/epaoswer/hazwaste/data/br03/national03.pdf)

wells are the most heavily regulated. They are also controversial. Many environmental groups have questioned the ultimate ecological safety of these wells, while community groups would like to see more public involvement in EPA and state decisions on injection wells. Environmental justice advocates have raised the issue of whether siting decisions disproportionately impact minority communities.[17]

The Resource Conservation and Recovery Act of 1976

The first major federal law dealing with hazardous waste was the 1976 amendments to the Solid Waste Disposal Act, called the Resource Conservation and Recovery Act (RCRA). RCRA was passed in some haste, the same year that TSCA was passed. This was before Congress, or anybody else for that matter, knew much about the extent of the hazardous waste problem. The concern at the time was that much hazardous material was being disposed of in standard municipal landfills, where it could potentially cause future damage to surrounding ecosystems or to people who might come into contact with it.

The Resource Conservation and Recovery Act put the federal government actively in the role of regulating land-based solid waste, especially hazardous solid wastes. RCRA deals for the most part with contemporaneous waste, that which is being generated today and must be handled in some way. It also put land-based disposal on a par with disposal into water and air. But land disposal has a potential problem that air and water disposal do not have, at least to the same degree. Substances put in landfills may persist for dozens, hundreds, or even millions of years in the case of radiation from nuclear waste. Rather than being dissipated or chemically converted, they may stay in their original form, posing a significant threat to humans and the surrounding environment in the event such substances leach from the landfill or are disturbed by excavation, construction, and the like. Table 11.3 describes briefly the different types of contaminated land problems in the United States.

Subtitle C of RCRA applies to hazardous wastes. It establishes the following procedures:

1. A definition of hazardous solid waste.

2. A manifest system for tracking hazardous waste from generation to disposal.

3. Operating requirements for generators of hazardous waste, and both operating and technical requirements for facilities that transport, store, or dispose of hazardous waste.

4. A permit system to enforce the standards set under (3).

5. Authorization for states to develop programs to implement programs of hazardous waste control.

The Definition of Hazardous Wastes. The materials that are left over from the processes of production and consumption vary along a continuum, from highly toxic and extremely dangerous at one end to totally benign at the

Table 11.3 Types of Contaminated Lands

Type	Description
Superfund National Priorities List Sites	Congress established the Superfund Program in 1980 to clean up abandoned hazardous waste sites throughout the United States. The most seriously contaminated sites are on the National Priorities List (NPL). As of October 2005, there were 1,237 sites on the NPL.
RCRA Corrective Action Sites	EPA and authorized states have identified 1,714 hazardous waste management facilities that are the most seriously contaminated and may pose significant threats to humans or the environment. Some RCRA Corrective Action sites are also identified by the Superfund Program as NPL sites.
Leaking Underground Storage Tanks	Petroleum and hazardous substances often are stored in underground storage tanks (USTs). EPA regulates many categories of UST systems, including those at gas stations, convenience stores, and bus depots. USTs that have failed due to faulty materials, installation, operating procedures, or maintenance systems are categorized as leaking underground storage tanks (LUSTs). LUSTs can contaminate soil, ground water, and sometimes drinking water. Vapors from UST releases can lead to explosions and other hazardous situations if those vapors migrate to a confined area such as a basement. LUSTs are the most common source of groundwater contamination, and petroleum is the most common groundwater contaminant. As of September 2005, there were more than 650,00 active (in use) underground storage tanks. Since 1984, 1.6 million underground storage tanks have been closed, and almost half a million cleanups have been initiated.
Accidental Spill Sites	Each year, thousands of oil and chemical spills occur on land and in water. Oil and gas materials that have spilled include drilling fluids, processed waters, and other wastes associated with the exploration, development, and production of crude oil or natural gas. Accurate national spill data are not available.
Land Contaminated with Radioactive and Other Hazardous Materials	Approximately 0.54 million acres of land spanning 129 sites in over 30 states are contaminated with radioactive and other hazardous materials as a result of activities associated with nuclear weapons production and research. Although DOE is the landlord at most of these sites, other parties, including other federal agencies, private parties, and one public university, also have legal responsibilities over these lands.
Brownfields	Brownfields are real property, the expansion, redevelopment, or reuse of which may be complicated by the presence or potential presence of a hazardous substance, pollutant, or contaminant. Brownfields are often found in

(continued)

Table 11.3 *(continued)*

Type	Description
	and around economically depressed neighborhoods. As Brownfields are cleaned and redeveloped, surrounding communities benefit from a reduction of health and environmental risks, more functional space, and improved economic conditions. A complete inventory of Brownfields does not exist. According to the General Accounting Office (1987), there are approximately 450,000 Brownfields nationwide. The EPA's national Brownfield tracking system includes a large volume of data on Brownfields across the nation, but does not track all of them. EPA's Brownfield Assessment Pilot Program includes data collected from over 400 pilot communities.
Some Military Bases	Some (exact number or percentage unknown) military bases are contaminated as a result of a variety of activities. A national assessment of land contaminated at military bases has not been conducted. However, under the Base Realignment and Closure (BRAC) laws, closed military bases undergo site investigation processes to determine extent of possible contamination and the need for site cleanup. Currently, 204 military installations that have been closed or realigned are undergoing environmental cleanup. These installations collectively occupy over 400,000 acres, though not all of this land is contaminated. Thirty-six of these installations are on the Superfund NPL list, and, of these, 32 are being cleaned up under the Fast Track program to make them available for other uses as quickly as possible.
Waste Management Sites that were Poorly Designed or Poorly Managed	Prior to the 1970s, untreated waste was typically placed in open pits or directly onto the land. Some of these early waste management sites are still contaminated. In other cases, improper management of facilities (that were typically used for other purposes such as manufacturing) resulted in site contamination. Federal and state cleanup efforts are now addressing those early land disposal units and poorly managed sites that are still contaminated.
Illegal Dumping Sites	Also known as "open dumping" or "midnight dumping," illegal dumping of such materials as construction waste, abandoned automobiles, appliances, household waste, and medical waste raises concerns for safety, property values, and quality of life. People tend to dump illegally because legal dumping costs money and/or is inconvenient. While a majority of illegally dumped waste is not hazardous, some of it is, creating contaminated lands.
Abandoned Mine Lands	Abandoned mine lands are sites that have historically been mined and have not been properly cleaned up. These aban-

doned or inactive mine sites may include disturbances or features ranging from exploration holes and trenches to full blown, large-scale mine openings, pits, waste dumps, and processing facilities. The Department of the Interior's (DOI) Bureau of Land Management (BLM) is presently aware of approximately 10,200 abandoned hardrock mines located within the roughly 264 million acres under its jurisdiction. Various government and private organizations have made estimates over the years about the total number of abandoned and inactive mines in the United States. Those estimates range from about 80,000 to hundreds of thousands of small to medium-sized sites. The BLM is attempting to identify, prioritize, and take appropriate actions on those historic mine sites that pose safety risks to the public or present serious threats to the environment.

Source: U.S. EPA, *EPA's Draft Report on the Environment 2003* (Washington, DC: EPA):B-4 to B-6.

other. Part of what RCRA had to do was break all these substances into two large categories: "hazardous wastes" and everything else. The act defines **hazardous waste** as: "a solid waste, or combination of solid wastes, which because of its quantity, concentration, or physical, chemical or infectious characteristics, may... pose a substantial present or potential hazard to human health or the environment when improperly treated, stored, transported, or disposed of, or otherwise managed...." The law also specifically excluded household waste from the definition.

RCRA gave EPA the job of specifying in more detail what wastes are to be considered hazardous. It had two ways of doing this: by listing specific materials known to be hazardous, and by establishing a set of criteria that can be used to decide if a substance is or is not hazardous. When the EPA began working on this, it identified nine possible criteria, but later narrowed this to just four: ignitability, corrosivity, reactivity, and toxicity.

Manifest System. While very large quantities of hazardous wastes are collectively disposed of in the United States each year, much of it occurs in small batches of relatively small quantities. The routes these wastes take from producers to users to transporters and finally to disposal sites can be very circuitous. Policy makers felt the strong need for a system that would make this complicated network more visible, so that it could be monitored and managed more effectively. This gave rise to the RCRA manifest system.

The **manifest system** requires essentially that as quantities of hazardous waste travel, they be accompanied by a form identifying the quantity, origin, and destination of the material. A transporter cannot accept waste without the accompanying manifest form. A storage facility cannot accept the waste without the same accompanying form. Originally the EPA was going to allow the states to develop their own manifest systems, but subsequently decided to develop a national system.

The manifest system applies only to hazardous waste that leaves the point where it is produced, which means that a very substantial proportion of all hazardous waste in the country does not fall under the system. One of the main reasons for creating the manifest system was to curb illegal dumping. Theoretically, if some quantity of hazardous waste unaccountably exits from the system, it should be traceable by virtue of a missing manifest. But it may be just as hard to find this as it is to find the missing waste itself, so the incentives for illegal dumping may not have been weakened very much through the manifest system.

Standards for the Handlers of Hazardous Waste. RCRA required EPA to establish performance standards for the activities of hazardous waste handlers, including record keeping, reporting, monitoring, and inspection; treatment, storage, and disposal methods; and location, design, and construction of hazardous waste facilities. Performance standards are the sets of operating conditions that all handlers are required to follow. A performance standard on location, for example, might require that hazardous waste disposal sites not be located near wetlands. A standard for record keeping might require that the operator of a disposal site maintain specific types of data about wastes accepted for disposal, and so on.

Permit System. The entire RCRA program is implemented with a permit program. Handlers of hazardous waste must obtain the necessary permits from the EPA or state authorities to be able to operate legally. This permit system is immensely complicated, owing to the vast number of different materials that are involved and the great multiplicity of methods for their handling and disposal.

Legacy Dumps and Superfund

RCRA deals primarily with active hazardous waste disposal sites. To deal with sites that were active in the past, but may be no longer, Congress in 1980 enacted the Comprehensive Environmental Response, Compensation, and Liability Act (CERCLA), known as **Superfund**. The passage of CERCLA is another case in which a statute was enacted largely in response to a single event that captured the public interest as well as the attention of Congress. In this case it was the Love Canal incident.

Love Canal. In the late nineteenth century in the city of Niagara Falls in western New York, an entrepreneur, William T. Love, dug a canal to convey water around the famous falls and generate electricity. His project was never completed, but many years later, in the 1940s, the canal excavation was used by the Hooker Chemical Company, quite legally at the time, to dispose of a large quantity of waste chemicals. When it was full, a shallow clay covering was placed over the top of the canal. Hooker then sold the land to the Niagara Falls School Board for a token fee, advising that although the site was suitable for a school or parking lot, any excavation of the area should be avoided.

Over the next decade or so, development encroached onto the site. The city first built an elementary school on the site in 1955. Roads followed, and then houses were built, so that by the early 1970s it had become a working-class neighborhood of modest houses whose backyards abutted an elongated empty lot, the old chemical dump.

Over the next eight years or so, residents began complaining of chemical seepage through basement walls, floors, and sump holes. Chemicals also showed up in sewers, rain puddles, and drainage ditches. Remnants of old disposal drums surfaced as holes began to open up in the field that was the former site of the canal. In early 1978 New York state officials and the EPA conducted air, soil, and water tests, which revealed the presence of a variety of chemicals throughout the environment. The resulting controversy involved residents; city, state, and federal officials; the governor of New York; President Jimmy Carter; scientists; the Hooker Company; the press; and others.[18]

What was difficult was trying to figure out what the health effects were, what should be done about it, and who was going to foot the bill for the remedies. Along the way there were dueling scientific studies, a rising crescendo of attention from the local and national press, increasingly concerned and militant homeowners who fought for public attention and redress, and embattled public agencies (especially the New York environmental and health agencies and the U.S. EPA) trying to effect some sort of resolution.

Ultimately, more than a thousand families were moved out of the Love Canal area, most at public expense. The elementary school was torn down. Major remediation efforts have been made at the site, and public funds were made available for purchasing and rehabilitating many of the boarded-up homes. During the 1990s families slowly moved back into the area, so it is once again a populous working-class area, but with a large fenced-off area where the old dump used to be.

There is ongoing controversy over the short- and long-term health effects among the residents of Love Canal. Many residents were convinced that they had suffered a variety of medical problems from exposure to the chemicals, from skin rashes to lethal cancers. Some studies by scientists seemed to confirm damage; for example, one controversial study seemed to indicate chromosome damage among residents of the area. But other respectable studies have shown no long-term impacts.

But although the health effects have been difficult to document, the political fallout from Love Canal was clear. It was a galvanizing event that moved an issue onto the front burner and created an opportunity for action. The EPA had been asking Congress for some time to enact new laws covering hazardous waste site cleanups. RCRA had been passed in 1976, but it was apparent that it was not suited to address problems such as Love Canal.

Love Canal created the conditions for getting a new law passed. Another impetus was that Jimmy Carter, a president who had pressed for more active environmental policy in the federal government, had been defeated in the presidential election of 1980 by Ronald Reagan, a conservative with basically an antiregulation stance. This heightened the incentive for proponents of congressional action to push through the necessary compromises. The result was the Comprehensive Environmental Response, Compensation and Liability Act (CERCLA) of 1980, commonly called Superfund.

Public concern clearly focused on the potential health impacts arising from exposure to the substances in these landfills. Exposure might be direct, as it was in Love Canal. Or it might come about through contamination of ground or surface waters, as happened in the well-known case in Woburn, Massachusetts.[19] The sites could also lead to contaminated air. Public fears were then, and still are, fueled by all that is unknown and hidden from view about the problem: where the dump sites are located, whether the hazardous wastes are actually migrating and causing contamination over a wider area, and the exact health threats posed by the various substances dumped in the sites. Since the problem first achieved prominence in the policy agenda in the 1970s, surveys continue to indicate that it ranks near the top in terms of public concern.

CERCLA.   The primary objective of CERCLA is to identify and clean up sites that have been contaminated by past hazardous waste disposal. It contains the following provisions:

1. A procedure for identifying sites where there is substantial risk of damage resulting from past hazardous waste disposal.

2. A procedure for remediating Superfund sites, either by the EPA or by firms that used the sites.

3. A financial fund to support EPA-led cleanup activities.

4. A liability system whereby past dumpers may be held liable for the costs of cleaning up the sites.

CERCLA has had a controversial history. Early in its life the federal courts ruled that Congress had intended a very aggressive liability policy toward those who had put chemicals in these sites. They could be held to a standard of **strict, joint, and several liability.** This meant that dumpers could be held liable even though their actions were legal at the time, and also that any single user of a site could be held liable for full cleanup costs regardless of the proportionate amount of material it had put in the site. For the environmental community this provision has been a positive one because it has put the initiative on the polluters to identify one another and pay the costs of the cleanup. For the regulated community it was regarded as too punitive, leading to open-ended liability and high costs. The result was that during the early years of Superfund, an enormous amount of litigation took place as regulators sought to get sites cleaned up and firms tried to reduce their financial liabilities.

Over time CERCLA has been amended and modified in an effort to make it more effective. In the Superfund Amendments and Reauthorization Act of 1986 (SARA), the fund was increased in size and changes were made to protect landowners who truly were not responsible for the presence of toxic materials. Many state "Superfund" programs have been developed to address sites that federal Superfund did not, and to introduce innovations into the process. One such program is prospective purchase agreements (PPAs), whereby private parties buying older industrial sites can be shielded from liability in return for private investment in cleanup and redevelopment. In 2002 Congress passed amendments to CERCLA called the Small Business Liability Relief and Brownfields Revitalization Act. This provided additional liability relief for some businesses, and codified the Brownfields program that the EPA had developed. In this program firms are given special incentives to redevelop sites that might have been contaminated in the past, the idea being to make these recycled sites more attractive for commercial and industrial development and reduce the pressure to develop pristine sites farther out.

Natural Resource Damages

CERCLA is best known for its goal of cleaning up hazardous waste sites. There is another important part of this statute. Section 107 of the law makes parties liable for ". . . damages for injury to, destruction of, or loss of natural resources, including the reasonable costs of assessing such injury . . ." due to the release of hazardous substances. The natural resources in question are resources owned by a governmental, or quasi-governmental, agency. The principle is that these resources are held by public agencies as trustees for the general citizenry, and in the event of **natural resource damages** due to a hazardous waste release, the perpetrators of the release may be held liable. This program is administered not by the EPA, but by the Department of the Interior (DOI). This agency has thus had the task of refining the meanings of the many ambiguous words and phrases in the law, and then pursuing those whose actions have caused damages. As in the other parts of CERCLA, the courts have been critical in deciding how the law may be implemented.

Summary

We live in a chemical society: Chemicals have become part of virtually every aspect of the modern industrial economy. There are major challenges in managing chemicals effectively and in the public interest. We discussed chemicals under three headings. The first was the use of chemicals in production and consumption. The major laws discussed were the Federal Insecticide, Fungicide, and Rodenticide Act (FIFRA), and the Toxic Substance Control Act (TSCA). FIFRA works through a registration system; all pesticides in use must be registered with the EPA. TSCA works through a pre-manufacturing notice system. Both laws make distinctions between existing and new chemicals, and address the latter more aggressively than the former. The second category was toxic emissions. Both the Clean Water Act and the Clean Air Act have sections dealing with toxic emissions. For the most part toxic emissions are controlled through technology-based effluent standards; in air the standard is maximum achievable control technology, and with water the standard is best available technology. We discussed the important Toxics Release Inventory, which gives interested citizens information about toxics stored or released in their communities. The third category was the disposal of hazardous wastes, essentially chemical leftovers. The two major laws here are the Resource Conservation and Recovery Act (RCRA) and the Comprehensive Environmental Response, Compensation, and Liability Act (CERCLA), also known as Superfund. RCRA deals with a contemporaneous hazardous waste, essentially by setting standards for those who handle or dispose of it, while CERCLA deals with legacy hazardous waste sites, largely by establishing a mechanism for identifying and cleaning up these sites.

Key Terms

balancing	permissible exposure levels
best available technology (BAT)	pesticide registration
hazardous waste	premanufacturing notice
manifest system	reasonable risk
maximum achievable control technology (MACT)	strict, joint, and several liability
	Superfund
natural resource damages	Toxic Release Inventory (TRI)

Questions for Further Discussion

1. What would the implications be for TSCA if companies applying for new chemical approval had to show, beyond a reasonable doubt, that the chemical was safe?

2. Discuss some of the major conceptual difficulties associated with doing a benefit-cost analysis of a regulation restricting the use of a particular chemical.

3. What is the "how clean is clean" debate? How might the debate be resolved?

4. What are the different policy approaches that could be taken to reduce the amount of hazardous waste that has to be disposed of?

Web Sites

The EPA offers many sites dealing with different aspects of the toxics problem, for example:

FIFRA

www.epa.gov/pesticides/about/index.htm

TSCA

www.epa.gov/oppt/newchems/tscasite.htm

NOAA has a site featuring issues related to toxic chemicals in coastal environments:

http://response.restoration.noaa.gov/cpr/cpr.html

A number of sites are available to help track TRI releases:
http://uspirg.org/uspirg.asp?id2=24464
http://www.scorecard.org/env-releases/us-map.tcl
www.epa.gov/tri

See also the sites of the:

Agency for Toxic Substances and Disease Registry
www.atsdr.cdc.gov/toxfaq.html

Pesticide Action Network
www.panna.org and www.pan-international.org

Additional Readings

Hird, John A., *Superfund: The Political Economy of Environmental Risk* (Baltimore: Johns Hopkins Press, 1994).

Lerner, Steve, *Diamond: A Struggle for Environmental Justice in Louisiana's Chemical Corridor* (Cambridge, MA: MIT Press, March 2005).

Linsky, Martin, ed., *Impact: How the Press Affects Federal Policymaking* (New York: Norton, 1986).

Mazur, A. C., *A Hazardous Inquiry: The Rashomon Effect at Love Canal* (Cambridge, MA: Harvard University Press, 1998).

Northeast States for Coordinated Air Use Management, *Mercury Emissions from Coal-Fired Power Plants: The Case for Regulatory Action* (Boston: NESCAUM, 2003).

Reisch, M., *Superfund and the Brownfields Issue*, Report 97-731 ENR, Congressional Research Service (January 2001).

Revesz, R. L., and R. B. Stewart, eds., *Analyzing Superfund: Economics, Science and Law* (Washington, DC: Resources for the Future, 1995).

Sigman, H., "The Pace of Progress at Superfund Sites: Policy Goals and Interest Group Influence," *Journal of Law and Economics* (April 2001).

U.S. Environmental Protection Agency, Superfund Emergency Response Program, *National Priorities List Site Totals by Status and Milestone* (February 6, 2003). http://epa.gov/superfund/sites/query/queryhtm/npltotal.htm.

U.S. General Accounting Office, *Hazardous and Nonhazardous Wastes: Demographics of People Living Near Waste Facilities*, GAO/RCED-95-84 (Washington, DC, 1995).

U.S. General Accounting Office, *Long-Term Coordinated Strategy Needed to Measure Exposures to Humans*, GAO/HEHS-00-80 (May 2000).

U.S. General Accounting Office, *Toxic Substances Control Act: EPA's Limited Progress in Regulating Toxic Chemicals*, GAO/T-RCED-94-212 (May 17, 1994).

Notes

[1] The book was *Silent Spring*, by Rachel Carson, and the chemical was DDT.

[2] U.S. EPA, *Pesticide Industry Sales and Usage, 1989 and 1999 Market Estimates*, Office of Pesticide Programs, August 2002 (www.epa.gov/oppbead1/pestsales/).

[3] The Insecticide Act of 1910.

[4] FIFRA, Section 136A, C5, as summarized in Nancy K. Kubasek and Gary S. Silverman, *Environmental Law*, 3rd ed. (Upper Saddle River, NJ: Prentice Hall, 2000):220.

[5] The graph in figure 11.1 shows what economists call "marginal" changes, i.e., the increase in total damages (costs) when pesticide use changes by a small amount, and the decrease in total benefits from this change. It is the trade-off between these two that represents the balancing problem. We will discuss this at greater length in chapter 16.

[6] The administration of FIFRA is largely the responsibility of the Office of Pesticide Programs within the EPA.

[7] David Roe and others, *Toxic Ignorance: The Continuing Absence of Basic Health Testing for Top-Selling Chemicals in the United States* (Environmental Defense Fund, 1997); National Research Council, *Toxicity Testing* (Washington, DC: National Academy Press, 1984).

[8] The Occupational Safety and Health Administration was established in the late 1960s with a mandate to improve the safety of the American workplace. During the 1980s and 1990s its annual budget averaged around $300 million, which it used for such tasks as workplace inspections, data collection and analysis, regulatory analysis, and accident inquiries. It is located in the U.S. Department of Labor. It is backstopped by the National Institute for Occupational Safety and Health (NIOSH), which is responsible for research underlying the establishment of workplace regulations.

[9] Previously there were several standards: for some chemicals it was "no unreasonable risk of adverse effects"; for carcinogenic chemicals it was outright prohibition.

[10] An additional wrinkle here is that to set the MACT floor, EPA must consider only the question of whether this is sufficiently protective of human health; if they move to set MACT lower than this they must proceed with a full benefit-cost analysis of the tighter standard. Another wrinkle is that the 1990 CAA contains what is called a "MACT hammer" provision. A hammer clause in a law is a default provision. In this case it says that if the EPA fails to issue a MACT standard within 18 months of the statutory deadline, sources must apply to their state authorities for a MACT determination.

[11] U.S. Environmental Protection Agency, *National Pollution Discharge Elimination System, NPDES Glossary,* http://cfpub1.epa.gov/npdes/glossary.cfm?program_id=0.

[12] NPDES, *Permit Writers Handbook.*

[13] EPCRA is actually Title III of SARA, the Superfund Amendments and Reauthorization Act of 1986, which we will discuss later in this chapter.

[14] At the end of the chapter some Web sites are listed.

[15] Solid waste is defined as "any garbage, refuse, sludge from a waste treatment plant, water supply treatment plant, or air pollution control facility and other discarded material, including solid, liquid, semisolid, or contained gaseous material resulting from industrial, commercial, mining, and agricultural operations, and from community activities" (http://www4.law.cornell.edu/uscode/unframed/42/6903.html).

[16] The injection well program, called the Underground Injection Control Program, is actually authorized under the Safe Drinking Water Act of 1974.

[17] See U.S. General Accounting Office, *Deep Injection Wells,* July 2003, www.gao.gov/atext/d03761.txt.

[18] For a good discussion of these events, see Judith A. Layzer, *The Environmental Case, Translating Values into Policy* (Washington, DC: Congressional Quarterly Press, 2002):52–77.

[19] The Woburn case of groundwater contamination is the subject of the book *A Civil Action,* and a film by the same name.

12

Nonhazardous Solid Waste

It is probably true that the average person gives relatively little thought each day to his or her environmental footprint. When we turn on the faucet, we expect to have clean water; when we flush the toilet, we don't worry much about what's happening to our wastes; when we drive down the highway, we usually don't mentally click off the pounds of various pollutants coming out of our tailpipes. But solid waste may be different. Each day the average American generates about 4.5 pounds of solid waste, of which most is nonhazardous waste. One of the main ways environmentalism has become more manifest in the lives of most people is in the daily actions needed to dispose of this part of their waste stream.

Solid waste is defined by RCRA as "any garbage, refuse, sludge from a waste treatment plant, water supply treatment plant, or air pollution control facility and other discarded material, including solid, liquid, semisolid, or contained gaseous material resulting from industrial, commercial, mining, and agricultural operations, and from community activities."[1] This is a broad definition, covering almost everything except uncontained gases. We talked in the previous chapter about the hazardous part of this waste stream. In this chapter we will discuss that part of the nonhazardous solid-waste stream that is called **municipal solid waste (MSW)**, which is trash, garbage, or other types of nonhazardous refuse generated by industries, commercial and institutional facilities, and households. It should be noted that the vast amount of nonhazardous solid waste from industry is not regarded as MSW; it consists primarily of very large amounts of wastewater that are held on-site in various types of impoundments. According to the EPA definition, MSW also does not include construction and demolition debris (much of which ends up in landfills), auto bodies, and sludge from wastewater treatment facilities. Nor does it include mining waste and agricultural waste (see table 12.1).

Of the total amount of MSW generated in the United States, about 60 percent comes from households and the rest from business and institutional sources. Figure 12.1 shows the trend over the last 40 years in amounts of MSW generated, total and per capita. Both trends are strongly up. Increased amounts of household waste seem to have been, so far, directly related to higher material standards of living. As shown in figure 12.1, the 4.5 pounds per person generated in 2003 represents about a 60 percent increase over 1960.[2] Note that over the last decade the per capita quantity of MSW has stayed about constant, although the total has increased because of population growth.

MSW—The System

MSW consists of a vast array of diverse material: discarded goods, packaging material, great quantities of waste paper, and so on. With this type of waste, the shift from a manufacturing to a more service-oriented economy does not have the same pollution-reduction potential as it does for industrial chemicals (at least so far), because of the material needs of a modern consumer economy. Nor is it easy to develop programs for decreasing these material flows. While production of the materials that eventually end up as MSW may or may not be centralized, the ultimate flows are highly dispersed throughout the population. Thus, to dematerialize the consumer economy to any great extent it is necessary to develop programs that work in this decentralized setting. This is one of the main reasons that MSW policies and regulations have for the most part been left to state and local authorities.

Table 12.1   Types of Nonhazardous Waste

Type	Description
Municipal Solid Waste	Municipal Solid Waste (MSW) is the waste discarded by households, hotels/motels, and commercial, institutional, and industrial sources. MSW typically consists of everyday items such as product packaging, grass clippings, furniture, clothing, bottles, food scraps, newspapers, appliances, paint, and batteries. It does not include wastewater. In 2003, 236 million tons of MSW were generated.[a]
Extraction Wastes	Extraction activities such as mining and mineral processing are large contributors to the total amount of waste generated and land contaminated in the U.S. EPA estimates that 5 billion tons of mining wastes are generated each year.

Industrial Nonhazardous Waste	Industrial nonhazardous waste is process waste associated with electric power generation and manufacturing of materials such as pulp and paper, iron and steel, glass, and concrete. This waste usually is not classified as either municipal waste or RCRA hazardous waste by federal or state laws. State, tribal, and some local governments have regulatory programs to manage industrial waste. EPA estimates that each year over 7.6 billion tons of industrial nonhazardous wastes are generated in the U.S.
Agricultural Waste	Agricultural solid waste is waste generated by the rearing of animals and the production and harvest of crops or trees. Animal waste, a large component of agricultural waste, includes waste from livestock, dairy, milk, and other animal-related agricultural and farming practices. Some of this waste is generated at sites called Confined Animal Feeding Operations (CAFOs). The waste associated with CAFOs results from congregating animals, feed, manure, dead animals, and production operations on a small land area. Animal waste and wastewater can enter water bodies from spills or breaks of waste storage structures (due to accidents or excessive rain), and nonagricultural application of manure to cropland. National estimates are not available.
Construction and Demolition Waste	Construction and demolition debris is waste generated during construction, renovation, and demolition projects. This type of waste generally consists of materials such as wood, concrete, steel, brick, and gypsum. (The MSW data in this report do not include construction and demolition debris, even though sometimes construction and demolition debris are considered MSW.) National estimates are not available.
Medical Waste	Medical waste is any solid waste generated during the diagnosis, treatment, or immunization of human beings or animals, in research, production, or testing. National estimates are not available.
Oil and Gas Waste	Oil and gas production wastes are the drilling fluids, process waters, and other wastes associated with the exploration, development, and production of crude oil or natural gas that are conditionally exempted from regulation as hazardous wastes. National estimates are not available.
Sludge	Sludge is the solid, semisolid, or liquid waste generated by municipal, commercial, or industrial wastewater treatment facilities. National estimates are not available.

[a]In addition, household hazardous waste is often handled as municipal solid waste.

Source: U.S. Environmental Protection Agency, *Draft Report on the Environment* (Washington, DC: EPA, 2003): B2–B3 (www.epa.gov/indicators).

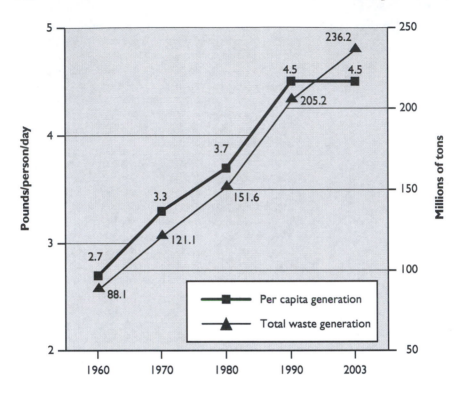

Source: U.S. EPA, *Basic Facts: Municipal Solid Waste* (www.epa.gov/epaoswer/non-hw/muncpl/facts.htm).

Figure 12.1   Trends in MSW Generation, 1960–2003

To get a general understanding of the flows involved consider the diagram in figure 12.2. It shows an extremely simple schematic of material flows
through an economy. The "economy" in this case is divided into just two
types of entities, producers and consumers. All virgin materials inputs are
assumed to flow from nature into the production sector. From this sector
there are two outflows of MSW: one represented by the materials content of
goods sold to consumers, the other as waste products (we are excluding process wastes here, just the flow of material included in what we know as
municipal solid waste). Of course there is a great deal of activity among
firms, much of which involves the transfer of materials that will end up as
MSW (e.g., packaging material used to ship products among firms). In the
interest of keeping the diagram simple, however, we have not included these
particular linkages.

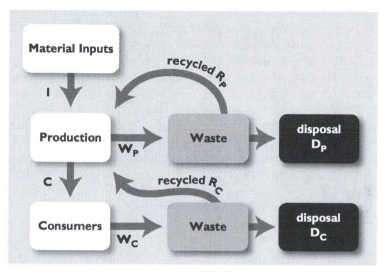

Figure 12.2   Schematic Showing MSW Flows

In the long run there must be a balance between what comes in and what goes out; that is, it must be the case that

$$I = D_p + D_c$$

It is also true that, in the production sector, there must be a similar balance:

$$\underbrace{C + W_p}_{\substack{\text{MSW flowing} \\ \text{out of the pro-} \\ \text{duction sector}}} = \underbrace{I + R_p + R_c}_{\substack{\text{MSW materials} \\ \text{flowing into the} \\ \text{production sector}}}$$

Both of these expressions, of course, involve time lags; many consumer products, for example, are durable to a certain extent, so the time between inputs and disposal may be quite long. In addition, if products are redesigned to be longer lasting, there will be a reduced requirement for raw materials for a given quantity of consumer goods, meaning less MSW eventually to have to deal with.

If we combine the two expressions above, we get

$$D_p + D_c = \underbrace{\underbrace{C + W_p}_{\substack{\text{"Source} \\ \text{Reduction"}}} - \left(R_p + R_c\right)}_{\text{"Waste Reduction"}}$$

The reduction of material coming from the production sector, either as waste (W_p) or incorporated in products (C), is known as **source reduction**.

For any given amount of material that is recycled, an increase in source reduction will reduce the quantities of material coming in, and therefore the quantity of materials that must ultimately be disposed of. Source reduction happens by reducing the amount of MSW generated by the producing sector of the economy (for example, less waste paper produced by commercial establishments), or by reducing the materials content of their outputs (for example, producing food products in a way that uses less packaging).

Source reduction plus recycling ($R_p + R_c$) is often termed **waste reduction**. Recycling essentially means reaching into the waste stream, either post-producer or post-consumer, and extracting materials to be returned as inputs into the system. Clearly, the greater the quantity of material recycled, the lesser the quantity to be buried or incinerated, other factors being equal.

Recycling is, in fact, a complicated phenomenon, involving an array of technical processes and exchange procedures. At one end are tag sales, where consumer products that would otherwise be disposed of are sold directly from one consumer to another.[3] At the other end are processes such as the extremely sophisticated international market in old newspapers, involving collectors, transporters, brokers, and complex chemical procedures by which it is rendered into usable newsprint.

Critical to recycling is the technology used to handle the MSW waste stream. The great flow of people into the suburbs during the last half of the twentieth century prompted the development of large bulk-trash pickup trucks that collected and mixed together all the items in the trash stream. Once everything is commingled in this way, it becomes very costly to separate out individual waste forms (glass bottles, for example) that might then be recycled. That, together with the relatively low prices of virgin materials, contributed to the very low recycling rates of the 1950s and 1960s. In recent years new technologies have been developed for separating trash, and a host of community recycling programs have enlisted consumers themselves to separate certain items to facilitate easier recycling.

Policies for Reducing MSW

The national Resource Conservation and Recovery Act (RCRA) gives the EPA oversight of some aspects of the process, particularly in setting standards for MSW landfills, which are less stringent than for hazardous waste landfills. And federal courts have decided important MSW cases, one of which had to do with whether states could legally block MSW imports originating in other states (they cannot). But most of the initiative has been left to states and local communities. To some extent this seems appropriate, because most, though not all, potential pollution problems traceable to MSW disposal are local in character. On the other hand, some aspects of the MSW problem are decidedly national in scope. One of the main components of the MSW stream, for example, is packaging material, and packaging technology and practices are chosen by national firms serving national, and international, markets. It would be hard for communities, even for individual states, to adopt packaging policies and standards that differ substantially from those of other states. In addition, the MSW waste stream increasingly involves interstate shipments, which at some point may call for federal action.

We will next review some of the technical options and policy approaches to achieving waste reduction, and later deal with issues related to MSW disposal.

Source Reduction

The challenge of source reduction is how to effect changes in technology and practices so that a given quantity of useful goods and services can be produced using less materials. Attention also needs to be directed at the quality of the material: a change to more easily handled materials (in terms of recycling or disposal), even without a change in quantity, is a positive step.

Some technical examples of source reduction are the following:

1. Designing products or packaging to reduce the quantity or the toxicity of the materials used, or to make them easier to reuse.

2. Reusing existing products or packaging; for example, refillable bottles, reusable pallets, and reconditioned barrels and drums.

3. Lengthening the lives of products such as tires, so fewer need to be produced and therefore disposed of.

4. Using packaging that reduces the amount of damage or spoilage to the product.

5. Managing nonproduct organic wastes (e.g., food scraps, yard trimmings) through on-site composting or other alternatives to disposal (e.g., leaving grass clippings on the lawn).

Policy approaches to source reduction can be categorized along the same lines as other types of environmental policy: command-and-control, incentive-based, and information-based/voluntary. Command-and-control policies work through regulatory specifications aimed at producers. A law specifying some maximum materials content for a product would be an example. A law requiring that consumers be offered a choice of buying in bulk, if it were to be passed, would also be an example.

One way to provide an incentive to producers to reduce packaging materials is to incorporate the costs of disposal in the total packaging costs to producers. For example, governments could tax packaging material by an amount equal to its disposal costs. Another approach is to make producers responsible for disposing of packaging material, in the form of producer take-back programs.

Producer Take-Back Programs.   In **take-back programs**, also known as **extended producer responsibility programs**, producers are required to accept back from consumers any packaging or product they may have sold or given them. The aim is to establish a clear return channel for consumers to use and to make the producers of the items responsible for disposing of them appropriately. By making producers responsible for waste handling, they will presumably have an incentive to think about reducing the waste potential of their products in their design and packaging.

Mandatory take-back programs have been started in many European countries. A classic example is the Green Dot plan undertaken in Germany. A number of products were designated for inclusion in the program. Producers, realizing that joint action would be far less costly, banded together to implement the program. They formed a separate company to handle the return of all the products. The company was supported by fees paid from producers of the various products. The products themselves were designated by a green dot, which told consumers that they could be returned to the special bins provided by the waste-handling company.

To date, most producer take-back programs in the United States have been voluntary. A number of companies have set up take-back programs, usually, but not always, limited to products sold by that company. Computer companies have moved in this direction. Ford and Saturn have bumper take-back programs. Kodak has a program for single-use cameras. Firms in the carpet industry have established an industry-wide take-back system. Some communities are trying to establish voluntary programs whereby goods bought from certain retailers can be taken back to participating take-back retailers.[4]

Some states are now moving in the direction of mandated take-back programs, especially for computers. Computer take-back legislation has been introduced in at least ten states, including California, Massachusetts, and Minnesota. A mandatory take-back program for rechargeable batteries has been started in Florida. Maine started a mandatory take-back program for mercury switches in cars.

The essential problem with take-back programs is that they create separate return channels for a designated set of products and packaging, basically duplicating the standard system for handling MSW. Under some circumstances, separate return channels may be established fairly efficiently. If everybody buys tires at specialized tire stores, it is relatively straightforward to make these stores responsible for accepting the used tires and returning them to manufacturers, using essentially the same distribution system that is in place for handling new tires, but in the opposite direction. But with products for which a new and specialized system has to be set up to implement a take-back program, costs are likely to be substantial. The OECD estimates, for example, that the disposal costs per ton of the Green Dot program were comparable to the costs of handling hazardous waste.[5]

Unit Pricing

Historically, communities have funded MSW collection systems out of general tax revenues. In this arrangement there is no relationship between the amount of MSW a household puts out on the curbside, and the amount of money it spends for disposal. In microeconomic terms, this amounts to households facing a zero price for MSW disposal. And any time the price of something is zero, people will use too much of it.

The essence of this problem has finally become apparent to many communities that are struggling with ever-increasing amounts of trash. The response has been to introduce **unit pricing**, a system that gives people an incentive to search for ways to reduce the amount of solid waste they produce. This is done by charging people for each unit (bag, pound, etc.) of trash they put on the curb, which naturally provides an incentive for families to reduce the number of bags of trash they set out. They can do this by recycling, by switching to products that have less waste, by putting food scraps in a compost pile, and so on. In general, unit pricing has led to substantial reductions in the total amount of trash in communities where it has been employed. Of course, no system is perfect. Increases in illegal dumping and difficulties with applying the plan to apartment buildings and other multiple-unit dwellings are problems that need to be addressed. Nevertheless, the new approach illustrates clearly the results that can be achieved when people are made responsible for (in this case, in economic terms) the solid waste they generate.[6]

Recycling

Studies show that unit pricing is more effective (leads to a larger reduction in trash collected) when it is accompanied by **recycling** programs. To analyze recycling, we can use our earlier notation to write the following expression for the production sector:

$$R_p + R_c + I = W_p + C$$

What this shows is that recycled MSW is an alternative to virgin materials to supply the material needs of production. The justification for recycling, in other words, is to lower the amount of virgin materials used, which must ultimately reduce by the same amount the quantities of materials requiring disposal.[7] The amount of MSW recycled in the United States has increased substantially over the last few decades. In 1960 the overall recycling rate was about 6 percent, while in 2004 it was about 30 percent (figure 12.3). This means that at the present time about 30 percent of the MSW waste stream (after source reduction) is diverted to recycling rather than going for disposal. Of course this is an aggregate number; it says nothing about the enormous variation in recycling rates among different components of the MSW system. Recycling varies by type of material, by production sector, and by location.

Recycling means reaching into the waste stream and diverting selected material back into the production process. In reality this normally involves a substantial series of steps: consumer or producer interception of material, sorting, transporting, some degree of reprocessing, and so on. In the early days of recycling programs public enthusiasm was expressed mostly at the front end of the process, the consumer sorting and material return that made the supply of recycles more abundant. Later, attention was also directed at the demand side, with steps taken to increase the use of recycled material in the production sector.

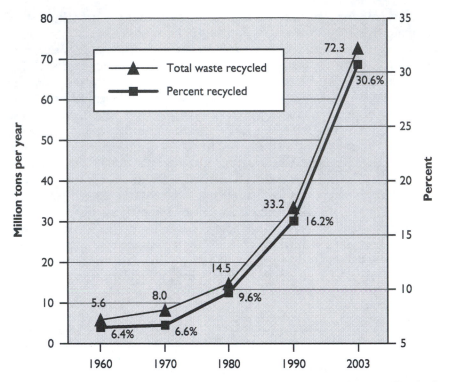

Source: U.S. EPA, *Basic Facts: Municipal Solid Waste* (www.epa.gov/epaoswer/non-hw/muncpl/facts.htm).

Figure 12.3 Waste Recycling Rates, 1960–2003

On the demand side there are different types of policies that might be pursued. One is to require public agencies to purchase materials with a minimum recycled content. An incentive policy would be to place a per-unit tax on virgin materials used in production; for example, a tax per ton of paper pulp coming directly from trees. This would alter the relative price of virgin and recycled materials in favor of the latter, and so lead to an increase in the recycling ratio. The ratio is equal to

$$(R_p + R_c)/(R_p + R_c + I)$$

As mentioned, however, most public recycling programs and regulations have been carried out at the local level, with policy action sometimes originating at the state level. So this works against the possibility of an overall national tax applied to virgin materials.

Community Recycling Programs. Perhaps the most direct attack on recycling has been the organization of community recycling programs, either voluntary or mandatory. Households are asked, or required, to separate certain recyclable materials (paper, glass, plastic, etc.) and put them out on the curb for pickup by a specialized collection crew. In 2001 there were 9,700 community curbside recycling collection programs reported in the United States.[8] In some cases consumers are asked to take the recyclables to a community collection point. MSW collection from small businesses is often included in these community programs. Trash from large businesses and institutions are normally handled through private contractors.

Community programs vary in terms of logistics, materials accepted, and financial incentives. In most of them consumers are asked to do a certain amount of presorting (separating aluminum, plastic, and paper, for example). In many communities special collection days have been established to separate household hazardous waste that would otherwise end up in an MSW landfill. Many communities have ventured into composting (yard scraps, food waste) as an extension of their recycling activities. Numerous states have enacted laws requiring, or encouraging, certain recycling targets by their communities.

In the enthusiasm to establish recycling programs in order to ease the strain on landfills, many communities initially overlooked the issue of whether there would be a market for the recycled material. Gradually, a market chain has developed for handling recycled material: sorters, handlers, brokers, reprocessors, and so on. In many cases public subsidies have been used to encourage the development of links in this chain. At present many communities earn some revenues through selling recycled material into the appropriate markets.

Deposit/Refund Programs.   Ten states have deposit/refund programs for containers.[9] California's system includes the refund, but involves no deposit. Such programs are targeted especially at carbonated drink containers, primarily beer and soft drinks. Deposit/refund is a combination tax/subsidy system. Consumers pay a small deposit charge on the containers at time of purchase; this money goes into a fund which is used to refund the tax when the containers are redeemed. The main argument for deposit/refund systems is to reduce the quantity of trash and roadside litter. It is also true that some states gain financially because not all the containers are redeemed; in other states, however, the unclaimed deposits stay in the hands of the industry.

Bottle bills have always been controversial; the beverage industry usually objects to the cost and hassle of operating redemption systems; the environmental community stresses their salutary impacts on litter and MSW reduction. In a number of states advocates are trying to extend current bottle-bill laws to include noncarbonated drink containers.

A continuing problem with most deposit/refund programs is that the deposit rate is established in law. This gives it a political sensitivity and makes it hard to change, and over time this can weaken the incentive effects of the program. Suppose a 5-cent deposit rate was established in 1980 and not changed since. From 1980 to 2004 the general price level has increased by a factor of about 2.3. Thus, the **real value** (market value adjusted for inflation) of the 5 cents in 1980 was only about 2 cents in 2004. Clearly this produces a much weaker incentive to redeem eligible containers under the program. This gives added importance to the need for periodic revisions and updating of these types of programs.

Managing the Waste Stream

After source reduction and recycling, there remains a quantity of MSW that must be managed in some way. These flows are the quantities represented by D_p and D_c in figure 12.2. These quantities are what is left over at the end of the process, and are clearly the result of all the decisions made back "up the line." It's also true, however, that how this final waste stream is handled will impact the incentives that influence these prior decisions. Suppose, for example, that the cost of disposing of MSW is getting higher over time (which it is). If this added cost were, for example, subsidized by local governments, it would have no strong direct influence on prior decisions; for example, decisions by manufacturers to reduce packaging materials. On the other hand, if rising costs are passed on to handlers, consumers, and producers, it will produce the appropriate incentive.

The two main technical means for handling $(D_p + D_c)$ are landfilling and incineration. In 2001, about 70 percent of total MSW generated ended up in the disposal stream; of this about 80 percent was landfilled and the rest incinerated.

MSW Landfills

The landfill situation in the United States has changed markedly in recent years. As figure 12.4 shows, there were almost 8,000 landfills in operation in 1988, but only about 1,850 in 2001, a 78 percent decrease in just 12 years. The likelihood is that this number will continue to decline, though probably at a decreasing rate.

MSW Landfill Standards. In earlier days when each town had its own town dump, standards for how these should be designed and operated were nonexistent. Not so today. The smaller number of landfills means that the average landfill has increased greatly in size. Virtually every state has established a strict set of standards governing MSW landfills and **transfer stations**. In addition the RCRA contains a number of standards applicable to such sites. These regulations cover all phases of the program: site selection and preparation, construction, operation, environmental monitoring, enforcement of landfill rules, and closure operations. Starting and operating an MSW landfill is now a complicated social, economic, and legal procedure, as exhibit 12.1 suggests.

The consolidation of landfills means much more MSW is being transported among states; generated in one state and transported to a landfill in another state. This has been accompanied by two seemingly inconsistent issues: some states seeking to ban the importation of MSW and other states trying to ban its exportation. States that have become host to new large land-

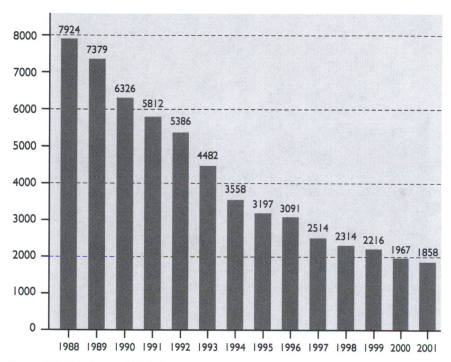

Source: U.S. EPA, *Municipal Solid Waste in the United States: 2001 Facts and Figures*, EPA 530-R-03-011 (2003):15.

Figure 12.4   Number of MSW Landfills in the United States

fills owned and operated by private companies may find themselves receiving substantial amounts of MSW from other states. Some have objected to this on the grounds that it makes their states environmental dumping grounds. The U.S. Supreme Court, however, has consistently ruled that individual states cannot exclude MSW imports from other states, because doing so would be in violation of the commerce clause of the U.S. Constitution (Article I, Section 8).

At the other end, some states have sought to restrict exports of their trash. Usually this occurs because the state, or some of its communities, has signed supply contracts with incinerators or recyclers. The latter, seeking to ensure a steady supply of input, often negotiates contracts specifying minimum quantities of MSW to be delivered to the facilities. Thus, if communities export their MSW it could threaten performance under these contracts. So many states have sought to enact what are called **flow-control** regulations, basically requiring communities to deliver their MSW to the local facilities that have contracted for the supply. In 1994 the Supreme Court ruled against flow control, saying it violated the commerce clause. But subsequent federal court cases have made it possible to develop programs that achieve

---

Exhibit 12.1
Typical State Permit Requirements for MSW Landfills

- a solid waste landfill plan approval
- a conditional-use zoning permit
- a highway department permit (for entrances on public roads and increased traffic)
- a construction permit (for landfill site preparation)
- a solid waste facilities permit
- a water discharge/water quality control permit
- an operation permit (for ongoing landfill operations)
- a mining permit for excavations
- building permits (to construct buildings on the landfill site)
- a fugitive dust permit
- an air emission permit
- a closure permit

Source: U.S. Environmental Protection Agency, *Decision Maker's Guide to Solid Waste Management*, EPA 530-R-95-023, Vol. II, Chap. 9 (1995):9–14.

---

some degree of flow control without violating legal standing. As a result, the majority of states now have flow-control programs in effect.[10]

Host Fees and Tipping Fees.   The other major trend in MSW landfills is privatization. Twenty years ago virtually all landfills were municipally owned. Today approximately a third of these are privately owned, and this is expected to increase as private entrepreneurs see opportunities to provide a service that will be in increasing demand. Growing privatization means that private companies must search out acceptable sites, suitable in terms of geology and hydrology, and acceptable to residents who live nearby. To gain acceptance by those living in the community, companies have made use of substantial **host fees**, payments made to the communities for the right to develop a landfill. Host fees normally involve direct payments to the towns, and often much more than this (see exhibit 12.2).

The other fee of importance at MSW landfills is **tipping fees**, charges levied, usually per ton of material, to those making use of the facilities. Table 12.2 shows recent experience on tipping fees in various parts of the United States. Tipping fees vary greatly from one part of the country to another—they are highest in the Northeast—and have increased substantially over the last twenty years (the national average increased about 300 percent from 1985 to 2002).

Exhibit 12.2
Host Fees at the Arbor Hills Landfill

The Arbor Hills landfill in Salem Township, Michigan, is operated by Browning Ferris Industries (BFI). It is a huge operation, accepting MSW not only from within the Township but also from throughout Michigan (10 percent of Michigan's trash ends up there) and from sources in Canada. To compensate people of Salem Township for accepting the landfill, BFI worked out the following agreement:

- Payment to the Township of 2.5 percent of all landfill revenues and 4 percent of all composting revenues. This amounts to an annual revenue of about $1.2 million for the Township.

- Revenue amounting to half the total BFI revenues generated from BFI sales of landfill gases and products.

- Free disposal of all Township MSW in the landfill, together with a BFI-provided drop-off site for recyclables and compostables.

- An agreement by BFI to keep its trucks (and the trucks of its other customers) from driving through the center of town.

- An agreement to control odor, dust, and litter from the landfill.

- An agreement to compensate Township residents for damages, such as groundwater contamination.

- A wider agreement with all the other towns of the county where the landfill is located, under which BFI will take all their MSW at a 15 percent discount on the normal tipping fee.

Source: Richard C. Porter, *The Economics of Waste* (Washington, DC: Resources for the Future, 2002):116–117.

Table 12.2   Average Landfill Tipping Fees, Selected Years ($ per ton)

Region		1985	1990	1995	2004
Northeast	CT, ME, MA, NH, NY, RI, VT	12.66	64.76	73.17	70.53
Mid-Atlantic	DE, MD, NJ, PA, VA, WV	16.99	40.75	45.68	46.29
South	AL, FL, GA, KY, MS, NC, SC, TN	3.24	16.92	28.50	30.97
Midwest	IL, IN, IA, MI, MN, MO, OH, WI	7.23	23.15	31.15	34.96
South Central	AZ, AR, LA, NM, OK, TX	7.24	12.05	20.30	24.06
West Central	CO, KS, MT, NE, ND, SD, UT, WY	5.36	11.06	23.29	24.13
West	AK, CA, HI, ID, NV, OR, WA	10.96	25.63	37.69	37.74
National		8.20	23.01	32.19	34.29

Source: National Solid Wastes Management Association, *NSWMA's 2005 Tipping Fee Survey* (Washington, DC, n.d.). Used with permission.

Higher tipping fees should send a signal back up the line to consumers, packagers, and producers to reduce the amounts of material that ultimately end up going to landfills. But this, of course, depends on how the system is structured, and thus whether the increased fees are being felt by decision makers. To the extent that municipalities pay tipping fees out of general revenues, of course, this price signal will be weakened so much that it will have little impact on decisions of consumers and producers.[11]

Some communities have sought to introduce **advance disposal fees (ADFs)** on material that will ultimately end up in the waste stream. Various ADFs have been put into effect around the United States, for drink containers, white goods (e.g., refrigerators), chemicals, computers, carpets, and other types of goods. These programs, sometimes called **extended financial responsibility**, have been adopted primarily to raise revenue, which can then be used, at least theoretically, to fund recycling and other disposal programs.

Incineration

About 15 percent of MSW in the United States was incinerated in 2001. Most of the facilities engaged in this activity are waste-to-energy operations, where MSW is burned and used to produce an energy product, normally steam or electricity. There is a small but growing number of operations that incinerate separated waste products such as used tires or wood scraps as a source of fuel for certain types of industrial boilers. All incinerators are subject to regulations on their emissions. Incinerating MSW results in a quantity of leftover ash that is about 25 percent by weight of the original fuel volume. This is normally landfilled. Incinerators, like landfills, have been the object of many community NIMBY (not in my backyard) fights.

Summary

There was a time when every town and city in the United States had its own town landfill (normally called the town dump) where residents disposed of their trash without giving it a second thought. Not so today. Demographic and economic growth have produced a great increase in the material trash that communities have to manage in some way. Thus, municipal solid waste (MSW) disposal has become a major problem, and the system has seen vast changes. There has been an important focus on waste reduction, consisting of both source reduction (reducing the amount of material used in products), and recycling. Programs include community recycling programs, producer take-back plans, and unit pricing. These appear to be having an impact, in that the amount of MSW per capita that needs to be disposed of has recently stopped increasing (see figure 12.1).

Disposal options consist of two tracks: landfilling and incineration. In the last 20 years there has been a great reduction in the number of landfills, with concomitant increase in their average size. There also has been a substantial evolution in the direction of privatization. One factor that will loom large in MSW management in future years is the costs of disposal, consisting of transportation costs and tipping fees at MSW landfills.

Key Terms

advance disposal fees (ADFs)
extended financial responsibility
extended producer responsibility
flow-control
host fees
municipal solid waste (MSW)
real value
recycling

solid waste
source reduction
take-back programs
tipping fees
transfer stations
unit pricing
waste reduction

Questions for Further Discussion

1. As a public policy target, how should a community determine the recycling rate it should try to reach?

2. The U.S. Supreme Court has ruled that MSW is a product like anything else, hence states may not restrict the interstate transport of this material. Do you think that this is a reasonable position?

3. "If a community can increase the proportion of MSW it recycles, it can reduce the amount that has to be disposed of in landfills and incinerators." Comment.

4. Suppose a ten-cent deposit fee was put into effect in 1975 and has never been changed. What is the real value of this fee today?

5. What is the relationship between the increasingly strict MSW landfill standards set by most states and the major consolidation in landfill sites over the last decade?

Web Sites

As with many other topics the EPA Web site has much useful information on handling MSW:

www.epa.gov/epaoswer/non-hw/muncpl

Since much of the policy initiative for MSW comes at the local level, there are a number of Web sites with this focus:

The Municipal Waste Management Association

www.usmayors.org/uscm/mwma/publicat.asp

Association of State and Territorial Solid Waste Management Officials

www.astswmo.org

Many environmental groups have sites containing useful information on MSW:

Soil and Water Conservation Society

www.swcs.org/

Zero Waste America
www.zerowasteamerica.org

National Recycling Coalition
www.nrc-recycle.org

Eco·cycle
www.ecocycle.org

In addition, there are private firms specializing in MSW:
Allied Waste Industries
http://investor.awin.com

Waste Management
www.wm.com

Additional Readings

Ackerman, F., *Why Do We Recycle? Markets, Values, and Policy* (Washington, DC: Island Press, 1997).

Bauer, S., and M. L. Miranda, *The Urban Performance of Unit Pricing: An Analysis of Variable Rates for Residential Garbage Collection in Urban Areas*, EPA Cooperative Agreement Report #CR822-927-010 (April 1996). http://www.epa.gov/epaoswer/non-hw/payt/pdf/upaperf1.pdf.

Curlee, T. R., S. M. Schexnayder, D. P. Vogt, A. K. Wolfe, M. P. Kelsay, and D. L. Feldman, *Waste-to-Energy in the United States: A Social and Economic Assessment* (Westport, CT: Quorum Books, 1994).

Jenkins, R. R., *The Economics of Solid Waste Reduction: The Impact of User Fees* (Cheltenham, UK and Northampton, MA: Edward Elgar, 1993).

Klein, Christine, "The Environmental Commerce Clause," *Harvard Environmental Law Review* 27, no. 1 (2003):1–70.

Porter, Richard C., *The Economics of Waste* (Washington, DC: Resources for the Future, 2002).

U.S. Environmental Protection Agency, *Municipal Solid Waste in the United States: 2001 Facts and Figures*, EPA 530-R-03-011 (Washington, DC: EPA, October 2003).

Notes

[1] See the text of RCRA at www4.law.cornell.edu/uscode/unframed/42/6903.html.

[2] Folks in less wealthy countries produce much less on a per capita basis. For example, per capita waste generation in India was about one pound in 1990. See Richard C. Porter, *The Economics of Waste* (Washington, DC: Resources for the Future, 2002):3.

[3] Of course, the tag sale has recently become substantially more sophisticated by virtue of the Internet and companies such as eBay.

[4] For example, see http://ottawa.ca/gc/takeitback.

[5] Organization for Economic Cooperation and Development, "Case Study on the German Packaging Ordinance" (Paris: OECD, 1998).

[6] See: U.S. Environmental Protection Agency, *Unit Pricing*, EPA/530-SW-91-005 (Washington, DC: EPA, February 1991).

[7] Recycling and source reduction are intimately related. Producers could increase the amount of recycled material used, and the proportion of total materials coming from recycled sources, without helping the problem. Suppose total materials use is 100, equally divided between recycled ($R_p + R_c$) and virgin materials (I). Suppose now I stays constant, but $R_p + R_c$ increase to 60. Then the recycled source proportion goes from 50 percent to about 55 percent,

an apparent gain. But I is still 50, meaning that there will still be the same amount of material to dispose of in the long run.

[8] This and other data in this chapter come largely from U.S. Environmental Protection Agency, *Municipal Solid Waste in the United States: 2001 Facts and Figures*, EPA 530-R-03-011 (Washington, DC: EPA, October 2003).

[9] These are Connecticut, Delaware, Iowa, Maine, Massachusetts, Michigan, New York, Oregon, Vermont, and Hawaii.

[10] See U.S. Environmental Protection Agency, *Flow Control and Municipal Solid Waste*, Report to Congress, EPA 530-R-95-008.

[11] We must also remember general effects of inflation: from 1985 to 2002 the general price level increased by about 80 percent, so a tipping fee of $15 in 1985 would have increased to about $27 just on the basis of general inflation. Of course, tipping fees increased by more than this.

⑬ Radiation

Radiation is fast-moving energy in the form of particles or rays. Certain types of radiation, called **ionizing radiation**, are of high enough energy to damage material that it encounters. There are three principal sources of ionizing radiation:

1. Incoming radiation from the sun, in the form of ultraviolet and gamma radiation. Exposure to ultraviolet radiation can cause damage such as sunburn and skin cancer.

2. Human-produced electromagnetic radiation. Most electromagnetic radiation produced by humans (e.g., radio waves) is non-ionizing; some, however, such as x-rays, can cause damage.

3. Radiation from certain radioactive material that is found in nature and may be augmented through processing.

Substances that emit ionizing radiation need to be handled in keeping with their potential to cause damage. In some cases this is not hard; for example, the radioactive material in some smoke detectors is shielded to prevent human exposure. In other cases it is much more difficult, as with the fuel in nuclear power plants, which is extremely radioactive and can kill those who are accidentally exposed to it.

Materials that emit radiation have several important characteristics. One is the energy of the radiation, which determines its damage potential. Another is the rate at which the radiation diminishes over time. As a material emits radiation, it will undergo radioactive decay, which diminishes the radiation coming from it. But not all substances decay at the same rate. A common method of measuring this rate is in terms of **half-life**, which is the length of time needed for half of the original material to decay and become radioactively dormant.

Radiation has three pathways through which it can cause damage in humans: inhalation, ingestion (in water or food), and direct exposure. In some cases cells in exposed tissues are damaged directly, as with cancer. In other cases radiation disrupts the genetic material governing cell reproduction. There are two types of exposure situations that have to be considered in managing radiation: workers who are occupationally exposed, and regular citizenry who can be exposed through background radiation, consumer products, or accidents.

There are two types of policy problems regarding radioactivity: (1) setting and enforcing standards for acceptable radiation exposure levels and (2) dealing with waste materials that are radioactive. It is evident that (2) also includes (1); that is, many of the standards established under (1) are directed at activities involving radioactive waste material disposal.

Setting Exposure Standards

Radiation dosage levels received by humans as a result of exposure are normally measured in **rems**. This is a measure that takes into account both the intensity and length of exposure. High-dose levels unequivocally cause health damages; damage from low-dose levels is less clear. Several radiation damage functions are shown in figure 13.1. The horizontal axis measures individual exposure, expressed in millirems per year (a millirem is 1/1,000 of a rem). The vertical axis measures excess cancer deaths; that is, cancer deaths above what would normally be expected in the absence of any radiation. Two functions are shown, one depicting a situation in which 500 people are exposed to the indicated exposure levels, and the other applying to 1,000 people. In other words, for 1,000 people exposed to a level of 5 rems (5,000 millirems), we would expect one cancer death, while for 500 people exposed to this number of rems the expected number of cancer fatalities would be half this amount.[1] The functions are shown as solid lines in their upper reaches because there is reasonably solid evidence from which to deduce the shape of the function in that region. This relationship has been reasonably well established from the experience of people who have been accidentally exposed to high levels of radiation.[2]

In their lower reaches, however, the functions are much less well-understood. There is little evidence that exposure to very low levels of radiation causes significant damage. If we simply draw a straight line back from the higher points (the assumption of linearity), we are assuming that there is damage even at very low levels of exposure. But the actual relationships might look like the lower of the two dotted segments. In this case low levels of exposure produce little damage. Scientific studies are not conclusive on whether low-level exposures cause adverse health effects among humans.

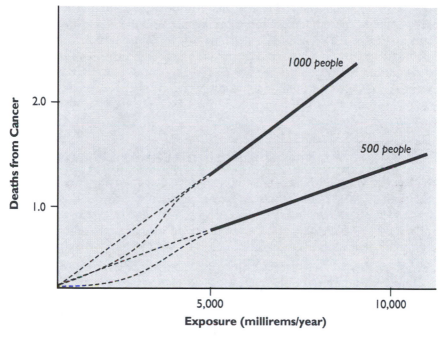

Figure 13.1   Radiation Damage Function

The average person in the United States is estimated to receive 360 millirems exposure per year, broken down as shown in table 13.1. Most of this (about 83 percent, as shown) is "background" radiation, which comes from the rays of the sun and from radioactive material in the earth's crust. Most of the rest is from medical sources, including x-rays and radiation therapy. If you believe that the function shown in figure 13.1 is truly linear, a 360 millirem exposure for 10,000 people would be expected to produce on average 7.2 cases of fatal cancer in a group of this size. Of course, there is controversy about whether a linear, no-threshold damage function is correct.

Table 13.1   Annual Dosage Levels of the Average American

Source	Dose (millirems[a]/year)
Background	
Radon	200
Other	100
X-rays	39
Nuclear medicine	14
Other[b]	7
Total	360

[a] One millirem equals 1/1,000 rem.
[b] Occupational exposure, exposure from nuclear power plants, exposure from consumer products (such as tobacco, smoke alarms, etc.).

Source: U.S. Nuclear Regulatory Commission, "How Does Radiation Affect the Public" (www.nrc.gov/what-we-do/radiation/affect.html).

The two federal agencies responsible for setting radiation exposure standards are the Environmental Protection Agency and the Nuclear Regulatory Commission (NRC). The NRC sets standards in connection with the operation of nuclear power plants and the handling of nuclear fuel, while the EPA sets standards for most other operations and exposures. They overlap to some extent in standards governing the handling and storage of spent nuclear fuel (see table 13.2).

Policy Issues in Radioactive Waste Disposal

Nuclear waste consists of material that emits radiation higher than normal background levels. Many different types of material are involved, some with very low levels of radiation that will quickly decay, and others that are highly radioactive and potentially lethal, with decay periods of thousands of years. It is typically divided into several categories. The two most important are:

1. *High-level waste.* This consists primarily of **spent nuclear fuel (SNF)**; that is, fuel rods removed from nuclear power plants; they are highly radioactive and will remain dangerously so for tens of thousands of years. This category also includes waste produced during spent fuel reprocessing.

2. *Low-level waste.* This includes a wide variety of nonnuclear material and items that become radioactive during their use (e.g., workers' clothing and tools at nuclear power plants, and materials used in medical programs

Table 13.2   Radiation Exposure Standards Established by Federal Agencies

Standard/Agency	Numerical Limit (millirems per year)
Nuclear power plants (NRC)	
General public	100
Workers	5,000
High-level waste operations (NRC)	100
Spent fuel, high-level waste, transuranic waste (EPA)	All pathways: 15
	Groundwater: 4
Proposed Yucca Mountain standards	
EPA	All pathways: 15
	Groundwater: 4
NRC	25
Low-level waste (NRC)	25
Drinking water (EPA)	Beta/photon: 4
Uranium fuel cycle (EPA)	25
Power plant decommissioning (NRC)	25

Source: U.S. General Accounting Office, *Radiation Standards: Scientific Basis Inconclusive, and EPA and NRC Disagreement Continues*, GAO/RCED-00-152 (Washington, DC: GAO, June 2000).

involving radiation). Low-level waste is subdivided as A, B, or C, depending on radioactivity and decay life. In general, low-level waste has substantially lower radioactivity and shorter decay life than other types.

Other recognized forms of radioactive waste are:

3. *Transuranic waste (TRU).* A type of low-activity waste resulting from nuclear weapons production; most is extremely long lived and potentially dangerous if handled incorrectly.

4. *Uranium mill tailings.* Residuals from uranium mining, low in radioactivity but high in quantity.

5. *Mixed waste.* Radioactive waste that is mixed with nonradioactive hazardous waste.

There are four substantial problem areas in the handling of radioactive waste in the United States:

1. Developing a system for handling the quantities of spent fuel from nuclear power plants and other high-level nuclear waste.

2. Handling the large quantities of low-level radioactive waste.

3. Cleaning up radioactive contamination resulting from the nuclear weapons program. This includes contamination at sites at which research and development, testing, and production took place.

4. Handling the very large quantities of material taken from decommissioned nuclear weapons.

The major federal statutes affecting these disposal problems are reviewed in table 13.3. The remainder of the chapter will discuss these problems at length.

Spent Nuclear Fuel

The technology for extracting useful energy from nuclear material was first developed in the early 1950s. Initially it focused on developing nuclear power plants for naval ships, especially submarines and aircraft carriers. Attention turned quickly to civilian uses, however, and was directed at nuclear-powered electricity generating plants. These would use nuclear fuel as the heat source to make the steam that would then drive the electric generators. Proponents of nuclear power said that nuclear plants would be able to generate electricity very cheaply (a catch phrase at the time was that nuclear power would be "too cheap to meter"). Furthermore, they would not produce the air pollutants characteristic of plants using coal or petroleum.

The first U.S. nuclear power plant (Dresden I in Illinois) began operating in 1960. Throughout the 1960s and early 1970s new licenses were awarded at a rapid rate, so that by 1985 there were 107 nuclear power plants in operation and 13 more under construction. But the expansion did not persist, because construction costs turned out to be much higher than originally projected, and the public had become much more concerned about safety issues after

Table 13.3   Significant U.S. Federal Laws Dealing with the Nuclear Industry and the Handling of Radioactive Waste

Legislation	Content
Atomic Energy Act of 1946	Created the Atomic Energy Commission (AEC) to conduct research and development on peaceful applications of nuclear energy.
Atomic Energy Act of 1954	Gave the AEC regulatory authority over the production and handling of nuclear material.
Energy Reorganization Act of 1974	Divided the AEC into two agencies: • Energy Research and Development Administration (ERDA), responsible for nuclear R and D. • Nuclear Regulatory Commission (NRC), responsible for the regulatory function of the AEC.
Energy Organization Act of 1977	Created the Department of Energy (DOE), which took over the functions of ERDA.
Low-Level Radioactive Waste Policy Act of 1980	Established rules and procedures by which states could form interstate compacts to build and operate low-level waste disposal facilities.
Nuclear Waste Policy Act of 1982	Authorized deep geological disposal of spent nuclear fuel; created a fund for financing development of a disposal site; established an office (the Office of Civilian Radioactive Waste Management) within DOE to carry this out; established the Nuclear Waste Technical Review Board.
Low-Level Radioactive Waste Policy Amendments Act of 1985	Postponed some of the deadlines in the earlier act; clarified responsibilities for waste handling.
Nuclear Waste Policy Amendments Act of 1987	Limited the possible high-level storage sites to one: Yucca Mountain in Nevada; authorized the DOE to develop a monitored retrievable storage (MRS) facility to store spent fuel temporarily.
Energy Policy Act of 1992	Required the EPA to write new standards for the Yucca Mountain repository.

the Three-Mile Island accident of 1979 and the Chernobyl disaster of 1986. Thus, new applications dwindled in the late 1980s and 1990s, and many plants that had previously been approved were never built. In 2004 about 20 percent of the electricity generated in the United States came from 104 active nuclear power plants.[3] In some countries (notably France and Japan) this percentage is much higher. Whether additional new plants will be built is difficult to predict within today's political climate (see exhibit 13.1).

A typical nuclear power plant produces 20 to 30 metric tons of spent nuclear fuel each year. Thus, as of 2002 there were about 47,000 metric tons of SNF in the United States, and by 2035 this is expected to reach 84,000

Exhibit 13.1
The Ebb and Flow of Nuclear Politics

Nuclear energy has engendered major political conflict since it was first harnessed in the early 1950s. On one side are the companies producing nuclear reactors, their political supporters, and public agencies set up in part to encourage the growth of a nuclear power industry. On the other side are environmental groups stressing the dangers of radiation pollution that could result from reactor accidents, their engineering and technical allies, and local groups, like the Clamshell Alliance in New England, formed to work against the siting of nuclear power plants. The relative influence of the two sides has waxed and waned through time as events have unfolded: energy shortages, economic factors, reactor accidents, and so on. Now the nuclear industry has enough power to extract subsidies from Congress; now the antinuclear forces have enough power to forestall particular projects.

At the present time the nuclear power industry is in a state of retrenchment: many of the existing plants have been decommissioned, and new ones have not been licensed. But forces continue to evolve. Increasing petroleum prices and growing concern about global warming have given the nuclear industry new opportunities to create political support for nuclear energy. But ongoing concerns about disposing of spent nuclear fuel, highly radioactive and dangerous, and of potential accidents at nuclear power plants, offer opportunities for the antinuclear forces to keep the brakes firmly on the revival of this industry.

---

metric tons. This material is extremely hot and highly radioactive. In addition it contains plutonium, which can be used to fashion nuclear weapons.

When nuclear power was being actively developed, officials recognized that there would be future problems with SNF disposal. But the enthusiasm to get this sector up and running overshadowed these concerns, and the issue was reserved for future consideration. The assumption at the time was that the disposal of SNF was a problem that could be solved if enough science was devoted to it. It was also vaguely assumed that the nuclear power industry would continue to expand and switch to breeder reactors (reactors that create more potential fuel than they originally used up), which would use the plutonium extracted from the SNF of the first generation of nuclear plants. But the nuclear power industry instead began to contract; the science of SNF disposal turned out to be much more difficult than originally thought, and the politics of the problem have evolved into a gigantic game of NIMBY, with the states as players.

When it became clear in the 1970s that the SNF problem would be one of waste disposal, not use, the first move was to turn to science for help. The National Research Council was commissioned by Congress to look into the problem and suggest a solution. Its report recommended deep geological repositories as the preferred technical option. These are deep underground storage sites where the geology ensures isolation of the SNF for the many thousands of years it would take for its radioactivity to decay to benign levels. This seemed quite straightforward, and some preliminary investigations had identified a number of potential sites for repositories of this sort.

Congress responded in 1982 with the Nuclear Waste Policy Act. It recognized that siting this type of facility would be contentious, and it tried to put in place, or at least appear to be putting in place, a process for rationally choosing an SNF site, or sites. The 1982 law:

1. Adopted geologic disposal as the preferred technology for long-term isolation of SNF.

2. Established a deadline of January 31, 1998 for the DOE to begin accepting SNF from commercial nuclear power plants for deposit in a storage facility.

3. Established a Nuclear Waste Fund, in which utilities would pay one mill (a tenth of a cent) per kilowatt-hour of nuclear electricity produced, to help pay for finding, developing, and operating a repository.

4. Established the Nuclear Waste Technical Review Board, an independent scientific body whose role was to make recommendations about SNF disposal based on available scientific evidence.

5. Identified a number of possible sites in the West and several in the eastern United States for further study (subsequently the president took the eastern sites and all but three of the western sites out of consideration).

The 1982 Nuclear Waste Policy Act is a good illustration of how seemingly good intentions, written into the law, can go awry. The law sought to establish a clear strategy for identifying and investigating repository sites. It consisted of a number of steps: site nomination, screening, selection, and characterization. Each step was supposedly clearly defined and based on accepted criteria. The thought was that there would perhaps be less room for political maneuvering if the process was clearly laid out from start to finish. This is not the way it worked, however. Rather, by laying out a long series of selection steps as it did, the law actually gave participants a number of points at which political jousting could take place over site selection. The process quickly devolved into a game of NIMBY, in which the states where possible sites were identified sought to get themselves taken off the list.

They were all successful, except for the state of Nevada. In 1987 Congress passed the Nuclear Waste Policy Amendments Act of that year. This law directed DOE to focus on only one site: **Yucca Mountain**, a geologic formation about 125 miles north of Las Vegas. Since that time, the Yucca Mountain site has become a scientific and political extravaganza, involving citizens and political bodies at every level, dueling scientists, and an increasingly aggressive nuclear power industry looking for a place to put its spent fuel.

To date, about $4 billion has been put into studying the geology of Yucca Mountain and establishing the infrastructure for a repository there. But the date for the site to begin accepting SNF has been continually extended. The original law called for a start date of 1998 but this was never feasible. Questions continue to be raised about the geology and hydrology of the region and how likely it would be that radiation could escape confinement and contaminate the surrounding region. Resolution of these questions was thought to be essentially a matter of doing more and better science on the site, but it has become clear that more science can not resolve all of the human factors involved in the site.

What is involved is a level of risk. People of Nevada would like there to be no risk from the repository. But zero risk is not possible. For example, scientists know that volcanic activity has sometimes occurred in this vicinity over past millennia. There is some probability that it could happen again. Scientists could venture a guess, say, one in a million over the next 1,000 years, but how should the people of Nevada respond to this?

Another problem is human encroachment. The repository will have to isolate the waste for 10,000 years before the material has decayed enough to be nondangerous. Things that took place thousands of years ago are the province of archeologists, who dig evidence out of the sand. Who is to say whether in 5,000 years, when this site has been long forgotten, somebody will decide that it is an excellent site on which to drill some test wells for petroleum (will we still be using fossil fuels for energy in 5,000 years?)? No amount of science can give a definitive answer to this question; the time period is too long to be encompassed by normal human thought processes.

As controversy has swirled around Yucca Mountain, and as the people of Nevada have fought against the site, its opening has been continuously pushed off into the future.[4] Other options have been considered, such as long-term storage of SNF at the site of the power plant that produced it, or chemical transformation to reduce its radioactivity. But the greatest interest still focuses on the Yucca Mountain repository. Recently President Bush sought to move the process along by coming out publicly in favor of the Yucca site.

As of 2006 the Yucca Mountain site in still being litigated. A number of lawsuits have been filed, most notably by the State of Nevada, and the case is being heard in the U.S. Court of Appeals for the District of Columbia Circuit. A number of issues are involved. One is whether Congress may constitutionally proceed with laws authorizing the project's go-ahead. Another issue is whether the EPA erred in using a 10,000-year life for its planning purposes. Congress had directed the EPA to follow the lead of the National Academy of Sciences on this, and the NAS had recommended using a 250,000-year life for planning the project.

Meanwhile, the delay in opening the Yucca repository, or any other national site, means that immense amounts of spent fuel are being stored on-site at nuclear plants. Some is in dry storage, and some is suspended in large tanks of water. The costs of this on-site storage are continuing to mount, and the federal government has become responsible for much of this expense because of the delay on the national repository. In addition, there are serious questions about the security of these dispersed storage operations.

Low-Level Radioactive Waste

Low-level radioactive waste (LLW) is essentially defined as waste that does not fit into any of the other categories of nuclear waste. It consists primarily of tools, clothing, equipment, containers, filters, fluids, and so forth that have been contaminated through their use in settings where radiation is present. The largest part of this comes from nuclear power plants and nuclear weapons sites. Other low-level waste comes from hospitals, research laboratories, and industries that utilize radioactive materials.

The amount of radioactive material in LLW is highly variable. Accordingly, low-level waste is classified into three categories:

1. *Class A*. Contains the lowest concentration of radioactive materials, generally with half-lives of less than 5 years.

2. *Class B*. The next lowest concentration of radioactive materials.

3. *Class C*. Contains the highest concentration of radioactive material that is allowed to be disposed of in a low-level disposal facility.

About one-third of the low-level radioactive waste comes from commercial operations (e.g., power plants and hospitals), while the rest comes from nuclear weapons sites operated by the U.S. Department of Energy. Disposal of the DOE material is the responsibility of the federal government, while commercial LLW is primarily the responsibility of the states. The history of state efforts to develop adequate disposal capacity for these wastes is a great example of how political inertia, perverse policy incentives, and contention among the states can stultify efforts to solve what ought to be a fairly tractable issue in public policy.

Until the 1960s, commercial radioactive waste was disposed of by the Atomic Energy Commission (AEC), a predecessor of the Department of Energy. In the 1960s, the AEC phased out of the business of taking commercial low-level waste, at which time responsibility shifted to the states. A number of commercial waste operators began operating about this time, but most of these were soon closed, primarily for safety reasons. A major problem existed for the individual states in establishing disposal facilities. The U.S. Constitution bars individual states from limiting interstate commerce, in particular from putting limits on goods and services flowing into a state from some other state. If an individual state were indeed to develop a repository for LLW, it would probably not be able to restrict shipments of LLW from other states, on the grounds that such a limit would constitute an unconstitutional restraint of trade.[5]

With states thus having a strong incentive not to act individually, Congress passed the Low-Level Radioactive Waste Policy Act of 1980. The objective of the law was to get states to act cooperatively and to limit the number of sites used for LLW disposal. It gave states the right to enter into **interstate compacts** to develop LLW disposal sites. As an incentive, the law states that, under certain conditions, states in a compact could limit both the inflow and outflow of LLW and/or impose surcharges on waste shipments from nonmember states. The act was amended in 1985 to prod states to move more energetically in forming compacts and opening new disposal sites.

At the present time there are 10 compacts encompassing 42 states (8 are unaffiliated). The compacts are shown in figure 13.2. The layout of these compacts illustrates the incentives built into the process. No state would want to open an individual site, because it would then legally have to accept LLW from other states. The way to forestall this is to be in a compact with at least two other states. The ideal would be to form a compact with several other states that would not need to dispose of large quantities of LLW. Then a state could garner the benefits of being in a compact, without bearing high costs. Thus, Texas is in a compact with Vermont. And South Dakota is part of the Southwestern compact with California and Arizona. In addition, compact formation can be expected to be a volatile process, as states try to maneuver for advantage with other states. Thus, a long-running conflict between South and North Carolina has affected the Southeast compact, while Nebraska withdrew from the Central compact.

The compacts (and some of the unaffiliated states) have spent collectively about $600 million attempting to locate and develop sites for handling LLW. None of these efforts has been successful. So the system that the earlier federal statutes were meant to encourage, a series of new regional disposal sites around the country, has simply not come to fruition.

Note: Shaded states are not affiliated with a compact.

Source: Produced by the Low-Level Radioactive Waste Forum, Inc., June 2005. Used with permission.

Figure 13.2   States' Membership in Compacts

The primary reasons for this appear to be the following:[6]

1. *Public and political opposition to new sites.* This is the NIMBY phenomenon in full swing. States want disposal capacity somewhere, but in every state there is vociferous opposition to siting a LLW facility there. This opposition has been expressed at many places in the process: community opposition in towns thought to contain possible sites, state legislatures, public licensing commissions, and so on.

2. *Continued access by almost all states to "legacy" disposal sites.* There are three of these sites currently accepting certain out-of-state LLW: Barnwell in South Carolina, Richland in Washington, and Envirocare (a private operation) in Utah. The history of each of these sites is complex, but the effect is that by continuing these sites, much of the pressure on states to find alternative facilities is greatly weakened. In some cases (e.g., North Carolina), temporary storage is being used in lieu of permanent disposal. South Carolina hopes to close Barnwell to outside users by 2008, the prospects of which have led some in Congress to propose changes to existing laws governing low-level waste.

3. *Reduction in the quantity of LLW.* Many states have had success in instituting programs to reduce the amounts of low-level wastes generated.

Cleaning Up After the Nuclear Weapons Program

The largest single environmental cleanup job currently underway in the United States is the decontamination and amelioration of the sites that were involved in nuclear weapons production. The cold war between the United States and other Western countries and the Soviet Union lasted roughly from 1950 to 1990. It involved many areas of contention and conflict, one of the hottest of which was a proliferation of nuclear weapons. Both sides produced and deployed a vast arsenal of nuclear weapons, primarily nuclear warheads attached to missiles of various types. At its most virulent stage (the late 1980s) the two sides each had many thousands of nuclear weapons aimed at one another or otherwise ready for use. As of now, roughly 70,000 nuclear warheads have been fabricated worldwide.

To produce this arsenal of nuclear weapons, the United States developed a vast complex of operations for mining, processing, manufacturing, and deploying the necessary nuclear material. At the height of this activity, more than 100 sites spread through 30 states were involved. Most of these sites are now contaminated to one degree or another. The extent of the contamination includes radioactive wastes that have been stored in various ways on these sites, contaminated buildings and equipment, and contaminated soil and groundwater. Several years ago it was estimated that the total cost of cleaning up this complex would be between $200 billion and $300 billion and that it would take 70 years to complete. Furthermore, some of the wastes will remain dangerously radioactive for thousands of years. As with all such estimates, the actual cost will no doubt be substantially higher when the cleanup is finally finished, if it ever is.

The issue prompts many important policy questions and controversies. Perhaps the most fundamental is why so much nuclear waste was created in the first place. The nuclear weapons program was carried out by numerous private contractors, but with direct oversight by relevant units within the Department of Defense. In theory, it should have been possible to build and operate the system with reasonably good safeguards against the various types of water, air, and land pollution that was to be expected. But this is not the way it worked out. Why?

This situation provides a prime example of how agencies whose ostensible goals are to work on behalf of the public nevertheless can contribute as much to environmental degradation as the more highly publicized pollution from the private sector. The ingredients were: (1) a citizenry that had been convinced of the need to quickly develop a vast nuclear arsenal to forestall threats from the Soviet Union, (2) a well-funded public agency with what it regarded as a strong mandate to move ahead rapidly without regard for the potential environmental effects of its actions, and (3) the absence of adequate environmental oversight, from either public agencies like the EPA or private groups, to monitor the situation and force the issue into the public arena. The result was a public program conducted without public scrutiny that only later was discovered to have produced massive amounts of environmental contamination.[7]

A second major question about nuclear weapons cleanup is why the problem has not received the public attention one might have thought it would given the amounts of money involved. The Office of Environmental Management (OEM) in the DOE has an annual budget of about $6 billion, as compared to a total EPA budget of about $7.5 billion in recent years. These numbers are similar in order of magnitude, yet the OEM budget receives far less scrutiny and generates far less controversy than the EPA budget. Nor is this likely to change soon. The OEM operation is responsible for cleaning up 114 sites that were involved with the nuclear weapons complex. By 2007 OEM plans to have completed cleanups at 37 sites. But these were the smallest and least difficult sites to deal with. The remaining sites are much larger and will require enormous amounts of money over many decades to adequately remediate them. So the budget of the OEM will have to be maintained at a very substantial level into the indefinite future.

Perhaps one reason that the nuclear weapons cleanup program has not received the public attention one might have expected is that they are all site specific, which makes them local problems but not necessarily national problems. An example of this is the Rocky Flats operation.

The Saga of Rocky Flats. Rocky Flats was a large nuclear weapons facility located about 15 miles northwest of Denver. It was built in the early 1950s, at the beginning of the nuclear standoff of the cold war. The fact that it was being built was no secret; at the time it was widely regarded as an economic stimulus for the local economy.[8] But the nature of the work, which involved the production and handling of large amounts of radioactive waste, was highly secret. The priority at the time was on meeting the perceived needs of the cold war nuclear buildup, not on developing a safe and sound method of handling nuclear waste.

Over time, however, the environmental implications of Rocky Flats gradually became more apparent. A series of accidents in the 1950s and 1960s were reported but given little press coverage. The surrounding population was largely ignorant about environmental damage that might have been caused by these events.

In the 1970s and 1980s, however, the site received increasing public scrutiny. Scientists began raising questions about possible impacts and studies were conducted. Activist groups like the Rocky Flats Action Group formed, both to publicize the problems stemming from the facility and to bring pressure to bear for dealing with them. Questions were raised about the continued need for the plant as the cold war ebbed. Major maneuvering occurred among the Department of Energy, the EPA, state and local environmental regulators, the FBI, the U.S. Congress and state legislatures, and private contractors over who would do what and how it would be paid for. The national and local press produced long investigative reports about the situation. The U.S. Congress responded in 1992 by passing the Federal Facilities Compliance Act, which requires that federal facilities meet the same environmental standards as private companies.

The Rocky Flats plant was shut down in 1989. Since then a cleanup and rehabilitation effort has been underway, though virtually every element of this effort has been plagued by controversy: how clean is clean enough, how to dispose of radioactive waste, how to find waste that is unaccounted for, what the site might be used for in the future, and so on. In 1997 DOE gave the site priority and estimated it would be remediated by 2006 at a cost of $7.5 billion. Two years later it upped the estimated cost to $168 billion, and current estimates are that the project will take in excess of $300 billion and last into the indefinite future.

Public Oversight and OEM.   Despite events like Rocky Flats, despite the large sums of money the OEM has spent, and will spend in the future, Congress and federal policy makers have spent relatively little time and effort on this program. The reasons for this are probably twofold. First, this is a series of local issues that are difficult to develop into a national issue. There has been substantial coverage of the issues by newspapers, particularly the local press, and attention given it by active environmental organizations, such as the Alliance for Nuclear Accountability and the Institute of Energy and Environmental Research. There may be 50 or 60 sites around the United States, but most people do not live next to one of them. Therefore, the national coalitions and alliances that are necessary to get Congress to move on the issue are hard to construct.

Second, much of the OEM cleanup is seen by local interests as useful primarily for its economic implications, not necessarily its environmental impact. The nuclear weapons complex created a large number of communities dependent on the money coming out of the federal budget. When weapons production stopped, site cleanup became a new vehicle for channeling federal dollars to these local economies. This reality has substantially muted any effort that might be made to evaluate the OEM program from the standpoint of, say, cost effectiveness.

If history is any guide, this situation is likely to persist until such time as there is a major crisis at one of the sites.[9]

Decommissioning Nuclear Weapons

A vital element of the nuclear program is actually decommissioning the nuclear weapons built earlier. As of 2004 the United States had about 10,000 warheads in existence, each of which has substantial amounts of highly radioactive material that could cause tremendous contamination if handled incorrectly. How fast the country reduces this arsenal depends on the weapons politics in Washington. The Bush administration proposed a reduction schedule that would reduce the stockpile to 6,000 warheads by 2012. On the other hand, it has also funded substantial programs for nuclear weapon research and production.

Existing weapons are distributed among a number of U.S. sites (Nevada, New Mexico, Georgia, Alaska) and overseas. The primary location for deprocessing these weapons is a facility in Amarillo, Texas. Of course, the issues are not only managing radioactive waste material from these weapons, but also the threat of nuclear terrorism.

Summary

Radiation occurs both naturally and as the result of human activities. Nuclear power plants and the nuclear weapons complex have produced large amounts of highly radioactive material that needs to be carefully handled to avoid exposing people to damaging radiation. In addition, the modern economy, particularly the health sector, produces large amounts of low-level waste that must be disposed of.

The nuclear power industry expanded in the 1970s and 1980s without adequate concern for disposing of the highly radioactive spent nuclear fuel that each reactor produces. The assumption was that the federal government, given money from the nuclear-power industry, would find a timely solution. This has not proved to be the case. After many years of study and political action, the focus is on long-term storage of spent fuel at the Yucca Mountain repository in Nevada. But it has been impossible to activate this site because of scientific and political problems. Meanwhile, the spent fuel is stored temporarily at the sites of the power plants where it was used.

Despite the vast amounts of money spent on cleaning up after the nuclear weapons buildup, the task remains huge and there is no indication of when, or even whether, it will ever be completed. Despite the size of the program it has not received the public attention that other major environmental problems have. One reason is that for most (but not all) people, the problem appears as one confined to a small number of remote areas of the country.

There has been little action by states to provide increased repository capacity for low-level nuclear waste. One reason for this is the substantial reduction in the amounts of LLW produced. Another is because of the perverse incentives the states have under the interstate compact system established under federal law.

Key Terms

half-life   rems
high-level radioactive waste   Rocky Flats
interstate compacts   spent nuclear fuel (SNF)
ionizing radiation   Yucca Mountain
low-level radioactive waste

Questions for Further Discussion

1. In what ways is nuclear radiation a local, regional, national, and global problem?

2. When the cold war was being ramped up, with thousands of nuclear weapons being developed, why was so little thought given to the future environmental problems it might produce?

3. Why has there been so little activity under the low-level waste provisions of the Low-Level Radioactive Waste Policy Act of 1980?

4. The rationale for developing the Yucca Mountain repository has been that with enough study, it could be changed from a political problem to a scientific problem in hydrogeology. Do you think this was realistic?

5. Almost as much money goes to cleaning up waste products from the nuclear weapons buildup each year as goes to the entire EPA budget. Yet it produces little public controversy. Why?

Web Sites

Numerous government agencies have informative Web sites on radiation issues, for example:

Nuclear Regulatory Commission
www.nrc.gov

See also the Web site of an NRC established center:

The Center for Nuclear Waste Regulatory Analyses
www.swri.edu/4org/d20/CNWRA.htm

Environmental Protection Agency
www.epa.gov/radiation

Department of Energy
www.em.doe.gov

In addition, there are many public and private groups who focus on nuclear matters, both waste issues and questions about nuclear weapons, for example:
American Nuclear Society
www.ans.org

Center for Nuclear and Toxic Waste Management
http://cnwm.berkeley.edu/

Nuclear Policy Research Institute
www.nuclearpolicy.org

Nuclear Information and Resource Service
www.nirs.org

Additional Readings

Benjamin, Richard, and Jeffrey Wagner, "Reconsidering the Law and Economics of Low-Level Radioactive Waste Management," Working Paper, Department of Economics, Rochester Institute of Technology (2005).

Congressional Budget Office, *Cleaning Up the Department of Energy's Nuclear Weapons Complex* (Washington, DC: CBO, May 1994).

Congressional Budget Office, Testimony on Environmental Cleanup Programs in the Departments of Defense and Energy (Washington, DC: CBO, March 1996). (www.cbo.gov/showdoc.cfm?index=4745&sequence=0).

Gerrard, M. B., *Whose Backyard, Whose Risk: Fear and Fairness in Toxic and Nuclear Waste Siting* (Cambridge, MA: MIT Press, 1994).

Holt, Mark, *Civilian Nuclear Waste Disposal*, CRS Report IB92059 (Washington, DC: CRS, January 11, 2002).

League of Women Voters Education Fund, *The Nuclear Waste Primer* (Washington, DC: LWV, 1993).

Makhijani, Arjun, Howard Hu, and Katherine Yih, eds., *Nuclear Wastelands: A Global Guide to Nuclear Weapons Production and Its Health and Environmental Effects* (Cambridge, MA: MIT Press, 1995).

Murray, Raymond, *Understanding Radioactive Waste*, 4th ed. (Columbus, OH: Battelle Press, 1994).

National Research Council, *The Disposal of Nuclear Waste on Land* (1957).

Probst, Katherine N., and Adam I. Lowe, *Cleaning Up the Nuclear Weapons Complex: Does Anybody Care?* (Washington, DC: Resources for the Future, January 2000).

Schwartz, Stephen I., ed., *Atomic Audit: The Costs and Consequences of U.S. Nuclear Weapons Since 1940* (Washington, DC: Brookings Institution, 1998).

U.S. Office of Technology Assessment, *Complex Cleanup: The Environmental Legacy of Nuclear Weapons Production* (Washington, DC: OTA, 1991).

Notes

[1] The expected number of cancer deaths is the average number of cancer deaths for a large number of groups of the indicated size.

[2] Exposure is sometimes measured in person rems, which is the number of individuals times the exposure of each one. 1,000 people each exposed to 50 rems equals 50,000 person rems; 1,000,000 people each exposed to .05 rems is also equal to 50,000 person rems; one person

exposed to 50 rems and one person exposed to 10 rems gives a total of 60 person rems. A reasonably well established relationship is that each 5,000 person rems will produce one cancer death.

3 There are also 23 nuclear power plants that have been permanently shut down.

4 Another issue with regard to the Yucca Mountain site is that it would require a substantial amount of SNF transportation, from nuclear power plants around the country to the repository site in Nevada. Transportation of this sort can never be entirely free from the risk of accident and release of radiation.

5 This problem also has come up in the interstate shipment of municipal solid waste (trash); see chapter 12.

6 This section draws heavily from General Accounting Office, *Low-Level Radioactive Wastes: States Are Not Developing Disposal Facilities*, GAO Report GAO/RCED-99-238 (Washington, DC: GAO, 1999); see also the GAO Report: *Low-Level Radioactive Waste: Disposal Availability Adequate in the Short Term, but Oversight Needed to Identify Any Future Shortfalls*, GAO-04-604 (Washington, DC: GAO, 2004).

7 This same pattern applied to the experience of many of the ex-socialist countries: economic decisions in the hands of bureaucrats who were insulated from public opinion, a great stress on economic development regardless of the cost, and a citizenry who had neither the information nor the means to question the process. And the environmental results were the same.

8 This section draws heavily from Judith A. Layzer, *The Environmental Case: Translating Values into Policy* (Washington, DC: Congressional Quarterly Press, 2002):78–101.

9 The most recent candidate for this has been the occupational and environmental hazards at the Paducah, Kentucky, gaseous diffusion plant. But although this was the subject of many newspaper stories, it was never elevated to the status of a national crisis.

SECTION IV
THE PROBLEMS

Thus far we have discussed the policy-making process, the participants, and the major policies. In this section we encounter another "p" word: problems. The word *problems* is used not only in the restricted sense of things that are broken and need fixing, but also in the sense of questions that need better answers, trends that need a more complete understanding, and potentials that ought to be more widely appreciated. This set of four chapters can not possibly include all the many detailed issues that inhabit the interior processes of public environmental policy. Instead we focus on four major types of issues: understanding the various consequences that policy can produce; discussing the growing role of incentive-based policies; investigating the role of formal analysis in policy making; and considering the trend back toward state-level initiatives in environmental policy.

14

Policy Consequences

Unforeseen, Special Interest, and Perverse

Environmental policy decisions are meant to be purposeful acts; they are meant to have consequences. But policy making in the real world is not the same as shooting arrows toward a target: clear objective and clear result in terms of whether that objective was attained. In the rough and tumble of policy making it should come as no surprise that actual consequences sometimes do not match supposed objectives. In this chapter we will discuss how this disconnect happens, and give examples. It is widely known that many aspects of policy making come under the heading of political theater. Much of the action is for public consumption, meant to convey to the citizenry that their political representatives are addressing pressing public concerns and interests. In this chapter we will bypass such posturing and instead focus on real-world policy consequences and their relationship to pollution-control objectives.

In the ensuing discussion we will see many examples of policy outcomes that are not what we would like, where "we" refers to the public at large. And though some of you might conclude that all, or most, public policy is misguided in some fashion, that most emphatically is not the intent of the discussion. In fact, there are many examples of effective environmental policy and

277

regulation over the last few decades. The lesson to be taken from this discussion is not that public policy seldom works, but that it will not be effective unless it is designed with thoughtfulness and, especially, transparency in its context and impacts.

Unforeseen Consequences

People are not omniscient, so public policies don't always work out the way they are intended. Oftentimes we know too little about certain ecological and environmental factors, but feel we must act anyway. The social aspects of environmental policies are especially difficult to foresee and thus can produce circumstances in which unintended and unforeseen consequences can occur.

Unforeseen consequences, particularly of the environmental type, have often accompanied new technologies, which themselves have been encouraged by public policies of various types. A classic case is CFCs (chlorofluorocarbons) and the global ozone shield. These substances were developed in the 1920s to substitute for refrigerants that were then in use. CFCs appeared to be much more benign and effective than the chemicals they replaced, and numerous localities enacted regulations requiring their adoption. They were soon used widely in home and industrial refrigeration, and enabled the development of air conditioning. CFCs also became widely used as propellants in aerosol spray cans. But at the time scientists had no real understanding of the impacts these substances might have on the earth's atmosphere. The ability of CFC molecules to react with and destroy atmospheric ozone was totally unforeseen at the time these synthetic chemicals were developed. Recent efforts to protect the ozone layer have produced a major international treaty aimed at reducing CFC use and substituting less harmful materials.[1]

Another well-known instance of unforeseen consequences occurred as the result of provisions in the Clean Air Act of 1970. As we learned in earlier chapters, this law called for a system of National Ambient Air Quality Standards, set by the EPA and implemented by the states. As part of this implementation, states established ground-level recording stations where the ambient quality of the air could be sampled. Of course the expectation behind the law was that states would enforce command-and-control type emission standards on polluters to achieve the desired improvement in recorded pollution levels. Unexpectedly, however, pollution-control authorities discovered that some major sources of airborne emissions, especially large fossil-fuel power plants, had a different and cheaper way of improving local air quality. They did this by building smokestacks substantially taller than they previously had been. What this did was move the point of emissions into the brisker winds that normally occur at higher altitudes. This meant that *local* air quality improvements could be obtained to some extent at the expense of reduced air quality at longer distances downwind. Congress attempted to deal with this problem in the CAA amendments of 1977.[2]

Are unforeseen consequences simply the result of policy makers not being well-informed, or not having enough time to figure out the full impacts of their actions? Sometimes this is the case.

1. Lead was first added to gasoline in the 1920s to enhance its antiknock characteristics. Nobody at that time foresaw that lead would become a major damaging pollutant several decades later.

2. Acreage controls on U.S. agriculture were introduced in the 1950s as a way of dealing with the substantial crop surpluses that federal price subsidies were producing. Few people at the time foresaw clearly the extent to which this would drive agriculture toward such heavy reliance on chemicals (fertilizers, pesticides), as farmers tried to increase their per acre yields to offset the federal restrictions on the number of acres they could harvest.

3. In mid-twentieth century, as the chemical age was gathering momentum, few people appreciated the problems that chemical disposal would entail, and the environmental contamination that could result if these chemicals were simply handled in traditional ways.

It is also the case that unforeseen consequences result from organizational or institutional factors that stand in the way of effective information flows. The Clean Air Act of 1990 required oxygenated gasoline in certain regions at certain times of the year to reduce automobile emissions. One of the substances approved as an oxygenate was MTBE (methyl-tertiary-butyl ether). But heavy use of MTBE in the 1990s led to substantial groundwater contamination, so that by the end of the decade many people were calling for its discontinuance. But the problematic nature of MTBE in gasoline had been know for some time. It had earlier been used as a power-enhancing gas additive, and in fact had caused some instances of groundwater pollution in the 1980s. Scientific studies done at this time highlighted the potential for MTBE to become a water contaminant. But the policy process can be a cumbersome undertaking; in this case, ". . . published research that warned of problems associated with MTBE-contaminated water supplies was available as early as 1986 and was not incorporated into the regulatory decision-making process focused on air quality, suggesting flaws in the process by which science is communicated and used within the regulatory rule-making process."[3] Unfortunately, the existence of relevant information does not guarantee that it will be introduced at the right time and the right place in the policy process.

Historically, an important source of problems of this type has been the way that many environmental agencies—federal, regional, and state—have been organized. The typical agency is structured along the lines of the main environmental media: air, water, land. It has, for example, an air pollution control division (or bureau or section) and a water pollution control division. The air division designs programs to reduce air pollution and measures progress by looking at changes in air quality. The water division does the same with respect to water quality. But in reducing emissions there may be many cross-media alternatives available to polluters; airborne emissions might be reduced, for example, by converting materials to a form that can be put into a nearby watercourse. In the other direction, material might be extracted from a wastewater stream and then sent to an incinerator. In this way, single-minded efforts by the different divisions to get pollution reductions in "their" media can produce incentives simply to shift emissions to a different media. This is not necessarily bad, if the damage caused in the new media is less than in the old. But if this is to happen by design rather than by accident, cross-media pollution-control impacts need to be recognized explicitly.

Special-Interest Consequences

We have noted many times how the making of public policy is a complex process of mixing and harmonizing the conflicting and contentious interests that have access at various points. The resulting statutes and regulatory documents are lengthy, detailed, and complex. It can come to pass, therefore, that a statute which has the stated objective of improving environmental quality in some dimension can also contain provisions that are primarily aimed at benefiting particular special interests.

We mentioned above the unintended consequences of provisions that mandated MTBE as an oxygenator in gasoline. If MTBE ultimately is banned, but an oxygenate is still required, this creates a substantially enlarged market for producers of ethanol. Thus, while overall air pollution control is the objective of the Clean Air Act, specific provisions written into the law can have great consequences for private interests, and part of the dynamics surrounding the passage and implementation of laws is driven by these special interests.

A celebrated case of special interests benefiting from environmental policy occurred in the Clean Air Act Amendments of 1977. In that law, Congress included a specific technology requirement for large, new power plants. These plants were required to install stack-gas scrubbers to reduce emissions of SO_2. This appeared to be a bold, environmentally sound, command-and-control type requirement. Indeed, many environmental groups actively supported its enactment. As exhibit 14.1 makes clear, however, the prime motivation for the requirement came from a special interest source, that of protecting the jobs of coal miners in the Midwest. Including a command-and-control requirement that had beneficial consequences for this group ultimately cost the rest of the country a substantial amount of money. Less expensive alternatives were available.

Are all environmental policies and regulations a compendium of requirements that benefit one special interest or another? There are those who may believe this. Part of the problem is that even in policies and regulations that are reasonably well thought out, special-interest provisions can be added, often in innocuous ways. But there is plenty of policy research that shows that policy makers, on average, bring to the process somewhat broader notions of the public interest. A case in point, to which we alluded in chapter

Exhibit 14.1
Environmental Policy and Politics

"... Congress sometimes makes it difficult or impossible to reduce the cost of meeting environmental goals. The most notorious example is the 1977 change in the Clean Air Act concerning coal-fired electric power plants.

"In 1971 the EPA promulgated a new source performance standard that required all new coal-fired power plants to emit no more than 1.2 pounds of SO_2 per each million BTUs of electricity produced. It was expected at that time that new plants would meet this standard by incorporating into their design sophisticated equipment known euphemistically as scrubbers—actually mini-chemical plants that remove SO_2 by injecting wet limestone into the flue gases, thereby trapping (or scrubbing) the SO_2 before it escapes. Most new plants, however, chose to meet the original new source performance standards by shifting to lower-sulfur coals from southern Appalachia or western states. This saved the affected utilities, and hence their customers, a good deal of money because for most plants scrubbing would have been considerably more expensive than fuel-switching (a scrubber can account for $200 million of the $1 billion or so required to build a new 1,000-megawatt coal-fired power plant).

"Letting new power plants meet the new source performance standard however best they saw fit created one problem: the future job prospects of miners of high-sulfur coal, primarily in the Midwest, were threatened. As a result, midwestern senators and congressmen—in concert with environmental groups—pushed through an amendment to the Clean Air Act in 1977 that in effect required any new coal-fired power plant not only to meet the original NSPS, but also to do so via technological means—that is, by scrubbing. According to the Congressional Budget Office, this one requirement will by the year 2000 cost rate payers $4.2 billion more *per year* in additional electricity costs than would be required to meet the same emissions standard using low-sulfur coal and allowing emissions trades between new and existing sources.

"How many jobs might this protectionist measure save? It is difficult to say, but one rough estimate put the number in the range of 5,000 to 10,000. If correct, this estimate implies an expenditure of $400,000 to $800,000 per year *per job saved*. Since coal miners typically earn about $40,000 annually, the 1977 amendment would appear to be quite foolish— the annual incomes of the miners in question could be guaranteed for less than one-tenth the cost associated with forced scrubbing. Such an approach would seem to be far more attractive than the route Congress chose."

Source: Excerpted from Paul R. Portney, "Air Pollution Policy," in Paul R. Portney, ed., *Public Policies for Environmental Protection* (Washington, DC: Resources for the Future, 1990):75–76.

11, is the Comprehensive Environmental Response, Compensation and Liability Act (CERCLA), known popularly as Superfund. This Act authorized the expenditure of a large amount of money to clean up old hazardous waste dump sites. When big funds materialize, politicians often try to steer dollars toward their districts and/or supporters. This tendency, one would think, would certainly have directed Superfund money toward politically favored groups. In fact, this doesn't appear to be the case. Instead, evidence shows that the EPA has targeted Superfund money on the worst hazardous waste sites; that is, they have tended to direct the money toward the biggest problems, which seems quite a rational thing to do.[4]

So while it is clear that private, special-interest consequences are not the sole driving force behind environmental policy, that is not to say that they are unimportant. Policy makers should strive to maintain a perspective on the real objectives of public policies, be aware of the kinds of policy circumstances that lend themselves to special-interest impacts (think command-and-control), and opt for transparency as much as is possible. It is certainly no help in this regard that federal and state pollution-control policies and regulations have become extremely lengthy and complex over the last few decades. This makes it very hard to be knowledgeable about all the details of the laws, and thus of the full range of impacts they may have.

Unlike the unforeseen consequences discussed in the previous section, special-interest consequences, however well or badly they coordinate with the primary objectives of a policy, are usually intended; they are included because they are expected to have specific impacts. Still another type of important policy consequence is that which runs directly counter to the stated objectives of the policy in question. As we will see in the next section, this type of impact is unfortunately quite common in the policy world.

Perverse Consequences

Perverse consequences are those that tend to go directly counter to the objectives of the policy or regulation in question. Why would policy makers write laws that have these perverse effects? It comes down to a matter of incentives. Throughout this book we talk about the adoption of incentive-based pollution-control programs. These are explicit attempts to take advantage of normal economic incentives to produce more cost-effective pollution control. But the issue of incentives is much broader than this. In fact, incentive issues exist in virtually all government policies and regulations, and the failure to recognize this often leads to the perverse consequences mentioned.

Let's take one example with which everyone is probably familiar, and a product that you may have at home: childproof medicine caps. Until the late 1960s, over-the-counter medicine and related products (pain relievers, vitamins) were sold in plastic containers with pop-tops that were easily flipped open. While most adults stored these products well out of reach of children, it came to the attention of policy makers that children were being poisoned when they overdosed on aspirin from bottles left on a countertop or some other accessible place. The development of the "childproof cap" seemed to be a solution. Even if a bottle was placed in an accessible location, children would be unable to open it, and therefore the rate of poisoning would plummet. Congress then passed a law in 1970—the Poison Prevention Packaging Act—requiring childproof caps on all analgesics (they are now so common that virtually all readers of this volume will only be familiar with this type of medicine cap). It seemed to be a simple, quick, technical solution to a straightforward problem.

Problem solved? A study several years after the implementation of the law found that child poisonings did not drop at all; indeed, there was some evidence that they had risen.[5] Why? Unbeknownst to policy makers at the time (and reasonably so, I think most would agree), the study found two behavioral responses by parents that mitigated and sometimes reversed the effects of the new caps. The study's author referred to these as the "lulling effect" of government regulation. First, parents were more likely to leave the bottles in accessible locations, "knowing" that their children could not open them. Therefore, rather than storing them high in a medicine cabinet, they might leave bottles unattended on a kitchen counter. Second, because the earliest caps were so difficult to open, even for adults, parents tended to leave the cap sitting on top of the bottle rather than tightening it. The results were bottles that were now more accessible and possibly easier to open than before. This perverse consequence resulted from a policy aimed at helping children that actually created incentives that exacerbated the problem. Subsequently, producers developed caps that were far easier to open by adults yet still difficult for children.[6]

In the above example, perverse consequences occurred when policy makers attempted to dictate a technical solution without fully considering the behavioral responses people would make. Governments can set regulations, but it is the decisions of private interests, businesses, and individuals that largely determine whether public goals like cleaner air and water are achieved. What is usually lacking on the part of policy makers is an accurate understanding of the full set of incentives that motivate behavior. Incentives are basically the benefits and costs impinging on people that lead them to act in certain ways. Perverse incentives are incentives that lead people away from the objectives of the policy or regulation.

Another example of perverse consequences involves water usage. People in developed nations like the United States use substantial amounts of water. In a typical suburban home, water is used for a wide variety of in-house and out-of-house purposes. Occasionally, communities face water shortages, because of dry weather, lack of snow, and so on. Some communities have dealt with water shortages by requiring all users to cut back consumption by a certain percentage. This sounds equitable, and is certainly a direct response to the problem. But notice the perverse aspect of this approach. The people who will least feel the effects of these restrictions are those who have used water profligately in the past; the people who will be most affected are those who had already reduced their water consumption prior to the restriction, because they are reducing from a smaller base. In order words, such restrictions reward the wasters and penalize the conservers. This perverse consequence stems from a policy that appears to treat everybody equally in a situation where they differ in an important way.

The Command-and-Control Approach

Perverse incentives are more common in environmental policy than is widely recognized. For the most part they stem from the historical attachment that policy makers have for command-and-control policies.

Most command-and-control standards operate through a preferred technology approach. Authorities identify an industry that is causing pollution. They study that industry (or more likely they hire a private contractor to study the industry) and identify a series of technology options that all firms in the industry might adopt. For each option they estimate its costs and its performance in terms of emissions. The study produces data like the following (real data will be much more complicated, of course, but this simplification captures the essence of it):

	Technology Options				
	A	B	C	D	E
Cost ($ mil per year)	10	20	40	100	400
Emissions (tons per year)	100	80	60	40	10

Now the authorities must choose one of these technologies and set the corresponding emission limits. Pollution-control laws typically contain language directing officials to select the "best available technology," the "best practicable technology," or "best conventional technology." The authorities have to decide what these phrases mean in the context of the data. Typically, they are interpreted in terms of cost; a "practical" technology, for example, would presumably be one that did not involve substantial costs, whereas "available" might imply a more high-tech, presumably more expensive, approach.

In the above example, authorities might select technology C as the one that best meets the criteria in the law. Implicitly or explicitly, they are setting an emission standard of 60 tons per year. The enforcement problem is now to get all firms in the industry to adopt technology C.

Getting Emissions and Cost Data. A command-and-control approach requires that the authorities develop reasonably accurate cost and emission data on which to base their decisions. The primary source for these data is the polluting industries themselves. There is no particular incentive for the firms in the industries to provide accurate information. In fact, they have an incentive to provide data to the authorities that make it appear that pollution control in their industry is going to be very costly, implying that the standards should not be too restrictive. It is common for members of the polluting community to appear before Congress and argue that proposed pollution-control regulations are going to be extremely costly and disruptive to their industries. Most persuasive to legislators is information that shows that regulations will result in job losses in their districts. Future pollution-control costs become matters of great controversy.

The problem is not that estimates of future costs have to be made; certainly they do, and in so doing industry data are important. The problem is that when setting very specific technology requirements in command-and-control regulations, problems about uncertain future costs become unduly magnified and controversial.

End-of-the-Pipe Bias.   Inevitably, the technology options identified by command-and-control authorities are simplifications in the sense that they concentrate on one, or a few, of the many dimensions of the total operations of firms within that industry. They do this because it is simply too complicated to include each and every facet of a firm's operations in the technology analyses. It is widely accepted that for many years the EPA's command-and-control regulations focused on "end-of-the-pipe" aspects of the operations. They addressed different ways of handling and treating emissions. It also has been widely recognized that in many cases the best way to reduce pollution is to go back into the earlier stages of a firm's operations and to make changes that will reduce the quantity of emissions that have to be handled at the end of the pipe.

Ideally, firms themselves would evaluate every stage of the whole production process to look for ways to reduce pollution throughout their operations. This is known as the "pollution prevention" perspective. But pollution prevention efforts have to be done opportunistically, on a case-by-case basis, using the special knowledge of the people who are actually running the operations, not by public regulators. So pollution prevention programs have been very hard to integrate into the command-and-control approach, and have existed mostly as add-ons that have had only modest success. At the federal level the first major effort at pollution prevention was the Pollution Prevention Act of 1990. Similar programs have been initiated by many of the states. In general they stress information disclosure, mandatory pollution prevention planning, and voluntary actions by polluters.[7]

Differentiated Control.   Consider a scenario in which public regulators tell the electric power industry that it has to reduce total SO_2 emissions by 50 percent over the next ten years. Contrast this with a command-and-control approach in which authorities mandate specific pollution-control technologies that power plants have to adopt (e.g., they all have to adopt stack-gas scrubbers). There is now a strong incentive for certain firms, or groups of firms, within the industry to ask authorities for exemption to the standards. Commonly, older firms in an industry request exemptions on the basis of the prohibitively high cost of retrofitting their plants. If they successfully argue their case, the result is **differentiated control**, which means that regulators place different pollution-control requirements on different sources within an industry.

At present, about half of America's electricity is generated in large coal-fired power plants, most of them built between 1950 and 1980. About a third of the CO_2 emitted in the country comes from these plants. They are responsible for about 60 percent of national SO_2 emissions, 25 percent of NO_x emissions, and about a third of total mercury emissions, besides numerous other airborne toxics. Replacing these coal-fired plants with modern gas-fired plants would reduce these pollutants by very substantial amounts. In the normal course of events, as plants age and their technologies become outdated, they are replaced with newer plants. But this is not happening in the case of coal-fired power plants. In fact, the amount of power generated by these plants is increasing, not decreasing. Some new plants are being built, but the old coal-fired plants persist.

Why don't we see a rapid move toward these newer, less-polluting power plants? Economics might be one explanation. The old coal-fired plants are completely paid off by this time, so the only costs associated with their use are the variable costs: fuel, labor, and so on. Generation costs vary from plant to plant, but appear to average about 2 cents per kilowatt hour (kWh). New gas-fired plants have costs of about 3–3.5 cents per kWh, which is less than what it costs to operate a new coal-fired plant (about 4 cents per kWh), but more than the costs of the old coal plants.

A closer look at the situation, however, shows that the problem is not so much plain economics as much as it is regulatory. The main reason why the older coal-fired plants continue to thrive is because of a perverse incentive of the Clean Air Act. The act has the effect of raising the costs of new cleaner technology and lowering the costs of the older, dirtier plants.

The culprit is differentiated control, which typically applies more stringent pollution control standards to new sources rather than existing sources. As we discussed in chapter 9, the 1970 CAA incorporated differentiated control through the provision called "new source performance standards" (NSPS). These standards applied to new or significantly modified sources. In nonattainment areas, state implementation plans (SIPs) require new sources to install technology consistent with the "lowest achievable emission rate" (LAER). Existing sources must install "reasonably available control technology" (RACT), which is less stringent than LAER.

The 1977 CAA amendments added the provision for new source review (NSR). NSR is meant to have a more sensitive trigger so that companies can not make substantial modifications to extend the lives of their plants without having to install more costly pollution-control technology.

The environmental community has in general staunchly supported NSR, on the grounds that it appears to represent a more aggressive approach to controlling emissions from these large power plants. It is sometimes associated with the notion of "technology forcing." **Technology forcing** means to apply pollution control standards that would be very costly to achieve with today's technology, in the hopes that companies will develop better (i.e., less costly) pollution-control techniques to meet the standards. Differentiated control would seem to lend itself to technology forcing because very stringent standards can be applied to new sources.

Aficionados of differentiated control also use economic arguments to support the practice. It is normally more costly to retrofit pollution-control technology into existing sources than to build them into new sources at the time they are being constructed. Furthermore, it is thought, in the normal course of events old sources wear out and are gradually replaced by new ones, so eventually the newer sources with more stringent pollution control will become predominant. It's important to recognize also that many of the "new" sources are actually old sources that have been substantially modified and upgraded with more efficient production technology. So the more restrictive pollution control standards apply to both brand new sources and old sources that are being substantially modified.

The huge problem with differentiated control, however, is that it creates perverse incentives. If a new plant will be subject to more costly pollution-control measures than an existing plant, a company may very well decide to hold onto the old plant to avoid the stricter requirements. In this way the system of differentiated control creates an incentive to continue to operate older, more polluting plants. The perverse incentive may run deeper because firms will have little incentive to voluntarily reduce emissions from existing sources, even though in many circumstances this might be done at modest cost. An example of how this affects power plant regulation is shown in exhibit 14.2.

Larry Parker and John Blodgett, of the Congressional Research Service, have studied the overall impact of NSR. They reveal that over the last decade or so, the utilization of the older coal-fired power plants has actually increased, rather than decreased, as you would expect with power plants that are aging. It clearly appears that many power companies are doing what is needed to extend the economic lives of these older plants without triggering NSR provisions of the CAA.[8]

CAFE Standards

Corporate Average Fuel Economy or **CAFE standards** are requirements placed on manufacturers' fleets of vehicles that require them to meet minimum fuel economy standards or else pay a financial penalty for exceeding prescribed levels. Currently, the CAFE standard for passenger cars is 27.5 miles per gallon, an average over all passenger cars sold by the manufacturer (the manufacturer can produce cars that exceed this standard as long as they are offset by cars that beat the standard). However, the CAFE standard is lower for light trucks, including sport utility vehicles (SUVs), at 20.7 mpg. Initially, it was thought that because light trucks (e.g., pickups) were used mainly for commercial purposes, the differential standards were justifiable.

Manufacturers, however, in response to the two-tiered standards, began aggressively marketing light trucks and SUVs. This was for two reasons.

Exhibit 14.2
Perverse Incentives Under New Source Review

"NSR can create perverse environmental incentives, especially when major technology advances make new plants much cleaner than old ones. A recent analysis by Byron Swift illustrates how NSR requirements can impede the adoption of clean and efficient energy technologies, such as combined heat and power (CHP) systems. In a modern CHP system, fuel is burned in a turbine to generate electricity, and the waste heat from combustion, which in conventional stand-alone generation systems is vented to the atmosphere, is used in commercial or industrial processes at the site. A new CHP installation using a gas-fired turbine with low-nitrogen oxide burners and no end-of-pipe emissions controls substantially reduces nitrogen oxide emissions from levels that would result from the continued operation of an existing onsite boiler to provide process heat and an offsite power plant to provide power. CHP also allows for a substantial reduction in the total primary energy input required to meet heat and power needs, yielding economic benefits and lower carbon dioxide emissions.

"Unfortunately, NSR rules pose a substantial deterrent to the spread of CHP technology. Potential users of CHP, typically existing industrial or commercial facilities with old onsite boilers, are subject to an uncertain and time-consuming NSR permitting process. In addition, NSR rules require the application of end-of-pipe control technology to an already clean turbine with very low emissions. This requirement can significantly increase the cost of a CHP project and removes only a small amount of pollution, resulting in a very high cost per ton of removal—upwards of $25,000 by Swift's estimate, or 25 to 75 times the cost of emissions reductions available from existing sources."

Source: Excerpted with permission from Howard K. Gruenspecht and Robert N. Stavins, "New Source Review Under the Clean Air Act: Ripe for Reform," *Resources* 147 (Washington, DC: Resources for the Future, Spring 2002):20. The research report referred to is: Byron Swift, "Grandfathering, New Source Review, and NO$_x$— Making Sense of a Flawed System," *Environment Reporter* 31, no. 29 (2000):1538–1546.

First, the lower costs of meeting less-stringent fuel economy (and emissions) standards made them more cost-effective. Second, by attracting buyers who would otherwise purchase mid-size or full-size sedans, car companies were able to reduce the portion of the passenger-car fleet devoted to the relatively less-efficient models, thereby improving their CAFE standard and reducing or eliminating any penalty charges. Therefore, the attempt to improve fuel economy and reduce gasoline consumption through CAFE standards served, in effect, to worsen the situation by giving manufacturers an incentive to sell less-efficient light trucks and SUVs to erstwhile car buyers.

How Do Perverse Incentives Arise?

As noted earlier, perverse consequences often result when policy makers rely on traditional command-and-control remedies without taking into account the various ways people might modify their behavior in response to the regulation. Another example from the CAFE program is illustrative. The objective of that program is to have an automobile fleet that gets better mileage, thereby reducing our dependence on foreign oil and producing fewer aggregate emissions from that fleet. This is a worthy objective; but the way we try to achieve it is important. When Congress simply mandates better mileage, it means that consumers will be buying cars that on average get better mileage. In other words, they are less expensive to drive per mile, assuming the price of gasoline is unchanged. But this means that people will, again on average, drive them more miles per year. So part, perhaps a large part, of the better miles-per-gallon performance of cars will be offset by the fact that they are driven more miles. The behavioral responses that people make to the regulation, in other words, work against the objectives of the program.

Another example that illustrates this phenomenon occurred in the mid-1990s in Mexico City. Authorities, trying to do something about the heavy air pollution there, decided that air quality could be substantially improved if the number of cars being driven into the city each day could be reduced. Using a straightforward command-and-control approach, they passed a regulation banning certain cars on certain days. They implemented a program that used license plate numbers to identify cars: If the last digit of the number was 1 or 2, the car was banned on Mondays; if the last digit was 3 or 4, the car was banned on Tuesdays; and so on. Thus, if license plate numbers were strictly random, this meant that there should be 20 percent fewer cars on each weekday (it did not apply to weekends). After this scheme had been in place for a few years, however, authorities found that the number of cars being driven into Mexico City had not decreased; in fact, it had actually increased somewhat. The reason is that thousands of commuters had reacted in a predictable way, by buying a second car—with an offsetting number on the plate—that they could use on certain days of the week. In this way the regulation, since it overlooked the behavioral responses that would follow, seems to have made the city's air pollution problem worse.

Sometimes perverse incentives will have special-interest effects. For example, air pollution regulations on "mobile sources" (e.g., automobiles) impose stringent standards on new cars without affecting older cars. Why? Because it is very expensive to retrofit older cars with new pollution-control technologies. Moreover, few politicians want to impose the equivalent of a significant tax on nearly every citizen by requiring all existing cars to be retrofitted. It is much easier to impose restrictions on things that don't yet exist—new cars—than on an existing fleet of millions of automobiles. The problem is that because advanced pollution-control technologies make new cars more costly, many people delay the purchase of a new car. And since older cars pollute much more heavily than new cars, the added incentive to keep one's old car serves to delay air quality improvements because of the aging fleet of existing automobiles. Therefore, while perverse incentives are destructive, the political logic that created them also protects them. Moreover, while the incentives may be perverse for society as a whole, significant benefits accrue to certain groups, like the owners of older automobiles, who get the benefits of cleaner air without the costs.

Summary

The primary purpose of environmental regulation is, or should be, to improve environmental quality in its many dimensions. But there are a number of other consequences that sometimes arise. In this chapter we discussed unforeseen consequences, special-interest consequences, and perverse consequences.

Unforeseen consequences are impacts, often negative, that were not anticipated when regulations were put into effect. Since policy makers are no more omniscient than anyone else, and our understanding of the environment is not complete, these can clearly occur. The appearance of MTBE contamination of local water supplies was not anticipated when this material was approved as a gasoline additive to combat air pollution. Reducing the likelihood of unforeseen consequences requires appropriate analysis of environmental actions and the organization of the policy process in a way that encourages a broad perspective on proposed policies and regulations.

Special-interest effects tend to favor one particular special interest; for example, the producers of gasoline additives benefit when the EPA mandates the use of additives. Most environmental regulations will have differential consequences for different economic groups; it is important to have transparency in the policy process and to make sure that special-interest consequences do not drive environmental policy.

Perverse consequences are policy outcomes that actually work against the stated objectives of the policy involved. They normally result from command-and-control measures that do not adequately take into account the behavioral responses that individuals and firms will make to the new regulation. Perverse incentives are surprisingly common in environmental policy. An increased adoption of well-designed incentive-based policies is one way of reducing perverse incentives.

Key Terms

CAFE standards   perverse consequences
differentiated control   special-interest consequences
end-of-pipe bias   technology forcing
incentive-based policy   unforeseen consequences

Questions for Further Discussion

1. Suppose a law was passed in a certain city requiring that every commuter carpool at least once a week. What would be some of the consequences (unforeseen, special interest, or perverse) of this law?

2. What steps might be taken to reduce the influence of special-interest impacts in environmental policy?

3. What steps might be taken to reduce the incidence of significant unforeseen consequences in environmental policy?

4. In what ways might the organizational structure of the EPA affect the incidence and seriousness of unforeseen consequences arising from environmental regulations?

Web Sites

There are few, if any, Web sites devoted exclusively to chronicling policy impacts. There are some sites where, amidst the other messages the site managers want to get out, policy impacts are sometimes discussed. From a conservative approach see:

www.CATO.org/research/nature-st.html

For a liberal view see:

www.greenpeace.org

Other relevant Web sites are:

Resources for the Future

www.rff.org

The Brookings Institute

www.brookings.org

Additional Readings

Ackerman, Bruce A., and William T. Hassler, *Clean Coal/Dirty Air* (New Haven, CT: Yale University Press, 1981).

Bryant, Bunyan, ed., *Environmental Justice, Issues, Policies, and Solutions* (Washington, DC: Island Press, 1995).

Bryner, Gary C., *Blue Skies, Green Politics: The Clean Air Act of 1990*, 2nd ed. (Washington, DC: CQ Press, 1995).

National Association of Public Administrators, *The Environment Goes to Market: The Implementation of Economic Incentives for Pollution Control* (Washington, DC: NAPA, 1994).

Pye-Smith, Charlie, *The Subsidy Scandal: How Your Government Wastes Your Money to Wreck Your Environment* (London: Earthscan, September 2002).

Sterner, Thomas, *Policy Instruments for Environmental and Natural Resource Management* (Washington, DC: Resources for the Future, 2003).

Notes

[1] We will deal with this in greater detail in chapter 18.

[2] See Regan J. R. Smith, "Playing the Acid Rain Game: A State's Remedies," *Environmental Law* 16 (1986):255 ff.

[3] David Stikkers, "The Unintended Consequences of Reformulated Gasoline," in Paul S. Fischbeck and R. Scott Farrow, eds., *Improving Regulation: Cases in Environment, Health and Safety* (Washington, DC: Resources for the Future, 2001):88.

[4] See, for example, John A. Hird, "Superfund Expenditures and Cleanup Priorities: Distributive Politics or Public Interest," *Journal of Policy Analysis and Management* 9 (1990):445–483; Thomas Stratmann, "The Politics of Superfund," in Terry L. Anderson, ed., *Political Environmentalism, Going Behind the Green Curtain* (Stanford, CA: Hoover Institution Press, 2000):239–262.

[5] W. Kip Viscusi, "The Lulling Effect: The Impact of Child-Resistant Packaging on Aspirin and Analgesic Ingestions," *American Economic Review* (1984):324–327.

[6] I am indebted to John Hird for this example.

[7] See James Boyd, "The Barriers to Corporate Pollution Prevention: An Analysis of Three Cases," in Paul S. Fischbeck and R. Scott Farrow, eds., *Improving Regulation: Cases in Environment, Health, and Safety* (Washington, DC: Resources for the Future, 2001).

[8] See Larry B. Parker and John E. Blodgett, "Air Quality and Electricity: Enforcing New Source Review," Congressional Research Service, RL30437 (Washington, DC, January 31, 2000).

15

Incentive-Based Environmental Policies

As we have noted throughout the book, most environmental policy actions undertaken to date, both in the United States and in other countries, have been designed on the basic principles of **command and control**. The authorities determine what kinds of pollution abatement actions they believe are best, according to whatever criteria they are using, then regulations are put in place requiring those actions by polluters. The regulations are enforced by standard social machinery, that is, inspectors, courts, fines, jails, and so on.

The popularity of command and control is based on several factors: the public health, nuisance-control orientation of early environmental laws; the legal/engineering culture that dominates the EPA and other policy agencies; and the technological reality that our ability to monitor emissions from specific sources has been relatively weak. One of the main downsides of this regulatory approach is that it encourages the perspective that pollution control is essentially a technological problem, one that can be solved by identifying appropriate techniques and requiring that they be adopted.

Command and control is effective when pollution sources are easy to distinguish, damages from pollution are significant, and the most appropriate pollution-control technologies are easily identified by regulators. But when

293

these conditions are not met, this approach can easily lead to cost ineffectiveness, technological lock-in, and perverse incentives.

The growing realization of these deficiencies has fostered something of a shift in thinking about environmental policy. It is not a shift that everybody embraces with enthusiasm, nor is it a change that has broad applicability to all areas of environmental policy. But it is happening both in the United States and abroad. One way to characterize this shift is a move from considering pollution control as a technological problem toward thinking of it as a behavioral problem. Instead of policies that require public agencies to identify, compel, and enforce actions by polluters, there is an effort to establish programs that harness the initiative and knowledge of the polluters themselves to find and adopt methods of reducing pollution. This effort reflects a growing interest in what are called incentive-based environmental programs.

Incentives in Pollution Control

Incentives are the array of benefits and costs, or rewards and penalties, that impinge on individuals and lead them to act in certain ways. In a sense, any environmental regulation, even a command-and-control regulation, contains incentives. Owners of a polluting enterprise have an incentive to adopt the approved technology to avoid whatever fines and penalties the EPA might impose for noncompliance. But the notion of designing environmental policies to take advantage of the inherent incentives of polluters is different. Here the important incentives are those leading polluters themselves to identify, develop, and adopt more cost-effective approaches to controlling emissions.

A good way to illustrate the importance of incentive-based policies is to discuss them in terms of one of the major policy problems they are designed to address. This is the problem of "information asymmetries."

Information Asymmetries and Incentives

Information asymmetries is a fancy way of saying that one person knows something that another person doesn't. In the real world they are not the exception but rather the rule; they exist everywhere. In the world of public policy, information asymmetries occur when the people being regulated, in our case polluters, have more and better information about pollution-control options and costs than the regulating authorities. When regulators set a performance standard, like emission limits, they have to take into account many things, one of which is the cost that industry or consumers will incur in meeting the standard. A standard that is "too" costly is simply not feasible; if it does happen to get written into law, it won't be implemented and, if authorities do try to enforce it, the courts won't uphold it. But what does "too" costly mean, and who decides when a proposed standard is too costly?

This is where information asymmetries become apparent. Suppose scientists and engineers working for the regulating agency know a lot about the technical features of the industry they are regulating. Suppose they know what technical options are available and have a good idea of what it would cost to develop and adopt them. By "have a good idea" we mean "know as much about it as the firms who will be regulated." This fit the situation in the early 1970s regarding automobile emissions: engineers at the EPA were very knowledgeable about the technologies available for reducing car emissions; in particular, they knew a lot about the potential of catalytic converters, having worked with them directly as well as having read about the work being done by Japanese car manufacturers. In fact, U.S. car companies had been dragging their feet in doing research on catalytic converters, so it is probably correct to say that the EPA had better information than the manufacturers. This made it possible for the EPA to set very challenging emission-reduction goals that were still within the range of feasibility for the car companies to meet. Although there was a great deal of political pushing and shoving between the EPA and the auto manufacturers, overall the process produced very substantial reductions in auto emissions (in emissions per mile, not necessarily in total emissions from the overall car fleet on the roads).[1]

But there are lots of situations where the EPA's information about pollution-control options is far worse than that possessed by the polluters; where there is, in other words, asymmetric information. Nothing is more common in pollution-control politics than members of the regulated community appearing before Congress or the EPA and arguing that a proposed standard will be far more costly than can be justified, or than they can afford. If the EPA does not have reliable, independent information on what these costs will likely be, how does it react? Propose a more relaxed standard? Enact the more stringent standard? Adjust the effort devoted to enforcement? Make the companies swear that the cost information they are providing is truthful?

As an example, consider the contemporary electric power industry. Major changes are taking place in this industry as a result of technological advances, deregulation, and shifts in the international petroleum market. It is hard for people in the industry itself to know how all these changes are going to impact pollution-control options. It is even more difficult, near impossible, for EPA regulators to get a good handle on this. If the EPA were to employ a conventional command-and-control approach, the likelihood that they could identify the most cost-effective[2] means of pollution control in the electric power industry is remote. That's because most of the knowledge about pollution-control technologies lies in the electric power industry itself. And there is no reliable way to get the industry to reveal all of this information to government regulators if the result is going to subject the industry to command-and-control types of regulations.

So a way has to be found to give the regulated community the incentive to use this experience and knowledge. This means a system that allows polluters to benefit themselves when they use their best knowledge and skills to develop and implement the most cost-effective pollution-control actions.

Types of Incentive-Based Policies

There are a number of policies that we can regard as designed to reshape the incentives of polluters. The main ones are:

- Emission charges
- Emission trading plans
  - Cap-and-trade programs
  - Project-based trading
  - Rate-based trading
- Emission subsidies

You might also regard **fines and penalties** as a type of incentive approach, and to some extent they are. If polluters are faced with the prospects of financial penalties for violating regulations, this would clearly act as a deterrent, if the fine is substantial enough. But fines and penalties have to be part of any type of pollution-control program (except those that are strictly voluntary). Establishing the most effective system of penalties is thus an issue in all policy approaches. In designing incentive-based programs, on the other hand, we are trying to actually provide incentives for polluters to look more deeply into their behavior to identify the most effective means of pollution control.

The following sections discuss how incentive-based policies work. Remember that in the real world there is always a difference between how a plan looks on paper and how it works in practice; between how it functions in theory and how it actually operates after all the hard questions of implementation have been encountered. Like anything else in the world of policy, incentive-based schemes have advantages and disadvantages; they work well in some circumstances but not in others.

Emission Charges

Think of a paper mill located on a river. It produces paper, a very useful product even in this supposedly digital age. But it also produces a substantial quantity of waste that has to be disposed of in some way. The nearby river offers a convenient solution; mix the waste material with water, perhaps treat it to some degree, then pipe it into the river. Nature, in the form of the flowing river, will not only move the wastes offsite, but will actually transform them in the process through the natural degradation abilities of the river water. In essence, the firm is receiving a very valuable service from nature but paying very little for it, basically only the cost of the pipe. The firm could not do this with any of its other productive inputs, so why should it be able to do this with the valuable resources of nature?

Extending this logic, it is reasonable to conclude that this paper mill, and all others in the same circumstances, should be charged for using this natural resource; they should be subject to an emission charge. An **emission charge** is simply a monetary charge per unit (ton, pound, kilogram, etc.) of material emitted. In the case of the paper mill it would probably be a charge per ton of biochemical oxygen demand (BOD), which is a measure of the amount of dissolved oxygen in the receiving waters that will be drawn upon to degrade the organic waste.

The incentive aspects of emission charges lie in the fact that they are designed simply to set the charge rate, not to dictate the means by which polluters try to reduce emissions to minimize the financial burden of the charge. Thus, it produces the incentive for firms to choose the most cost-effective methods of pollution control, using their knowledge of and experience with technical and operational options and accompanying costs.

The Politics of Emission Charges

The idea of pollution charges has been around for a long time. Many years ago economists showed that pollution could be regulated in an efficient and cost-effective manner by using a system of emission charges set at the correct level.[3] From a political standpoint, however, the idea has not been popular, at least in the United States. Who wants to have to pay for something that they have been getting free?

The polluting community (not just the business community but also the community of consumers whose cars, for example, pollute the air) has historically looked on emission charges the way people typically look at taxes in general—as burdensome and to a large extent unwarranted, or at least too high. In the early 1970s President Nixon proposed a charge system for BOD, lead in gasoline, and SO_2 emissions from power plants and other large industrial sources. These proposals went nowhere. More recently President Clinton proposed a tax on the carbon content of fuels in order to reduce CO_2 emissions. It also went nowhere.

The environmental community itself has never been particularly attracted to the idea of emission charges. If pollution is seen as a moral issue, a price-based approach to its control is probably going to be regarded with great skepticism. Rather than focus on its pollution-fighting potential, many environmentalists have characterized emission charges as a "pay-to-pollute" system that doesn't recognize pollution as an illegal activity.

Emission Charges in Practice

Nevertheless, the use of emission charges appears to be growing in some pollution-control applications. One is in the area of municipal solid waste (MSW), discussed in chapter 12. A growing number of communities are using volume or weight-based fees, called unit-based prices, for the disposal of household MSW. These are being used not only to provide an incentive to dispose of smaller quantities of MSW, but also to generate funds for running the collection and recycling programs.

Another area is industrial discharges to publicly operated treatment works (POTWs). Over the last decade there has been a trend toward POTWs setting fees for accepting industrial waste, fees that are based on the quantity of wastes sent to the treatment plant. In effect these function like emission charges.[4] Although their primary objective is to finance the waste-treatment facility, not to reduce overall emissions, they do make industrial plant managers more sensitive to finding ways to reduce emissions that are less expensive than the fees they have to pay at the POTW. To this extent they function somewhat like emission charges.

A number of European countries have instituted emission charges. Finland and Norway have charges on CO_2 emissions from selected sources. A number have charges on fuels and electricity, which have the effect of reducing consumption of these commodities. France and Germany have charges on waterborne emissions; Switzerland has a charge on aircraft engine noise.[5]

Cap-and-Trade Programs

The other incentive-based approach to pollution control goes under several names, the most common being **cap and trade**. Most everyone understands intuitively what it means to put a cap on total emissions, but it is not as widely understood how trading is supposed to work and what it is supposed to achieve.

The Origins of Trading in Pollution Control

It will be useful to look at how emission trading came about as a major policy option. From a strictly conceptual point of view, economists were talking about the idea back in the 1960s.[6] From the standpoint of application, the idea of trading arose in the 1970s as a practical response to an obvious problem: how to limit overall emissions in a growing economy.

Think about the following very simple example: Suppose you operate a small firm in a community that derives its water from a groundwater aquifer. Your business requires inputs of water in order to produce your output, perhaps it is flowers. The town decision makers are concerned about water supplies in the near future, and passes an ordinance putting a limit on the maximum amount of water any one firm can withdraw from the system annually. This is a hardship for you because you have a growing business that will need considerably more water in the future. You have a friend, on the other hand, who owns and operates a firm that is probably going to be using less water in the future because the demand for its output is expected to shrink.

Suppose you wanted to find a way to get a larger water allocation. One way would be to go to the water department and convince its director to grant you an increase. You might try to enlist the help of your brother-in-law, who works in the road division but knows some folks in water. If you can put enough pressure on them maybe they will increase your allocation. The outcome will apparently depend on how much influence you can exert, and how adamant the water agency turns out to be.

But you, being clever, see another possibility.[7] You go to the water committee and say: "Look, suppose I can get another firm in town to reduce its water use, so that you can reduce its allotment by 10,000 gallons per year. If I do this, will you increase my allocation by 10,000 gallons per year?" The water agency, not wanting to stifle economic growth, might say: "Sure, we would like to accommodate a growing, vibrant community, so we will do it if you can get your friend to go along." Note that such a deal produces no change in the aggregate quantity of water withdrawn, just a reallocation of individual limits.

This fictitious scenario is similar to the situation in southern California in the 1970s, except that there it concerned air pollution. Because of the region's diminished air quality, authorities put a serious clamp on new sources because they would add to airborne emissions of SO_2, NO_x, and so on. But that created a dilemma: how to accommodate a growing economy without worsening the air pollution problem. The answer local officials came up with (with the participation of the U.S. EPA) was to let potential new sources procure emission reductions from existing sources to offset their new emissions. In fact, these arrangements became known as the **offset program**.

In the scenario with the water supply, you would ask your friend for an offset that would allow you to increase your water allocation. But how do you persuade your friend to give you the offset? You might appeal to your many years of friendship and mutual respect. If that didn't work, you could offer to pay some modest amount for the water offset. If you did that, you would actually be buying (and your friend would be selling) a water withdrawal permit; you would in fact be trading.

The offset program developed along these principles, allowing for economic growth but putting a limit on total emissions. As the concept expanded in the 1970s, offsets could be used among plants owned by the same company (what became known as the **bubble program**), or by plants owned by different companies. In some cases offsets could be banked, that is, put aside for future use if needed. What gradually developed was a large market in offsets, with many buyers (firms wanting to expand operations, or new firms) and many sellers (firms going out of business, moving to another location, or firms that already had found a way to reduce their emissions).

How Cap and Trade Works

Cap and trade is simply an extension of the offset idea. Authorities first establish an overall limit (cap) on annual[8] emissions. This aggregate level of emissions is then allocated out among the various sources, usually by creating emission permits and giving each source a certain number of permits. The sources are then allowed to trade permits among themselves, at whatever prices they agree on.

We can illustrate the process with an example; the details are in table 15.1. There are two sources of an air pollutant, source A and source B. Perhaps they are power plants emitting SO_2. Current emissions are 50 tons per

Table 15.1   Cap-and-Trade Program

	Source A	Source B	Total
Current emissions	50	50	100
Unit costs of reduction	10	30	
Desired reduction (established by authorities)			80
Equiproportionate reduction			
Total emissions	40	40	
Emission control costs	100	300	400
Costs per ton reduced			20
Cap and trade			
Discharge permits issued by authorities	40	40	
Emissions after B buys 10 permits from A	30	50	
Emission control costs	200	0	200
Costs per ton reduced			10

year from each source. The plants, we assume, have somewhat different production technologies; perhaps one is newer than the other, or they use different fuels. The impact of this is that they have different emission control costs: If source A reduces emissions, it will cost $10 per ton, while it will cost source B $30 per ton to reduce emissions.

The first step is for authorities to determine the total cap on emissions. Let's assume this is set at 80 tons. Now suppose that, in the spirit of command and control, we require equiproportionate emission reductions from the two sources. To meet our overall target of 80 tons total, each source will have to reduce emissions by 10 tons. This will cost source A $100 and source B $300, for a total of $400. Thus, in this case the cost per ton of emissions reduced will be $20.

But now let's introduce the trade part of cap and trade. To do this the authorities issue emission permits for 40 tons to each source. A permit is essentially a piece of paper entitling the holder to emit one ton of emissions. Thus, with their new permit holdings, and assuming they do nothing to change them, each source would be entitled to emit a maximum of 40 tons. But they can each do better by trading permits. Suppose they can buy or sell permits among themselves at a price of $20 per permit (we will revisit the issue of price below).

Suppose source A sells 10 permits to source B. Source A now holds 30 permits, and to be legal it must now reduce its emissions to 30 tons. Source B now has 50 permits, so it doesn't have to reduce its emissions at all. Total control costs are $200 for A and $0 for B, for a total of $200. In this case the costs per ton of total emissions reduced is $10, half what it was under an equiproportionate approach. By trading permits, the sources have redistributed the overall 20-ton emission reduction. Source A, with lower unit costs of reduction, ends up taking on the full 20-ton reduction.

The reason this is called an incentive-based program is that it harnesses the natural instincts of companies to find economic gains, in this case leading to permit trading and a redistribution of the overall reduction. In the process, of course, the permits are traded. This means bought and sold, of course, not simply passed about from one to the other. With such trading the price established for the permits is obviously critical.

If source B can buy a permit for anything less than $30 it will be better off doing so, as that is its unit cost of reducing emissions. Likewise, if source A can sell permits for anything over $10, it will be better off doing so, because its costs of emission reduction are only $10. This is why, in the example above, we used a price of $20, half way between $10 and $30. But any permit price in this range would work; the amount that each source would gain would change, but not the fact that they both gain by trading.

Of course, this is just a simple two-source example. In real world cap-and-trade programs there are likely to be hundreds, or possibly thousands, of participants. There is a lot more trading, and markets for emission permits on which prices are established through conventional forces of supply and demand. Exhibit 15.1 discusses a proposed cap-and-trade program for particulate matter.

Implementing Cap-and-Trade Programs

In our simple example, cap and trade looks to be a straightforward plan to encourage cost-effective pollution control. As with any type of public policy, however, there are a host of political and administrative problems associated with the design and implementation of these programs.

It is probably fair to say that the environmental community historically has not been enthusiastic about cap-and-trade programs, for a number of reasons. One is philosophical, the idea that awarding a certain number of emission permits to a firm implies that society in some sense approves of that level of pollution, or that firms are entitled to that level of emissions. Other objections are more practical: that it is overly complicated, that firms will be able to profit from emission reductions they would have made anyway, and that trading may create hot spots, or geographical concentration of permit hold-

---

Exhibit 15.1
Emissions Trading Among Measures Recommended to Control Fine Particles

"In a draft guidance for states, the Environmental Protection Agency suggests they use 'nontraditional' measures, such as emissions trading or pollution fees, to control emissions of fine particles.

"The guidance is being developed to help states come into attainment with a new federal air quality standard for particulate matter being implemented by EPA.

"EPA is scheduled to designate nonattainment areas by Dec. 31 for the new standard, which for the first time regulates particles smaller than 2.5 microns in diameter (PM-2.5).

"The agency announced April 23 that 18 states and the District of Columbia recommended that EPA designate 145 counties within their boundaries as nonattainment areas.

"Fine particles are emitted from a variety of sources, including diesel engines and from burning coal at power plants. According to EPA, fine particles contribute to cardiac and respiratory problems.

"EPA said the draft guidance is intended to give states a larger menu of options for controlling fine particles than traditional measures such as emissions controls on large stationary sources like power plants.

"The agency has undertaken a variety of measures to control particulate matter, including measures to require cleaner-burning diesel engines and a proposed rule to limit sulfur dioxide and nitrogen oxide emissions from power plants using emissions trading.

"EPA circulated the guidance in early May to the State and Territorial Air Pollution Program Administrators and Association of Local Air Pollution Control Officials (STAPPA/ALAPCO), and it is expecting comments from the group by May 28, according to an agency official. The agency wants to make the guidance available to states when it makes final nonattainment zone designations, the official said.

"According to the draft guidance, nontraditional approaches may allow larger emissions reductions at lower cost than traditional measures and also allow control measures to be tailored to individual sources.

"Nontraditional measures can provide incentives for sources to make continuous emissions reductions, the draft guidance says, unlike traditional measures which require specific sources to meet specific limits but provide no incentive to do more.

"Emissions trading, such as EPA's acid rain program to control sulfur dioxide, takes advantage of the fact that some pollution sources are able to reduce emissions at a lower cost than others, the guidance says.

"According to the guidance, emissions trading allows a source with higher emissions control costs effectively to pay a lower-cost source to reduce emissions beyond the required limit. This achieves the largest emissions reductions at the lowest cost with benefits for both sources.

"The guidance offers examples of state-based emissions trading programs that other states could emulate. For example, the rights to burn dry grass are subject to trading in Spokane, Wash. Some communities in Colorado use tradeable permits to allow the installation of new wood stoves only if permits for existing stoves are retired."

ings. In the latter case, pollution could actually get worse in some regions although in the aggregate, emission levels would improve.

In recent years it seems also fair to say that more members of the environmental community have recognized the benefits of cap and trade. One environmental group, Environmental Defense, has been a primary force among NGOs in encouraging cap-and-trade programs.[9]

Setting the Cap. Although this is an incentive-based scheme, it all starts with a political/administrative decision about what the overall cap should be. Environmentalists want small caps; sources in the polluting industry normally want larger ones. The present fight over national programs to control emissions of SO_2, NO_x, and perhaps CO_2, is largely one about how restrictive to make the caps, in terms of total emissions, and the time frame for compliance. The Bush administration proposal has larger caps and longer times to compliance than the alternative proposal put forth by the Democrats and backed by many environmental groups. These are shown in table 15.2.[10]

In most programs the "cap" is not one number that is unchanging, but rather an initial cap set for a period of years followed by caps that gradually decline over time. This obviously creates more possibilities, for example a high initial cap that declines rapidly, or a lower initial cap with a slower decline.

Distributing the Initial Permits. Having set the overall cap, the next job is to allocate it among the firms that are participating in the program. In the first phase of the SO_2 program in the 1990 Clean Air Act Amendments, for example, the allocation was to about 500 large power plants in the eastern United States. Here the political implications of cap and trade are at their most intense. Emission permits will presumably become valuable items after a program commences, so naturally everybody wants as many permits as they can get in their initial allocation; permits they don't need can then be sold. Of course, some of the participants may have enough political clout to obtain more permits, in which case other parties will get fewer, or the cap will have to increase.

The states themselves may be heavily involved in the initial allocation in programs involving sources in several states. Each state will normally want "its" firms to be abundantly endowed with permits, so that major cutbacks will not be necessary and so they can be sellers rather than buyers of permits. Much of the politicking over the 1990 CAA program for SO_2 trading was spearheaded by the states, as they sought to get more permits for their resident industries. Some of the upper Midwest states (Minnesota, Wisconsin) threatened to have their senators and congresspeople vote against the plan unless some of the large power plants in their states were given more permits. The strategy worked, and the plants were given more permits.

The way to avoid a free-for-all in the initial permit allocation is to use a formula that tries to incorporate the important factors on which awards should be based; for example, the output of the plant (big plants should presumably get more permits than small ones), historic SO_2 emissions (plants

Table 15.2 Legislative Comparison of Multipollutant Proposals S. 150, S. 131, and S. 843

Features	S. 150—Jeffords (109th)	S. 131—Clear Skies (109th)[a]	S. 843—Carper (108th)
Affected Facilities	Electricity-generating facilities with a nameplate capacity of 15 MW or more	Electricity-generating facilities with a nameplate capacity of 25 MW or more	Electricity-generating facilities with a nameplate capacity greater than 25 MW
National Annual Allowance Allocation Caps			
Sulfur Dioxide (SO_2)	2.25 million tons in 2010 Split into two regions[b]	4.5 million tons in 2010 3.0 million tons in 2018	4.5 million tons in 2009 3.5 million tons in 2013 2.25 million tons in 2016
Nitrogen Oxides (NO_x)	1.51 million tons in 2010	2.19 million tons in 2008 1.79 million tons in 2018 Split into two regions[c]	1.87 million tons in 2009 1.7 million tons in 2013
Mercury	5 tons in 2009 Facility-specific emissions limitations without trading	34 tons in 2010 15 tons in 2018	24 tons in 2009 10 tons in 2013 Facility-specific limitations apply[d]
Carbon Dioxide (CO_2)	2.05 billion tons in 2010[e]	No CO_2 policy	2.57+ billion tons in 2009[f] 2.47+ billion tons in 2013[g] + additional tonnage through sequestration incentives

[a] Because of the political stalemate in Congress on these competing plans, the Bush administration in 2005 promulgated two regulatory plans: the Clean Air Interstate Rule and the Clean Air Mercury Rule, which together incorporate most the provisions of the Clear Skies proposal.

[b] Under S. 150, the western region has a 0.275 million ton cap on SO_2 and the nonwestern region has a 1.975 million ton cap on SO_2.

[c] Under S. 131, the western region has a 0.715 million ton cap on NO_x and the eastern region has a 1.475 million ton cap on NO_x. The eastern NO_x cap is reduced to 1.074 million tons in 2018.

[d] For S. 843, from 2009 to 2012, mercury emissions cannot exceed 50% of the total mercury present in delivered coal at each affected facility. After 2012, the percentage drops to 30%. Also, emissions may not exceed an output-based rate determined by the administrator. The CO_2 cap is specified in S. 150 and it approximates 1990 level CO_2 emissions from the electricity sector.

[f] The S. 843 2009 allowance cap is equal to 2006 electricity sector CO_2 emissions as projected by EIA in the most recent report as of date of enactment. The number shown is EIA's *AEO 2003* projection for 2006.

[g] The S. 843 2013 emissions cap is equal to actual 2001 electricity sector CO_2 emissions. The number shown is EIA's *AEO 2003* projection for 2001.

Source: David Lankton, Billy Pizer, Karen Palmer, and Dallas Burtraw, "Legislative Comparison of Multipollutant Proposals S. 150, S. 131 and S. 843 Version 6/3/05." (Washington, DC: Resources for the Future). www.rff.org/multipollutant/. Used with permission.

with higher emissions perhaps should get more permits than plants with lower emissions—or should they?), and so on. While this is a reasonable approach, it has to be recognized that any formula will tend to benefit some sources and put others at a disadvantage. Thus, one can expect political wrangling over the formula.

It also needs to be recognized that there can be perverse incentives lurking in the allocation procedure. Suppose, for example, that firms in an industry expect to be faced with a cap-and-trade program for one of their major pollutants. Suppose further that they think permits will be awarded based in part on the historic emission levels of the firms. They clearly have a disincentive to reduce emissions prior to the program; in fact, they would have an incentive to increase emissions in order to qualify for a larger initial allocation of permits.

Setting Trading Rules. As we saw in the earlier example, the trading part of cap and trade is what ultimately leads to cost-effective pollution control. But there has to be rules governing the trading. Who may trade? How much may they trade? Does the EPA or any other authority have to approve trades? Can permits be leased for short periods of time as well as traded permanently? What happens to a trade if the selling party does not reduce its emissions? Can a permit applicable to emissions in one year be banked for use in future years? These and many other trading questions have to be answered, fashioned into regulations, then enforced.

Perhaps the most fundamental question is the first: Who may trade? Markets work best when the number of potential traders is relatively large. But unless the applicable pollution problem is truly nationwide in its origins, the logic of cap and trade would suggest some limitation on the geographical locations of traders. If authorities create a cap-and-trade program to address industrial emissions in southern California, for example, there probably is no point in allowing trades between firms in Los Angeles and firms in New York. On the other hand, the Title IV program for controlling SO_2 emissions from power plants is indeed a nationwide program; trades have been made between sources in far distant states.

Another interesting question is whether anybody ought to be allowed to buy and sell permits, not just polluters. If, for example, environmental groups are legally allowed to buy permits, the total number of permits in circulation could be reduced over time, leading to commensurate reductions in total emissions, at least in the long run. Most cap-and-trade programs do permit trades by nonpolluters; anybody can buy Title IV SO_2 permits, for example.[11]

The Hot Spot Problem

One major concern in emission permit trading programs is the possibility of creating **hot spots**. Cap-and-trade programs put a limit on total emissions, but when trading takes place among spatially spread out sources, there can be a shift in the regional distribution of emissions. If all or most of the sources in one area are permit sellers, and all or most of the sources in another area are buyers, people living downwind (or downstream) from this second group could actually experience an increase in air (or water) pollution. The 1990 SO_2 trading program, for example, applies to power plants spread throughout many states. Suppose that, hypothetically, all of those in Ohio and Indiana buy permits from plants elsewhere in the country. It is conceivable that total SO_2 emissions from these two states could increase, even as emissions elsewhere went down. Regions downwind from these two states would be exposed to air that had more SO_2 in it than before the program. Exhibit 15.2 bears on this problem and suggests that in the SO_2 program, at least, the hot spot problem has not materialized.

With the push to extend trading to many new pollution situations, however, the hot spot problem is still something to be concerned about. Trading programs in waterborne emissions may be more prone to creating hot spots because of lower levels of mixing within water resources. For example, suppose trading is allowed among industrial sources of water pollution around Long Island Sound. The problem is that there may be substantial differences in localized levels of pollution, because all emissions into the Sound are not uniformly mixed throughout. Thus, local hot spots could appear as a result of the trading.

Other Forms of Incentive-Based Programs

The recent policy emphasis in the United States and elsewhere has been on cap-and-trade programs. A number of eastern states have banded together in an attempt to inaugurate a cap-and-trade program to control CO_2 emissions to combat global warming. The European nations have put in place a

---

Exhibit 15.2
A Conclusion on Hot Spots in the 1990 Clean Air Act
SO_2 Trading Program

"Although trading programs do not guarantee reductions at each source, the data show that they have achieved consistent results between regions, and have also led to proportionately greater reductions at higher-emitting plants. The SO_2 trading program in particular significantly reduced existing hot spots by causing disproportionate reductions in the Midwest. This finding is attributable both to the allocation method used in Title IV and for the tendency in trading programs for the largest sources to reduce emission the most. These findings indicate that cap-and-trade programs similar to those evaluated would not be expected to lead to emissions concentrations or hot spots."

Source: Excerpted from Bureau of National Affairs, "Emission Trading and Hot Spots: A Review of Major Programs," *Environment Reporter* 35, no. 19 (2004):1035.

major cap-and-trade program to control greenhouse gases, and the principles of cap-and-trade have been introduced into the Kyoto process. There are, however, other types of incentive programs.

Other Forms of Trading

There are several other types of trading programs in addition to cap and trade. These go under the names of (1) project-based trading and (2) rate-based trading.

In project-based trading each source is given a baseline quantity of emissions and then may buy or sell credits to cover emissions higher or lower than the baseline. Suppose, for example, a source is given a baseline emission quantity of 1,000 tons per year. If it then reduces its emissions to 800 tons, it may trade its 200-ton credit to some other source whose emission rate is above its baseline level. Project-based trading does not require setting an overall emission level (the cap), nor an original permit allocation level for each source. It does require setting baseline levels, however, and doing this will normally be controversial. One problem often encountered is whether to set the baseline on the basis of some historical emissions performance, or on the basis of expected future emissions if the trading program were not in existence. The administrative aspects of this type of trading program will be substantially different than those under cap-and-trade programs.

Under a rate-based system, standards are set for emissions per unit of output (e.g., emissions per million kilowatt hours of electricity generated). Trading is then allowed in these units. These are somewhat more complicated to administrate, and more problematical in terms of achieving reductions in overall emission levels in an industry or region.[12]

Subsidies and the Environment

There is another sense in which incentives are important for improving the environment. In the complex world of public regulation, some firms and industries often end up receiving public subsidies. These **subsidies** can be overt or covert, involving direct cash payments from the government, or favorable regulations that have the effect of increasing the incomes of the affected firms or industries. Various political justifications are used for subsidies, such as the need to save jobs or the strategic importance of the industry. In effect, subsidy programs become incentives that shape the way industries perform and grow. They also can have major impacts on the environmental effects of these industries. So in many cases an effective way of reducing these environmental impacts is to reduce the subsidies.

Perhaps the clearest example of this is agriculture. Over the years, public programs designed to support the incomes of farmers have had a major impact on farm operations. They have helped to produce a heavily industrialized, chemically dependent agriculture, designed to maximize per acre or per animal yields. This has led to a number of pollution problems, notably fertilizer runoff, pesticide contamination, and concentration of animal wastes.

From an analytical perspective it is usually difficult to determine the exact contribution to a pollution problem caused by subsidies of various forms. The political problem of eliminating subsidies is even harder.

Political Aspects of Incentive-Based Programs

Although incentive-based environmental policies are becoming popular, they are not about to replace entirely the command-and-control apparatus in pollution control. That structure, and the thousands of regulations it has produced, will persist for a long time. Not only is the command-and-control mentality enduring, but the organizational machinery that has evolved to implement the regulations can not be rapidly changed. More importantly, there are many cases of pollution control that do not lend themselves directly to incentive-based solutions.

In addition, not everybody within the policy struggle is convinced that incentive-based programs are the best way to proceed. Incentive-based programs have been much touted by economists, who have always put great emphasis on efficiency and cost effectiveness. The potential cost savings from incentive-based plans are persuasive for many policy advocates who approach the issue of pollution control from an economics perspective.

Many environmental groups, on the other hand, look at incentive-based measures with little enthusiasm, if not outright hostility. Part of it is simply political combat; if firms in the regulated community are in favor of cap and trade, as they often are, then the environmental community needs to be wary. For environmentalists, the flexibility that is touted as the main advantage of cap and trade is actually one of the main drawbacks. Polluters seeking relief from environmental regulations often put their pleas in the form of a need for added flexibility. Environmental advocates are worried that giving polluters added flexibility can actually give them more ways to avoid significant emission cutbacks.

Summary

Recent years have seen an evolution in environmental policy. Although the historic emphasis on command-and-control regulations continues to exist, there is an evolution toward incentive-based pollution-control programs. Such programs attempt to harness the cost-reducing incentives that profit-driven firms normally have, and direct it toward the adoption of more cost-effective pollution-control measures. By including the regulated community in the search for effective pollution control, approaches attempt to balance the information asymmetries inherent in command-and-control measures.

The two main types of incentive-based programs are emission charges and emission trading. Pollution charges have never had very strong political backing, for the same reason that there has never been strong support for any type of new tax. In at least one area, however, charges are becoming more common: This is in the handling of household waste. Around the country many communities have moved in the direction of unit-based pricing for household solid waste, both to raise money and to give households an incentive to reduce their waste streams.

Emission trading programs, on the other hand, are becoming more popular, gaining supporters in both the environmental and regulated communities. The main approach is cap and trade, in which authorities set an overall cap on total emissions, but allow trading among firms to redistribute the individual cutbacks in a cost-effective way. In theory, cap-and-trade programs produce more pollution control per dollar of program cost than the standard command-and-control plan. Cap and trade is not a magic panacea, however. It fits some pollution-control problems better than others, and requires a well-thought strategy for allocating permits, establishing trading rules, and minimizing the potential for hot spots.

Key Terms

bubble program	hot spots
cap and trade	information asymmetries
command and control	offset program
emission charge	subsidies
fines and penalties	

Questions for Further Discussion

1. Pick a pollution-control problem (e.g., vehicle emissions, power plants, pulp mills). Discuss the information asymmetries that public regulators have in developing pollution-control measures for that problem.

2. One of the major differences between command-and-control and incentive-based measures is how they impact future technical change in pollution-control technologies. Explain.

3. How might you design a cap-and-trade program to deal with tailpipe emissions from automobiles?

4. "Uncontrolled markets are the cause of the problem. So how can we expect to use markets successfully to correct environmental pollution problems?" Comment.

5. The Kyoto Protocol contains provisions for a global trading system in CO_2 emission permits. What might you foresee as potential problems in such a global trading system?

Web Sites

The U.S. EPA publishes volumes of material about incentive-based programs. One of these is "Tools of the Trade: A Guide to Designing and Oper-

ating a Cap-and-Trade Program for Pollution Control," available at:
www.epa.gov/airmarkets/international/tools.pdf

On water quality trading:
www.epa.gov/owow/watershed/trading/tradingpolicy.html

The EPA's program in economic incentives for pollution control has much useful information:
www.yosemite.epa.gov/ee/epa/eed.nsf/webpages/homepage

Also see the Web sites of:

Resources for the Future, which reports on much research on incentive-based approaches
www.rff.org

Environmental Defense, which has strongly represented incentive-based type programs in policy debates
www.ed.org

Other useful information is available at:
www.oecd.org (click on environment)
http://pdf.wri.org/incentives_overviewdoc.pdf

The Center for Clean Air Policy encourages incentive-based approaches to air pollution problems:
www.ccap.org

Foundation for Research on Economics and the Environment:
www.free-eco.org

Additional Readings

Ackerman, Bruce A., and Richard B. Stewart, "Reforming Environmental Law: The Democratic Case for Market Incentives," *Columbia Journal of Environmental Law* 13 (1988):171–199.

Anderson, Frederick R. et al., *Environmental Improvements Through Economic Incentives* (Baltimore, MD: Johns Hopkins University Press, 1978).

Anderson, Robert, *The U.S. Experience with Economic Incentives in Environmental Pollution Control Policy* (Washington, DC: Environmental Law Institute, 1997).

Cole, Daniel H., *Pollution and Property: Comparing Ownership Institutions for Environmental Protection* (Cambridge: Cambridge University Press, 2002).

Dower, Roger C., and Mary Beth Zimmerman, *The Right Climate for Carbon Taxes: Creating Economic Incentives to Protect the Atmosphere* (Washington, DC: World Resources Institute, August 1992).

Environmental Law Institute, *Effluent Charges on Air and Water Pollution*, ELI Monograph Series (Washington, DC: ELI, 1973).

Hahn, Robert W., and Robert N. Stavins, "Incentive-Based Environmental Regulation: A New Era for an Old Idea?" *Ecology Law Quarterly* 18, no. 1 (1991):1–42.

National Association of Public Administration (NAPA), *The Environment Goes to Market: The Implementation of Economic Incentives for Pollution Control* (Washington, DC: NAPA, 1994).

Organization for Economic Cooperation and Development, *Domestic Transferable Permits for Environmental Management* (Paris: OECD, 2001).

Organization for Economic Cooperation and Development, *Implementing Domestic Tradeable Permits for Environmental Protection* (Paris: OECD, 1999).

Organization for Economic Cooperation and Development, *Improving the Environment Through Reducing Subsidies*, 3 vols. (Paris OECD, 1999).

Organization for Economic Cooperation and Development, *Taxation and the Environment: Complementary Policies* (Paris: OECD, 1993).

Organization for Economic Cooperation and Development, *Environmental Policy: How to Apply Economic Instruments* (Paris OECD, 1991).

Raymond, Leigh, *Private Rights in Public Resources Equity and Property Allocation in Market-Based Environmental Policy* (Washington, DC: Resources for the Future, 2003).

Reppeto, Robert L. et al., *Green Fees: How a Tax Shift Can Work for the Environment and the Economy* (World Resources Institute, 1992).

Schelling, Thomas C., ed., *Incentives for Environmental Protection* (Cambridge, MA: MIT Press, 1983).

U.S. Environmental Protection Agency, *The U.S. Experience with Economic Incentives for Protecting the Environment*, EPA-240-R-01-001 (January 2001). http://www.epa.gov/economics/.

U.S. Environmental Protection Agency, *Economic Incentives, Options for Environmental Protection*, 21P-2001 (Washington, DC: EPA, March 1991).

U.S. Environmental Protection Agency, *Economic Disincentives for Pollution Control: Legal, Political and Administrative Dimensions*, EPA-600/5-74-026 (Washington, DC: EPA, 1974).

Wallart, Nicolas, *The Political Economy of Environmental Taxes* (Cheltenham, UK and Northampton, MA: Edward Elgar, 1999).

Notes

[1] This course of events was very well described by David Gerard and Lester B. Lave, *Implementing Technology-Forcing Policies: The 1970 Clean Air Act Amendments and the Introduction of Advanced Automobile Emissions Control* (Carnegie Mellon University, Center for the Study and Improvement of Regulation, 2003).

[2] "Cost effective" means the biggest bang for the buck. Suppose I have two possible pollution-control measures: one costs $11 million and will reduce total emissions by 500 tons per year; the other costs $15 million and will produce a reduction of 750 tons per year. The second program is more cost effective because it costs $20,000 per ton to reduce emissions, while the first costs $22,000 per ton.

[3] See, for example, Edwin Johnson, "A Study in the Economics of Water Quality Management," *Water Resources Research* 3, no. 2, Second Quarterly (1967).

[4] Winston Harrington, *Regulating Industrial Water Pollution in the United States* (Washington, DC: Resources for the Future, n.d.).

[5] Barry C. Field, and Martha K. Field, *Environmental Economics: An Introduction*, 4th ed. (New York: McGraw-Hill, 2006):234.

[6] For example, see J. H. Dales, *Pollution, Property and Prices* (University of Toronto Press, 1968).

[7] There is a third option, that of simply taking more than your entitlement, hoping either to stay undetected or to be able to appeal to the judge when you get penalized for overuse. We will overlook this possibility.

[8] It could be some other time period, monthly, quarterly, etc.

[9] One ED economist, Dan Dudek, was instrumental in designing the Title IV program for trading SO_2 permits, and has continued to promote trading programs in the United States and around the world.

[10] The bills reported are all Senate Bills. Comparable bills have been introduced in the House, though there are differences. For example, the "Climate Stewardship Act," introduced in the

House by John Olver and colleagues, proposes trading programs for, among other substances, CO_2, methane, nitrous oxide, and sulfur hexafluoride.

[11] If you would like to buy a permit, or portion of a permit, perhaps for a gift, there are Web sites where you can do so. One of these is the Clean Air Conservancy: www.cleanairconservancy.org/. Carbon offsets can be purchased through Terra Pass, Inc. at www.terrapass.com.

[12] More extensive discussions of the different types of trading programs appear in *Tools of the Trade: A Guide to Designing and Operating a Cap and Trade Program for Pollution Control*, EPA 430-B-03-002 (Washington, DC: EPA, June 2003).

16

Policy Analysis

Principles, Roles, and Controversies

One of the significant ongoing struggles in federal (and state) environmental policy is whether, and how, some degree of formal policy analysis ought to be incorporated into the policy decision process. By formal analysis we mean explicit attempts to account for the social consequences of policies and regulations, in a spirit of openness and using reasonably objective analytical methods. Put this way, what could be controversial about more and better policy analysis? It would appear to be a necessary step in making rational policy decisions. But the policy world is a political world, one of ambition and influence, where political interests can often thrive on ambiguity and obscurity. On the other hand, good policies can sometimes be hamstrung when impossible standards of analytical clarity are demanded.

In this chapter we will do two things: (1) describe the main types of analysis involved in evaluating environmental policy, and (2) discuss the pros and cons that have been put forth by participants in the policy-analysis controversy. No one should doubt that there is a real struggle underway. Several decades ago President Reagan issued an executive order requiring benefit-cost analysis for all major federal regulations. President Clinton issued his own executive order, relaxing the requirement somewhat. With the rise of conservative forces in Congress, more and more interest is being expressed in that body for policy analysis. The environmental community is split. For

example, one published argument against analysis is titled *Sophisticated Sabotage: The Intellectual Games Used to Subvert Responsible Regulation.*[1] But there are
many in the movement who believe more and better analysis would be useful.

Benefit-Cost Analysis

The most comprehensive, and generic, type of analysis used to evaluate
public programs is benefit-cost analysis. The basic format for this analysis
was developed fifty years ago, primarily to evaluate federal water resource
development projects (especially large dams and their related systems). Since
then it has been applied more widely, one application of which is its use in
evaluating pollution-control policies and regulations.

The Basic Idea

The essence of **benefit-cost analysis** is to identify and place a value on all
of the consequences of a particular project or regulation. Some of those consequences are costs, for example, the costs of building a hazardous-waste
incinerator or the costs of complying with a new regulation. Some of the consequences are benefits, for example, the reduction in damages from pollutants
being introduced into the environment. The underlying principle is that these
projects or regulations involve trade-offs; one cannot have the benefits without the costs. The justification for doing the analysis is to show policy makers
the nature of the trade-offs inherent in the particular policy decision.

Figure 16.1 depicts the valuations of benefits and costs; for example,
those that might flow from a regulation requiring communities to achieve a
certain recycling rate for their municipal solid waste. The recycling rate, running from zero to 100 percent, is indexed along the horizontal axis, while
costs are indexed along the vertical axis. The two curves illustrate the benefits
and costs of achieving varying levels of recycling. So, for example, a recycling
rate of r_1 percent would entail costs of $\$c_1$ and benefits of $\$b_1$, and net benefits of $\$b_1 - \$c_1$. The functions show the essential aspects of the trade-off: A
higher recycling rate will indeed produce greater benefits, but at higher costs.

A benefit-cost analysis may be used to evaluate a predetermined policy.
For example, suppose authorities have chosen a target recycling rate of r_2.
The job of the analyst is then to determine what the benefits and costs of that
target would be. Or a benefit-cost analysis might be used to help identify a
worthwhile target in the first place. If one knew enough about the two curves
shown in the figure, one could identify the recycling rate that gives the maximum net benefits. For example, net benefits at r_2 exceed those at a recycling
rate of r_1.

Steps in a Benefit-Cost Analysis

Every benefit-cost analysis involves particular attention to the unique
project or regulation to which it is being applied, so every analysis will have

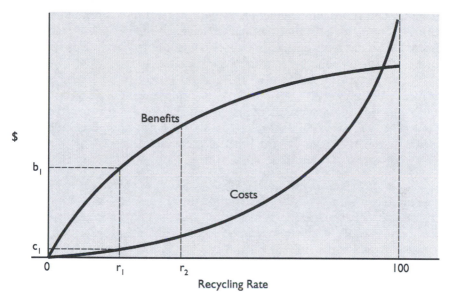

Figure 16.1   Benefits and Costs of Recycling

some unique elements. But there is a basic structure that every benefit-cost analysis conforms to, more or less. It involves the following steps:

1. Initial Specification.   This involves specifying clearly the project or regulation to be studied. One cannot analyze what has been unclearly described.

2. Measuring Consequences.   This requires determining the full impacts, both costs and benefits, in physical terms. Suppose the project involves the construction of a series of offshore wind turbines to generate electricity. The project must be completely specified in terms of such factors as construction schedule, operating procedures, maintenance and repair requirements, and the expected schedule of power production over time. In this case it will be necessary to address the question of what type of power production the turbines will replace when they are operating (this is the problem of establishing a **baseline**: what would have happened in the absence of the project). Another need in this case is a full description of the visual (scenic) impairment the turbines would produce, numbers of affected people, sight-lines impact, and so on.

If what is being evaluated is a regulation, prospectively or retrospectively, the requirements are somewhat different. In this case the analyst must determine the flow over time of factors that are impacted by the regulation, and compare these with what would have happened in its absence. Suppose, for example, that the regulation is an emission standard; firms in a particular industry will be subject to a maximum rate of emissions, which itself will decline over time according to a specified schedule. The analyst must now determine how firms will respond to the new requirement in terms of the technical and procedural changes they will make in their operations. To do this, of course, requires that the analyst have substantial knowledge of the technological characteristics of the firms in this industry, as well as economic factors affecting the market in which they operate.

The other critical factor is to determine how changes in emissions levels from this industry will affect ambient conditions in the environment; how much will ambient water or air quality be affected by the performance of the firms. The next step is to determine the health or other impacts on humans (and nonhuman elements of the impacted ecosystem) stemming from these changes in ambient conditions.

3. Valuing Benefits and Costs. This requires expressing the flows of benefits and costs identified in Step 2 in terms of comparable value. This is a critical step. If benefits are to be compared to costs, they must be expressed in common terms. Typically this means expressing them in monetary terms, not because money is the only consideration, but because it provides the most readily available and flexible metric for describing a large and diverse set of consequences. For the wind turbine project, for example, one needs to add the engineering, construction, and operating costs of the installation, with the environmental costs of scenic degradation. Benefits would include the value of the generated power, together with the reduced damage from air pollutants coming from fossil plants.

In the example of the pollution-control regulation, analysts must determine the value of the costs to private firms of reducing emissions, and the value of the benefits to society from having less air pollution. The public costs of implementing the regulation may also be important.

Valuation is a major problem in most cases of environmental pollution control. Electricity is easily valued because it is traded in a market, where prices are easy to observe. But there are few markets where environmental quality is traded in a direct way that would unambiguously reveal its social value. What is the value of an otherwise scenic vista disrupted with large, whirling wind turbines? What is the value of lowering the probability of respiratory illness due to particulate matter in the ambient air? It's clear that these items have great value; what is difficult is arriving at a commonly accepted measure of those values. Economists and others have devoted much effort at developing techniques for valuing these types of environmental factors.

4. Comparing Benefits and Costs. The final step is comparing the benefits with the costs. There are several ways of doing this: net benefits, which are simply benefits minus costs, and the benefit-cost ratio, which is total benefits divided by total costs. The resulting index can be used to help determine whether to undertake a program (e.g., tighten the emission standard because the estimated benefits of doing so exceed the estimated costs), how to design the program (e.g., reduce the size of the turbine project to ten structures, because this is the size that will give maximum net benefits), or to compare one program with another (e.g., tightening the SO_2 standard will yield lower net benefits than tightening the ozone standard).

Risk Analysis

The evaluation of pollution-control benefits (and sometimes costs) is complicated by the fact that the impacts of reducing ambient levels of pollution are **probabilistic**. In a probabilistic relationship, outcomes are uncertain. If we take a random sample of 100 people who have started to smoke, we would expect that, on average and over time, about 20 of them will die of lung cancer.[2] Note that this is not 100 percent; some who smoke won't get lung cancer. On the other hand, a few nonsmokers will get lung cancer. And we can not determine at the outset exactly which individuals will get lung cancer. On an individual basis, we can say that a random person who begins (and continues) to smoke has a 20 percent chance of getting lung cancer in his or her lifetime. People who smoke are exposing themselves to a risk level of this magnitude.

The effects of environmental pollutants on people are probabilistic in this way. People who are exposed to air pollution of certain types are at higher risk (i.e., higher than if they were not so exposed) of contracting various types of diseases, such as bronchitis and lung cancer. People who are exposed to certain kinds of chemicals in the workplace, or in their drinking water, are at risk of disease. Thus, the control of environmental pollutants is very much a matter of controlling the levels of risk to which people are exposed.

This brings up a host of difficult questions about levels of risk, how people respond to risk, how much they want to protect themselves against risks of various types, how best to reduce risk levels, and so on. Over the last few decades, researchers and policy makers have developed an elaborate set of concepts and procedures for addressing such questions under the rubric of risk analysis.

Risk analysis is basically composed of two general questions: (1) If some chemical or substance or operating procedure is to be used in our economy/society, how much risk will people be exposed to? (2) Depending on our answer to question (1), what do we feel about this level of risk, and what might we want to do about it? In particular, should we undertake steps to lower this risk and, if so, what steps should we take? The first of these questions is called **risk assessment**. The second is called **risk management**.

Risk Assessment

The four basic steps in risk assessment are:

- hazard identification
- dose-response analysis
- exposure analysis
- risk characterization

Hazard Identification. **Hazard identification** means determining whether a particular chemical or operating practice represents a risk of some unknown amount. It means separating those things that are risky from those that are not.

Dose-Response Analysis. In a dose-response study the objective is to identify the relationship between dose, measured in the quantity of a contaminant in the environment, and response, measured in terms of some type of health impact. From a conceptual standpoint this relationship could take on a number of different forms, as depicted in figure 16.2. Relationship A begins at the origin and extends to the right in a linear fashion; each increase of a certain amount in dose level leads to the same numerical increase in response level. Note that the response indicator is in terms of the proportion of individuals who contract a given disease. This reflects the probabilistic nature of the relationship. Another dimension of this is that the function A (and the others as well) are statistical relationships; they express the number of cases which, on average, would occur in a group of 100 people.

Relationship B is a nonlinear one; it increases at an increasing rate. Low-dose levels do not produce much of a response, but as doses get higher, their impact increases sharply; near its end it is going up almost vertically. Relationship B also displays another very important characteristic: It has a threshold. This is a dose level below which the response is zero. In this case the

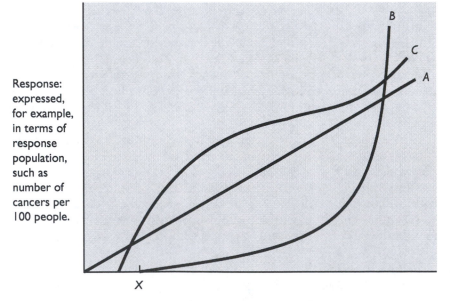

Response: expressed, for example, in terms of response population, such as number of cancers per 100 people.

Dose: level of a contaminant in the environment, expressed, for example, in parts per million (ppm), or micrograms per liter (µg/L).

Figure 16.2   Hypothetical Dose-Response Function

threshold is the dose level indicated by x. Threshold levels, whether they exist for particular contaminants, and, if so, what they are, represent one of the controversial aspects of risk analysis. Congress frequently directs the EPA to set exposure standards at levels that will "protect the public health," or some similar language, without telling the agency what this means. If thresholds exist for contaminants, and if these thresholds are at reasonable levels (i.e., not extremely close to zero), the agency might just set the standard at the threshold level. But if there is no threshold, or one exists but it is very tiny, this strategy is not available and some other approach will have to be used, with political ramifications.

Relationship C is another nonlinear dose-response function with a threshold. But it is also more complicated in shape. It increases rapidly at low levels, then less rapidly, and finally rapidly again at high-dose levels.

There are two primary sources of data used to identify dose-response relationships: laboratory experiments and epidemiological studies. Laboratory experiments have traditionally worked by exposing groups of small animals, such as mice and rats, to controlled dose levels (quantity and duration) and then recording the response in terms of the number of disease conditions that result. Since it is a laboratory setting, close control can be exercised over the test procedure, which makes it possible to isolate cause and effect fairly clearly, and draw conclusions about toxicity with relatively high confidence. Nevertheless there are a number of significant problems with this type of research:

1. Tests are conducted on animals, not on humans, for obvious reasons. Is it valid to extrapolate from mice or other lab animals to humans?

2. Test doses are normally very high, usually many times higher in proportion to body weight, what a normal human will be exposed to in real life. Usually the extrapolation to low-dose levels is made under the assumption that the dose-response function is linear. How accurate is this assumption?

Epidemiology is the study of human populations in their normal settings in which analysts try to deduce dose-response relationships by using statistical analysis to link exposure levels to experience in terms of the incidence of disease. This approach has an advantage in that it looks for impacts among humans, so there is no need to extrapolate from lab tests on nonhuman organisms. Its major drawback is that the environments in which humans live, work, and play have many dimensions, and it is difficult to single out any one factor (exposure to a particular chemical, for example) and measure its impact separate from all the other factors that affect human health. Researchers attempt to overcome these difficulties by finding populations that have reasonably clear exposure characteristics so they can be compared to similar populations without the characteristics, and then employing powerful statistical tools to analyze the data. Exhibit 16.1, which contains excerpts from a recent work of the National Research Council, will help you gain some appreciation of this approach. The EPA recently has been embroiled in the politics/science of changing the maximum contaminant

Exhibit 16.1
Epidemiological Evidence About Dose-Response from Studies on the Relation of Cancer to Arsenic in Drinking Water

". . . In this section, detailed summaries and evaluations are presented of two of the recently completed studies that have adequate data to contribute to quantitative assessment of risk—one for urinary-tract cancers in Taiwan (Chiou et al. 2001) and the other for lung cancer in Chile (Ferreccio et al. 2000). . . .

"Chiou et al. (2001) conducted a prospective cohort study of 8,102 persons in the Lanyang basin of northeastern Taiwan, a region where arsenic-contaminated shallow wells were used for drinking water from the late-1940s through the mid-1990s. All cohort members had used shallow private wells for their primary drinking-water supply. Subjects were interviewed at home between October 1991 and September 1994. There were 4,586 homes represented in the study and 3,901 well-water samples taken and analyzed for arsenic with the use of hydride generation with flame atomic absorption spectrometry. . . . The interview included information on history of well-water consumption, residential history, sociodemographic characteristics, cigarette smoking, personal and family medical history, occupation, and other potential risk factors. Subjects were followed for cancer incidence from the time of enrollment (1991 to 1994) through December 31, 1996, with the use of multiple resources. Detailed analyses of total urinary cancer (includes kidney, bladder, and urethral cancer) and specifically of the most common cell type of urinary cancer, transitional cell carcinoma (TCC), are presented. Nine subjects were diagnosed with bladder cancer, eight with kidney cancer, and one with both. Among those 18 subjects with urinary-tract cancer, 17 had pathological confirmation, and 11 were diagnosed with TCC. . . .

"In a region of northern Chile with a history of increased concentrations of arsenic in drinking water, Ferreccio et al. (2000) conducted a case-control study of incident lung cancer. Eligible cases included all lung cancer cases diagnosed in the eight public hospitals in regions I, II, and III from November 1994 through July 1996. There were 217 eligible subjects identified, and 151 (70%) participated. Nonparticipation was largely due to inability to locate the subject. Controls were selected from the hospitals where the lung cancer cases were diagnosed. Two control series were selected: cancers other than lung cancer and noncancer controls. Another set of similarly identified controls was selected for a parallel study of incident bladder cancer. Cases and controls were interviewed regarding residential history, socioeconomic status, occupational history (to ascertain employment in copper smelting), and smoking."

Source: Excerpted from National Research Council, *Arsenic in Drinking Water, 2001 Update* (Washington, DC: National Academy Press, 2001):37–50.

level (MCL) of arsenic in public drinking water systems. The current MCL is 50 micrograms per liter (μg/L). This was originally set by the U.S. Public Health Service back in 1942. At the time there was a recognition that high arsenic levels had adverse health impacts, but relatively little was known about them. In other words, arsenic had been identified as a hazard, but we knew little about the dose-response relationship; how much arsenic produces how much of what types of disease? In the last couple of decades there has been a lot of research on this relationship. The primary responses have been identified as lung and bladder cancers and, more recently, hypertension and diabetes.

Exposure Analysis. Exposure analysis refers to research aimed at discovering how much a given population would, in its normal activities, be exposed to a particular chemical or risk situation. A substance that has strongly adverse health impacts, in the dose-response sense, may not be a big problem if people ordinarily are not exposed to it. Conversely, a weakly toxic substance could nevertheless have an important social impact if a very large proportion of the population is exposed to it.

Consider again the case of arsenic in drinking water. Even though dose-response research has shown that arsenic in drinking water can cause, say, bladder cancer, in order to know how much risk people are exposed to from this source we must know how much arsenic is in fact in U.S. drinking water. Since all drinking water is not the same, this means getting samples of drinking water from many different sources, public and private, and having them tested for arsenic. But even this is not enough. To calculate true exposure we must also know how much water people typically consume, and this means doing survey work to study peoples' water consumption habits.

Different types of chemicals and practices require different types of exposure analysis. Studying the exposure to arsenic in drinking water requires the data mentioned above. Studying exposure to arsenic in building materials (arsenic is present in lumber-treating materials) requires a different type of data. Exposure to the ionizing radiation in x-rays requires still another type of data, and so on.

Risk Characterization. Once the first three steps of risk assessment have been completed, analysts evaluate them in combination in order to characterize the risk that people are under from exposure to that particular substance.

From a regulatory standpoint, another level of analysis is needed. In order to formulate adequate regulations, policy makers need an answer to the question: If a standard was set at some level (an MCL in drinking water, a prohibition of a certain substance to treat lumber, a limit on the number of x-rays a person should receive each year), what will be the impact in terms of reduced risk as compared to the current situation? Table 16.1 contains risk characterization data from the National Research Council's study of arsenic in drinking water.

Chapter Sixteen

Table 16.1 **Estimates[a] of Excess Lifetime Risk (Incidence per 10,000 People) of Lung Cancer and Bladder Cancer for U.S. Populations Exposed at Various Concentrations of Arsenic in Drinking Water[b,c]**

Arsenic Concentration (µg/L)	Bladder Cancer		Lung Cancer	
	Females	Males	Females	Males
3	4	7	5	4
5	6	11	9	7
10	12	23	18	14
20	24	45	36	27

[a] The estimates are the central point estimates from the distribution of risks calculated using a particular statistical model and data set (see note b).

[b] Estimates were calculated using data from individuals in the region of southwestern Taiwan where arsenic is endemic, data from an external comparison group from the overall southwestern Taiwan area, and U.S. age-adjusted cancer incidence data. The risks are estimated using what the subcommittee considered reasonable assumptions: a U.S. resident weighs 70 kg, compared with 50 kg for the typical Taiwanese, and the typical Taiwanese drinks just over 2 liters of water per day, compared with 1 liter per day in the United States; therefore, it assumes that the Taiwanese exposure per kilogram of body weight is approximately 3 times that of the United States. It is possible to get higher and lower estimates using other assumptions. Risk estimates are rounded to the nearest integer. All 95% confidence limits are less than ±12% of the maximum-likelihood estimate and are not presented. Those confidence limits reflect statistical variability in the population incidence estimates only, a narrow range that primarily reflects the relatively large sample size of the data modeled. As such, they are not indicative of the true uncertainty associated with the estimates.

[c] If Taiwanese baseline cancer rates are used instead of U.S. data to estimate the risk, the corresponding risk estimates (incidence per 10,000) for arsenic at concentrations of 3, 5, 10, and 20 µg/L of drinking water are as follows: female bladder cancer, 2, 4, 8 and 15; male bladder cancer, 2, 3, 7, and 13; female lung cancer, 2, 3, 6, and 12; and male lung cancer, 2, 3, 6, and 11.

Source: From National Research Council, *Arsenic in Drinking Water, 2001 Update* (Washington, DC: National Academy Press, 2001):12.

Risk Management

Knowing what the risk is from some environmental factor does not immediately dictate what to do about it. To make a reasoned decision about this, two more types of information are required: (1) how people value risk reduction, and (2) how much risk reduction will result from the different policy steps that might be taken.

Risk Valuation. While the work of risk assessment is the province of physical and health scientists, the work of risk valuation falls primarily to economists. The question they must answer is: How much do people value risk reductions like those produced by pollution-control regulations? To some policy advocates this is not a particularly useful question; for them it is enough to know that pollution increases health risks and thus something should be done to reduce it. The essence of policy analysis in this case, however, is to recognize that reducing risks involves costs to society, and whether these costs in any particular instance are outweighed by the value people place on the reduced risk.

Valuing risk reductions has become an important subspecialty within environmental economics. Different techniques have been used, such as analysis of employment data to deduce how people implicitly value risky jobs; and direct surveys to ask people questions about how they feel about risk. It is not surprising that this is a complicated line of research. People are surrounded by risk in their everyday lives. How they perceive and balance these risks is often not obvious, even to themselves. So deducing, for example, how much people would value a regulation that lowered the risk of getting chronic bronchitis from 1 in 200,000 to 1 in 500,000, is very hard.

Risk Regulation. It is also not easy under normal circumstances to know how much risk reduction will result from particular environmental regulations. Suppose, for example, the EPA estimates that a pesticide currently in use leads to five excess cancer deaths among the U.S. population each year. One might suppose that a ban on this chemical would result in five fewer cancer deaths each year. This may or may not be the case, however. If this pesticide is banned, growers may turn to some other practice or chemical, which will likely entail some degree of risk. Depending on the size of this alternative risk, the total number of excess cancer deaths could do anything—decrease, increase, or stay the same.

Regulating risk usually involves some type of **comparative risk** analysis; that is, examining the risks associated with different courses of action, or different types of regulation. This type of analysis answers questions such as: How much reduction in risk would be obtained by shifting resources from outdoor air pollution to the control of indoor air pollution? If officials simply capped an old landfill rather than excavated the material and carted it away, what are the risks of contaminating nearby groundwater resources?

Other Types of Analysis

It is fair to say that risk analysis has become a dominant tool in environmental policy analysis, and that benefit-cost analysis has produced the greatest public controversies through the years. Within the policy-generating agencies there are several other forms of analysis widely used.

Cost-Effectiveness Analysis

From a benefit-cost perspective it is usually the benefits that are hardest to evaluate, because finding an acceptable and practical procedure for estimating the value of environmental improvements is difficult and controversial. In a **cost-effectiveness analysis**, the benefits of a program are not evaluated; rather the costs of attaining some specified objective are estimated. In effect a cost-effectiveness analysis is half a benefit-cost analysis, with the more controversial part left out. We may not be able to agree on what a cleaner environment is worth to the average person. Regardless of that, however, we should all be able to agree that for the resources we are devoting to environmental protection, we should be getting the greatest improvement possible. In other words, are our targets, in terms of air, water and land pollution, being achieved in a cost-effective way?

Cost-effectiveness studies are often done with a comparative motive. When there are a number of different ways to reach an objective, we want to know how they compare in terms of cost. Exhibit 16.2 provides an example of this. Here the stated objective is to reduce aggregate gasoline consumption by ten percent, and there are two possible approaches evaluated: (1) establishing tighter CAFE standards, or (2) a higher tax on gas. CAFE stands for "corporate average fuel economy," and refers to the mandated mileage goals the automakers have to meet with their new cars. Note that there are two types of CAFE programs studied, one with trading and one without. As we discussed in the previous chapter, trading is a way of achieving more cost-effective pollution control. In the case of automobile mileage, trading is between automakers based on the relative costs to them of producing better-mileage cars.

Environmental Impact Statements

One of the early federal environmental statutes of note was the National Environmental Policy Act (NEPA) of 1969 (though it was actually signed into law on January 1, 1970). The intent of the law is to require federal agencies to introduce environmental considerations into their decision making. The vehicle for this is the **environmental impact statement (EIS)**, an analysis that all agencies must do for any project they undertake (including those they fund). An EIS must be done for any project that is expected to have a significant impact on the environment.[3] These statements must contain:

1. A description of the expected environmental impacts of the proposed action.

2. Alternatives to the proposed action, including no action.

3. An analysis of any irreversible and irretrievable commitments of resources the action would produce.

4. An analysis of long-run cumulative effects stemming from the action.

NEPA also created the Council on Environmental Quality, an executive agency whose job is to manage the EIS process and publish an annual report on the state of the environment.

EISs are largely the work of natural scientists, such as biologists, hydrologists, and ecologists. The main task is to clarify the linkages that will spread the impact of the project or plan through the ecosystem and to estimate the quantitative and qualitative repercussions it will have on the various elements of that system. NEPA does not prohibit agencies from undertaking actions that will harm the environment, only that they must identify and disclose these effects prior to the action. Many states have passed similar laws applying to actions within their borders.

Exhibit 16.2
Cost Effectiveness Analysis: Achieving a Reduction in Gasoline Consumption of 10 Percent by Fuel Economy Standards or a Gasoline Tax

Proponents of increasing corporate average fuel economy (CAFE) standards for passenger vehicles see the policy as a relatively low cost and proven way to decrease the United States' dependence on oil and emissions of carbon dioxide (the predominant greenhouse gas). Opponents argue that CAFE standards are a costly and cumbersome way to reduce gasoline consumption, that they interfere with the market and unduly burden U.S. business, and (because they may encourage more driving and alter vehicle design) that they may compromise the safety of motorists.

CAFE standards are currently 27.5 miles per gallon (mpg) for cars and 20.7 mpg for light trucks. The standard for cars has not changed since 1990, and the truck standard has been fixed since 1996 but is scheduled to increase to 22.2 mpg by 2007. The average fuel economy of each manufacturer's fleets of cars and light trucks must meet those standards, or the firm will be subject to a fine. All major automakers currently meet or exceed the standards.

This issue brief focuses on the economic costs of CAFE standards and compares them with the costs of a gasoline tax that would reduce gasoline consumption by the same amount. The Congressional Budget Office (CBO) estimates that a 10 percent reduction in gasoline consumption could be achieved at a lower cost by an increase in the gasoline tax than by an increase in CAFE standards. Furthermore, an increase in the gasoline tax would reduce driving, leading to less traffic congestion and fewer accidents.

Estimated Costs of Achieving a
Ten Percent Reduction in Gas Consumption

| | CAFE Standards | | |
	Without Trading	With Trading	Gasoline Tax
Policy	31.3 mpg for cars 24.5 mpg for light trucks		46-cent-per-gallon increase
	(billions of dollars)		
Total Costs to the Economy[a]	3.6	3.0	2.9
Producers' costs	1.2	0.8	0.5
Consumers' costs	2.4	2.2	2.4

[a] For producers, costs are measured as reductions in total profits, whereas for consumers, they include both higher prices and the reduction in welfare for consumers who chose not to buy a new vehicle because of the higher prices.

Note: CAFE = corporate average fuel economy; mpg = miles per gallon.

Source: U.S. Congressional Budget Office, *The Economic Costs of Fuel Economy Standards Versus a Gasoline Tax*, December 2003. http://www.cbo.gov/showdoc.cfm?index=4917& sequence=0.

Policy Analysis Issues

Benefit-cost analysis would seem to be the voice of sweet reason: Why wouldn't we want to evaluate as best as possible the expected positive and negative consequences of proposed policies or regulations? And even if we decide that it is too difficult or involved to measure benefits accurately, surely everyone can agree that cost-effectiveness analysis is appropriate. Is there anybody who doesn't want to get the biggest bang for the buck from pollution-control expenditures? Similarly, shouldn't we attempt to ascertain the value of risk reduction that environmental regulations produce? It is unlikely that policy should aim to eliminate risk entirely; not only would it cost too much, but it is not even clear what that would mean.

Unfortunately, things are not that straightforward. In policy struggles, knowledge is power. Even apparent, or tentative knowledge, may confer power on its possessor. In fact, many people have objected to moving toward basing policy decisions more closely on the results of policy analytics. Some objections are based on principles, some on practicality, some on political grounds.

Ethical Objections

Some who object to the use of policy analysis do so on ethical grounds. Ethical rules are behavioral commandments of right or wrong that are not subject to trade-off or compromise. Maintaining the quality of the environment impresses many as an ethical or moral issue that ought to be pursued whatever the cost. On these grounds, it is not legitimate to base environmental decisions on such estimates as the value of human lives saved as a result of particular environmental regulations. To do so is to put environmental policy too much under the influence of economic analysis and its practitioners, who know the "price of everything but the value of nothing."[4]

Moral strictures work through guilt, and there are many environmental problems where a greater sense of guilt would lead to more effective actions. But guilt, and the ability to direct it toward certain ends, may never obviate the need for making judgments about what ought to be done, and how. When it comes to cleaning the air over a certain city, for example, people will undoubtedly agree that it is a moral end to pursue, but also will want to know what particular level of cleanliness ought to be pursued, and the most cost-effective way of doing so.

Analytical Techniques

The fundamental basis of benefit-cost analysis is to estimate both benefits and costs and to compare them. It is a political fact of life, however, that different groups will be more heavily invested in one side than the other. Those seeking more stringent environmental regulations will put greater stress on the benefits produced; those in the regulated community can be counted on to emphasize the cost side of the equation. Any technique that implies giving equal weight to both sides may find few supporters. Both sides will have major objections.

Objections have been raised to many of the techniques used for benefit-cost analysis. Most analyses, for example, involve **discounting** future values. This is based on the common-sense observation that under normal circumstances people will place a higher value on a dollar of benefits today than on an IOU that promises to pay a dollar only at some future time. Although normal people behave this way, it's not clear that governments should make decisions this way, because it appears to devalue future generations relative to those alive today.

Most benefit-cost analysis and risk analysis treat everybody the same. A dollar's worth of net benefits to one person, or reduced risk to one person, is treated as equivalent in value to those amounts accruing to any other person. Participants in the environmental policy struggle will usually be sensitive to the distributional aspects of that policy. The whole basis for **environmental justice** is that environmental regulations and pollution-control activities frequently work to the relative advantage of higher income citizens, and to the relative disadvantage of low-income people and people of color. The objection to analysis on these grounds often stems from the idea that less-well off groups in society ought to be treated more liberally than more privileged groups. Of course the answer to this is that, in the course of any policy analysis, it is possible to distinguish groups in different circumstances, which could be used to inform regulatory decisions.

Analytical Difficulties.   The political aspects of benefit-cost analysis to a large extent play off the analytical difficulties inherent in applying it to environmental cases. The fact is that environmental impacts are usually a lot harder to value than technical and market-related factors. Often this means that in a benefit-cost analysis it is much more difficult to value benefits than costs. Suppose the object of analysis is a new air pollution regulation. Estimating its costs is a matter of estimating how much the regulated community will have to spend to meet the new requirement. This means costing out the new technologies and practices these firms will put in place, for which there may be relatively good data in engineering studies, cost surveys, and the like. But as to benefits, the job is to value the improvements in air quality produced by the new regulation. What value do people put on having cleaner air? Cleaner air is normally be expected to have positive health impacts. But this just transfers the question: How much do people value improvements in health?

What this usually means is that cost estimates often have the appearance of being more reliable, and more objective, than benefit estimates. So these analyses may often seem to offer better ammunition for those concerned about costs, than for those whose focus is on the benefits of pollution control.

This criticism of benefit-cost analysis techniques does not apply to cost-effectiveness analysis because here no attempt is made to value benefits. But for full benefit-cost analysis this represents a real issue; benefit-cost analyses that are limited only to the most easily quantified impacts are not necessarily the best guides to action. Eliminating analysis is also undesirable, because then decisions are made purely on the basis of politics. It is best, then, for policy makers to use the analysis for what it does say and recognize that it may not include everything.

The Politicization of Policy Analysis

The policy process is a political process in which groups and ideas contend for influence and the greater representation of their views. In this struggle information can be a weapon. It tends to confer power on those who possess it and hinders those who don't. So the contenders are not neutral about what they would prefer studies to show. The regulated community would like to see costs estimated as very high. The environmental community would like benefits to be valued very highly. A regulatory agency would like the studies to indicate that their activities are socially worthwhile. Politicians seek out studies whose conclusions support their position.

There are any number of cases in the past where studies have been clearly swayed and biased according to the predilections of the policy participants for whom the studies were done. This has led many observers to question the very basis for doing policy analysis: If it is going to produce biased results slanted to support one position or another, why should such studies be given any credence? Of course, the answer is that if studies typically incorporate misleading analysis, the best course of action is not to do without any analysis, but to institute procedures and protocols that would tend to produce good policy analysis.

Environmental Analysis in the Private Sector

Our discussion of environmental analysis has been in terms of the public sector. Public agencies faced with implementing laws must find some way, formal or informal, of evaluating the consequences of their actions. Environmental analysis also occurs in the private sector. Private firms routinely do all kinds of analysis to help them in decision making: market analysis, analysis of strategic alternatives, financial analysis, and so on. To some extent environmental values may be introduced as simple add-ons to current procedures. For example, if a firm is required to add a new end-of-the-pipe treatment process that will have little impact elsewhere in the business, the analytical job may be fairly straightforward. It amounts to estimating the cost of a new process or machine, and adding this to the firm's operating costs.

But when actions require integrating environmental initiatives more thoroughly into business operations, analysis becomes more difficult. Consider the issue of pollution prevention. As mentioned in chapter 12, pollution prevention consists of firms making various process, input, or production changes so as to reduce the quantity of residuals needing to be treated, recycled, or discharged. **Pollution prevention (P2)** looks back up the operation line, directly into the firms' operating producers, for changes that are more fundamental than end-of-the-pipe residual handling procedures. Many see this as a promising way to achieve major reductions in firms' environmental footprints. And it is undoubtedly true that in the long run, if we wish environmental concerns to permeate through the many layers of decision making that characterize any significant economic enterprise, we have to find ways to make it happen.

One factor that is sometimes overlooked by P2 advocates is the need to be able to quantify prospective P2 investments so they can be evaluated on an equal footing with other financial decisions that firms routinely make. When firms evaluate the implications of undertaking environmentally related changes, they look at the benefits *to them* of reducing emissions, not the benefits to society. This means essentially extending a firm's cost-accounting practices to encompass the environmentally related changes in its operations. This is not necessarily easy to do. One recent study of pollution prevention activities by firms draws the following conclusions:

> . . . significant information barriers confront corporate financial decision makers. Their presence underscores the continued importance of improved environmental cost accounting methods to better estimate environment-related financial benefits. Improved data collection, estimation, and evaluation techniques can only improve corporate decision making. Corporations know this, of course. The cost of better information is the best explanation for why there isn't more of it. Focusing on the costs of information itself might be a particularly fruitful approach to encouraging pollution prevention.
>
> . . . government promotion of state-of-the-art accounting practices, actuarial analysis, and materials accounting tools are likely to concretely benefit firms that are increasingly concerned with environment-related costs and opportunities.[5]

This study also concludes that the specific types of environmental regulations that are applied to polluting firms can make a significant difference in terms of incentives to engage in P2. To the extent that regulations require specific technology-based steps to reduce emissions, these incentives may be weakened; if the regulations permit a certain amount of flexibility and room to maneuver, P2 efforts may be encouraged.

Summary

There is an ongoing controversy in environmental policy regarding the role of formal policy analysis. Should it be required for new regulations, recommended, or perhaps not relied upon at all? There are different points of view on the question, but recent trends are in the direction of relying more heavily on formal analysis to evaluate policy alternatives.

The primary mode of analysis is benefit-cost analysis. This essentially involves estimating all of the consequences of a policy or regulation and then valuing these so they may be compared in terms of net benefits or a benefit-cost ratio. Much of the controversy about benefit-cost analysis stems from the difficulties of estimating the values of benefits. While the costs of a regulation may often be hard to estimate, most concern focuses on the difficulties of measuring benefits. The benefits of environmental improvements, though real, do not have a direct market with which to evaluate them. This uncertainty makes some approaches to benefit-cost analysis controversial.

Because of the inherent uncertainty associated with the benefits flowing from environmental improvements, much work has gone into the development of risk analysis, which includes both assessing risks (e.g., the risk of getting chronic bronchitis if you breathe heavy doses of SO_2) and then putting a value on risk reduction.

One type of analysis that is less controversial, and therefore to be encouraged, is cost-effectiveness analysis. In cost-effectiveness analysis benefits are stated in nonmonetary terms (e.g., a 10 percent reduction in energy use; a 15 percent reduction in a particular water pollutant), while costs are evaluated as they would be in benefit-costs analysis. Cost-effectiveness analysis is usually done for comparative purposes so that, given several policy alternatives, it is possible to identify the one which, for a given program cost, achieves a greater amount of the objective.

Key Terms

baseline	environmental justice
benefit-cost analysis	epidemiology
comparative risk	exposure analysis
cost-effectiveness analysis	pollution prevention (P2)
discounting	probabilistic
dose-response analysis	risk assessment
environmental impact statement (EIS)	risk management

Questions for Further Discussion

1. Some people think that benefit-cost analysis is inappropriate in public decision making because it tries to short circuit the essential political judgments that need to go into policy decisions. Discuss.

2. Many environmental regulations are recommended because they will diminish health impacts of a polluted environment. How might we proceed to estimate the value of improved health?

3. If you were director of the Office of Management and Budget, would you require the various agencies to justify their regulatory decisions with benefit-cost analyses?

4. "Benefit-cost analyses can be rigged to give you any answer you may want." Comment.

5. On what possible grounds might a public agency decide to go forward with a regulation even though a benefit-cost analysis has estimated that it will have negative net benefits?

Web Sites

The National Center for Environmental Economics is a group within EPA that works on developing policy analysis tools:

www.yosemite.epa.gov/ee/epa/eed.nsf/webpages/homepage

See also other government agencies:
Office of Management and Budget
www.whitehouse.gov/omb/circulars/A094/A094.html

Department of Agriculture
www.usda.gov/agency/oce/

See "benefit cost analyses" in the:
Concise Encyclopedia of Economics
www.econlib.org/library/CCE.html

The National Center for Environmental Decision-Making Research has relevant material:

www.ncedr.org/tools/othertools/costbenefit/lead.htm

A good source for completed environmental impact statements is the Transportation Library of Northwestern University:

www.library.northwestern.edu/transportation/searcheis.html

Additional Readings

Abelson, P. W., *Project Appraisal and Valuation of the Environment* (New York: St. Martin's Press, 1996.

Bartelmus, Peter, and Eberhard K. Seifert, eds., *Green Accounting* (Ashgate: The International Library of Environmental Economics and Policy, August 2003).

Boroush, Mark, *Understanding Risk Analysis: A Short Guide for Health, Safety, and Environmental Policy Making* (Washington, DC: Resources for the Future and the American Chemical Society, October 1998). Internet edition: www.rff.org/rff/publications/loader.cfm?url=/commonspot/security/getfile.cfm&PageID=14418

Bregman, Jacob, *Environmental Impact Statements,* 2nd ed. (Taylor and Francis Group, 2006).
(www.environetbase.com/ejournals/books/book_summary/summary.asp?id=16).

Dixon, John, Louise Fallon Scura, Richard Carpenter, and Paul B. Sherman, eds., *Economic Analysis of Environmental Impacts*, 2nd ed. (London: Earthscan, November 1994).

Farrell, Alexander E., and Jill Jäger, eds., *Assessments of Regional and Global Environmental Risks: Designing Processes for the Effective Use of Science in Decisionmaking* (Washington, DC: Resources for the Future, February 2005).

Finkel, A., and D. Golding, eds., *Worst Things First: The Debate Over Risk-Based National Environmental Priorities* (Washington, DC: Resources for the Future, 1991).

Glasson, J., R. Therivel, and A. Chadwick, *Introduction to Environmental Impact Assessment* (London: Routledge, 2005).

Gray, Wayne B., ed., *Economic Costs and Consequences of Environmental Regulation* (Ashgate: The International Library of Environmental Economics and Policy, 2002).

Hamilton, James T., and W. Kip Viscusi, *Calculating Risks? The Spatial and Political Dimensions of Hazardous Waste Policy* (Cambridge, MA: MIT Press, 1999).

Hanley, Nick, and Clive L. Spash, *Cost-Benefit Analysis and the Environment* (London: Edward Elgar, 1993).

Irwin, Lewis G., *The Policy Analyst's Handbook: Rational Problem Solving in a Political World* (Armonk, NY: M. E. Sharpe, 2003).

Loomis, John, and Gloria Helfand, *Environmental Policy Analysis for Decision Making* (Kluwer Academic Publishers, November 2001).

Lutter, Randall, and Jason F. Shogren, *Painting the White House Green: Rationalizing Environmental Policy Inside the Executive Office of the President* (Washington, DC: Resources for the Future, April 2004).

Morgenstern, Richard D., ed., *Economic Analysis at EPA: Assessing Regulatory Impact* (Washington, DC: Resources for the Future, 1997).

Office of Management and Budget, "Draft 2003 Report to Congress on the Costs and Benefits of Federal Regulations," *Federal Register*, February 3, 2003.

U.S. Environmental Protection Agency, *Final Report to Congress on the Benefits and Costs of the Clean Air Act, 1970-1990*, EPA 410-R-99-002.

U.S. Environmental Protection Agency, *Final Report to Congress on the Benefits and Costs of the Clean Air Act, 1990-2010*, EPA 410-R-99-01.

U.S. Environmental Protection Agency, *Guidelines for Preparing Economic Analyses*, EPA-240-R-00-003, September 2000. http://www.epa.gov/economics/.

Viscusi, W. Kip, *Rational Risk Policy* (Oxford: Oxford University Press, 1998).

Visgilio, Gerald, and Diane Whitelaw, *Our Backyard: A Quest for Environmental Justice* (Lanham, MD: Rowman and Littlefield, 2003).

Walker, K., and J. B. Wiener, "Recycling Lead," in *Risk versus Risk: Tradeoffs in Protecting Health and the Environment*, eds. J. D. Graham and J. B. Wiener (Cambridge, MA: Harvard University Press, 1995).

White, Allen, Deborah Savage, Julia Brady, Dmitri Cavander, and Lori Lach, *Environmental Cost Accounting for Capital Budgeting: A Benchmark Survey of Management Accountants*, EPA/742/R-95/005, Office of Pollution Prevention and Toxics (Washington, DC: EPA, 1995).

Notes

[1] By Thomas O. McGarity, Sidney Shapiro, and David Bollier (Washington, DC: Environmental Law Institute, 2004).

[2] This is a rough estimate; the actual number depends on how heavy a smoker is, how they smoke, and other factors. We use this for illustrative purposes.

[3] To determine if a project or plan will have a significant environmental impact, NEPA calls for agencies to conduct environmental assessments.

[4] This is the title of a recent critique of environmental policy, Frank Ackerman and Lisa Heinzerling, *Priceless: On Knowing the Price of Everything and the Value of Nothing* (The New Press, 2004).

[5] James Boyd, "The Barriers to Corporate Pollution Prevention: An Analysis of Three Case Studies," in Paul S. Fishbeck and R. Scott Farrow, eds., *Improving Regulation* (Washington, DC: Resources for the Future, 2001):110–111.

17

Decentralization

The Role of the States

One of the major themes in American political history is the interplay between the states and the central government. The U.S. Constitution specifies our system as a federal structure, a collection of individual states that surrender certain powers to a central governmental body. Throughout our country's history, battles have been fought, politically and militarily, over the division of powers, rights, and responsibilities between the state governments and the federal government in Washington. The waxing and waning of this conflict is destined to be a permanent feature of American politics and policy.

Prior to 1970 the main initiative for environmental policy in the country lay with the states. The federal role was perceived as backing up the states, especially in providing the scientific and legal help they might need to develop environmental regulations applicable to their own situations. Then came the 1970s and the rapid ascendancy of the federal effort in pollution control. Initiative passed to the U.S. Congress and the EPA.

But in recent years the centralization/decentralization debate has gained a higher profile in the political and policy arenas.[1] This has occurred on both sides of the political spectrum. Conservatives have questioned the propriety and need for a national legislature and regulatory agency to specify rules for many environmental problems that are actually localized in terms of their origin and impacts. For many liberals, the need for state and regional action arises because of a perceived failure at the national level to come to grips with certain fundamental environmental problems, such as global warming and reductions in emissions of greenhouse gases.

One thing is certain. Most states now have legal and administrative expertise in environmental matters that were absent thirty years ago. The result is that many of them have become more responsive and aggressive in environmental regulation. The political and policy balance between federal and state authorities may be shifting. The states are going to be major actors in environmental policy for the foreseeable future.

Actions at the State Level

There are two types of actions that states can take regarding environmental regulation: (1) participation in federal laws, and (2) development of a separate body of laws and regulations applicable to their own citizenries.

Participation in Federal Laws

Federal and state policy authorities do not exist in separate and nonoverlapping spheres. In fact, the two arenas are closely related.

Political Representation.   States represent themselves as federal policy is being formed, working to shape that policy in ways that are congenial to the perceived needs of their voters. This can be done by using the various avenues of influence: lobbying to shape regulations, funding studies, organizing coalitions, and so on. It also can be done, and has been done recently, by resorting to the courts, bringing suits against the EPA or polluters themselves. The Northeast states, led by New York, have recently resorted to the courts to get a number of Midwest power plants, grandfathered in when the 1970 Clean Air Act was passed, to reduce their emissions.

Implementing Federal Laws.   When the major federal pollution-control laws were framed, they were constructed on the assumption that, while the federal EPA would set the requirements, implementation and enforcement would largely be carried out by the individual states. As of the present time, about three-fourths of the federal programs whose implementation could be delegated to the individual states are so delegated. Thus, for example, the permit programs of the Clean Air Act, Clean Water Act, and the Resource Conservation and Recovery Act are for the most part operated by the states, according to procedures and mandates established in Washington. We will discuss below some of the problems this can create.

Pursuing State Laws and Regulations

Virtually every state has an active output of statutes, regulations, and programs designed to address its environmental pollution problems. There are several motivating factors involved. For one, national programs often aim at the most egregious cases of pollution, leaving the states to grapple with lower-level problems. For example, every state in the country has a Super-fund-type program for cleaning up hazardous-waste-contaminated sites that are not deemed bad enough by the EPA to get on the National Priorities List and qualify for national cleanup. In addition, there are some areas of environmental regulation that historically have been left to the states, especially land-use control and municipal solid waste management.

Another reason states are actively involved in environmental protection is that many people see state action as a potential substitute for federal action. Thus, if action on environmental issues is thwarted at the federal level, people may look to the states to initiate action. In the last few years, for example, federal authorities under the Bush administration have moved toward less aggressive federal pollution-control measures. In response, some states have initiated more vigorous state regulations. One area where this has been especially prominent is in the control of greenhouse gases. At the federal level the administration has avoided meaningful steps toward reducing CO_2 emissions, the major greenhouse gas, primarily because of the impact this would have on the fossil fuel sectors of the economy. As a result a number of states, most notably California, have taken the initiative to undertake programs for addressing this problem.

Federal laws tend to address problems common to all states, but each state also has unique environmental problems that call for local attention and action. The special problem of air pollution in southern California is well known, but virtually every state has an analogous, though perhaps less serious, situation. Massachusetts has the special water problems of Cape Cod; Florida has the special issue of Lake Okeechobee; Louisiana has the Mississippi Delta; Texas has the pollution problems along its border with Mexico, and so on.

Another factor behind the growth of state action is the rise of what has been called **place-based environmental advocacy and action**.[2] This is local action stemming from a community desire to maintain and enhance local environmental resources. The emphasis is not on general, overarching laws of higher bodies, but on actions that local communities can take to protect their environmental resources. As we discussed in chapter 4, the rise of these local-ized, resource-based environmental groups has been especially rapid in recent years, which has given momentum to the shift from federal to lower-level political action.

Interstate Cooperation

Action at the subfederal level does not necessarily mean individual states acting alone. Groups of states often act jointly to address regional issues. Cooperative action among states can be pursued in a number of ways.

Adoption of Uniform Laws.   If a number of states enact the same laws and regulations on a particular environmental issue, it can have an important national impact. The **opt-in provisions** of mobile-source tailpipe standards under the Clean Air Act are an example. The law allows other states to adopt the more stringent California standards. As more and more states have done so, the California standards move toward becoming, in effect, national standards.

Multi-State Legal Action.   By acting jointly in legal cases, for example in suits against the EPA or polluters themselves, states can work toward achieving common objectives.

Interstate Compacts.   An interstate compact is a formal, legally enforceable agreement entered into by several states for the pursuit of some goal. An example is the Great Lakes Compact, authorized by Congress in 1955 and acting to protect the water and land resources of the Great Lakes-St. Lawrence system.

Multi-State Scientific and Policy Analysis.   States can work together, sometimes under the auspices of authorizing federal law, to carry out joint studies and to develop common policy positions on important environmental issues. A good example is the Ozone Transport Commission, a group of thirteen northeastern states created under the Clean Air Act. Its roles are to develop regional approaches to reducing ground-level ozone in its area, and to advise the EPA on ozone transport issues (i.e., problems related to the migration of ozone pollution from its point of origin in the Midwest into states of the Northeast).

Constitutional Issues

The Constitution establishes the basic framework for determining when federal actions take precedence over state actions and when state actions can be undertaken without fear of being overruled by federal authorities. It specifies that any power not explicitly delegated to the central government, or expressly forbidden, is reserved to the states.

The Commerce Clause

One power that has been given to the federal government (in Section 8, Article I of the Constitution) is the power to regulate interstate commerce. It allows Congress to regulate commerce among the states. This **interstate commerce clause** has been interpreted in two ways, as allowing the federal government to regulate activities affecting interstate trade, and as specifically prohibiting any states from interfering with interstate commerce. The first of these provides the rationale for federal environmental laws, as these laws can be interpreted as initiatives to regulate interstate commerce. The second essentially forecloses any environmental action undertaken by a state if that action can be shown to have an impact on the free movement of goods and services among the states.

One area where this has come into play has been in potential interstate shipments of solid waste, either hazardous waste (HW) or nonhazardous (municipal solid waste, MSW). With greater consolidation of landfill sites around the country, coupled with still huge production of HW and MSW, much more of this is being shipped among states. Efforts by individual states to exclude importation from other states have been found to be a violation of the commerce clause, as have efforts by some states to reduce exports of such waste for flow-control purposes.

Of course, it could be argued that any state-level environmental regulation interferes with interstate commerce since it presumably increases the production costs of in-state producers. For the most part the courts have resorted to a **balancing approach**, comparing the benefits such regulations would confer on state residents to the burden imposed on interstate shipments.[3]

The Supremacy Doctrine

Another constitutional provision with great importance in environmental matters is the **supremacy doctrine**. Article 6 of the Constitution says that federal law "shall be the supreme Law of the Land." From this supremacy clause there has developed through the years the law related to **federal preemption**. This law essentially specifies the conditions under which federal laws preempt state laws. These conditions are basically the following:

1. When the state law is in direct conflict with a federal law. Thus, for example, states may not enforce laws calling for weaker emission standards than are contained in federal pollution control laws. In many cases they may invoke stricter standards, however.

2. When federal regulation of an activity has become so pervasive that Congress has essentially left no rationale for state action. Thus, for example, major federal laws governing pollution by ships in coastal waters essentially place this problem out of reach of state laws. See also the case discussed in exhibit 17.1, which refers to federal preemption of laws regarding mileage requirements for cars.

Preemption at the State Level

Just as federal laws may preempt state laws, so too state actions can preempt those of local communities. These issues are framed in the same way, that is, for any particular environmental issue, should the state take action, thereby preempting local initiative; or should it be left to the individual communities to make their own determinations and decisions?

Local Pesticide Laws. Communities around the country have become greatly concerned with the large-scale local use of pesticides, which may threaten environmental and human health. Huge amounts of pesticides are applied every year to golf courses, lawns, school grounds, and so on, not only to control pests in a technical sense, but also for aesthetic purposes. Many local groups have sought to pass ordinances that would limit, in one way or another, excess pesticide use. Towns have sometimes passed such laws to protect groundwater supplies. School districts have sometimes enacted rules limiting pesticide applications on school grounds. Sometimes laws have been

enacted at county levels, for example a county-wide law requiring that pesticide applicators notify abutting property owners.[4]

Exhibit 17.1
A Federal Preemption Case

In 1992 the Maryland legislature passed a statute to encourage car owners to use more fuel-efficient, and therefore less polluting, cars. Under the
law, new and used passenger cars would be taxed on the basis of the mileage they got. Starting in 1995, cars getting less than 27 miles per gallon
(mpg) would be taxed $50 per mpg they fell below this 27 mpg threshold.
Cars obtaining more than 35 mpg would get a credit of $50 per mpg above
this threshold. This sounds like an excellent way of giving Maryland car
owners an incentive to buy and use cars that produce lower emissions, thus
leading to less mobile-source air pollution in the state. Unfortunately, the
program never went into effect, and the reason was federal preemption.

In 1975 the U.S. Congress passed the Energy Policy and Conservation
Act (EPCA). This was during the oil supply disruption caused by the OPEC
export embargo, so Congress felt the need to respond. A major part of
the EPCA was the CAFE (corporate average fuel economy) program. The
law mandates that auto companies produce cars that achieve certain minimum mileage, on average. The statute is written specifically to preempt
any state action relating to automobile mileage standards. Federal regulators, and auto manufacturers, wanted to forestall individual states from
establishing 50 different mileage standards.

When the Maryland law was being crafted, the question of whether it
was preempted by the federal CAFE program was raised. The Maryland
program had the objective of reducing air pollution, which the CAFE program did not. But the Maryland program was specifically linked to automobile mileage performance, and would obviously have an impact on the
average mileage of the fleet of cars being driven in that state.

The Maryland program precipitated some political pushing and shoving
between federal and state authorities. The National Highway Transportation
and Safety Administration took the position that the Maryland program was
indeed preempted by CAFE. The Maryland attorney general took the position that it was not, because it was aimed at pollution control, not mileage
enhancement.[a] The result of this controversy was that the Maryland program
was never put into effect primarily because of major uncertainties about
whether it would precipitate a preemption battle. (Another reason for its
abandonment was probably the practical complications of administering it.)

[a] For a discussion of this case see Rachel L. Chanin, "California's Authority to Regulate Mobile Source Greenhouse Gas Emissions," *New York University Annual Survey of American Law* 58 (2003):699–754.

The question is, when do state pesticide laws preempt local laws of this type? The pesticide industry—producers, appliers, etc.—have lobbied heavily in favor of state preemption. They can then focus their lobbying at the state level, and not have to deal with a plethora of different local laws.

Conceptual Issues

Environmental problems come in all varieties, from managing a neighborhood landfill to responding to global warming. It is impossible to draw conclusions in the abstract about the extent to which environmental policy making ought to be decentralized. The question needs to be posed, and answered, in terms of specific environmental problems.

Consider a case at one end of the spectrum, an instance of strictly local pollution, where environmental spillovers do not travel from an originating state to any other state. An example might be the water quality of the Biscayne Aquifer, the large groundwater source for southeastern Florida. The pollution that tends to degrade this aquifer is generated entirely within Florida, primarily from agricultural and domestic sources. One could argue that this case, and similar ones elsewhere, is best approached with a decentralized policy system, in which each state manages the environmental resource the way it regards as appropriate. Local problems of this type are amenable to local solutions.

At the other end of the spectrum are emissions that migrate to other states. Airborne emissions of SO_2 in the Midwest affect all states to the east. Emissions of CO_2 from anywhere in the United States are uniformly mixed in the atmosphere and affect global warming for everybody, both in this country and elsewhere in the world. In this case we have a strong argument for a national approach to environmental policy. No individual state has control over its ambient CO_2 level. Joint action is necessary. In some cases regional action by groups of states might be preferable, if the problem is strictly regional. But in cases where regional policy institutions are not well developed, action at the national level would be required.

Thus, one of the factors affecting the desirability of decentralization is the nature of the environmental problem being addressed. Another component is the technological nature of the regulatory solution. Mobile-source air pollution is very much a state/regional phenomenon. The air quality in most cities is degraded primarily by the traffic in each city. But the main object of control, automobiles and their tailpipe emissions, are produced and distributed in a national market. While it would be technically feasible to have different tailpipe standards in every metropolitan area, it would not be particularly efficient to do so. It may be feasible to have large groups of states acting in concert, an approach somewhere between complete centralization and complete decentralization. This is in general the situation we now have in the United States.

Political Gaming

A situation that seems to argue for a degree of centralization in environmental policy is when states try to gain an advantage by playing off the environmental decisions of neighboring states. If individual states were left to set their own pollution-control standards, they might have an incentive to weaken them. Why? Most states regard themselves as being in economic competition with other states. Thus, they pursue growth agendas, to increase the economic security of their residents and to accommodate demographic growth. By making their environmental standards less restrictive, the thinking goes, they can attract businesses into the state, as well as hold on to those already there. This phenomenon is known as the **race to the bottom**:[5] Economic competition among the states leads to progressive relaxation of environmental standards, until every state has standards that are the same as the weakest among them.

If there is, in fact, a strong urge leading to a race to the bottom, then decentralizing environmental policy could have negative ramifications for environmental quality. But how pervasive is this phenomenon? There is evidence on both sides. States that have definite pro-business attitudes, and apparently lax environmental standards are part of the package, include Louisiana and Texas. States with aggressive environmental attitudes, no doubt more aggressive than federal authorities, include Massachusetts, California, and New York. Table 17.1 contains data that give a comparative perspective of resources devoted by the states to environmental protection. The data show state environmental expenditures per capita for 1993 and vary enormously, from a low of $18.6 in Ohio to a high of $338.8 in Alaska.

These data do not speak directly to the question of whether some states have deliberately weakened environmental standards to attract economic growth. The approach of each state is affected by the nature of the environmental problems faced, the environmental expertise in the various public agencies and political bodies, and the environmental values among the population.

Thus, it should be no surprise that research into the race-to-the-bottom problem over the last few decades has yielded mixed conclusions. Some studies report that certain businesses tend to locate in states with relatively lax environmental standards, and some studies report no such phenomenon.[6] To some extent it may be a matter of perceptions. In a survey of state environmental officials, Kirsten Engel found that some 88 percent of them agreed that "concern over industry location and siting affects environmental decision making in their state."[7]

The Battle Over Unfunded Mandates

One of the arenas for the struggle between federal authorities and the states has been the battle over **unfunded federal mandates**. An unfunded fed-

Table 17.1   State Environmental Expenditures Per Capita, 1994*

	$/person		$/person
Alaska	338.8	Kentucky	41.3
Wyoming	189.7	Tennessee	40.9
Vermont	91.6	Maryland	39.5
Montana	82.6	South Carolina	38.1
Idaho	80.6	Texas	38.1
Delaware	77.4	Missouri	36.8
Colorado	74.2	New Hampshire	35.1
Nevada	73.6	Illinois	34.3
California	66.9	New Mexico	33.7
Oregon	62.3	Florida	33.6
South Dakota	62.2	Nebraska	32.8
Maine	61.5	Massachusetts	32.2
Louisiana	60.8	Iowa	31.8
North Dakota	57.6	Alabama	30.1
Washington	56.2	New York	28.5
West Virginia	53.8	Virginia	25.1
Rhode Island	53.6	Oklahoma	25.0
Utah	52.3	Hawaii	24.5
Minnesota	51.4	North Carolina	23.9
Wisconsin	48.2	Arizona	22.9
Pennsylvania	44.7	Georgia	22.4
New Jersey	43.8	Michigan	20.8
Connecticut	42.7	Indiana	19.8
Arkansas	42.2	Kansas	19.4
Mississippi	42.1	Ohio	18.6

* Although these are somewhat old, no more recent data are available. The Environmental Council of the States reports that, on an aggregate level, current expenditures per capita for environmental purposes are about the same as they were in 1993.

Source: The Council of State Governments, *Resource Guide to State Environmental Management*, 4th ed. (Lexington, KY: CSG, 1996).

eral mandate is a federal directive for the states to undertake certain actions, but without sufficient federal funds to pay for them. The states must, therefore, come up with the resources to pay for, in whole or in part, the programs required by federal laws. A classic unfunded mandate is the recent No Child Left Behind Law, which mandates that states put in place a substantial testing program for schoolchildren. State authorities have complained loudly about the lack of federal funding for the testing program itself and for the educational improvements needed to achieve the standards of the law.

In the environmental area unfunded federal mandates have also been major objects of contention. The Safe Drinking Water Act sets maximum contaminant levels that municipalities are expected to meet in their drinking water systems, but does not involve reimbursement for the costs of meeting these standards. States have also complained about the local costs of waste-water treatment facilities, of meeting unreasonably high cleanup standards in Brownfield cases, and other issues.

Unfunded mandates have a political life and an economic life. In the political arena, the phenomenon itself results from the natural tendency for politicians to take credit for the benefits of public policy and avoid the responsibility for the costs. Federal legislators can point to the benefits that will derive from federal laws, while pushing the costs off onto others. Opposition to unfunded federal mandates led in 1995 to the passage of the federal Unfunded Mandates Reform Act, which is supposed to make it more difficult for Congress to push costs onto states and localities.

From a policy-effectiveness point of view, there are countervailing tendencies. On the one hand, one can certainly argue that localities ought, in fact, pay the costs of pollution control if sources within that area are solely responsible for it, especially if the pollution drifts over to another state or locality. This is an example of what in Europe is called the **polluter-pays principle**; that polluters themselves should be responsible for the damages they cause, and that this cost ought not to be foisted onto somebody else, for example the general public.

On the other hand, if there are no environmental spillovers, one could argue that states and localities themselves should determine the relevant environmental standards they should strive for. In this case it's not the lack of funding that is at major issue, but the fact that federal authorities are setting the standards rather than letting them be set locally.

States as Policy Innovators

There is another reason for thinking that environmental policy ought to be subject to some degree of decentralization. With the growth of state-level environmental expertise that this tends to produce, states can function effectively as sources of innovation of new policy initiatives. The hard-core nature of environmental politics at the national level sometimes stifles the introduction of new ideas into national environmental regulation. Opposing positions get more deeply entrenched, powerful coalitions can head off new ideas. Though difficult, federal innovation is not impossible, since we know that innovation does happen in Washington.

But there are fifty states, so there are substantial opportunities for new ideas to be fully developed and then either spread to other states (e.g., bottle bills), or incorporated into federal laws. For example, DDT was first banned by Wisconsin; this later became a national effort. The Federal Strip Mining Control and Reclamation Act of 1977 was substantially modeled after the Pennsylvania strip mining reclamation law. The federal toxics release inventory program is an idea that originated with programs in New Jersey and Maryland.

The Case of California

California occupies a special role in the debate over federal-state relationships on environmental policy, particularly in air pollution control. California instituted controls on automobile emissions for the first time in 1960, well before the federal standards began. It was motivated by the special air pollution problems of the Los Angeles basin, where urban smog was first recognized. In recognition of this, the 1967 Clean Air Act Amendments granted California a waiver from federal standards, allowing it to adopt more stringent tailpipe standards if it so chose, which it has. In general, through the years, cars sold in California have had to meet tailpipe emission standards that are substantially more restrictive than those established for the rest of the country.

The California exemption was included in the major 1970 rewrite of the CAA. Also included, however, was the continued prohibition against other states developing their own standards. The auto companies continued to be alarmed at the prospect of having to produce cars with different emission specifications for every state. In the 1977 CAA amendments, however, rationality prevailed. Congress reasoned that if the car companies were already making two types of cars (in terms of emission performance), one type for California and the other for everywhere else, there was no reason to disallow making the California cars available to markets in other states. Thus, in the 1977 law they included an "opt-in" provision, whereby other states can adopt, as of 1990, tailpipe standards identical to those of California.

This gave the California standards much greater significance on the national level. One impact was to lead the main automakers to adopt a voluntary program whereby they produced lower emission vehicles earlier than they would have otherwise. The intent was to try to keep states from adopting the California standards under the opt-in rules. Nevertheless, by 2000, four states (New York, Massachusetts, Vermont, and Maine) had adopted the California standards, and more are threatening to do so. The upshot is that this puts the California Air Resources Board (CARB) in a very powerful position with respect to initiating changes in tailpipe emission standards that the EPA establishes for the rest of the country under the CAA.

A similar effort is being launched to reduce CO_2 emissions and thus reduce the threat of global warming. With little action, or an aversion to action, on the national level, a number of states have taken their own steps to limit greenhouse gases from industrial sources. Massachusetts was one of the first, introducing a cap-and-trade program for CO_2 emissions, as well as several other types of emissions, from large power plants. But California has become the first to attempt to reduce CO_2 from the transportation sector, a major producer of greenhouse gases. In 2002 it passed a law requiring automobiles to reduce CO_2 emissions in future cars sold in that state. This law has been vigorously challenged by auto manufacturers on the grounds that the only practicable way of doing this is by building cars that get better mileage, but federal law preempts individual states from setting their own mileage requirements.[8]

Summary

Before about 1970, environmental policy was highly decentralized among the states. With the establishment of the EPA and major federal laws of the early 1970s, it became much more centralized, with initiative and responsibilities shifting to Washington. In the last decade or so, the issue of decentralization has become a topic of major concern; while nobody expects the EPA to fade away anytime soon, the growing environmental expertise and interests of the states have led many of them to become more assertive in environmental policy matters. The question of how environmental policy initiatives and responsibilities should be divided among federal, state, and local governments is now a front-burner issue.

The U.S. Constitution sets a basic framework for our federal government; those matters not specifically given by the Constitution to the federal government are reserved for the states. This applies to matters of interstate commerce, the management of which is expressly stated as a federal responsibility. In effect this provides the fundamental justification for federal environmental laws, and restricts the latitude of state environmental laws. Also important is the supremacy clause of the Constitution, which allows the federal government to preempt certain areas of environmental regulation.

From a conceptual point of view, the question of whether a particular environmental problem is best approached with a centralized or decentralized policy ought to depend on a number of factors: the extent to which environmental impacts spill over from one state to another, the economic inefficiencies that could result if states individually try to regulate essentially national economic markets, the extent to which states might be motivated to use environmental policy as a competitive factor vis-à-vis other states, and the nature of the political struggle that typically goes on between federal authorities and the states.

One important justification for having a system that is decentralized to some extent is to get the advantages of states' ability to innovate in environmental regulation. At the federal level, powerful coalitions can make it difficult (though not impossible) to introduce new approaches to environmental regulation. It may be easier to do this at the state level; in fact, many programs that get written into federal laws are programs that have been first tried at the state level.

Key Terms

balancing approach	polluter-pays principle
federal preemption	race to the bottom
interstate commerce clause	supremacy doctrine
opt-in provisions	unfunded federal mandates
place-based environmental advocacy and action	

Questions for Further Discussion

1. From a conceptual point of view, what are the important factors that should determine whether a particular environmental issue is more properly a federal issue or a state and local issue?

2. What guidance does the U.S. Constitution give in dividing the overall task of environmental regulation between federal authorities and the states?

3. What factors might make it easier for states to develop innovative environmental regulations than it is for the federal government?

4. Why is California such an important state when it comes to air pollution control?

5. What are the various ways that groups of states may operate together in environmental matters?

Web Sites

The prime site for state activities is the Council of State Governments:
www.csg.org

and particularly its environmental program:
www.csg.org/CSG/policy/enviro/default.aspx

Its Ecos (standing for environmental communiqué of the states) site has lots of information on state environmental programs:
www.csg.org/pubs/pubs_ecos.aspx

Another Ecos site is the Environmental Council of the States:
www.ecos.org

The Environmental Law Institute offers many studies and reports on state environmental programs, especially through its Center for State, Local and Regional Environmental Programs:
www.eli.org
www2.eli.org/research/statecenter/htm

Additional Readings

Bernstein, Tobie, *State and Local Indoor Air Quality Programs: Five Case Studies* (Washington, DC: Environmental Law Institute, 1997).

Butler, Henry R., and Jonathan R. Macey, *Using Federalism to Improve Environmental Policy* (Washington, DC: AEI Press, 1996).

Environmental Law Institute, *An Analysis of State Superfund Programs, 50-State Study, 2001 Update* (Washington, DC: ELI, November 2002).

Environmental Law Institute, *Fresh Air: Innovative State and Local Programs for Improving Air Quality* (Washington, DC: ELI, December 1997).

Keiner, Suellen T., *The New Air Permitting Program: The Role of the States* (Washington, DC: Environmental Law Institute, 1992).

Lowry, William R., *The Dimensions of Federalism: State Governments and Pollution Control Policies* (Durham, NC: Duke University Press, 1992).

Murray, Paula C., and David B. Spence, "Fair Weather Federalism and America's Waste Disposal Crisis," *Harvard Environmental Law Review* 27, no. 1 (2003):71–103.

Rechtschaffen, Clifford, and David L. Markell, *Reinventing Environmental Enforcement and the State/Federal Relationship* (Washington, DC: ELI, 2003).

Ringquist, Evan J., *Environmental Protection at the State Level: Politics and Progress in Controlling Pollution* (Armonk, NY: M. E. Sharpe, 1993).

Scheberle, Denise, *Federalism and Environmental Policy: Trust and the Politics of Implementation* (Washington, DC: Georgetown University Press, 1998).

Notes

[1] Environmental decentralization also goes by other names, e.g., environmental federalism, devolution, defederalization, and civic environmentalism.

[2] Sometimes called community-based action.

[3] See Frona M. Powell, *Law and the Environment* (St. Paul, MN: West Educational Publishing, 1998):167–169.

[4] For information about many of these initiatives, see the Web site of Beyond Pesticides, www.beyondpesticides.org.

[5] The conflict over globalization also features a concern about a race to the bottom, but in this case the racers are countries rather than states. We will discuss this in Chapter 20.

[6] Wallace E. Oates, "A Reconsideration of Environmental Federalism," Discussion Paper 01-54 (Washington, DC: Resources for the Future, November 2001).

[7] Kirsten H. Engel, "State Environmental Standard Setting: Is There a Race and Is It to the Bottom?" *Hastings Law Journal* 48 (1997):271–398.

[8] The law is the Motor Vehicle Information and Cost Savings Act, part of the Energy Policy and Conservation Act of 1975. This law established the Corporate Average Fuel Economy (CAFE) program whereby Congress establishes minimum average mileage standards for new cars.

SECTION V
INTERNATIONAL
ISSUES

In this last section of the book we deal with some issues in international environmental policy. The world is shrinking, and events in one country are more and more likely to affect people in others. In addition, we now more fully appreciate that there is truly a global environment that has to be nurtured and improved. Thus, the future will undoubtedly see greater emphasis on international environmental issues. The section contains three chapters: chapter 18 deals with the issue of maintaining the global atmosphere, chapter 19 with some of the basics of international agreements, and chapter 20 with the thorny issue of globalization and the environment.

18

Global Environmental Problems

Throughout history the main perspective of humans has been local, and the environmental problems that have made themselves manifest have been local in nature: neighborhood smoke from a factory, smells and sanitary effects from local herds of horses, the contamination of the town well, and so on. As human populations have multiplied and spread, many local problems have been transformed into regional and national issues. More recently, continued demographic and economic growth, the shrinking of the earth in terms of transportation and communication, and the expansion of scientific perspectives and capabilities have made us realize that some environmental problems are truly global in extent. There is such a thing as the global environment, capable of being disrupted by the activities of humans.[1]

In this chapter we will deal with two cases of global environmental pollution and its control: the protection of the earth's ozone shield, and the response to the global greenhouse effect. Both of these involve the human-induced disruption of the radiation balance between the earth and its cosmic environment. Both are problems that can be tackled effectively only by collective action among all peoples of the world, as fractured as they may be along geographical, political, social, economic, and cultural lines.

The Ozone Layer

Ozone (O_3) leads two different lives in the environment. At the earth's surface it is an air pollutant, the primary constituent of smog, produced by the interaction of emissions of volatile organic compounds (VOCs) and nitrogen oxides (NO_x) that react in the presence of sunlight. A major part of the Clean Air Act is aimed at controlling ground-level ozone. But most of the ozone in the earth's atmosphere is located in the stratosphere, a zone extending from about 10 km to 50 km above ground level. This stratospheric ozone is critical in maintaining the earth's radiation balance. The atmosphere surrounding the earth essentially acts as a filter for incoming electromagnetic radiation. The atmospheric gas responsible for this is ozone, which blocks a large percentage of incoming low-wavelength, or ultraviolet, radiation.

The Scientific Problem

Several decades ago scientific evidence began to indicate that the ozone content of the atmosphere was showing signs of diminishing. In the mid-1980s a substantial hole appeared in the ozone layer over Antarctica. More recently, significant ozone reduction has been found throughout the entire stratosphere, including those areas over the more populated parts of the world. In the 1970s scientists discovered the cause of this phenomenon. It had been known for some time that the chemical content of the atmosphere has been changing at a rapid rate and on a global scale. Ozone disappearance was linked to the accumulation of chlorine in the stratosphere. Chlorine was found to insert itself into what was normally a balanced process of ozone production and destruction, vastly increasing the rate of ozone destruction. The source of the chlorine turned out to be a variety of manufactured chemicals which, released at ground level, slowly migrated up to higher altitudes. The culprits are substances called **halocarbons**, chemicals composed of carbon atoms in combination with atoms of chlorine, fluorine, iodine, and bromine. The primary halocarbons are called **chlorofluorocarbons (CFCs)**, which have molecules consisting of combinations of carbon, fluorine, and chlorine atoms. Another subgroup is the halons, composed of these elements plus bromine atoms; bromine, in fact, acts similarly to chlorine in breaking down ozone molecules. Carbon tetrachloride and methyl chloroform are also implicated in ozone destruction.

CFCs were developed in the 1930s as a replacement for the refrigerants in use at the time. Unlike those they replaced, CFCs are extremely stable, nontoxic, and inert relative to the electrical and mechanical machinery in which they are used. Thus, their use spread quickly as refrigerants and also as propellants for aerosols (hair sprays, deodorants, insecticides), industrial agents for making polyurethane and polystyrene foams, and industrial cleaning agents and solvents. Halons are widely used as fire suppressors. When these substances were introduced, attention was exclusively focused on their benefits; there was no evidence that they could have long-term impacts on the atmosphere. But the very stable nature of these gases allows them to migrate very slowly in the atmosphere. After surface release, they drift up through the troposphere into the stratosphere, where they begin a long process of ozone destruction.

Several years ago it was thought that ozone depletion might confine itself to small parts of the stratosphere, in which case damages from the increasing surface flux of ultraviolet radiation would be limited. But recently strong evidence has appeared that significant ozone depletion now occurs periodically over large portions of the world's highly populated regions. Thus, damages are likely to be much more widespread.

Current research indicates that there are two main sources of damage to humans: health impacts and agricultural crop losses. Health damages are related to the increased incidence of skin cancers and eye disease. The dose-response relationships developed by the EPA indicate that for each 1 percent increase in UV_B radiation, basal-cell and squamous-cell cancer cases would increase by 1 percent and 2 percent, respectively, while melanoma skin cancers would increase by less than 1 percent and cataracts by about 0.2 percent. Increased UV_B radiation also can be expected to increase food production costs because of the physical damages it produces in growing plants. Damages also are expected in other parts of the earth's physical ecosystem.

Policy Responses

Ozone depletion is one global problem in which countries of the world have mounted an effective response. In 1970 the United States and several other countries took unilateral action, banning CFCs in aerosols, though not in refrigerants. But continued scientific evidence motivated more action at the international level; in fact, this is a good example of a case where the accumulating results of scientific work tended to drive policy response, as table 18.1 illustrates.

Under the auspices of the United Nations, 24 nations in 1987 signed the **Montreal Protocol on Substances That Deplete the Ozone Layer**. There was another important factor that facilitated the Montreal Protocol: competition among the large, international chemical companies. If ozone-depleting substances were phased out, the path was cleared for companies to develop alternatives, and the company or companies that could do this the fastest would have a major commercial advantage. Several large U.S. firms at the time saw themselves in this position, and were instrumental in getting U.S. political approval for the agreement. As we will discuss later, this is one of the missing elements so far in the approach to combat global warming.

The Montreal agreement committed the signatory nations to phasing out the production and consumption of ozone-depleting substances. Soon after the original agreement was signed, it became clear that the problem was getting worse, partly because several large CFC-producing countries had not signed the original agreement. In subsequent amendments countries agreed

Table 18.1 Calendar of Scientific Activities and Policy Responses on the Issue of Atmospheric Ozone

Science		Responses	
1974	Researchers put forth the theory that CFCs may destroy significant amounts of atmospheric ozone.		
1976	The U.S. National Academy of Sciences releases a report predicting significant ozone depletion.		The SST (supersonic transport) debate.
		1978	CFCs are banned as propellants in nonessential aerosols in the U.S.
1980	Research efforts are institutionalized NASA—science EPA—policy NAS—integration State—treaties		The UNEP Governing Council calls for reductions in CFC-11 and CFC-12.
		1982	UNEP convenes experts to prepare a Global Framework Convention for the Protection of the Ozone Layer.
1985	Members of a British scientific team present evidence of significant ozone depletion over Antarctica (the "ozone hole").		The Vienna Convention for the Protection of the Ozone Layer is opened for signature.
1987	Scientific evidence is presented showing that chlorine chemicals are the primary cause of ozone depletion.		The Montreal Protocol on Substances That Deplete the Ozone Layer is opened for signature.
1988	Ozone losses over the northern hemisphere are reported.		
		1989	European countries and the United States agree to faster action for phasing out CFCs, but developing countries oppose the new timetable.
		1990	The parties to the Montreal Protocol agree to a faster timetable for reducing CFC production and consumption.
1991	The World Meteorological Organization reports that the rate of depletion in stratospheric ozone is much faster than predicted.		
		1992–1994	Further meetings of the Montreal Protocol countries are held to step up timetables for reducing CFCs and HCFCs.

to phase out the production of CFCs completely by the year 2000, to add carbon tetrachloride and methyl chloroform to the list, and to introduce a long-term schedule for phasing out HCFCs. As of 2006, the agreement had been ratified by 188 countries, including India and China.[2]

Table 18.2 shows the consumption freeze and phaseout schedules for the main ozone-depleting substances covered in the agreement. One of its important features is that it treats developed and developing countries differently: the latter have delayed phaseout schedules relative to the former, in deference to their needs to foster economic growth. The agreement also created a fund, fed by contributions from the developed world, to help finance CFC-reducing technological changes in the developing world.

The Montreal Protocol appears to have been reasonably successful so far. "The total combined abundance of ozone-depleting compounds in the lower atmosphere peaked in 1994 and is now slowly declining. Total chlorine is declining, but total bromine is increasing."[3] This result is probably related to the effectiveness of the Montreal Protocol. The scientific data on stratospheric ozone levels are less conclusive, however. The extent of the Antarctic ozone hole peaked in 2000, and over the next few years started to decrease in size. At mid-decade it had started to increase again, perhaps due to other factors. It will apparently be some time before the earth's ozone shield is fully repaired.

Table 18.2   Phaseout Schedules Contained in the Montreal Protocol and Subsequent Amendments

Substance	Developed Countries		Developing Countries	
	Consumption Freeze	**Phaseout**	**Consumption Freeze**	**Phaseout**
Chlorofluorocarbons (CFC)	July 1, 1989	Jan. 1, 1996	July 1, 1999	Jan. 1, 2010
Halons	—	Jan. 1, 1994	Jan. 1, 2002	Jan. 1, 2010
Other Fully Halogenated CFCs	—	Jan. 1, 1996	—	Jan. 1, 2010
Carbon Tetrachloride	—	Jan. 1, 1996	—	Jan. 1, 2010
Methyl Chloroform	Jan. 1, 1993	Jan. 1, 1996	Jan. 1, 2003	Jan. 1, 2015
Hydrochloro-fluorocarbons (HCFCs)	Jan. 1, 1996	Jan. 1, 2030	Jan. 1, 2016	Jan. 1, 2040
Methyl Bromide	Jan. 1, 1995	Jan. 1, 2005	Jan. 1, 2002	Jan. 1, 2015

Source: United Nations Development Program, Montreal Protocol, Phase-Out Targets (www.undp.org/Montrealprotocol/Montreal.htm).

Global Warming

The second great problem of the world environment is **global warming**, sometimes called the greenhouse effect. The earth receives massive amounts of radiation from sun and space; it also emits radiation back into space. The balance between incoming and outgoing radiation drives a number of physical parameters on and above the surface of the globe. Critical in determining this balance is the chemical composition of the earth's atmosphere. Certain gases in the atmosphere, such as CO_2 and water vapor, trap heat, similar in effect to a greenhouse. This heat is what makes life on earth possible; without it the earth would be a frigid rock drifting through space. Changes in the composition of the atmosphere will change its heat-trapping capabilities. This will presumably lead to increases in mean temperatures at and above the earth's surface, and a host of other impacts that are driven by these temperature changes. This will have far-reaching impacts on humans and every other element of the earth's ecosystem.

The Science

Scientific attention to this problem goes back to the early nineteenth century. In 1827 a French scientist, Jean Baptiste Fourier, explained how the chemical content of the global atmosphere allowed it to warm the earth's surface, making it habitable by humans and other organisms. Other scientists in the nineteenth and early twentieth centuries[4] identified the possible problems that could result if the atmosphere was changed through human activities.

But major scientific resources were not devoted to studying the greenhouse effect until midway through the twentieth century. Since then, scientists around the world have been at work probing and analyzing the many physical dimensions of the global greenhouse phenomenon. Thousands of studies and reports have been published, and more will appear in the future, as we try to understand more fully the very complex atmospheric dynamics involved and the role that humans play.

The main scientific questions are the following:

1. Are mean surface (and atmospheric) temperatures increasing around the world?
2. How much of the increase is related to human activity?
3. How much change can we expect in the future under different scenarios for greenhouse gas (GHG)?
4. What will be the ecological impacts of global warming for different countries and groups of people?
5. What actions can and should we take to respond to the threat of global warming?

Interpreting the Past. Questions (1) and (2) deal with what has happened to date. On the first of these questions there is a strong consensus among scientists that global surface temperatures are indeed increasing. The general conclusion is that during the twentieth century global average surface temperatures rose by 0.6 ± 0.2°C.

How much of this increase can be attributed to humans? The scientific consensus on this is also strong, though there are still a few naysayers. Studies have concluded that as of the end of the twentieth century, the global atmosphere contained about 365 ppm of CO_2, whereas in the 1,000 years before the industrial revolution the atmospheric content of CO_2 varied between 270 and 290 ppm. Atmospheric concentrations of other greenhouse gases also have increased.

The chief culprit is human-caused increases in emissions of CO_2 stemming from the use of fossil fuels in the modern economy. Under normal circumstances (i.e., without humans), an enormous amount of CO_2, about 800 billion tons per year, cycles through the global biosphere. It is emitted and absorbed such that the atmospheric content of CO_2 stays roughly constant. Over the last 150 years, as a result of the industrial revolution and the accompanying use of fossil fuels, human activities have substantially increased the total amount of CO_2 emissions, today about 25 billion tons per year. Much of this is absorbed in oceans and biomass, but a substantial amount has contributed to a buildup of CO_2 in the earth's atmosphere.

Although CO_2 is the primary greenhouse gas, other gases are of growing importance. These are methane (CH_4), nitrous oxide (N_2O), hydrofluorocarbons (HFCs), perfluorocarbons (PFCs), and sulfur hexafluoride (SF_6), which originate from a wide variety of human activities. These substances differ in a number of important respects that have important implications for responding to the threat of global warming. They differ in terms of their heat-trapping ability and in their residence time in the atmosphere. For example, the heat-trapping impact of CH_4 is about 30 times more powerful than that of CO_2, but the estimated residence time of CO_2 is about 250 years, while that of CH_4 is only 10 to 15 years. There is substantial agreement among scientists that humans have produced most (i.e., between 70 and 90 percent) of the observed increases in global temperature.

The Future. Question (3) above addresses the future. To predict the future one has to look not only at physical processes but also projected human responses. This is speculative. We don't know for sure how fast humans will respond and what actions they will take. In a situation like this a common approach is to lay out a number of possible **future scenarios**, each based on different assumptions about future human actions. The assumptions have to do with factors such as population growth, economic developments, and technological changes that might occur, for example in automobiles or electric power generation.

The Intergovernmental Panel on Climate Change (discussed below) recently developed a series of scenarios on quantities of GHG emissions that might occur in the future. Some of the results are shown in table 18.3. Future

**Table 18.3   Future GHG Emissions Scenarios, Based on Population
and Economic Growth and Energy Use**

Type	1990	2020	2050	2100
CO_2 emissions from fossil fuel use (GtC/yr.)				
Scenario I	6.0	11.2	23.1	30.3
Scenario II	6.0	11.0	16.5	28.9
Scenario III	6.0	10.0	11.7	5.2
Scenario IV	6.0	9.0	11.2	13.8
Methane (MtCH$_4$/yr.)				
Scenario I	310	416	630	735
Scenario II	310	424	598	889
Scenario III	310	377	359	236
Scenario IV	310	384	505	597
Nitrous Oxide (MtN/yr.)				
Scenario I	6.7	9.3	14.5	16.6
Scenario II	6.7	9.6	12.0	16.5
Scenario III	6.7	8.1	8.3	5.7
Scenario IV	6.7	6.1	6.3	6.9

Note: GtC/yr.: gigatons carbon per year; MtCH$_4$/yr.: million tons CH_4 per year; MtN/yr.: million tons nitrogen per year

Scenarios are as follows:

Scenario I describes a future world of very rapid economic growth, global population that peaks in mid-century and declines thereafter, and the rapid introduction of new and more efficient fossil-based technologies. Major underlying themes are convergence among regions, capacity building, and increased cultural and social interactions, with a substantial reduction in regional differences in per capita income.

Scenario II describes a very heterogeneous world. The underlying theme is self-reliance and preservation of local identities. Fertility patterns across regions converge very slowly, which results in continuously increasing global population. Economic development is primarily regionally oriented and per capita economic growth and technological change are more fragmented and slower than in other storylines.

Scenario III describes a convergent world with the same global population that peaks in mid-century and declines thereafter, as in Scenario I, but with rapid changes in economic structures toward a service and information economy, with reductions in material intensity, and the introduction of clean and resource-efficient technologies. The emphasis is on global solutions to economic, social, and environmental sustainability, including improved equity, but without additional climate initiatives.

Scenario IV describes a world in which the emphasis is on local solutions to economic, social, and environmental sustainability. It is a world with continuously increasing global population at a rate lower than Scenario II, intermediate levels of economic development, and less rapid and more diverse technological change than in Scenarios I or III. While the scenario is also oriented toward environmental protection and social equity, it focus is the on local and regional levels.

Source: Intergovernmental Panel on Climate Change, *Special Report on Emission Scenarios* (Geneva: IPCC, 2000). Excerpted from Table 3a, pp. 17–20. Used with permission of the publisher.

emissions of CO_2, CH_4, and N_2O are shown for four different scenarios. The basis for each scenario is described in the footnote to the table. Note several things. First, there are substantial differences among the scenarios in terms of emissions, from which we can conclude that the future actions we take can have a substantial impact on future emissions. Second, all but one of the scenarios involves continued increases in the emissions of these gases. Scenario III is the only one implying a decrease in global emissions. But this scenario is based on an assumption that countries around the globe rapidly transition to service-based economies and rapidly adopt clean and resource efficient technologies.

On the assumption that future GHG emissions continue to increase as in Scenarios I or II, the expectation is that global temperatures will increase 1.4°C to 5.8°C above 1990 levels by 2100.

Impacts. Which then brings us to question (4), what can we expect from these changes in terms of impacts on humans and other elements of the global ecosystem? To answer this requires two steps. The first is to deduce the specific meteorological changes that will result, in terms of temperature (e.g., frequency of heat waves and droughts), storms, precipitation, and sea levels and temperatures. These impacts will not be uniform around the world, but will vary substantially by latitude and longitude. The second step is to translate these physical changes into the impacts they might have for humans. Table 18.4 is a brief summary of these possible impacts.

One problem that substantially complicates the job of getting worldwide policy response to global warming is that these impacts will not be uniform across all countries. Higher latitude countries, for example, will be impacted differently than more tropical countries. It is conceivable that some countries may even be favorably affected in terms of such things as agricultural productivity and water availability.

What Can Be Done? Question (5) concerns the possible actions we might take in response to the global warming threat. Very broadly, there exists two types of strategies: mitigation and adaptation. Mitigation means taking steps to reduce future temperature increases and the meteorological impacts they would produce. Adaptation means to take steps to reduce the impacts of whatever temperature increases do occur. Obviously these strategies are not mutually exclusive. We can do some of both if that is what is called for.

Mitigation can be pursued in two ways: by reducing the emissions of greenhouse gases, and by increasing the capacity of the earth's ecosystem to absorb the primary GHG, carbon dioxide, and permanently sequester the associated carbon.

If the world continues to develop along a fossil-intensive energy path similar to the one it has followed over the last few centuries, atmospheric levels of CO_2 are expected to reach about 950 ppm by 2100. A very aggressive worldwide effort to combat global warming could probably reduce the increase to about 520 ppm by 2100. Thus, even an immediate and bold effort to combat the problem can not forestall a significant CO_2 buildup. Realistically, aggressive action is unlikely to be pursued unless something very major happens to grab the attention of 6 billion people around the world. Most likely, whatever steps are adopted will be intermediate ones, somewhere between doing nothing and an all-out effort. Therefore, the most likely scenario for the future is an increase in CO_2 concentrations to somewhere

Table 18.4   Possible Effects of Climate Change

Energy demand
Increased energy demand for cooling; reduced demand for heating. (Very likely) Net effect varies by region and climate change scenario.

Coastal zone inundation
Low-lying coastal areas in developing countries would be inundated by sea level rise: a 45 cm rise would inundate 11 percent of Bangladesh and affect 5.5 million people; with a 100 cm rise, inundation increases to 21 percent and the population affected to 13.5 million. Indonesia and Vietnam would also be severely affected, as well as a number of small island countries. (Likely)

Exposure to storm surge
Global population affected by flooding during coastal storms will increase by 75 to 200 million.

Human health
Increased heat-related injuries and mortality and decreased cold-related ones. For developed countries in temperate regions, evidence suggests a net improvement. (Medium) Moderate increase in global population exposed to malaria, dengue fever, and other insect-borne disease. (Medium to likely) Increase in prevalence of water-borne diseases, such as cholera. (Medium) Increase in ground-level ozone. (Medium)

Water supplies
Many arid areas will have a net decrease in available water.

Agriculture
Many crops in temperate regions benefit from higher carbon dioxide concentrations from moderate increases in temperature, but would be hurt by larger increases. Effect varies strongly by region and crop. Tropical crops would generally be hurt. Small positive effect in developed countries; small negative effect in developing countries. Low to medium confidence: 5 to 67 percent.

Extinction of species
Species that are endangered or vulnerable will become rarer or extinct. The number of species affected depends on the amount of warming and regional changes in precipitation. (Likely)

Ecosystem loss
How ecosystems respond to long-term changes is poorly understood. Climate change will affect the mix of plant and animal species in ecosystems. (Likely to occur, but with a substantial lag)

Source: Warwick J. McKibbin, and Peter J. Wilcoxen, "The Role of Economics in Climate Change Policy," *Journal of Economic Perspectives* 16, no. 2 (Spring 2002):114. Used with permission.

between 500 and 950 ppm, with whatever climate impacts this has. Similar reasoning applies to most of the other greenhouse gases.

The Politics of Global Warming

The global greenhouse problem is a classic case in which the controversy is not just about how to respond. A major part of the conflict revolves around the science, not only disagreement over what the scientific results are in the objective sense, but especially in organizing and introducing these results into the political/policy process.

Organizing and Communicating the Science. Scientists are spread throughout research institutions, government agencies, universities, and private firms. They communicate among themselves and publish papers in technical journals and reports. Sometimes individual scientists are in the position to make influential pronouncements or produce influential reports.[5] Instrumental in this information channel are science writers in the media, and publications that take it upon themselves to interpret scientific results to a wider audience (e.g., *Scientific American*). Statements of scientists can often be magnified in impact if they come from groups of scientists with special credentials. For example, in 1989 a group of 49 Nobel Prize winners and 700 members of the **National Academy of Sciences** issued a joint statement asserting that there was broad agreement among scientists on the nature and causes of the global greenhouse effect. The **World Meteorological Organization (WMO)** of the United Nations has been instrumental in pulling scientists together to produce joint statements.

The First World Climate Conference was organized in 1979 under the auspices of the United Nations. Out of this grew the World Climate Program, which gave impetus to internationally coordinated studies of climate change. In 1985 the World Meteorological Organization, the **United Nations Environment Program (UNEP)**, and the **International Council of Scientific Unions** organized the International Conference on the Assessment of the Role of Carbon Dioxide and of Other Greenhouse Gases in Climate Variations and Associated Impacts. In 1988, WMO, UNEP, and Environment Canada sponsored the World Conference on the Changing Atmosphere. These conferences were held for the purpose not only of getting scientists together to exchange views, but also were public events that invited media coverage and publicity; thus, they were important in the continuing process of communicating the work and concerns of scientists to policy makers and the public at large.

While it is important to get scientists to interact among themselves and produce the impetus for further work, it is critical to communicate scientific results to the nonscientific public to convince people of the seriousness of the problem, to put scientific results in terms people can understand, and to motivate policy makers toward action. A major development in scientific communication came in 1988 with the establishment of the **Intergovernmental Panel on Climate Change (IPCC)**. This was a joint effort by the U.N. Environment Program and the WMO. Its mission is to bring together groups of scientists to assess the state of our understanding of the greenhouse effect and communicate this to policy makers around the world. The IPCC's work is organized under three headings: (1) assessing the existing scientific literature on climate change and developing a scientific consensus on these results; (2) assessing the potential environmental and socioeconomic impacts of these changes; and (3) formulating and analyzing a variety of response actions available to policy leaders.

The IPCC has become the preeminent international organization for getting scientific results into the public arena. It has issued a series of definitive assessment reports (1992, 1996, and 2001) and a large number of special reports on various aspects of the phenomenon. It has especially focused on developing a consensus among scientists about the extent and likely repercussions that will flow from climate change. In its last report, IPCC strengthened its previous conclusions that warming is occurring and that human activity is causing most of it, and increased its estimates of future temperature changes, to between 2.7 and just under 11 degrees Fahrenheit over the next 100 years.

In the U.S. Global Change Research Act of 1990 (P.L. 101-606), the United States Global Change Research Program (USGCRP) was charged with the responsibility for undertaking a scientific assessment of the potential consequences of global change on the United States. The act requires the federal interagency Committee for Global Change Research of the National Science and Technology Council to "prepare and submit to the President and the Congress an assessment which analyzes current trends in global change, both human-induced and natural, and projects major trends for the subsequent 25 to 100 years."[6]

The National Politics of Global Warming

Science is one thing and politics is another, and in this case the science is not pushing a policy response as strongly as it did in the case of the ozone hole. This is changing, however. On one side, urging a more aggressive public response, are environmental groups, science communication groups,[7] and many politicians and policy officials. On the other side, urging a cautious, wait-and-see position, are business groups and their allies among political and policy officials. In between is the vast U.S. public, which has not yet become overtly concerned about the issue. The Clinton administration made a major effort in the 1990s to heighten public awareness and concern about global warming, but this was not particularly successful, as we discussed in chapter 5.[8] Doing something about global warming means making major changes in our fossil-fuel-based economic system, and there is great resistance to this among both consumers and economic interests. Barring some short-term cataclysm, only continued growth in public concern will lead to a state of affairs where the necessary reforms can be pushed through.

Within Congress a bipartisan group of senators has sought to develop a plan for a market-based program to reduce U.S. carbon dioxide emissions.

The object has been to reduce total emissions to 2000 levels by 2010. It was defeated in the Senate in 2003, and again in 2005. The National Commission on Energy Policy has put forth an alternative, but so far Congress has not taken action on it.

Meanwhile the domestic politics of global warming are changing. Many in the business community are foreseeing the necessity of moving to a carbon-constrained energy system. The insurance sector is increasingly concerned about the higher losses that would result from changed meteorological and hydrological patterns. The renewable energy sector is gaining increased interest. Into the policy vacuum at the national level have stepped the states, a number of which have tried to initiate programs aimed at reducing emissions of greenhouse gases, especially CO_2. See the discussion in exhibit 18.1.

The International Arena: Kyoto and Beyond

The greenhouse effect is truly a global phenomenon; every country contributes to the problem, though in different degrees, and any effective mitigation effort is going to require the majority of countries to participate in the solution. The international dimensions of the problem, coupled with the great economic and cultural differences among countries, make it particularly difficult to address global warming in a concerted manner. For example:

1. Among developed countries, some are agreeable to undertaking costly steps to reduce greenhouse gases, and some are not. Many European countries are in the first group, while the United States, which happens to be the largest emitter of CO_2, is in the second group.

2. Differences also exist between developed and developing countries (sometimes called the North-South split). Many in the developing world take the position that the developed countries have been most responsible for the problem, which is true, and therefore ought to lead the way in solving it. Some in the developed world counter that with the expected growth of many large countries that are now classified as developing (e.g., India and China), their GHG emissions will grow rapidly in the near future (this is also true), so they ought to be prepared to take steps now to control these emissions.

3. Some countries will be harshly impacted by global warming while others will not. If the sea level rises through thermal expansion, many small island nations may find themselves effectively inundated. This threat has led them to organize the Alliance of Small Island States to represent their views more forcefully. On the other hand, there may be some countries who will benefit from a modest amount of global warming; for example, by improving agricultural productivity.

The Kyoto Protocol. As part of the **Earth Summit** of 1992, delegates from participating states endorsed the United Nations Framework Convention on Climate Change, which essentially was a statement of the seriousness

---

Exhibit 18.1
The Regional Greenhouse Gas Initiative

At the national level, policies to limit greenhouse gases have been effectively stymied by political opposition. This will eventually change, but there is no knowing when. Meanwhile some of the states have initiated actions to control these emissions. Many have started programs to encourage renewable energy; California has proposed a standard for tailpipe CO_2 emissions for automobiles in that state. In a significant regional effort, nine northeastern states have banded together to start a cap-and-trade program among themselves aimed at reducing greenhouse gases. Called the Regional Greenhouse Gas Initiative (RGGI), it was launched in 2003 and is applicable in its initial stages to CO_2 emissions coming from power plants, with plans later to expand it to other gases and other economic sectors.

The RGGI was developed with great care and deliberation to deal with the many economic and equity issues that have to be resolved. The objective is for states to meet future goals for CO_2 emission reductions by allocating CO_2 emission permits among the power plants located in these states. These plants would then be allowed to trade permits among themselves. As we discussed in chapter 15, this allows a more cost-effective reduction in CO_2 emissions, at least in principle.

There are many ongoing problems that have to be addressed as the program is implemented. One is the question of possible "leakage"; if generating plants in these states have higher electricity production costs because of the program, will consumers simply try to buy more power from outside the region, leading to increased CO_2 emissions elsewhere? How can the program be designed so that eventually it could be expanded to include other states and other economic sectors? Is it possible that the program might be designed so that eventually trading might take place with sources in other countries?

One of the major benefits of the RGGI is that it serves as a laboratory for studying the impacts of design and implementation factors in CO_2 cap-and-trade programs. There is widespread feeling that eventually there will be a national, comprehensive greenhouse gas trading program in the United States. The RGGI can provide useful data and experience for designing such a program.

---

of the problem and the need to do something about it. This treaty called for *voluntary* reductions in greenhouse gas emissions. By the mid-1990s, however, it became apparent that voluntary reductions would not produce the targeted emission goals. In 1997 another international meeting was convened, held in Kyoto, Japan, and attended by delegates from 171 countries. This international effort produced the **Kyoto Protocol**, which committed a group of developed countries to *binding* reductions in greenhouse gas emissions, to be achieved by 2008–2012. It is the political economy of the Kyoto Protocol that has dominated international discussions of global warming policy over the last few years. The commitments are in terms of aggregate anthropogenic CO_2-equivalent emissions, expressed as a percentage of 1990 emissions in the various countries. The agreements contain commitments from 39 industrialized countries and one country group, the European Union (EU). Thus, the protocol is essentially an agreement among European countries, the former communist countries of Eastern Europe, and the United States, Canada, Russia, and Japan. The agreed-upon reductions are shown in exhibit 18.2.

The Kyoto Protocol came into force on February 16, 2005, after being ratified by the requisite number of countries. The United States is not one of them, however. Although President Clinton signed the treaty in 1997, it was not ratified by Congress. President George W. Bush withdrew from the convention in 2001, claiming it would hurt the U.S. economy. A major rationale for this is that the agreement requires relatively large cutbacks of greenhouse gases by countries of the developed world, but none, either now or in the future, by developing countries such as India and China. Nor are there any substantial incentives built into the protocol that would lead these countries to commit to substantial GHG reductions in the future. It has become apparent also that achieving the Kyoto-mandated reductions will be difficult for those countries that ratified the treaty; a number of them have already slowed their efforts in the face of the costs of achieving the Kyoto targets.

Other questions about the Kyoto agreement are being addressed in a series of meetings among the signatory countries. These include enforcement issues and the introduction and use of **flexibility mechanisms** that would presumably help countries meet their cutback targets with a lower overall cost. Such mechanisms include:

1. *International emission trading.* Annex B countries may alter their GHG cutback responsibilities by buying or selling emission quantities among themselves.[9] Thus, one country could cut emissions by more than is required, and sell the excess to another country, which may then reduce emissions by a smaller amount.

2. *Joint implementation.* Annex B countries may undertake joint projects (e.g., a reforestation project in the United States partly funded by another country) and transfer emission allowances on the basis of the projects.

3. *Clean development mechanism.* Annex B countries can finance emission reductions in non-Annex B countries and gain credits toward their GHG cutback responsibilities.

The trading possibilities inherent in these flexibility mechanisms have encouraged the growth of a substantial number of private-sector firms that specialize in promoting and carrying out these trades.[10]

Questions abound over whether the Kyoto Protocol will have much of an impact on worldwide GHG emissions. Many people have pointed out its

Exhibit 18.2
The Kyoto Protocol for Limiting Greenhouse Gas Emissions

At a conference held in December 1997 in Kyoto, Japan, the parties to the United Nations Framework Convention on Climate Change agreed to an historic protocol to reduce emissions of greenhouse gases into the Earth's atmosphere toward the objective of forestalling the phenomenon of global warming.

Key aspects of the protocol include emission reduction targets for industrialized countries, and timetables for reaching them. The specific limits vary from country to country, as indicated. For most key industrial countries the reductions are about 8 percent (7 percent for the United States).

The framework for these targets includes the following:

- Emissions targets are to be reached over a five-year budget period rather than by a single year. Allowing emissions to be averaged across a budget period increases flexibility by helping to smooth out short-term fluctuations in economic performance or weather, either of which could spike emissions in a particular year.

- The first budget period will be 2008–2012. The parties rejected budget periods beginning as early as 2003, as neither realistic nor achievable. Having a full decade before the start of the binding period will allow more time for companies to make the transition to greater energy efficiency and/or lower carbon technologies.

- The emissions targets include all six major greenhouse gases: carbon dioxide, methane, nitrous oxide, and three synthetic substitutes for ozone-depleting CFCs that are highly potent and long-lasting in the atmosphere.

- Activities that absorb carbon, such as planting trees, will be used as off-sets against emissions targets. "Sinks" were also included in the interest of encouraging activities like afforestation and reforestation. Accounting for the role of forests is critical to a comprehensive and environmentally responsible approach to climate change. It also provides the private sector with low-cost opportunities to reduce emissions.

	Quantity of Emissions (in CO_2 equivalents) as Percentage of Emissions in Base Year
Australia	108
Austria	92
Belgium	92
Bulgaria	92
Canada	94
Croatia	95
Czech Republic	92
Denmark	92
Estonia	92
European Community	92
Finland	92
France	92
Germany	92
Greece	92
Hungary	94
Iceland	110
Ireland	92
Italy	92
Japan	94
Latvia	92
Liechtenstein	92
Lithuania	92
Luxembourg	92
Monaco	92
Netherlands	92
New Zealand	100
Norway	101
Poland	94
Portugal	92
Romania	92
Russia	100
Slovakia	92
Slovenia	92
Spain	92
Sweden	92
Switzerland	92
Ukraine	100
United Kingdom	92
United States	93

Sources: U.S. Environmental Protection Agency, "Fact Sheet on the Kyoto Protocol" (Washington, DC: EPA, October 1999):2; United Nations, "Framework Convention on Climate Change" (New York: UN, March 18, 1998):30.

flaws.[11] Many others have taken the position that it is a useful first step in what promises to be a very long-term effort over the next few decades to reduce greenhouse gas emissions from the developed world, and accommodate growth without massive increases in these emissions from countries in the developing world.

Summary

As the world population and economy grow, the scale of environmental impacts is increasing. Some of our most important issues concern the effects humans are having on the global environment. In this chapter we considered two of these: the degradation of the stratospheric ozone layer and global warming.

Stratospheric ozone depletion has come about as an inadvertent and unforeseen consequence of new chemicals introduced many decades ago. These chemicals were instrumental in facilitating the massive increase in refrigeration and air conditioning that has occurred over the last 50 years, but also led to the chemical destruction of substantial parts of the stratospheric ozone layer. The international response to this has been the Montreal Protocol, which incorporates a gradual phaseout in the production and consumption of the chemicals, first among countries of the developed world, followed by those of the developing world.

The other major global problem is the greenhouse effect; that is, the gradual warming of mean temperatures at the earth's surface because of a buildup of pollutants in the earth's atmosphere. The most important of these emissions is carbon dioxide (CO_2), produced as a normal by-product of fossil fuel use. Steps to reduce these emissions have been controversial and difficult because the modern economy essentially runs on fossil fuels. While scientific evidence for the global warming phenomenon accumulates, it has been hard to produce a large enough political coalition at the national level to undertake action. So far, most action in the United States has occurred in the states. On the international level the focus is on the Kyoto Protocol, a 1997 agreement that committed developed countries to cutbacks in emissions of greenhouse gases. Although the protocol went into effect in 2005, there has been very little success in getting significant cuts in GHGs among countries that have ratified the agreement (which does not include the U.S.). Substantial changes and incentives will be required in the future. One of these will have to be the inclusion of the developing world in future agreements.

Key Terms

chlorofluorocarbons (CFCs)
Earth Summit
flexibility mechanisms
future scenarios
global warming
halocarbons
Intergovernmental Panel
  on Climate Change (IPCC)
International Council
  of Scientific Unions

Kyoto Protocol
Montreal Protocol on Substances
  that Deplete the Ozone Layer
National Academy of Sciences
United Nations Environment
  Program (UNEP)
World Meteorological
  Organization (WMO)

Questions for Further Discussion

1. How might we institute some type of policy analysis in order to foresee more clearly problems such as the inadvertent destruction of the earth's stratospheric ozone shield?

2. Why was it relatively easy to get agreement in the United States on the Montreal Protocol, as compared to the difficulties of getting agreement with the Kyoto Protocol?

3. Why are ordinary citizens in general apparently unconcerned with the prospects of global warming?

4. What are the pros and cons of the Kyoto Protocol?

5. If you could rewrite the Kyoto Protocol, how would you do it?

Web Sites

There are hundreds of sites dealing with global warming and other global environmental issues. Naturally, the EPA has an extensive site:
  www.yosemite.epa.gov/oar/globalwarming.nsf/content/index.html

Other government agencies with sites include the National Oceanographic and Atmospheric Administration:
  www.climate.noaa.gov/

The Intergovernmental Panel on Climate Change maintains a site:
  www.ipcc.ch

as does virtually every environmental organization; for example:
World Wildlife Fund
  www.panda.org/about_wwf/what_we_do/climate_change

There are many business-related sites:
The Global Climate Coalition
  www.globalclimate.org

There are many sites that present guides to the hundreds of sites on the issue of global warming:
Global Warming Links
www.autobahn.mb.ca/~het/globalwarming
Similar sites are readily available on the topic of ozone depletion; for example:
www.europa.eu.int/comm/environment/ozone/links.htm

Additional Readings

Baranzini, Andrea, and Philippe Thalmann, eds., *Voluntary Approaches in Climate Policy* (London: Edward Elgar, July 2004).

Barrett, Scott, "Political Economy of the Kyoto Protocol," in Dieter Helm, ed., *Environmental Policy Objectives, Instruments, and Implementation* (New York: Oxford University Press, 2000).

Boehmer-Christiansen, Sonja, and Aynsley Kellow, *International Environmental Policy: Interests and the Failure of the Kyoto Process* (London: Edward Elgar, 2003).

Environmental Law Institute, *Reporting on Climate Change: Understanding the Science*, 3rd ed. (Washington, DC: ELI, 2003).

Greenpeace, *Guide to the Kyoto Protocol* (Greenpeace International, October 1998). (http://archive.greenpeace.org/climate/politics/reports/kppop.pdf).

Griffin, James M., ed., *Global Climate Change: The Science, Economics, and Politics* (London: Edward Elgar, 2003).

Immerwahr, John, *Waiting for a Signal: Public Attitudes toward Global Warming, the Environment and Geophysical Research*, American Geophysical Union, Electronic Publication, 1999 (http://www.agu.org/sci_soc/attitude_study.html).

Intergovernmental Panel on Climate Change, IPCC Third Assessment Report, *Climate Change 2001* (Geneva, Switzerland: IPCC, 2002).

Lipschutz, Ronnie, *Global Environmental Politics, Power, Perspectives, and Practice* (Washington, DC: Congressional Quarterly Press, 2004).

Mendelsohn, Robert, and James F. Neumann, eds., *The Impacts of Climate Change on the United States Economy* (Cambridge: Cambridge University Press, 1999).

National Academy of Sciences, *Policy Implications of Greenhouse Warming* (Washington, DC: National Academy Press, 1991).

National Research Council, *Climate Change Science: An Analysis of Some Key Questions* (Committee on the Science of Climate Change, 2001).

Nordhaus, William D., *Economic and Policy Issues in Climate Change* (Washington, DC: Resources for the Future, 1998).

Okonski, Kendra, ed., *Adapt or Die: The Science, Politics and Economics of Climate Change* (London: Profile Books, 2003).

Organization for Economic Cooperation and Development, *Action Against Climate Change: The Kyoto Protocol and Beyond* (Paris: OECD, 1999).

Rabe, Barry G., *Greenhouse and State House: The Evolving State Government Role in Climate Change* (Pew Center on Global Climate Change, November 2002).

Swingland, Ian R., ed., *Capturing Carbon and Conserving Biodiversity: The Market Approach* (London: Earthscan, May 2003).

Toman, Michael A., ed., *Climate Change Economics and Policy* (Washington, DC: Resources for the Future, 2001).

United Nations, Department of Public Information, *Planning, Designing and Implementing Policies to Control Ozone Depleting Substances under the Montreal Protocol: A Handbook of Policy Setting at the National Level*, E.03.111.D.32, 9280723111, n.d.

United Nations Environment Program, *Global Environment Outlook 3* (London: Earthscan, August 2002).

U.S. Congressional Budget Office, "The Economics of Climate Change: A Primer" (Washington, DC: CBO, April 2003). (www.cbo.gov/showdoc.cfm?index=4171&sequence=0).

U.S. Global Climate Research Program, *Climate Change Impacts on the United States: The Potential Consequences of Climate Variability and Change* (November 2000).

van Ierland, Ekko C., Joyeeta Gupta, and Marcel T. J. Kok, eds., *Issues in International Climate Policy: Theory and Policy* (London: Edward Elgar, June 2003).

Young, Zoe, *A New Green Order? The World Bank and the Politics of the Global Environment Facility* (London: Earthscan, January 2003).

Notes

[1] Instances of global environmental impacts may be very old; there is some evidence that Roman lead smelting activities increased airborne lead levels around the world 1,500 years ago.

[2] Not all of these have ratified all of the subsequent amendments, however. For ratification status see www.unep.org/ozone/Treaties_and_Ratification/2C_ratificationTable.asp.

[3] World Meteorological Association, "Scientific Assessment of Atmospheric Ozone," 1998.

[4] The first climate "model" used to predict the impacts of atmospheric change was done by a Swedish chemist named Svante Arrhenius in 1895.

[5] For example, in 1988 James Hansen, a scientist at the National Aeronautics and Space Agency, gave very influential testimony before the Senate Energy and Natural Resources Committee, in which he identified global warming as a serious threat and sought to summarize the state of our knowledge about it.

[6] The official Web site for this assessment is www.nacc.usgcrp.gov.

[7] Such as the Union of Concerned Scientists.

[8] More recently, Clinton's vice president and later presidential candidate Al Gore has sponsored a major film on the problem in an attempt to heighten public awareness. The film, *An Inconvenient Truth*, is based on a book of the same name, written by Gore.

[9] Annex B countries are those that have committed to some cutback in GHG emissions.

[10] Simply search the Web under "emissions trading" to find the names and business objectives of many of these firms.

[11] As one astute observer has written: "The essential problem with the Kyoto approach is that it provides poor incentives for participation and compliance. The minimum participation clause is set at such a low level that the agreement can enter into force while limiting the emissions of less than a third of the global total. The compliance mechanism, negotiated years after the emission limits were agreed upon, essentially requires that noncomplying countries punish themselves for failing to comply—a provision that is unlikely to influence behavior. The likely outcome will be an agreement that fails to enter into force, or an agreement that enters into force but is not implemented, or an agreement that enters into force and is implemented but only because it requires that countries do next to nothing about limiting their emissions." [Scott Barrett, "Towards a Better Climate Treaty," *World Economics* 3, no. 2 (April–June 2002):35–45.]

19

International Environmental Agreements

In the last chapter we discussed two global environmental problems and the joint efforts countries are pursuing to address them, in one case the Montreal Protocol and in the other the Kyoto Protocol. But there are several other international environmental agreements of note, and the future will undoubtedly see many new ones. In this chapter, therefore, we will look at the general question of how countries come together to carry out joint action through agreements of one type or another. This, in effect, puts us into a totally different policy setting. Within any single country, environmental policy is made and, especially, enforced through the standard governmental machinery: legislatures, courts, inspectors, and so forth. Similar institutions are not available on the international level. There we have countries interacting as sovereign entities, each trying to advance its own interests, within a much more amorphous institutional setting.

In this chapter we will cover a range of issues that bear on the inclinations and abilities of countries to enter into international agreements. We will consider the institutional and legal context of these agreements, the incentives facing countries that negotiate and implement the agreements, and some of the political facts of life that determine their success.[1]

The Variety of International Environmental Agreements

Over the last few years, controversy surrounding the Kyoto Protocol has dominated political discussion and the environmental news media. But there are actually hundreds of international agreements applicable to environmental assets. A selected list is presented in table 19.1. This list highlights pollution-related agreements; it does not include many of the strictly natural resource agreements; for example, treaties covering the management of regional fisheries.

International environmental problems run the full gamut of national ones: air, water, hazardous wastes, and so on. What transforms a domestic problem into an international one is the presence of international borders running through the affected environmental resource such as an airshed or watershed. Effective action then usually requires coordinated action among groups of countries. This may range from relatively simple bilateral agreements (e.g., agreement between the U.S. and Canada on water quality issues

Table 19.1   Selected International Environmental Agreements

Agreement	Date of Adoption	Date of Entry into Force	Number of Signatories (* includes EU)
Marine Pollution—General			
International Convention for the Prevention of Pollution of the Sea by Oil	1954	1958	69
International Convention on Civil Liability for Oil Pollution Damage	1969	1975	64
Convention on the Prevention of Marine Pollution by Dumping of Wastes and Other Matter	1972	1975	82
International Convention for the Prevention of Pollution from Ships	1973	1983	113
International Convention on Oil Pollution, Preparedness, Response and Cooperation	1990	1995	55
Marine Pollution—Regional			
Convention on the Protection of the Marine Environment of the Baltic Sea Area	1974	1980	10*
Convention for the Protection of the Mediterranean Sea against Pollution[a]	1976	1978	21*
Convention for the Protection of the Marine Environment and Coastal Area of the South-East Pacific	1981	1986	5

Agreement	Date of Adoption	Date of Entry into Force	Number of Signatories (* includes EU)
Marine Pollution—Regional (continued)			
Convention for the Protection and Development of the Marine Environment of the Wider Caribbean Region	1983	1986	23*
Convention for the Protection, Management, and Development of the Marine and Coastal Environment of the Eastern African Region	1985	1996	8*
Convention for the Protection of the Natural Resources and Environment of the South Pacific Region	1986	1990	15
Convention on the Protection of the Black Sea Against Pollution	1992	1994	6
Marine Fisheries			
Convention for the Establishment of an Inter-American Tropical Tuna Commission	1949	1950	11
Convention on Fishing and Conservation of the Living Resources of the High Seas	1958	1966	57
International Convention for the Conservation of Atlantic Tunas	1966	1969	35*
Convention for the Conservation of Salmon in the North Atlantic Ocean	1982	1983	8*
South Pacific Fisheries Treaty	1987	1988	12
Marine Mammal			
International Convention for the Regulation of Whaling	1946	1948	40
Inter-American Convention for the Protection and Conservation of Sea Turtles	1996	Not yet in force	6
Agreement on the International Dolphin Conservation Program	1998	1999	7
Other Marine			
Convention on the Continental Shelf	1958	1964	77
Convention on the High Seas	1958	1962	78
United Nations Convention on the Law of the Sea	1982	1994	171*
Freshwater Fisheries			
Convention for the Establishment of the Lake Victoria Fisheries Organization	1994	1996	3
International Rivers, Lakes, and Groundwaters			
Convention on the Protection and Use of Transboundary Watercourses and International Lakes	1992	1996	30*
Convention on Cooperation for Protection and Sustainable Use of the Danube	1994	1998	12

(continued)

Table 19.1 *(continued)*

Agreement	Date of Adoption	Date of Entry into Force	Number of Signatories (* includes EU)
Air and Atmospheric Pollution			
Convention on Long-Range Transboundary Air Pollution	1979	1983	49*
Protocol on Long-Term Financing of the Cooperative Program for Monitoring and Evaluation of the Long-Range Transmission of Air Pollutants in Europe	1984	1988	38*
Vienna Convention for Protection of the Ozone Layer	1985	1988	176*
United Nations Framework Convention on Climate Change	1992	1994	189*
Kyoto Protocol	1997	Feb. 2005	84*
Transportation of Hazardous Materials			
Basel Convention on the Control of Transboundary Movements of Hazardous Wastes and Their Disposal	1989	1992	142*
Regional Agreement on Transboundary Movement of Hazardous Wastes in the Central American Region	1992	1994	6
Nature and Wildlife			
Convention for the Protection of Birds Useful to Agriculture	1902	1905	10
African Convention on the Conservation of Nature and Natural Resources	1968	1969	43
Convention on International Trade in Endangered Species of Wild Fauna and Flora	1973	1975	155
Convention on the Conservation of European Wildlife and Natural Habitats	1979	1982	44*
Convention on Biological Diversity	1992	1993	178*
Antarctica			
The Antarctic Treaty	1959	1961	44
Protocol to the Antarctic Treaty on Environmental Protection	1991	1998	38
Plant Protection			
International Plant Protection Convention	1951	1952	111
International Convention for the Protection of New Varieties of Plants	1961	1968	46

[a] Later renamed the Convention for the Protection of the Marine Environment and the Coastal Region of the Mediterranean.

Source: Excerpted from Scott Barrett, *Environment and Statecraft, The Strategy of Environmental Treaty-Making* (Oxford University Press, 2003): 165–194. Used with permission.

in the Great Lakes), to multilateral (e.g., an agreement among countries through which the Rhine River runs to reduce pollution levels in the river), to global (e.g., the U.N. Convention on the Law of the Sea, which deals with, among other things, pollution of the world's oceans).

Institutions of International Action—Organizations

Effective international action requires an effective set of institutions. Institutions is a general word, applying to all the governance paraphernalia that nations use to arrange their relationships to one another. We will discuss two types of institutions: the organizations—public, private, national, and international—that foster action; and the international legal system, such as it is, that guides and shapes these actions.

National Organizations

The major actors in international environmental affairs are the countries themselves. For better or for worse, the world is divided into nations, and the main preoccupation of each on the world stage is to look out for its own interests. Every country has its own organizational structure. In the United States the Department of State is supposed to have the preeminent role in international affairs, although other agencies also have interests. Its present organizational arrangement includes a Bureau of Oceans and International Environmental and Scientific Affairs, the jurisdiction of which includes both natural resource and environmental issues. The agency would be expected to have a lead role in negotiating any international environmental agreements for the country, dealing with their counterparts in other countries.

The U.S. Environmental Protection Agency has an Office of International Affairs, one role of which is devoted to activity on international environmental treaties. This includes monitoring, researching, and reporting on these treaties. Other executive agencies also have an international outlook; the U.S. Department of Energy, for example, is involved in anything that substantially impacts energy production and consumption, such as Kyoto. The U.S. Department of Agriculture is involved in matters related to the nation's farmers and food processors. Each country has its own ratification process for entering into international treaties. The United States is somewhat unique in that the Constitution requires this to be done through a two-thirds vote of the U.S. Senate.[2] This makes the U.S. Congress one of the preeminent players in international environmental treaties involving the United States.

Other countries have their own modes of international action, involving some mix of political organizations and authorities, public agencies, and private groups.

International Organizations

Existing in the international space between national governments is a host of international groups: secretariats, working groups, conferences of parties, scientific groups, regional associations, and so on. These comprise a main part of the institutional structure for negotiating and implementing international agreements.

The United Nations and Its Environment Program. The United Nations is a key player in any international action. The U.N. Environment Program (UNEP) was established in 1972 at the U.N. Conference on the Human Environment, known as the Stockholm Conference. It is based in Nairobi, Kenya. Its primary activities involve ". . . the dissemination of information, the cultivation of understanding, and collaboration with the environmental programs of other agencies";[3] in short, a "catalytic" role that highlights environmental priorities and encourages international cooperation. It pursues an effort in monitoring and reporting in order to highlight growing environmental problems around the world. One of its efforts has been to sponsor the Intergovernmental Panel on Climate Change (IPCC, discussed in the last chapter), the preeminent international scientific agency working on global warming. UNEP was a principal force behind the U.N. Conference on Environment and Development in Rio de Janeiro in 1992. It has sponsored a number of international conferences, groups of policy makers brought together to study problems and suggest appropriate courses of action; for example, the U.N. Commission on Sustainable Development, which came out of the Rio conference.

Other International Organizations. Besides the U.N. there are many other international organizations that play a role in international agreements. There are a number of regional groupings, such as the Association of Southeast Asian Nations (ASEAN) and the European Union (EU), whose agendas include environmental matters. There are groupings of countries based on economic status, such as the G7/G8[4] and the G77.[5] The Organization for Economic Cooperation and Development (OECD) in Paris is an organization of developed economies that carries out a strong consultative role in, among other things, environmental matters. Its spin-off group, the International Energy Agency, draws together representatives of 26 countries and focuses particularly on energy issues. The World Conservation Union brings together a group of public and private groups to focus on natural resource conservation issues with international significance. There exists a number of groups, formed under the auspices of the U.N. and others, whose work includes sponsoring and/or communicating the work of environmental scientists on a host of issues. The economic research of the International Bank for Reconstruction and Development (known as the World Bank) should also be mentioned.

Nongovernmental Organizations (NGOs). Hundreds of private groups operate in the international environmental arena. They are popularly called

nongovernmental organizations (NGOs). International NGOs try to project and represent their interests in the settings where international negotiations and programs take place. But their activities go well beyond this. There are many who pursue a research/information agenda with the intent of shining the spotlight on important environmental problems around the world; examples are the World Resources Institute and the International Institute for Environment and Development. Others are very active in actually helping governments, particularly those of the developing world, plan and implement programs; examples are the World Wildlife Fund and Environmental Defense. Others are primarily for the purpose of encouraging research on international environmental issues; these include the World Conservation Union and the International Council of Scientific Unions.

Implementing Bodies

International agreements, if they are to have any effect, must have people or groups established or designated to oversee implementation. In many cases this may be a free-standing commission under the overall governance of the participating countries. The Danube Commission, for example, is an organization established to implement the various agreements among the countries that are riparian to that great river. The International Joint Commission was established to manage the various agreements between the United States and Canada on resource and environmental issues along their long border.

Implementation groups may be located within other organizations. The Convention for the Protection of the Mediterranean Sea Against Pollution is managed by a group within the U.N. Environment Program, as are many others.

International Legal Institutions

It is not quite right to say that there are no legal institutions at the international level. There are, but they are quite different from national legal systems. International law governing environmental effects flowing among countries, and agreements that may be entered into by these countries, are actually a set of customs and procedures that are looked upon as obligations. Normally we think of international obligations as arising in two ways: (1) through the informal force of international customs to which countries adhere even in the absence of explicit agreements to do so, and (2) through formal treaties and other agreements that are meant to mandate specific actions on the part of participating countries.

Customary Law

One of the main concepts that orders the interrelationships among sovereign nations is **customary law**. This may sound like an oxymoron; *custom* means habitual behavior, while a *law* is a rule that compels behavior. In fact, customary law combines these elements; it refers to precedents from past experience that countries tacitly agree to regard as obligatory. "Obligatory" in this case is weaker than the obligation of citizens to obey the laws of their country; it is more like correct behavior that countries come to expect of one another even though there is no direct way of enforcing it.

An example of customary law is territorial limits in offshore waters. For a long time a country's sovereignty was regarded as extending out only three miles from its shores. This was customary law in the sense that it was never formally set out in a treaty, but was accepted by most countries as a binding commitment. Recently this custom changed; now the accepted limit is 12 miles with a 200-mile exclusive economic zone (EEZ). This is now codified more formally in the Law of the Sea treaty.

The role of customary law has been well described in the following terms:

> Custom identifies the players, delineates their territories, and invests players with rights to act. . . . However, custom also imposes responsibilities. It lets states decide for themselves whether they want to participate in international treaties, but it requires that states make sincere efforts to cooperate. It allows states to act as they please, but it also requires that states be good neighbors and "take adequate steps to control and regulate sources of serious global environmental pollution or transboundary harm within their territory or subject to their jurisdiction."[6]

Formal Agreements

A formal international agreement is an explicit statement of joint action that is meant to commit the participating countries to specified actions. These normally are written documents agreed to by participants, and to which they can refer (or argue over) to determine the nature and extent of their commitments.

International agreements come in several forms:

1. A **treaty** is a fully developed agreement specifying problems, actions to be undertaken by signatories, steps to be taken under implementation and enforcement, and so on.

2. A **convention** is an agreement in which countries define a problem and jointly commit to addressing it, but without specifying exactly the concrete steps that will be undertaken to meet its objectives.

3. A **protocol** is an agreement that attempts to fill in some of the details of a convention: what specific actions the signatories will undertake, what institutions will be established to implement the agreement, and so on.

To this list we might add the idea of unions. A union is a group of countries that agrees to form collective institutions and yield some degree of sovereignty to those institutions; for example, to create regulations that would be binding in each country of the union. The most important contemporary example of this is the European Union, which we will discuss later.

Of course, there are no police on the international level. There does exist an international court (the International Court of Justice, known as the World Court, based in the Hague[7]). The court lacks the power of a national court; it can hear only those cases that countries voluntarily agree to have taken up, and of course has no direct way to enforce any of its decisions. Perhaps its only means of influence is the international stigma that may attach to countries who lose cases before the court.

Political Factors in International Agreements

Thirteen global environmental treaties have been negotiated over the last three decades; the United States is a party to seven of them. Of the others, the one currently receiving the most publicity is the Kyoto Protocol, which the U.S. Congress has specifically declined to ratify.[8] One important reason that the United States has not been at the forefront of many of these efforts relates to the dispersed style of decision making that characterizes Washington politics.

Negotiating global treaties brings together almost 200 countries that are extremely diverse in their economic, demographic, cultural, and political characteristics. It is very hard in these circumstances to gain wide agreement on details; it is much easier to gain acceptance of somewhat vague principles and objectives, and leave the details to later, especially details about how the agreements are to be implemented and enforced. The Kyoto Protocol, for example, establishes targets for greenhouse gas cutbacks, but says virtually nothing about how these cutbacks might be enforced. Thus, it is not surprising that the agreement has had little impact on actual emissions so far, and is not expected to have much influence in the future.

In many countries, vaguely worded international agreements are somewhat easy to ratify because of the way that technical environmental decisions are centralized. Not so in the United States. The "devil is in the details," and unless the details of implementation are reasonably clear and acceptable, it is easy for coalitions of affected groups to forestall ratification. In addition, treaties, once ratified, become law, and in the litigious atmosphere of U.S. environmental policy, the regulated community could expect court challenges aimed at implementing treaty provisions. This is another reason why global environmental agreements are difficult to get ratified in the U.S. Congress.[9]

Another political fact of life affecting international environmental agreements is the divide that exists between developed and developing countries. The former are trying to maintain economic prosperity; the latter are trying to spur economic growth and catch up. Developing countries fear that the richer countries will use environmental treaties and regulations to put them at an economic disadvantage. According to this thinking, the rich countries have the wealth to absorb environmental costs; the poorer countries do not. One of the reasons most developing countries acceded to the Montreal Protocol was that specific steps were included to reduce their implementation costs. On the other hand, one reason why developing countries were not included in the Kyoto Protocol was their fear that it would severely hamper their economic growth. In addition, countries of the developing world are very sensitive to being "used" in the efforts of the developed countries to arrange matters to their advantage (see, for example, exhibit 19.1).

Exhibit 19.1
The Politics of the Basel Convention

In the 1980s there were several prominent cases where hazardous wastes originating in countries of the developed world were illegally and surreptitiously shipped to developing countries, in particular African countries, for disposal. This created a huge public outcry around the world because it looked like the former colonial powers were trying to take advantage of the weak political and economic situations of some of the developing countries. Many of them, in conjunction with international NGOs such as Greenpeace, worked through the UNEP to produce the Basel Convention on the Control of Transboundary Movements of Hazardous Wastes and their Disposal, approved in 1989 by 161 countries. As of 2006, it has been ratified by all but three of these original signatory countries.[a]

The original negotiations were contentious. Some countries, chiefly African nations, and NGOs wanted a complete ban on international hazardous waste shipments. Their position was (and is) that this was the only effective way to make sure that hazardous wastes of the developed world didn't somehow end up being dumped in developing countries. The other side, primarily composed of countries in the developed world, wanted to install a regulatory system based on notification and consent; shipments would be allowed if there was adequate notification given to international authorities and if the recipient countries gave legitimate consent. Their concern was to install a system that would not disrupt the substantial world trade in "leftovers," such as scrap steel and used ships, destined for sorting and recycling. The developing world was actually split on the issue; many wanted the ban, but some were in favor of notification and consent.

When the Basel Convention was finally approved, it contained the notification and consent provision. This was not the end of the controversy, however. Political struggle has continued, largely fueled by the efforts of the growing group of countries that want a ban. Advocates say this is still the best way to protect against abuses such as mislabeled waste and sham recycling schemes. Opponents of the ban still emphasize the potentially negative impacts of a ban on some recycling industries. Advocates of the ban say it will apply only to material contaminated with toxic substances, not to material that is free of such material.

The signing of conventions is usually followed by periodic meetings of the participants in order to develop protocols that address the details of the agreement. These are normally called Conferences of the Parties (COPs). Advocates of the ban introduced in COP-3 (1995) an amendment to the Basel Convention that would incorporate a ban on hazardous waste shipments (with numerous exceptions). It will become effective when ratified by two-thirds of the 62 countries who were at the meeting. As of 2006 it had been ratified by 61 countries. Only three of these are African countries; the largest collection is from western Europe. So the politics of the ban are changing. Even if the ban is finally approved, major questions linger. The Convention has been effective in stopping the egregious cases of hazardous waste shipments from developed to developing countries, but it must still deal with issues of legitimate trade in used materials (for example, used mobile phones—in 2000 about 400 million new mobile phones were manufactured, with an average expected useful life of between 1 and 2 years).

[a] Afghanistan, Haiti, and the United States.

Source: Based in part on Jonathan Krueger, "The Basel Convention and Transboundary Movements of Hazardous Waste," The Royal Institute of International Affairs, 1999 (see www.ciaonet.org; ciao stands for Columbia International Affairs Online).

Incentive Aspects of International Agreements

Developing and implementing an international environmental agreement (IEA) requires coordinated action by sovereign states. While there may be positive and negative rewards (carrots and sticks) associated with joining an IEA, there is no compulsion in the same sense as there normally is with a domestic law or regulation. So participation in an IEA is largely a voluntary act; states have to be convinced that acceding to an agreement will be in their individual best interests. This means that, however beneficial an IEA might be for the world as a whole, each country's decision to participate will be based on its individual motives and incentives. We will discuss these incentives in two types of environmental situations:

1. In some cases, the activities of one country affect the environment of other countries more than it impacts its own environment. This is the classic case of environmental pollution that is transmitted downstream or downwind from the polluter to those who suffer the damage. What makes it an international problem is the presence of a national border (or borders) between emitters and those experiencing the damage. Thus we will call these **cross-border effects**.

2. In other cases, emissions from each country contribute equally to a global condition that impacts all countries, including those from where the pollu-

tion originated. This situation applies to the global problems of deterioration of the ozone layer and the global greenhouse effect. Certain regional problems also have this character, for example the pollution of the Mediterranean Sea by countries that border it. We will call these **generalized effects**.

Cross-Border Effects

The countries of Europe have modern economies with substantial industrial, energy, and transportation sectors. This implies airborne emissions of both conventional and hazardous pollutants which, although decreasing in recent years in the aggregate, still remain considerable. The prevailing winds in Europe are from the west and southwest. These winds transport emissions from upwind countries, such as the United Kingdom, across international borders where they impact downwind countries, such as the Scandinavian countries. The result is a fairly conventional physical problem of air pollution, severely complicated by the fact that to manage it effectively requires some sort of international agreement.

While this case involves several countries, an environmental problem doesn't have to be big to be an international problem. An early case that led to the development of international law and custom on environmental issues involved a single smelter in Trail, Canada (province of British Columbia), the emissions from which were damaging crops across the border in the United States. The international tribunal convened to hear the case ruled in favor of the farmers, and stated that ". . . no state has the right to use or permit the use of its territory in such a manner as to cause injury by fumes in or to the territory of another."[10] This statement was embodied in the Declaration of the 1972 United Nations Conference on the Human Environment (the first "earth summit"), which covered all types of transboundary pollution.

Most international agreements seek to incorporate what is called the **polluter-pays principle**, which simply means that polluters themselves should be responsible for bearing the costs of rectifying cross-border pollution effects. But in the international arena there is no way of forcing the responsible countries to honor this obligation. Because international agreements are voluntary, it may be assumed that individual countries will never sign an agreement that is contrary to their self-interests. In other words, each potential signatory must regard the agreement as leaving them at least as well off as they would be without it. The implication of this is that agreements must frequently shift partially to a **victim-pays principle**. In this case the country or countries where the damage is experienced will have to compensate the polluting country to some extent so that the latter will have an incentive to join the agreement and take the necessary steps to reduce emissions.

When more than one country is responsible for the pollution, an additional factor comes into play, that of potential **free-riding** behavior among the polluters. Consider a case where the emissions from several countries are causing harm in another country. Emissions need to be reduced, but a certain percentage reduction in total emissions does not necessarily imply that each country has to cut back by that percentage. Each country naturally will want to limit its own emission reduction in the hope that more of the pollution-reduction burden will fall on the other polluting countries. Of course, if each of the polluting countries tries to free ride, the total amount of pollution reduction is likely to be relatively small, unless some means can be found to overcome this incentive.

Generalized Effects

The incentive to free ride is also likely to be strong in cases where pollution has generalized impacts over every country (sometimes called **reciprocal impacts**). In such cases, each country's emissions contribute in like fashion to the overall impact. This does not imply that all countries will experience the same level of impacts, only that the impacts each country does experience are a function of the overall level of global emissions.

Suppose country "A" is trying to decide whether to invest $10 billion in reducing CO_2 emissions. These emissions contribute to global temperature increases. Suppose that the proposed action is part of a multilateral effort by countries all around the world to reduce global emissions by getting each country to reduce its emissions. There are three interesting situations that might occur. The following tabulation shows the benefits and costs to country A in each of these cases:

Situation	Costs	Benefits	Net Benefits
1. All countries agree to reduce emissions.	10	20	10
2. No agreement is reached.	0	-5	-5
3. All other countries agree to reduce emissions, but country A does not.	0	19	19

If all countries follow the agreement, country A devotes $10 billion to control costs and then experiences, for example, $20 billion in benefits. The net benefit to country A in this case is $10 billion.

If there is no agreement, however, country A has no control costs. But it now experiences negative benefits, in the form of environmental costs, of $5 billion. Its net benefit in this case is -$5 billion. It would seem rational, therefore, for country A to be part of the global agreement.

But there is a third possible situation. Country A may try to take advantage of an agreement entered into by all the other countries. It could do so by staying out of the agreement and experiencing zero control costs. Its benefits would then appear to be $19 billion (a billion less than if it were to join the agreement because it won't be cutting back its own emissions), so its net benefit would be $19 billion. It can gain with an agreement, but it could gain even more by staying out of the agreement. In this case it is free riding on the control efforts of the others.

Obviously, if one country perceives that it could gain by trying to free ride, other countries will reach the same conclusion. But in that case there would be no agreement.

The control costs that a country experiences can be affected in three ways:

1. In the choices it makes about reducing its own emissions; for example, through strict command-and-control measures or through greater reliance on incentive-based policies. This factor is important whether or not a country is part of a large multilateral agreement.

2. Through the rules chosen in an international agreement as to how overall emission reductions will be distributed among countries.

3. By payments made by some countries to others as part of an international agreement to help offset costs in the recipient countries. These are transfer payments, sometimes called, in the jargon of economics, **side payments**.

Side payments can take many forms. In the Montreal Protocol, the advanced economies agreed to help the developing countries through **technology transfer**, a process whereby the recipient countries are aided financially and technically to adopt technologies produced in the developed countries, in this case for reducing CFC use.

Numerical examples such as that used in the last section are useful to depict the incentives facing individual countries that might be considering an international environmental agreement. But it is impossible to use them to predict the results of such agreements because international negotiations on environmental treaties are only one dimension of the full set of interactions among countries. How an individual country behaves in bargaining over, for example, a treaty reducing CO_2 emissions depends not only on the merits of that particular problem but on the whole gamut of international relationships in which it is involved. If it is involved simultaneously in negotiations on other matters, it may be more concerned with the total outcome and be willing to compromise in some areas in return for concessions in others. Thus, this concern with the net outcome of all these negotiations could dictate a position on any one issue quite different from what one would expect solely on the basis of the merits of that particular case. John Krutilla's study of the agreement between the United States and Canada over use of the Columbia River, for example, indicates that the distribution of costs in the treaty was primarily related to the desire of the United States to stimulate economic development in Canada.[11] In addition, when a country is involved in many negotiations, it may be concerned particularly with shoring up its reputation as a hard bargainer, which may lead it to behave in certain cases in ways that look to be inconsistent with its self-interest. The outcomes of treaty negotiations depend on context and the **strategic possibilities** available at that time, which is another reason we use the simple examples of the previous section for depicting the underlying economic logic of international agreements and not for actually predicting events.

Summary

Increasing levels of economic growth and globalization have produced significant global and regional environmental problems. This ongoing trend means there is an increasing need for joint action by the countries of the world. Achieving effective international action is much more difficult than getting effective national action because international agreements, treaties, conventions, and protocols do not enjoy the same level of implementation and enforcement institutions as are available on the national level.

Most of the international environmental agreements negotiated in recent years have been spearheaded by the United Nations Environment Program. Besides the usual national negotiating organizations, such as the U.S. State Department and the EPA, the international arena has seen the appearance of a large NGO (nongovernmental organization) sector. These groups have taken an active role in international actions, not simply in arguing for more effective agreements, but also in pursuing action programs in individual countries.

International agreements must be crafted such that each country perceives its best interest as served by joining. This means that negotiators must understand the incentives facing each country for taking various types of environmental actions. A distinction can be made between classic cross-border effects where the actions of some states affect the environment of states downstream or downwind; and environmental impacts that have generalized effects. With global warming, for example, the emissions of greenhouse gases by individual countries contribute to a problem that affects everyone. In cases like this, any particular country's incentive to "free ride" at the expense of other countries must be forestalled if an international agreement is to produce meaningful results.

Key Terms

convention	protocol
cross-border effects	reciprocal impacts
customary law	side payments
free-riding	strategic possibilities
generalized effects	technology transfer
nongovernmental	treaty
organizations (NGOs)	victim-pays principle
polluter-pays principle	

Questions for Further Discussion

1. Burden sharing is a major problem in concluding international environmental agreements. How should burdens be shared in global warming agreements?

2. What is free riding in the context of international agreements, and what might be some ways of overcoming it?

3. What is the difference between the Montreal Protocol and the Kyoto Protocol in terms of factors that made the former quite effective and the latter very ineffective?

4. "Side payments" in the form of technology transfers are often given to developing countries to lower the costs to them of joining international environmental agreements. What other types of side payments might be effective in this regard?

5. "International environmental agreements are very much shaped by the fact that enforcement on the international level is difficult, if not impossible." Discuss.

Web Sites

The EPA has a Web site dealing with international issues:
www.epa.gov/ebtpages/internationalcooperation.html

as does the U.S. Department of State:
www.state.gov/g/oes/

For tracking down the language and status of international environmental agreements, see ENTRI (Environmental Treaties and Resource Indicator):
http://sedac.ciesin.columbia.edu/entri/

and a Web site put together by Ronald Mitchell called International Environmental Agreements:
http://iea.uoregon.edu/

The Environmental Liaison Center tries to coordinate among the hundreds of NGOs active at the international level:
www.elci.org

Most international treaties have their own Web site; for example, the Basel Convention:
www.basel.int

and the Convention on International Trade in Endangered Species of Wild Fauna and Flora:
www.cites.org

For a journal devoted to international environmental agreements, see:
International Environmental Agreements: Politics, Law and Economics
www.environmental-center.com/magazine/kluwer/inea

Additional Readings

Barrett, Scott, *Environment and Statecraft: The Strategy of Environmental Treaty-Making* (New York: Oxford University Press, 2003).

Brown Weiss, E., and H. K. Jacobson, eds., *Engaging Countries: Strengthening Compliance with International Environmental Accords* (Cambridge: MIT Press, 1998).

Elliott, Lorraine, *The Global Politics of the Environment*, 2nd ed. (Washington Square: New York University Press, 2004).

Garcia-Johnson, Ronie, *Exporting Environmentalism: U.S. Multinational Chemical Corporations in Brazil and Mexico* (Cambridge: MIT Press, 2000).

Hecht, Joy E., *National Environmental Accounting: Bridging the Gap between Ecology and Economy* (Washington, DC: Resources for the Future, January 2005).

Hough, Peter, *The Global Politics of Pesticides: Forging Consensus from Conflicting Interests* (London: Earthscan, November 1998).

Kirton, John J., and Michael J. Trebilcock, eds., *Hard Choices, Soft Law: Voluntary Standards in Global Trade, Environment and Social Governance* (Brookfield, VT: Ashgate, December 2004).

Malone, Linda A., and Scott Pasternack, *Defending the Environment: Civil Society Strategies to Enforce International Environmental Law* (Washington, DC: Island Press, 2006).

Steinberg, Richard H., *The Greening of Trade Law: International Trade Organizations and Environmental Issues* (Lanham, MD: Rowman and Littlefield, 2002).

Victor, David G., Kal Raustiala, and Eugene B. Skolnikoff, eds., *The Implementation and Effectiveness of International Environmental Commitments: Theory and Practice* (Cambridge: MIT Press, 1998).

Notes

[1] In writing this chapter I have drawn heavily from two works: Scott Barrett, *Environment and Statecraft: The Strategy of Environmental Treaty-Making* (New York: Oxford University Press, 2003); and Lorraine Elliott, *The Global Politics of the Environment*, 2nd ed. (New York University Press, 2004).

[2] There are other types of international agreements that do not require Senate ratification. For a discussion of these matters see: www.//rx.com/features/ustreaty.htm #b5-6.

[3] Lynton Keith Caldwell, *International Environmental Policy*, 3rd ed. (Durham and London: Duke University Press, 1996): 83.

[4] The G7/G8 is a group of developed countries who meet regularly to discuss common problems, especially economic problems. The G7 includes France, Britain, Germany, Japan, Italy, Canada, and the United States; the G8 includes the G7 plus Russia.

[5] The G77 is a group of developing countries formed primarily to promote their economic interests in international settings.

[6] P. W. Birnie and A. E. Boyle, *International Law and the Environment* (Oxford: Clarendon Press, 1992): 89.

[7] ww.icj-cij.org

[8] The other agreements to which the U.S. is not a party are: The Bonn Convention on Conservation of Migratory Species; the Convention on Biological Diversity; the Convention on the Law of the Sea; the Rotterdam Convention on Prior Informed Consent Procedure for Certain Hazardous Chemicals and Pesticides in International Trade; and the Stockholm Convention on Persistent Organic Pollutants.

[9] For a good discussion of these points see J. W. Anderson, "U.S. Has No Role in U.N. Treaty Process," *Resources* 148 (Washington, DC: Resources for the Future, Summer 2002): 12–16.

[10] Quoted in William A. Nitze, "Acid-Rain: A United States Perspective," in Daniel Barstow Magraw, ed., *International Law and Pollution* (Philadelphia: University of Pennsylvania Press, 1991): 346.

[11] John V. Krutilla, *The Columbia River Treaty: A Study of the Economics of International River Basin Development* (Baltimore, MD: Johns Hopkins Press, 1968).

20

Globalization and the Environment

F_{ew} economic stories have caught the public attention and imagination more in recent years than the phenomenon called **globalization**. Globalization appears to involve inexorable, worldwide forces that are producing fundamental changes in the way people live. Proponents point out the advantages of globalization and the positive impacts it can have on the welfare of people in diverse circumstances around the world. Critics stress the economic and social threats to which many people will be exposed as globalization rolls onward in apparently ever strengthening waves.

Our subject in this chapter will be the environmental implications of globalization. We will first look at the kinds of changes that globalization entails, then discuss a number of ways in which globalization and environmental policy issues appear to be closely interwoven.

What Is Globalization?

Globalization is primarily an economic phenomenon, but it has diverse economic and social consequences. In essence it refers to greater economic exchange among the peoples and countries of the world. **Economic integration** is a process by which local economies become more closely tied together into an expanding set of regional, national, and international economies. This type of process has been going on for a long time.

When the first European settlers established communities in seventeenth-century New England, the towns were not well integrated with one another. Transportation of goods and of people was difficult, so the communities were quite independent and tended to regulate their own economic activities. Of course, this changed fairly rapidly. Roads were built, better modes of transportation were developed, and the economies of the communities became much more intertwined. People traveled more easily and intercommunity trading of goods and services increased sharply. Today it is hard to tell where one community stops and the next begins.

Before the twentieth century, countries were in somewhat the same situation as those early American communities. International trade took place, but at modest levels. The natural resources on which nations drew to support their economic development came largely from within their own borders. The money that was used to finance roads and railroads came largely from the savings of their own citizens. This has all changed. The fuel you now put in your gas tank probably came from somewhere else in the world. The money you put into your retirement account is likely to be loaned out to somebody in, say, Thailand, who wants to start a new business (there, not here), or speculate on the Thai stock market. The person you call to reserve an airline ticket might be sitting at a desk in another country.

Much of the impetus for global integration comes from vast changes in the costs of transportation and communication. A hundred years ago it could be a chore traveling from one town to another. Today you can hop on a jet and in 24 hours go from Manhattan to some of the most remote spots on earth. Tens of thousands of ships, increasingly gigantic in size, transport resources and goods throughout the world. And thanks to digital systems, instant international communication is now commonplace, even among communities that were once very remote from one another.

Globalization as Fact and as Policy

We should distinguish between the facts of globalization and the policy steps we, and others around the world, should take on the issue. Globalization as fact is manifest. Increasing quantities of the world's production enter international commerce. Technological change continues to drive down the cost of international communication and transportation, thus continuing to drive down what economists call the **transactions** costs of international commerce.

People continue to be more mobile throughout the world, as tourists bent on international travel and as migrants moving to change their economic and social prospects. These movements of people will continue to propel the forces of globalization.

Globalization is also a policy issue. How do we evaluate its impacts, especially its impacts on the environment? And what specific steps should we take to encourage it, to discourage it, and to shape it, in the U.S. and elsewhere? Some important dimensions of the globalization issue include the following.

Trade Liberalization. This means reducing barriers to economic exchange among people in different countries. Chief among these are transportation costs, which continue to go down. But it also refers to reducing human-erected barriers, such as tariffs, import or export quotas, and various other types of restrictions that countries often use to try to insulate themselves, or protect themselves, from the international economy. The benefits of trade liberalization are expected to be the added income and economic security that accrues to people in the trading countries. But there can be costs in terms of economic dislocation and reduced economic security for some people.

Liberalization of International Financial Markets. This means reducing the barriers to moving money among countries, letting people in one country invest in other countries, either by trading financial assets in other countries or actually investing in production or distribution facilities there. The objective is to have a system where financial flows can be easily shifted toward the most productive opportunities regardless of what particular country they happen to be in. Theory and experience tell us that more fluid and flexible financial institutions are essential for economic development. But experience also shows that uncontrolled international financial flows can wreck havoc in certain situations.

Changes in Economic Institutions. Globalization is often thought to involve a general predisposition for shifting economic activity toward private sector and market-oriented institutions. This has been stressed especially in the developing world, where substantial fractions of the economies have been run by state-owned and/or operated firms.

Reducing Barriers to the International Movement of People. In addition to increasing flows of goods and services, globalization involves more movement of people among countries. One aspect of this is a substantial increase in international business travel and tourism, which brings people of different cultures together. More importantly, emigration and immigration shift people permanently. These movements are driven especially by income and wealth differences among countries, and they normally have not only economic consequences but also political and cultural ones. Few countries opt for complete freedom of movement in or out; the policy issue is determining what restrictions are appropriate.

Further Dimensions of Globalization

The benefits of globalization are the increased opportunities it provides for people to obtain greater wealth and economic security. However, these benefits are not equally distributed, as critics have stressed.

Significant Realignments in Political Power.   Many observers feel that globalization will have important local political impacts, especially shifting political power away from national governments and toward international bodies. Two types of institutions are singled out: multinational companies and international policy bodies. By opening up their economies to the full forces of international commerce, nations may give large international companies (the multinationals) greater power over domestic economic policy, at the expense of local authorities. This would not necessarily be bad if these multinational companies had the interests of the local citizenry at heart, but they normally do not.

Globalization may also shift political power toward large international agencies such as the World Bank, the International Monetary Fund (IMF), and the World Trade Organization (WTO). These agencies, critics assert, are dominated by the interests of the developed countries. They are also dominated, critics contend, by people whose major concern is spurring economic development, at the expense of environmental values.

Greater Inequalities in Income and Wealth.   A major point of contention on globalization is whether it is leading to greater levels of **economic inequality** among and within countries. Critics say it does; others say it doesn't. In fact, the distribution of income and wealth and its connection with trade and economic development has been much studied. In a recent well-documented study, several economists have concluded that, while there have been small changes in the worldwide distribution of wealth over the last fifty years, they are nowhere near the extreme changes that took place in the first half of the nineteenth century, when some countries were embracing the industrial revolution aggressively.[1] Furthermore, most of the worldwide change in inequality is related to growing differences between countries, not within them. Which indicates that some communities and countries may be made worse off.

Cultural and Economic Homogenization.   The term cultural homogenization means increased attachment to the "cultural products" of the developed world, especially American products. Likewise, economic homogenization usually refers to a situation in which people strive to achieve a material standard of living characteristic of the developed world as opposed to the local, subsistence-based economies of much of the developing world.[2]

On Sorting Out Cause and Effects

As the above comments suggest, while globalization is obviously a major force in the world, the extent and direction of its impacts are matters of great controversy. In sorting out the causes and effects of these events it is important to guard against several modes of thought. One is to attribute everything that happens to globalization. The problem with this is that there are many other profound changes taking place around the world: political, social, religious, and so on. These developments are important drivers of world events in their own right. For example, we have seen a profound demographic revolution in the last 50 years; for every world citizen at the beginning of this time there are now 2.5 people. Much of the turmoil and conflict around the world can be attributed to this population explosion. Some have argued that integration of world economies may have had the effect of actually ameliorating the impacts of this phenomenon.

In analyzing the impacts of globalization, we must also guard against drawing general conclusions based on anecdotal evidence. It is abundantly clear that globalization does not benefit everyone. But looking at the circumstances of individual components may not be a reliable way to draw conclusions about overall trends. For example, reading a story about a highly polluting company relocating to a developing country doesn't necessarily mean that low-income countries are becoming havens for polluting firms headquartered elsewhere. To find out whether this incident is part of a larger trend we have to look at all the data in a comprehensive way.

But it is important also to keep in mind the opposite tendency: looking only at averages without breaking these down to examine subgroups of populations. The movement of averages (e.g., rising average income levels) can sometimes mask the fact that important subgroups of a population are moving in the opposite direction. A drop in the average levels of urban air pollution, for example, doesn't necessarily mean that air pollution in each and every urban area has been reduced.

The Politics of Globalization

The growth of national economies and the expansion of international trade have been accompanied by deforestation, depletion of fisheries, increased air pollution, and other environmental impacts throughout the world. It is only natural for people to link these events in a system of cause and effect. Some people take it a step further; that if economic integration and international trade could be discouraged, it would have a salutary effect on environmental quality around the world. And so the battle has been joined, between those who regard liberalized trade as a way of generating economic stimulus for growing populations around the world, especially populations of poor people, and those who regard it as a snare and delusion, which will lead to social disruption and environmental diminishment.

The fields of battle are diverse. The press has highlighted the episodes of direct action (Seattle 1999, Washington, D.C. 2000) where anti-globalization groups have taken to the streets to agitate for their views. Primary targets have been the large international organizations whose activities figure prominently in the encouragement of trade liberalization: The World Bank, the International Monetary Fund (IMF), and the World Trade Organization (WTO).[3] Conflict has erupted even within these organizations, between supporters of the traditional ways of conducting business and those pushing for new methods and procedures that acknowledge some of the concerns of their critics. Sometimes these conflicts become media events in themselves, as happened recently when a former chief economist of the World Bank wrote a book that is highly critical of its procedures.[4]

Needless to say the business community is heavily involved in the issue of globalization, since the business sector is one of the primary drivers of trade and international investment. The proportion of world economic output that enters into international trade is steadily increasing. Local entrepreneurs are normally drawn to the potential offered by external markets. But they are like everybody else; they would prefer to have more of the benefits and less of the costs. So they argue for opening up export markets, but also for protection from competitive imports. One of their main arguments is that foreign production is often cheaper because it takes place in countries with weaker environmental regulations. Environmental issues thus get mixed into the political fray that takes place on trade liberalization.

In recent years hundreds of public interest groups and direct action groups have focused on globalization issues. Many have an anti-globalization agenda and stress the environmental costs of increasing international integration. Established groups such as the Sierra Club, Greenpeace, the World Wildlife Fund, and Friends of the Earth have studied issues related to globalization. New groups have formed specifically around the globalization phenomenon. The activities of these groups include everything from research to lobbying to direct action to working with foreign governments on environmental issues.

Environmental Impacts of Globalization

Globalization clearly will have diverse impacts. Economic impacts loom large: Will it enhance economic wealth and security around the world? Social impacts are important: Will it erode valuable aspects of national and local cultures? And for our purposes, will trade liberalization and the resulting integration of national economies exacerbate environmental problems? If so, which ones, and could steps be taken to lessen this impact? Conversely, are there any environmental problems that might be ameliorated by globalization?

The important connections between globalization and environmental quality are the following:

1. Increased trade can be expected to produce higher total output and incomes in the trading countries. Or can it? The economic notion behind trade is the theory of comparative advantage. Countries can specialize in the economic activities they are good at (in the relative, not absolute, sense). By so doing, simple economic theory indicates they can increase their livelihoods above the level they could attain if they were to remain outside the international trading system. For the most part, economic studies confirm the stimulating effect of external trade; countries that trade extensively have healthier economies than those that don't.

But do the higher levels of output stimulated by trade lead to greater environmental damage? While the theory of comparative advantage says there are mutual gains for countries that engage in trade, it doesn't deal directly with environmental impacts. In fact, it is easy to find cases where increased trade has led to very substantial environmental damages, some so severe that they may threaten the long-term economic health of the countries involved. Exhibit 20.1 discusses a particularly egregious case of this.

2. Different countries may be expected to set different environmental standards for a variety of reasons. Does this lead to an unfair trade advantage for firms in the countries with lower standards because their costs are lower? If so, will this produce a "race to the bottom" in which each coun-

---

Exhibit 20.1
The Plundering of Nauru

Nauru is a tiny (8-square-mile) speck of an island in the western Pacific, home historically to about 10,000 people, but since reduced by the depredation of colonialism and WW II to about 600 souls. In the early 1900s a valuable deposit of phosphate was discovered on the island. One might think that this would have been a great boon to the people of Nauru, whose livelihoods had been sorely constrained by the natural limits of the island. The extraction and export of phosphate should have been a source of rising incomes and improved welfare. It has not, however.

For many years extraction and export was controlled by colonial powers, chiefly Australia. Net incomes (revenues minus costs) went chiefly to these powers, not to the local people. More importantly, scant attention was given to the environmental consequences of the extraction operation.

The people of Nauru achieved independence in 1968, by which time twothirds of the phosphate was gone. Phosphate continued to be extracted and exported, now under local control, and several funds were set up to rehabilitate the land and provide for social services. But money distributed to the local population was not wisely spent. In effect the incomes from the resource extraction were squandered, so today Nauru is sinking back into impoverishment, this time with an environment that has been seriously degraded.

Nauru is clearly a case where an open economy and world trade did not lead to sustainable economic growth. Instead it led to very substantial environmental destruction. Thus the simple idea that more trade means higher incomes, which means better environmental quality, is flawed. At the very least it points to the absolute necessity of having strong regulatory and institutional structures to protect the environment when countries open themselves to the demands of the international market.

Source: A good article on Nauru is "Paradise Well and Truly Lost," *Economist* (December 22, 2001).

try tries to help its firms compete by lowering environmental standards? Will countries with lower standards attract greater investment by firms in high-polluting industries? If so, what implications does this have for environmental quality in these countries?

3. In some cases increased trade might lead to greater cross-border pollution. For example, the North American Free Trade Agreement between the United States, Mexico, and Canada could stimulate industrial growth along the Mexican-American border to the advantage of certain firms in the agreement. This could lead in some cases to increasing cross-border environmental impacts. To some extent this is a variant of point (1) above, except in this case pollution runs across the borders of the trading countries.

4. When the GDP of a country becomes more oriented to trade, it may become more vulnerable to trade sanctions. Trade sanctions for environmental reasons then become a real possibility, and questions arise about when these are appropriate and when they are not. Environmental groups may promote trade sanctions to pressure exporting countries into adopting more stringent environmental regulations. Economic groups in one country may encourage or support environment-related trade sanctions as a way of protecting themselves against the competition of imports.

Trade, Growth, and the Environment

Economic analysis has shown pretty conclusively that countries which are more open to trade generally grow faster than countries that are less open. Trade, in other words, is a stimulus to rising output and incomes (remember, on average, not necessarily for everybody). So does rising economic output in growing economies produce greater or lesser amounts of pollution? Nobody should be surprised that the answer to this is complicated.

If everything else were constant, of course, increased economic activity would imply more pollution. More inputs would be used, more outputs produced, and the quantity of leftovers would increase. While this may be true in the short run, it is not true in the long run because growth and rising incomes cause things to change.

One thing that changes with economic growth is the sectoral composition of total output. Newly modernizing economies will normally rely on basic manufacturing and resource-based industries, sectors that normally produce relatively high emissions per unit of output. But as they develop, most economies evolve toward more service-type sectors, and these normally produce substantially fewer residuals to go into the environment. So normal sectoral shifts associated with growth can reduce the environmental impacts of developing economies.

Another important factor is that environmental quality is what economists call a "normal" good. **Normal goods** are those that people want more of as their income and economic security increase. (Conversely, the demand for **inferior goods** decreases as incomes increase.) As incomes improve, people want a cleaner environment—cleaner water and cleaner air, lower levels of trash, and so on. And higher incomes give them the means to reduce the environmental impacts of their economies. Naturally this is not a panacea that happens overnight. Furthermore, improved environmental quality normally involves political action of some type, and countries differ a lot in terms of how easy it is to mount successful political efforts to improve the environment.

In fact, considerable effort has gone into studying the relationship between economic growth and environmental quality factors in countries around the world. Some typical results are shown in figure 20.1. These results reflect the comparative experiences of many countries around the world, correlating their income levels (in terms of income per capita) with observed levels of six important environmental conditions:

- contaminated drinking water
- inadequate domestic sewage systems
- particulate matter in the air
- sulfur dioxide in the air
- municipal solid waste
- carbon dioxide emissions

The data indicate that for clean drinking water and access to sewage systems, the impact of higher incomes is unambiguously positive: as incomes improve people get better performance on these factors. For particulate matter and sulfur dioxide the impacts are more complicated. Initially, higher incomes lead to more particulates and SO_2 exposure, probably because in the initial stages of development there is normally greater reliance on "smoke-stack" types of industries. As incomes continue to rise, however, these two factors show improvements, for both of the reasons discussed above: sectoral changes in the economy and greater demands for cleaner air.

In terms of municipal solid waste and CO_2 emissions, the relationship is unambiguously negative; higher incomes lead consistently to larger amounts of household trash (per capita) and larger CO_2 emissions (per capita).

Where do we stand, then, on the trade $\rightarrow$ income $\rightarrow$ environmental quality linkage? For some environmental pollutants increased trade, if it leads to improved incomes, will have positive environmental effects; some will be felt immediately and others will be realized more gradually. But there are a few pollutants for which this is not true: economic growth has been historically associated with continued increases in CO_2, for example, meaning that trade-related growth will make the problem of global warming substantially worse than it is.

The complexity of the trade/income/environmental quality relationship is well illustrated by the issue of global warming. As the developing countries work to modernize their economies, increase trade, raise average incomes, and improve their general standard of living, they will emit more CO_2. These increased emissions will exacerbate the global warming problem at the same time developed countries are being asked to reduce CO_2 emissions to address the problem. But are the developed countries, with their relative affluence and high standard of living, in any position to ask developing countries to forego economic growth and relegate their citizenry to a lower standard of living? This is ethically dubious, and probably not even practical given the normal human propensity for self-improvement.

The saving grace, perhaps, is to note that the relationship of income to CO_2 emissions is an historical one; it is something that has characterized eco-

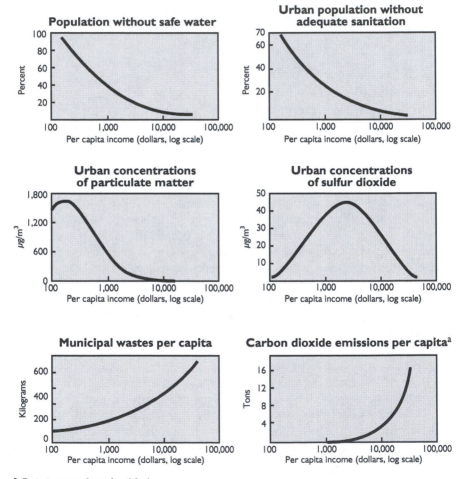

^a Emissions are from fossil fuels.

Source: World Bank, World Development Report 1992, *Development and Environment* (New York: Oxford University Press for the World Bank, 1992): 11.

**Figure 20.1   Relationship Between Income Per Capita and Six
                 Environmental Pollutants Among Countries of the World**

nomic development to date because of our reliance on fossil fuels. But in the future we may be able to break the link between growth and CO_2 output by shifting to low-carbon fuels, more fuel-efficient machines, and non-fossil-based energy sources.

Globalization and a "Race to the Bottom"

Opponents of globalization sometimes paint a bleak picture about the impact it might have on environmental regulations throughout the world. The supposed scenario goes something like this: trade and finance liberalization increases international commerce and the flow of investment among countries. More people around the world, in both developed and developing countries, become dependent on international markets for their livelihoods and prosperity. In an increasingly competitive world economy, countries and regions look for ways of boosting the competitiveness of their local businesses. This means trying to find ways of lowering the costs of production and distribution. Governments are pressured to relax environmental regulations so that firms can avoid costly pollution-control measures. Countries that have had higher environmental standards have to lower them to keep their businesses from fleeing to countries with the lower standards. Pollution levels surge as countries engage in competitive lowering of their environmental standards in order to give their own firms an advantage in international markets.

The phrase sometimes used to describe this phenomenon is **race to the bottom**, a progressive weakening of environmental standards brought on by the need to be competitive in an increasingly integrated world economy.[5]

Is this concern well founded? Are we actually seeing a general race to the bottom in environmental regulations as a result of globalization? There has been a lot of close analysis of this question in the last decade or so, and the clear answer is: no. Around the world we see general improvements in environmental quality and increasingly stringent environmental regulations. There has been many an anecdote that globalization critics can point to in apparent support of their argument. But anecdotes do not make trends, and the trends are clearly in the other direction. More integrated economies grow faster, and the higher incomes and wealth this produces leads societies to pursue more stringent standards, not weaker ones.

This can be seen explicitly in figure 20.2. It shows the correlation across countries between their income levels and the stringency of their air pollution control regulations. That correlation is clearly positive—higher incomes are associated with higher standards, not lower ones. Many other studies have found corroborating evidence: the race-to-the-bottom hypothesis, as a generalized phenomenon, is false. If the diagnosis is wrong, so is the implied prescription: that countries should either restrict trade, or all agree to adopt the same set of environmental standards governing their industries.

But let us not be overly glib about this relationship. Environmental pollution from industrial firms are externalities, impacts that take place away from the perpetrators, downstream or downwind. Getting polluters to do some-

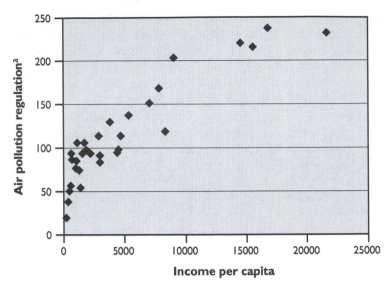

[a] Index of environmental performance in combatting air pollution using responses to a question-naire sent to government, business, and nongovernmental organizations.

Source: Data from Dasgupta, S., A. Mody, S. Roy, and D. Wheeler, "Environmental Regulation and Development: A Cross Country Empirical Analysis," World Bank Policy Research Department Working Paper No. 1448 (March 1995). Used with permission.

Figure 20.2   Relationship Between Income Levels and the Stringency of Environmental Regulations, 31 Countries, 1990

thing about these effects doesn't just happen automatically as a country's economy grows. It requires also the development of legal structures and the growth of politically active groups who will raise the necessary questions and work for their resolution. These laws and groups are more likely to material-ize in situations where the economic welfare of people is improving.

The Pollution-Haven Issue

Closely allied to the race-to-the-bottom idea is the pollution-haven hypothesis. Integration of international capital markets implies, among other things, that firms in one country can more easily invest in operations, either their own or those of other firms, in other countries. With capital being more mobile as a result, many have expressed fears that heavily polluting firms in countries of the developed world, rather than undertaking the costs of lower-ing their emissions, would pick up and relocate to countries of the developing world, where effective environmental standards are less restrictive. Countries with lower standards would thus tend to attract firms with relatively large emissions; they would become, in other words, **pollution havens**.

Is there any credence in the pollution-haven hypothesis? Is there evidence that this process is underway? There is no question that there is some amount of truth in the pollution-haven hypothesis. An example is the ship-breaking industry. Every year hundreds of very large, old, oceangoing tankers and freighters are dismantled; the separated parts and materials are recycled. This activity is currently concentrated in coastal enclaves located in several developing countries, India and Bangladesh in particular. One of the attractions of these locations is that there are no effective environmental regulations governing the activity; to this extent it is a pollution-haven story. Beyond this, however, it is largely a story of low labor costs; the work is extremely labor intensive and supplies of low-wage labor are abundant in these locations. This highlights the main problem with trying to determine the validity of the pollution-haven thesis; while weaker environmental regulations are clearly a plus if you are trying to decide where to locate a dirty industrial enterprise, other factors, especially labor and transportation costs, are also primary criteria.

The behavior of multinational firms in developing countries is also an issue. Suppose a large manufacturing firm in a developed country is moving to a developing country. Suppose further that environmental standards in the two countries differ. They are quite strict in the firm's home country and much less so in the adopted country, either because the standards themselves are weaker or because they are badly enforced or both. Which standards should the firm follow in its new home? There are two extreme points of view on this. One is that the company should seek to adopt the local practices with respect to acceptable emission controls and emissions. This means recognition of local laws, as well as "normal" behavior vis-à-vis the local authorities who enforce these laws. The other is that the firm should continue to follow the stricter pollution-control practices of its original country, with the same technology and practices that would have governed its operations had it not moved. But there is also intermediate ground. A company may, for example, move toward local standards, but operate with a progressive attitude; that is, it could obey local rules even though they may not be energetically enforced, or showcase new pollution-control methods that local firms might be persuaded to adopt, and so on.

Environmental Regulations as Trade Restrictions

Globalization critics also fear that governmental efforts to liberalize trade will make it more difficult for individual countries to enact certain types of environmental regulations. In this view, environmental regulations affecting imports may be judged illegal because they tend to act as restraints on trade.

The basic framework agreement among countries governing the rules of trade is contained in the agreement establishing the World Trade Organization (WTO). Article XX of the WTO agreement is the one most applicable to environmental matters. It says that trade limitations are not allowed, except in those cases where they are:

(b) necessary to protect human, animal or plant life or health; . . . [or] (g) relating to the conservation of exhaustible natural resources if such measures are made effective in conjunction with restrictions on domestic production or consumption . . .

Though relatively clear, the wording of Article XX does not unambiguously cover every circumstance. Suppose producers in another country employ methods that U.S. environmental groups believe to be environmentally harmful. If the environment being harmed is within, or contiguous to, the territory of the United States so that it harms U.S. citizens directly, trade restrictions would be okay under the WTO. But suppose the environment in question is actually within the producing country, or perhaps in a third country, rather than in the United States. Then the trade restriction would probably be judged illegal (at least in terms of the WTO agreement) despite the fact that U.S. environmentalists felt very strongly about it.

Thus, there are many environmental groups and interests that feel WTO efforts to relax trade restrictions will undermine a country's individual ability to protect important environmental assets by acting against those who would damage these assets. A well-known controversy along these lines has been the U.S. import ban on tuna coming from Mexico, on grounds of protecting dolphins in the eastern Pacific tuna fishery (see exhibit 20.2). The Marine Mammal Protection Act (MMPA) became law in the United States in 1972. One of its major objectives is to minimize the killing of marine mammals during commercial fishing operations. In the eastern Pacific Ocean, certain species of dolphins accompany schools of commercially valuable tuna, and if the tuna are caught using certain traditional methods, large numbers of dolphins will also be caught and killed. The MMPA governs U.S. tuna-fishing practices to prevent, or reduce, this incidental dolphin kill. It also restricts imports of yellowfin tuna from other countries that use standard purse-seine techniques, unless their dolphin kills are within 1.25 times the U.S. average for the same.

The United States imposed a ban on tuna imports from Mexico in 1990, citing these MMPA provisions. The GATT dispute resolution panel ruled that this was a violation of the rules governing trade restrictions. Among other things, the panel said, the ban violated Article XX because that article is not supposed to be applied extrajurisdictionally; in other words, it could not be applied to resources outside the territorial jurisdiction of the country invoking the import ban. A few years later the issue was again considered by a GATT panel. And it again ruled that the U.S. ban on tuna from Mexico violated the terms of GATT, although their reasoning was slightly different. Nevertheless, Congress enacted the International Dolphin Conservation Act of 1992, prohibiting the importation of any tuna that was not "dolphin safe," i.e., caught by methods that did not result in dolphin deaths.

Since then there has been an ongoing struggle between interests who would like to see these import restrictions relaxed and those who want them continued. The former maintain that the restrictions are not only counter to the WTO agreement, but ineffectual; furthermore, they say, there are better

Exhibit 20.2
Conflicts Over Environmental Regulations

"Conflict is prevalent between advocates of economic and trade priorities and those defending environmental and consumer protection, public health, and preservation of biological species. In principle, these conflicts need not be irreconcilable; in practice, they often are. Foresight into some of the political problems that implementation of the Rio agreements[a] may encounter may be obtained from experience with trade and environment-related treaties or agreements. An illustrative case in point appeared in the *New York Times* of Monday, December 14, 1990. A full-page appeal entitled 'SABOTAGE! of American's Health, Food Safety, and Environmental Laws—George Bush and the Secret Side of Free Trade,' was endorsed by twenty-one nongovernmental civic action organizations including the Sierra Club, Greenpeace, the Humane Society of the United States, and the National Consumer League. The purpose was to arouse citizen opposition to provisions of the North American Free Trade Agreement (NAFTA) and the 'Uruguay Round' of the General Agreement on Tariffs and Trade (GATT) that might prevent the United States from barring the importation of environmentally harmful products. This opposition was fueled by the GATT ruling in the tuna-dolphin controversy, in which enforcement of the U.S. Marine Mammal Protection Act was held to be in violation of GATT agreements and discriminatory against Mexican fishermen, whose nets trapped many dolphin.

"Representatives of developing countries have complained since the Stockholm Conference that developed countries used environmental restrictions to prevent importation of their products in order to protect home industries from competition. At Stockholm the developing countries claimed compensation for discrimination based on alleged environmental protection. But countries seeking global trade may also be motivated to raise their environmental standards, especially in relation to exports.

"Perhaps the objectives and priorities of free trade can be reconciled with the goals and values implicit in UNCED. Compromise rather than compensation or reconciliation seems more likely, because two different sets of assumptions and two dissimilar paradigms are in confrontation. The Declaration of Rio represents a broad, albeit sometimes indeterminate, public commitment. The trade agreements represent a much smaller, but more explicit set of objectives advanced by interests that have had an 'inside track' in the course of national policy making."

[a] The Rio Agreements are those negotiated at the U.N. Conference on Environment and Development, Rio de Janeiro, 1992.

Source: Excerpted from Lynton Keith Caldwell, *International Environmental Policy*, 3rd ed. (Durham and London: Duke University Press, 1996): 114. Used with permission.

ways of reducing dolphin deaths, such as working with the fishing fleets of other nations to help them develop better procedures for reducing dolphin deaths. Supporters of the trade restrictions believe they are still an effective way of enhancing overall protection for dolphins. Another issue is that dolphin-safe fishing methods may have negative impacts on other species of fish as well as sea turtles. The issue, in fact, has split the environmental community, with some groups in favor of lifting the ban and others opposed.

The Case of NAFTA

The WTO agreement is worldwide in scope, meant to apply to trade-related issues for all the countries of the world. There also have been many bilateral or regional trade agreements among smaller groups of countries, and these have had, and will continue to have, important environmental implications. From the standpoint of the United States and its neighbors, one of the most important is NAFTA. **NAFTA** stands for the **North American Free Trade Agreement**, an agreement negotiated among the United States, Canada, and Mexico primarily to reduce tariffs and other barriers to trade among the three countries. NAFTA is meant to stimulate the economies of these three countries by expanding markets for the goods and services they produce, or might produce in the future. Environmental concerns played an important role in the NAFTA negotiations. There were, and still are, substantial differences of opinion about how NAFTA will impact environmental quality in the participating countries. Indeed, differences of opinion on this matter split the environmental community. Sierra Club, Greenpeace, and others were against it; Audubon, World Wildlife Fund, the Environmental Defense Fund, and others were in favor of it.

The specific concerns related to NAFTA are:

1. Increased pollution in the countries, especially Mexico, because of increased economic activity accompanied by pollution-control regulations that are too lax, or are not sufficiently enforced.

2. Increased cross-border pollution as a result of the economic stimulus NAFTA apparently gives to the Maquiladora program. The Maquiladora program allows firms in Mexico to import production supplies and equipment duty free if the resulting output is exported. Although there are few limits on where these firms may locate in Mexico, in practice they have concentrated near the Mexico/U.S. border.

3. Pressure for reduced environmental standards, particularly in the United States and Canada, so firms in those countries can better compete in a liberalized trade environment. This is the familiar "race-to-the-bottom" argument.

It is not easy to find unambiguous and definitive information on the environmental effects of NAFTA. The political combat surrounding NAFTA is ongoing, so information tends to be presented to support particular political positions rather than to provide objective analysis of the situation. It is also true that environmental issues, though important, are not the main points of contention in the NAFTA conflict; the main issue is the effect on wages and employment on both sides of the U.S./Mexico border.

The common perspective at the time of the NAFTA negotiations, especially among U.S. environmental interests, was that environmental regulations in Mexico were substantially weaker than in the other two countries. While laws might be on the books, there was a serious problem with enforcement. This would have several effects, according to NAFTA critics. Foremost, it meant that increased economic activity in Mexico would have large environmental impacts. Not only would there be increased pressure on Mexican wildlife, forests, and energy resources, but the added air and water pollution would be significant. This is a familiar argument; for any given regulatory regime, more economic activity implies more pollution. But the way to attack this is by tightening regulations, not by suppressing economic activity. Having said this, one should not underestimate the difficulty of doing this. An enormous amount of political energy and activity will be needed to introduce effective environmental regulations into a situation where polluters have been operating without them, and where they will be seen as threatening the economic livelihoods of many people, including many poor people. Moreover, the perception of weaker environmental restrictions in Mexico fuels the concern that American and Canadian firms will relocate to Mexico in search of a pollution haven.

As regards the Maquiladora program, there has been a substantial industrial growth of this type in the borderlands area of Mexico. Initially a large part of this was in the clothing industry, while more recently the largest components are chemicals and electronics assembly firms. Much of this growth occurred before NAFTA, and much afterward. There is no doubt that the growth of Maquiladora firms has led to more pollution in the border area, but whether this is more or less in proportion to non-Maquiladora industry in Mexico is still an open question. The other unanswered question is whether NAFTA has indeed led to higher Maquiladora growth, or whether the latter was caused by other non-NAFTA events.[6]

Summary

Globalization is a process of integrating the economies of the world, involving increasing international flows of goods and services, financial assets, and people. The ways in which the growing world market has affected people in different countries is a major public policy concern. So are the environmental impacts that globalization produces. All else being equal, greater economic activity will produce greater environmental damage. However, with globalization all factors are not going to be equal. As people take advantage of the world market to increase their income and wealth, they will want better environmental quality and will be willing to devote more time and effort to putting in place public policies and regulations that will bring this about. As economies grow they change, evolving from high-polluting manufacturing sectors to lower-polluting service sectors. While opening up economies to world trade has produced some egregious cases of environmental degradation (e.g., Nauru), probably the best, if not the only, way to reduce these in number and intensity is to put in place effective political/regulatory structures.

Key Terms

economic inequality
economic integration
globalization
inferior goods
normal goods

North American Free
  Trade Agreement (NAFTA)
pollution havens
race to the bottom
trade liberalization
transactions costs

Questions for Further Discussion

1. Which of the many aspects of globalization do you think will have the most long-term impact on environmental assets around the world?

2. What is the connection among globalization, government policies, and environmental quality changes in the developing countries confronted with large-scale global economic integration?

3. How might globalization (economic integration) of the envirotech industry be a positive force for environmental protection in the countries of the world?

4. What do we mean by a "race to the bottom" in environmental regulations? Has this happened among the states in the U.S.? Is this experience relevant to the countries of the world?

5. Article XX of the WTO Agreement may not be explicit enough to be applied unambiguously in cases of environmental assets. Can you think of any ways to make it more explicit?

Web Sites

There are hundreds of Web sites that deal with various aspects of globalization and the environment. Many of the established sites have globalization sections:

World Resources Institute
www.wri.org

There are sites that stress anti-globalization views:

Global Exchange
www.globalexchange.org

International Forum on Globalization
www.ifg.org

Sites that are pro-globalization:

World Economic Forum
www.weforum.org

CATO Center for Trade Policy Studies
www.freetrade.org

Sites that attempt to pull together diverse views on globalization:
Commission on Globalization
www.commissiononglobalization.org

Sites that can be used to locate other sites:
The Globalization Web site
www.emory.edu/soc/globalization

Globalization Guide
www.globalizationguide.org

Additional Readings

Clapp, Jennifer, and Peter Dauvergne, *Paths to a Green World: The Political Economy of the Global Environment* (Cambridge: MIT Press, 2005).

Haas, Peter M., ed., *Environment in the New Global Economy*, The International Library of Writings on the New Global Economy Series No. 1 (London: Edward Elgar, December 2003).

Feenstra, Robert C., "Integration of Trade and Disintegration of Production in the Global Economy," *Journal of Economic Perspectives* 12 (1998): 31–50.

Kozul-Wright, Richard, and Robert Rowthorn, eds., *Transnational Corporations and the Global Economy* (New York: St. Martins Press, 1998).

Krugman, Paul, "Growing World Trade: Causes and Consequences," *Brookings Papers on Economic Activity* 1 (1995): 327–362.

Leonard, H. J., *Pollution and the Struggle for World Product* (Cambridge: Cambridge University Press, 1988).

Lofdahl, Corey L., *Environmental Impacts of Globalization and Trade* (Cambridge: MIT Press, 2002).

Mani, M., and D. Wheeler, "In Search of Pollution Havens? Dirty Industry in the World Economy, 1960–1995," *Journal of Environment and Development* (Fall 1998).

Michie, Jonathan, ed., *The Handbook of Globalisation* (London: Edward Elgar, December 2003).

Panayotou, Theodore, "Economic Growth and the Environment," Working Paper No. 56, Harvard University, Center for International Development, July 2000.

Rodrick, Dani, *Has Globalization Gone Too Far?* (Washington, DC: Institute for International Economics, 1997).

Steinberg, Richard H., ed., *The Greening of Trade Law: International Trade Organizations and Environmental Issues* (Lanham, MD: Rowman & Littlefield, January 2002).

Tisdell, Clem, and Raj Kumar Sen, eds., *Economic Globalisation, Social Conflicts, Labour and Environmental Issues* (London: Edward Elgar, March 2004).

Wheeler, David B., *Greening Industry: New Roles for Communities, Markets and Governments* (New York: Oxford University Press for the World Bank, 2000).

Williamson, Jeffrey G., "Globalization, Labor Markets and Policy Backlash in the Past," *Journal of Economic Perspectives* 12 (1998): 51–72.

World Commission on Environment and Development, *Our Common Future (The "Bruntland Report")* (Oxford: Oxford University Press, 1987).

Zaelke, D., P. Orbuch, and R. F. Housman, eds., *Trade and the Environment: Law, Economics and Policy* (Washington, DC: Island Press, 1993).

Notes

[1] François Bourquignon and Christian Morrisson, "Inequality Among World Citizens: 1820–1992," *American Economic Review* 92, no. 4 (September 2002): 727–744.

[2] See the various papers in Jerry Mander and Edward Goldsmith, eds., *The Case Against the Global Economy, and for a Turn Toward the Local* (San Francisco: Sierra Club Books, 1996).

[3] The World Bank (or, more precisely, the International Bank for Reconstruction and Development) was set up by the developed countries to help countries in the developing world undertake projects that will trigger economic development. One of its principal activities is development loans using funds raised in the developed countries. The IMF was established with the primary goal of helping countries stabilize their exchange rates and deal with international financial flows. These two institutions were founded at the end of WW II. The WTO, established in 1994, is an international organization whose goal is to encourage trade liberalization around the globe; it incorporates the General Agreement on Tariffs and Trade (GATT), an agreement initiated in the 1940s, as well as some new elements such as a global protocol on intellectual property rights.

[4] Joseph E. Stiglitz, *Globalization and Its Discontents* (New York: W. W. Norton, 2002). For a shorter version see: www.prospect.org/print/viz/1/Stiglitz-j.html.

[5] A particularly acrid version of the race-to-the-bottom idea was expressed by Ralph Nader during his 2001 presidential run:

> Among the most fetid examples of political cowardice and collusion between elected representatives and big business of the past thirty-five years are the passage of the North American Free Trade Agreement (NAFTA) and the revised General Agreement on Tariffs and Trade (GATT) into federal law. These agreements have little to do with the benefits of trade for citizens of member countries. The agreements were designed, largely by corporate lobbyists, as a "pull-down" mechanism and to facilitate the movement of capital across national boundaries. Such one-dimensional monetized logic tramples long-standing efforts around the world— some very successful—to protect the environment because environmental safeguards are very often considered "nontariff barriers to trade" and thus become targets for removal. Five years of WTO operation have made clear what a grave threat the trade organization is to the world environment.

Quoted in David A. Wheeler, *Prospects for an Environmental Race to the Bottom* (World Bank, October 2000): 1.

[6] For example, see William C. Gruben, "Was NAFTA Behind Mexico's High Maquiladora Growth?" Federal Reserve Bank of Dallas, Economic and Financial Review, Third Quarter (2001): 11–21.

Glossary

Numbers in parentheses indicate main chapter(s) in which term appears.

Administrative law (6)   The area of the law dealing with the actions of administrative and regulatory public agencies (such as the EPA).

Advance disposal fees (ADFs) (12)   A front-end charge on materials to cover their eventual disposal costs.

Alternative policy responses (3)   The different types of policies and regulations that can be aimed at particular pollution-control targets.

Ambient conditions (2)   Quantities of pollutants in the ambient environment, either air, water, or land.

Ambient standards (8)   Legal never-exceed levels put on the allowable amount of a pollutant in the environment.

Averaging (2)   The averaging of numerous ambient indices to determine an overall index.

Balancing (11) (17)   The weighing of both benefits and costs to determine the appropriate pollution-control target.

Baseline (16)   The level of a pollutant that is used for comparison when evaluating some performance measure.

Before/after comparison (2)   Comparing the results of a policy or regulation with conditions that existed before that policy or regulation was put in place.

Behavioral problem (1)   A problem that can be best analyzed in terms of the human decisions that are made that contribute to it or to its solution.

Benefit-cost analysis (BCA) (16)   Analysis to estimate all of the expected (or actual) benefits and costs of a policy or regulation.

Best available technology (BAT) (11)   A stringent technology-based effluent standard based on the "very best" technology for pollution control that is currently capable of being achieved.

Best-practicable control technology (9) A technology-based effluent standard taking into consideration the costs and benefits of the designated technology.

Bicameral legislative body (5) A legislature consisting of two bodies, such as a senate and a house of representatives.

Biochemical oxygen demand (BOD) (2) (10) The dissolved oxygen used up as organic matter is decomposed in a body of water.

Biosolids (10) Waste material left over after domestic wastewater is treated.

Bubble program (15) A system whereby multiple emission points (e.g., smokestacks) are treated as a single source for pollution-control purposes.

Bully pulpit (5) The ability of the president to attract attention and an audience when making public statements.

Corporate Average Fuel Economy (CAFE) standards (14) Federal requirement that automobile fleets produced by manufacturers achieve a specified minimum miles per gallon in performance.

Cap-and-trade programs (9) (15) Pollution control strategy in which the overall level of emissions is capped at some maximum, while polluters are allowed to trade individual emission allowances and thus redistribute the overall emission cap.

Chlorofluorocarbons (CFCs) (18) Materials implicated in the destruction of the earth's stratospheric ozone layer.

Citizen suits (6) Situations where private individuals or groups take legal action against polluters for violating pollution-control regulations.

Coalitions (3) (4) Groups coming together to jointly support a proposal or action.

Command and control (CAC) (1) (8) (15) Policies where regulatory authorities set performance or technology standards which are then enforced through standard legal means.

Common law (6) That body of law in which decisions are based on precedents established in previous cases that are similar to the one under consideration.

Community-based action (17) Action undertaken at the local level to support, or counter, activities of polluters in the community.

Comparative risk (16) The study of different policy options in terms of the degree of risk to which people are exposed under each option.

Consent decree (6) A judgment by a court that normally specifies remedial action parties must take, and may involve fines and penalties.

Constitutional law (6) Legal doctrines regarding how provisions of the U.S. Constitution are interpreted and enforced.

Convention (19) An international agreement that sets broad goals and procedures but does not cover details about actions countries must take.

Conventional pollutants (2) (10) Nontoxic pollutants; in the case of water includes biochemical oxygen demand, suspended solids, and fecal coliform.

Cost effectiveness (2) The degree to which a policy or regulation achieves the maximum impact for the cost incurred.

Cost-effectiveness analysis (16) An outcome in which, for a given cost, the maximum output (e.g., maximum amount of pollution control) is achieved.

Court system (6) The federal and state systems of trial, appeals, and special courts.

Criteria pollutants (2) (9) Air pollutants for which the EPA sets ambient air quality standards (SO_2, NO_x, lead, ozone, CO, and particulate matter).

Cross-border effects (19) Situations in which there is a political border (usually an international border) between the source of a pollutant and the people who suffer damage from it.

Customary law (19)   International customs and procedures that have become widely accepted among countries even though there is no formal way to enforce them.

Damage function (9)   A function showing the relationship between the degree of exposure to a pollutant and the amount of damage suffered.

Decentralization (17)   Shifting the responsibility for pollution control to lower levels of government (e.g., from federal to state levels, or from state to local).

Devolution (1)   Shifting some government functions from higher to lower levels (e.g., from federal to state levels).

Differentiated control (14)   Situation in which some sources are subjected to different pollution-control requirements than others.

Direct discharge (2)   Waterborne discharges that go directly from polluters into a water body (rather than through a treatment facility).

Direct pollutants (10)   Pollutants that are discharged directly from industrial polluters into bodies of water.

Discounting (16)   The process by which benefits and costs in different time periods are adjusted to reflect the differential value people normally place on these benefits and costs.

Dose-response analysis (16)   A study showing how subjects (laboratory animals, people) react to varying levels of a particular pollutant.

Earth Summit (18)   International meeting in 1992 sponsored by the United Nations and other agencies to highlight environmental problems and work toward their resolution. Delegates endorsed the Framework Convention on Climate Change.

Economic inequality (20)   A situation in which different people find themselves in different economic circumstances, e.g., in terms of family incomes.

Economic integration (20)   Movement towards increasing economic exchange among countries of the world.

Elite theory (3)   Idea that a small group of well-connected people are able to bias political results in ways that serve their particular interests.

Emission charges (or taxes) (9) (15)   A per-unit monetary charge placed on emissions of a particular pollutant.

Emissions (2)   Flow of pollutants from a source or group of sources.

End-of-pipe bias (14)   Pollution-control regulations that emphasize treatment of effluent at the end of the production process.

Enforcement (5) (6)   Administrative and legal means used to implement environmental regulations.

Environmental impact statement (16)   Study showing the environmental impacts of government programs.

Environmental interest groups (4)   Private political groups representing environmental interests.

Environmental justice (4) (6) (16)   Assuring that the benefits and costs of environmental policies are equitably distributed.

Environmental policy (1)   Public policy for protecting the environment.

Environmental sciences (7)   Biological, physical, and social sciences that focus on environmental resources.

Epidemiology (16)   The study of how causal agents (such as pollutants) affect groups of people.

Executive order (5) (8)   Legal order by president (or governor) specifying certain actions.

Exposure (1) (16)   The extent to which humans and other organisms are laid open to possible damage by pollution.

Exposure analysis (16)   Determination of how many people, or other elements of the environment, are exposed to a particular pollutant.

Extended financial responsibility (12)   Making polluters responsible for disposal costs of their products or wastes.

Extended producer responsibility (12)   Situation where producers take responsibility for providing for disposal of their products.

Federal preemption (17)   Situation in which constitutional interpretation gives federal authorities the right to take initiative in certain policy areas.

Fines and penalties (15)   Standard means of enforcing environmental laws.

Flexibility mechanisms (18)   Provisions for trading offsets and taking joint action by countries involved in Kyoto Protocol.

Flow control (12)   Local communities limiting trash exports in order to meet supply commitments to local handling companies.

Framing (5)   Providing a perspective for understanding or interpreting a particular policy position.

Free-riding (19)   Enjoying the benefits of something without bearing one's rightful share of its cost.

Functional model (3)   A model of the political process based on the different functions that are performed in reaching and enforcing agreements.

Generalized effects (19)   Pollution effects that impact everybody, e.g., global warming.

Global warming (18)   The gradual increase in the mean temperature at and above the earth's surface through the accumulation of human-produced gases in the atmosphere.

Globalization (20)   Closer integration of economies among countries of the world.

Government institutions (1)   Organizations, laws, and customs by which governments function.

Greenhouse gases (9)   Gases that accumulate in the atmosphere and cause global warming, primarily carbon dioxide.

Half-life (13)   The time it takes for radiation to be reduced by 50 percent.

Halocarbons (18)   Substances partially responsible for depletion of the ozone layer.

Hazard identification (16)   Identification of substances that pose some risk to humans or nonhuman organisms.

Hazardous air pollutants (HAPs) (9)   Chemical air pollutants other than the criteria pollutants.

Hazardous waste (2) (11)   Waste deemed particularly dangerous and in need of special handling.

Health impacts (18)   Impacts of pollutants on various dimensions of human health.

High-level radioactive waste (HLRW) (13)   Waste with levels of radioactivity high enough to cause clear damage.

Host fees (12)   Fees paid by operators of waste landfills to communities in which they are located.

Hot spots (15)   Locations where total emissions increase because sources in that region have procured additional tradable emission permits.

Impaired waters (10)   Water bodies whose quality is below that specified in water-quality plans.

Implementation process (3)   Steps taken to put policies and regulations into effect.

Incentive-based policies (8) (14) (15)   Policies designed to give polluters an incentive to find the most cost-effective means of pollution control.

Indirect discharge (2)   Waterborne industrial pollutants that are routed through a publicly owned treatment facility.

Indoor air pollutants (9)   Air pollutants within confined spaces such as homes, factories, and office buildings.

Inferior goods (20)   Goods for which demand diminishes as incomes rise.

Information asymmetries (8) (15)   When two parties to a transaction (e.g., the regulator and the regulated) have different amounts of information about the nature and characteristics of the transaction.

Information-based policies (8)   Policies based on providing pollution-related information to citizens so they may take appropriate action.

Information technology (4)   Computer-based methods of handling digital data.

Institution (1) (3)   Customs, laws, and organizations that provide the social foundation for economic, political, and social life.

Intergovernmental Panel on Climate Change (IPCC) (18)   International panel of scientists established by the U.N. to focus on global warming.

International action (1)   Activities taken by countries with an international focus.

International Council of Scientific Unions (18)   An amalgamation of many international scientific unions, or groups of scientists, focusing on particular problems.

Interstate Commerce Clause (6) (17)   Constitutional provision giving federal government the responsibility for regulating commerce among the states.

Interstate compacts (13)   Agreements by two or more states to act together toward resolving a common problem.

Ionizing radiation (13)   Radiation that can cause damage.

Kyoto Protocol (18)   Agreement negotiated by countries of the world to reduce emissions of CO_2 and other greenhouse gases.

Litigious society (1)   A society that commonly resorts to the courts to settle conflicts.

Lobbying (4)   Activity devoted to representing one's policy views in the political process.

Low-level radioactive waste (LLRW) (13)   Waste that has very low levels of radiation.

Manifest system (11)   System for creating a paper trail for hazardous waste.

Maximum achievable control technology (MACT) (9) (11)   Technology-based emission standards applied to hazardous air pollutants, based on the emission reductions of the best-performing sources.

Maximum contaminant level (MCL) (10)   Maximum levels of particular pollutants allowed in drinking water.

Mobile sources (9)   Pollutant sources that are not location specific, such as cars, ships, trains, and airplanes.

Monitoring (9)   Measuring and recording emissions or ambient contaminant levels.

Montreal Protocol (18)   Agreement negotiated by the countries of the world to reduce the emissions of substances that destroy the earth's stratospheric ozone shield.

Municipal solid waste (MSW) (2) (12)   Household and office trash.

National Academy of Sciences (7) (18)   Group established by Congress to advise federal government on scientific issues.

National Ambient Air Quality Standards (NAAQS) (2)   Ambient air pollution standards for the criteria pollutants, set by EPA.

National ambient concentration (2)   Average of ambient concentration levels from several spots around the country.

National Council for Science and the Environment (NCSE) (7)   Broad-based consortium of organizations working to improve the scientific basis of environmental decision making.

National Institute of Environmental Health Sciences (7)   Unit in the National Institutes of Health devoted to studying the environment-health link.

National Laboratories (7) Publicly funded research institutes established by the federal government.

National Research Council (7) Organization that is the principal operating agency of the National Academy of Sciences.

Natural resource damages (11) Estimates made under CERCLA of damages caused by accidental pollution releases.

NIMBY (4) Not in my backyard.

Nonattainment areas (6) (9) Regions in which air pollution is worse than applicable National Ambient Air Quality Standards.

Nonconventional pollutants (10) Certain water pollutants, like chlorine, that are classified as neither conventional nor toxic.

Nondelegation doctrine (6) Constitutional provision regulating the conditions under which Congress may delegate certain actions and decisions to administrative agencies.

Nongovernmental organizations (NGOs) (19) Private organizations that act in the political and policy arena, especially in the international setting.

Nonpoint source (10) A pollutant that is emitted in a diffuse manner.

Normal goods (20) Goods for which demand increases as incomes rise.

Normative analysis (1) The analysis of what ought to be.

North American Free Trade Agreement (NAFTA) (20) International trade agreement between Canada, Mexico, and the United States.

Notice of proposed rule making (NOPR) (5) Public notice given by a federal agency such as the EPA that it intends to issue a regulation on a specific case.

Office of Technology Assessment (OTA) (7) Organization established by Congress to study ways that technological change is affecting U.S. economy and society; dismantled in 1995.

Offset program (15) Pollution control in which polluters, if they plan to increase their emissions, must procure offsetting emission reductions from other sources.

Opt-in provisions (17) Legal provision allowing other states to adopt California's mobile source emission standards.

Ozone-depleting substances (9) Air pollutants, like chlorofluorocarbons (CFCs), that destroy ozone in the stratosphere.

Performance standards (8) Legal requirements specifying maximum emissions or emission rates.

Permissible exposure levels (PELs) (11) Regulatory limits established by OSHA on allowable levels of pollutant in workplaces.

Permit system (9) Pollution-control system implemented by requiring polluters to obtain emission permits as a condition of operation.

Perverse consequences (14) Consequences of statutes or regulations that are opposite to the stated objectives of these statutes and regulations.

Perverse incentives (14) Incentives that inadvertently lead polluters into actions that conflict with the objectives of the laws.

Pesticide registration (11) Provision under Federal Insecticide, Fungicide and Rodenticide Act that requires new pesticides to be registered with EPA before they may be used.

Place-based environmentalism (4) (17) Environmental movement concentrating on unique local issues.

Pluralism (3) Political doctrine holding that in an open political system, alternative policy views are represented by a diversity of interests and groups.

Plurality voting (4)   Winner-take-all voting system that awards victory to candidate with the most votes.

Point source (10)   Emissions stemming from a discrete and concentrated release point.

Policy (1)   Collective political action eventuating in public action or regulation.

Policy cycle (3)   A series of steps in the policy process through which a proposal originates and evolves toward enactment and implementation.

Policy instruments (8)   Different types of policies that are possible to attack various pollution problems.

Political agenda (3)   Priority ranking for public policy and political issues.

Political capital (5)   The store of political influence a president (or other politician) may generate through political actions.

Political economy (3)   The idea that politics is an extension of economic behavior in which everybody is trying to maximize their own net benefits.

Political model (3)   View of the policy process that stresses the political influences shaping policy outcomes.

Political theater (5)   Political actions undertaken primarily to communicate political images rather than substantive policy outputs.

Political/policy culture (3)   Pervasiveness of political and policy considerations among political actors.

Politics (3)   The art of representing one's views and interests within the arena of collective decision making.

Polluter-pays principle (17) (19)   Doctrine that polluters should be responsible for the costs of pollution control.

Pollution havens (20)   Countries or states that attract heavy polluters through having relatively lenient pollution-control laws.

Pollution prevention (P2) (8)   Reducing pollution by changing the production system so that lower quantities of residuals are generated.

Positive analysis (1)   The analysis of what is, especially in the sense of what the facts are, and of which causes lead to which effects.

Premanufacturing notice (11)   Prior notice to EPA required by chemical producers or users under the Toxic Substances Control Act.

Primary standards (9)   Human-health related standards under the National Ambient Air Quality Standards setting program.

Primary treatment (2)   First stage of wastewater treatment that removes about 30-40 percent of organic matter.

Proportional representation (4)   System of voting in which the number of seats in a legislative body awarded to a party reflects the proportion of the total vote won.

Protocol (19)   An international agreement that determines details of an international convention.

Public opinion (1) (4)   Views of the general public regarding preferred positions on various public issues.

Public policy (1)   Collective action on regulatory and administrative actions to be pursued by public agencies.

Publicly owned treatment works (POTWs) (10)   Municipally owned waste treatment facilities handling domestic and industrial waterborne wastes.

Pretreatment program (10)   Regulations covering required pretreatment for industrial waste sent to publicly owned treatment works.

Race to the bottom (17) (20)   A phenomenon in which individual states, or countries, enact increasingly lax environmental laws in an attempt to stimulate economic growth.

Radiation (9) (13)   Energy traveling through space, such as sunlight, infra-red, and gamma rays.

Rational model (3)   View of policy process that regards it as a reasoned choice of alternatives best designed to achieve desired results.

Real value (12)   Value after adjusting for normal inflation.

Reasonable risk (11)   Concept in some environmental laws that objective should be a "reasonable" level of exposure to risks.

Reasonably available control technology (RACT) (9)   A technology-based effluent standard based on technology regarded as available at reasonable cost.

Reciprocal impacts (19)   Another name for generalized impacts.

Recycling (12)   The reuse of materials that would otherwise end up in the waste stream.

Regulated industries (4)   Private firms subject to environmental regulations.

Regulations (3) (8)   Performance specifications required by EPA enactments and having the force of law.

Rems (13)   Common way of measuring exposure to radiation.

Research institutes (7)   Public and private organizations whose primary activity is to do research on environmental (or other) issues.

Research universities (7)   Universities in which faculty and staff conduct research as well as teach.

Risk assessment (16)   Steps taken to evaluate the degree of risk people might be exposed to through the exposure to certain materials and practices.

Risk management (16)   Steps taken to manage the risk to which people are exposed.

Rocky Flats (13)   Facility in Colorado that was contaminated with nuclear radiation resulting from its work in nuclear weapons production.

Scientific advisory groups (7)   Groups composed of nongovernmental members who offer advice to agencies on policy matters.

Scientific method (7)   Standard scientific procedure of hypothesis making and testing and the accumulation of knowledge.

Scientific publications (7)   Publications such as journals and books that normally feature scientific results.

Secondary standards (9)   Standards set under the National Ambient Air Quality Standards to achieve human welfare objectives that are not related to human health.

Secondary treatment (2)   The second stage of municipal wastewater treatment processes that can extract up to 80 to 90 percent of the organic waste.

Sectoral change (2)   When the broad makeup of the national economy changes, e.g., reductions in the size of the manufacturing sector, increases in the size of the service sector.

Sewage sludge program (10)   Program designed to dispose of the sludge left over from municipal wastewater treatment.

Side payments (19)   Payments (in money or some other form) that induces a country to participate in a political agreement.

Solid waste (12)   All solid, liquid, or contained gaseous material, divided into hazardous and nonhazardous.

Source reduction (12)   The reduction of material produced in the production process, either incorporated in output product or leftover material.

Special-interest consequences (14)   Provisions put into statutes and regulations that benefit particular economic or political interests.

Spent nuclear fuel (13)   Highly radioactive leftover nuclear fuel rods after they have been used in nuclear power plants.

State implementation plans (SIPs) (9)   Plans developed by the states to bring their air quality into conformance with the National Ambient Air Quality Standards.

State revolving fund (SRF) (10)   Reimbursable funds used by states to finance waste treatment facilities and drinking water system improvements.

Stationary sources (9)   Nonmobile sources of air pollutants, such as factories and power plants.

Strategic possibilities (19)   Temporary political conditions that make it possible to progress on some dimension of environmental policy.

Strict, joint and several liability (6) (11)   Standard of liability used in the Superfund program.

Subsidies (15)   Payments made to induce compliance to an environmental regulation.

Superfund (11)   Nickname for the Comprehensive Environmental Response, Compensation and Liability Act of 1980.

Supremacy doctrine (6)   Constitutional provision specifying that federal laws, when constitutional on other grounds, represent the supreme law of the country.

Take-back programs (12)   Programs requiring producers to take back their products from consumers after their useful life.

Taking (6)   Government appropriation of private property.

Technological problem (1)   A problem that can be solved by using the appropriate technology of production, distribution, or disposal.

Technology standard (8)   Legal requirement specifying the use of some specific pollution-control technology or practice.

Technology transfer (19)   The transfer of pollution-control technologies from developed to developing countries.

Technology-based approach (10)   Policy approach that in effect dictates certain pollution-control technology adoptions by polluters.

Technology-based effluent standard (TBES) (9)   An emission standard set on the basis of an approved pollution-control technology.

Tertiary treatment (2)   A final stage in wastewater treatment that is capable of increasing the removal of organic material to 95–99 percent.

Threshold (9) (13)   A quantity of ambient pollutant below which there is no discernible effect on humans or other elements of the environment.

Tipping fees (12)   Fees paid to landfill operators for the right to dump waste in that location.

Total maximum daily load (TMDL) (10)   The total pollution load a water body may accept and still meet water quality goals.

Toxic materials (2)   Solid waste materials that have been designated as capable of producing toxic effects in people or nonhuman organisms.

Toxic pollutants (2) (10)   Pollutants having potentially toxic impacts.

Toxic Release Inventory (TRI) (2) (11)   Program that records and publishes information on quantities of toxic releases by industrial sources.

Trade liberalization (20)   Taking steps to reduce barriers that stand in the way of international trade.

Transaction costs (20)   Costs of negotiating and implementing a transaction.

Transfer stations (12)   Facilities where solid wastes collected in a community are transferred to landfills elsewhere.

Treaty (19)   International agreement that specifies both objectives and the means of achieving them.

Unforeseen consequences (14)   Policy outcomes that were initially unexpected.

Unfunded federal mandates (17) Statutory requirements that one level of government (e.g., federal) places on lower levels (e.g., states) without the financial aid to help offset the costs of meeting them.

Union of Concerned Scientists (7) A private group that seeks to build bridges between scientists and the policy process.

Unit pricing (12) Charging a price per unit of municipal solid waste.

United Nations Environment Program (UNEP) (18) A program started in 1972 to coordinate international environmental actions, headquartered in Nairobi, Kenya.

Victim-pays principle (19) Idea that victims of pollution should pay polluters to reduce their emissions.

Waste reduction (12) Source reduction plus recycling.

Wastewater (10) Waste containing water after it has been treated to some extent.

Water quality standards (2) Emission and ambient pollution standards applied to bodies of water or to wastewater.

With/without comparison (2) Comparing the results of a program with what would likely have occurred if the program had not been pursued.

World Meteorological Organization (18) An agency of the United Nations focusing on issues pertaining to the earth's atmosphere.

Yucca Mountain (13) Location in Nevada chosen as site for nation's underground repository of high-level nuclear waste; has not yet begun to accept waste, pending legal challenges.

Index